Encyclopedia of THEATRE MUSIC

Random House · *New York*

ENCYCLOPEDIA

OF

THEATRE

MUSIC

A comprehensive listing of
more than 4000 songs from
Broadway and Hollywood: 1900–1960

BY
RICHARD LEWINE
AND
ALFRED
SIMON

ACKNOWLEDGMENT

The task of compiling information about more than 4000 songs would have been far greater without the co-operation of others. We are especially indebted to Tom Maturo, of Chappell & Co.; to the Music Division of the New York Public Library; to ASCAP; to Eugene Brigati and to Charles Gaynor. For their generous permission to reproduce original manuscripts we wish to thank Irving Berlin, Betty Kern Cummings, Ira Gershwin, Cole Porter, Richard Rodgers, Kay Swift and Vincent Youmans, Jr.

EDITORS' NOTE

In the compilation of these listings it seemed practical to establish certain ground rules. Primarily, only published songs from productions which opened in New York are included. In certain cases we have also listed songs which, though published, were dropped from shows on pre-Broadway tours—and these are so noted. Lastly, when writers collaborated on both words and music, their names are shown in a continuous line, rather than under the respective column headings.

CONTENTS

No art form is so distinctively American as musical comedy. It is, of course, a distillation of other forms—operetta, straight plays, vaudeville—but its sophisticated whole is completely and uniquely ours. And we are—and should be—especially possessive about our musical comedy songs. They may have fifth or sixth cousins in comic opera and in Tin Pan Alley, but they resemble none of them. The sound of a theatre overture is quite unlike any other musical sound in the world.

Inevitably theatre music has its devoted, in fact its fanatical, disciples. Let the party pianist presiding over an evening of Gershwin, Kern, Porter and Rodgers receive one ill-advised request for "Red Sails in the Sunset," and neither he nor the flock can be expected to act with reason or sanity. For the tribe has its dogma, its folklore and its unwritten laws—and can be ruthless with the uninformed. Some of the elders can sing, play, or at least recite, from the Princess Theatre shows of Kern, Bolton and Wodehouse; others, by the accident of having been born too late, begin with songs from the early Garrick Gaieties. But they are as one at heart in their nostalgic devotion. They make no claim that *all* theatre songs are worth remembering but they will swear to you that the good ones actually improve with age. The fire has been kept burning, not just by this passionate cult, but by thousands of others who will undoubtedly continue to sing, play, record and rerecord the songs into immortality.

What we have here undertaken is the first complete alphabetical listing of published songs from every musical show that has opened on Broadway since 1925. Certain off-Broadway scores have also, in our opinion, merited inclusion. Theatre songs before 1925 are in a separate, and selective, listing, and there is a further compilation of songs written for motion pictures by theatre composers—songs which have the unmistakable flavor of the Broadway stage. All of this, we hope, will be of value to those who use—or just have deep affection for—show music.

Early in the game our publisher pointed out that this would involve enormous work and no chance whatever of book-club selection or best-seller lists. This has not deterred us. Proof, if you need it, of how far some of these fanatics will go.

PART ONE

Theatre
Songs
1900-1924

THEATRE
SONGS

1900-1924

THE ANCESTRY of American musical theatre has long been the subject of conjecture. Some feel that its actual beginnings were with the production of *The Black Crook* in New York in 1866; others that its roots are deep in the comic operas of Strauss, Offenbach and Gilbert and Sullivan. Still others trace it to Harrigan and Hart, who wrote, produced and acted in their own shows before the turn of the century—or to Lew Dockstader's Minstrels. Its heritage is complex, to say the least, and in its blood line are probably some of all these antecedents.

The first American stage musicals of any distinction were the operettas of Victor Herbert, and later of Rudolf Friml and Sigmund Romberg. Though melodious and popular, they were cumbersome affairs, heavy in both costuming and sentiment; and, like their European cousins, they were characterized by lilting waltzes, stirring male choruses, romantic duets and interminable misunderstandings.

The advent of World War I marked the first major change. It not only ended a charming and untroubled way of life, it ended as well a reflection of that life on the stage. Operettas of the *mittel-Europa* school, such as *The Student Prince* and *Bitter Sweet*, continued to appear and were well received, largely because of their melodic scores. But the transparent and candy-coated libretto was on the way out.

Another kind of musical, the vaudeville and "girl" show, was fast disappearing. These were often vehicles for a star such as George M. Cohan or Raymond Hitchcock, light-hearted and simple affairs, with songs that were dropped in without regard to, sometimes at the expense of, the story line. These, too, had reached the end of their heyday.

It was in the late "teens" that audiences first became aware of a new musical stage. Jerome Kern had already written several enduring theatre songs, among them "They Didn't Believe Me" (1914) and "Babes in the Wood"

3

(1915), and Irving Berlin, by this time a successful writer of commercial "pop" songs, arrived on the scene with scores for *Watch Your Step* and *Stop! Look! Listen!* But it was with the era of the Princess Theatre shows that musical comedy, as we now know it, emerged. These Kern-Bolton-Wodehouse musicals were distinctly different from anything that had gone before. Book, lyrics and music were now of one design and seemed to have received more than passing attention from their authors. Their very existence implied intelligence on the part of the audience.

Any discussion of these beginnings must, therefore, make more than passing reference to Jerome Kern. No other theatre composer was to exert so profound an influence on the form, or to have so far-reaching an effect on the theatre composers who would follow him. Richard Rodgers, in an article for the *New York Times*, once wrote: "Kern was typical of what was, and still is, good in our general maturity in this country in that he had his musical roots in the fertile middle-European and English school of operetta writing, and amalgamated it with everything that was fresh in the American scene to give us something wonderfully new and clear in music writing in the world. Actually he was a giant with one foot in Europe and the other in America. Before he died, he picked up the European foot and planted it squarely alongside the American one."

Another writer on the subject was George Gershwin, who, in a letter to his biographer, Isaac Goldberg, said: "Kern was the first composer who made me conscious that most popular music was of inferior quality and that musical-comedy music was made of better material. I followed Kern's work and studied each song that he composed. I paid him the tribute of frank imitation and many things I wrote at this time [1916] sounded as though Kern had written them himself." Certainly many others, Vincent Youmans, Cole Porter and Louis Hirsch, in addition to Rodgers and Gershwin, were to carry the new form further, each with his own individual and highly polished style. But it was Kern, more than anyone, who presided over the beginnings.

The early twenties were the golden—and pre-inflationary—days of the musical theatre. The public could, and did, patronize thirty to forty musical shows a season. The songs they heard in those years were a giant step ahead of their vaudeville and Tin Pan Alley forebears. Melodies, harmonies and lyrics demanded more than casual listening, and the attentive theatregoer was hearing fresh song forms and imaginative rhymes

The theatre composer flourished and so did the lyricist. Oscar Hammerstein II, then in his twenties and fresh from Columbia varsity shows and a brief apprenticeship as a stage manager, was an early practitioner of the new art, the intelligent lyric. So were Otto Harbach, B. G. DeSylva, Anne Caldwell and—still writing as "Arthur Francis"—Ira Gershwin.

The revue, another staple in the theatregoer's diet, was undergoing its own transition. What had traditionally been a collection of popular songs, vaudeville and show girls, intended solely to brace the tired businessman, was becoming a forum from which to satirize and comment. Irving Berlin's Music Box Revues, the Ziegfeld Follies and George White's Scandals—five of them with scores by George Gershwin—retained the show girls, but their songs and sketches were of distinctly better stuff.

They were years of exciting theatrical exploration. It is significant that many of the songs are still, three and four decades later, constantly performed. The section that follows lists many of these pre-1925 songs, some of them more popular than ever, others which we believe will be well worth rediscovering.

THEATRE SONGS 1900–1924

TITLE	COMPOSER	LYRICIST	SHOW	YEAR
Absinthe Frappé	Victor Herbert	Glen MacDonough	It Happened in Nordland	1904
Ah, Sweet Mystery of Life	Victor Herbert	Rida Johnson Young	Naughty Marietta	1910
Alice Blue Gown	Harry Tierney	Joseph McCarthy	Irene	1919
Alice in Wonderland	Irving Berlin	Irving Berlin	The Century Girl	1916
All Lanes Must Reach a Turning	Jerome Kern	Howard Dietz	Dear Sir	1924
Allah's Holiday	Rudolf Friml	Otto Harbach	Katinka	1915
And I Am All Alone	Jerome Kern	Jerome Kern, P. G. Wodehouse	Have a Heart	1917
Any Old Place with You	Richard Rodgers	Lorenz Hart	A Lonely Romeo	1919
April Blossoms	Vincent Youmans, Herbert Stothart	Otto Harbach, Oscar Hammerstein II	Wildflower	1923
April Showers	Louis Silvers	B. G. DeSylva	Bombo	1921
Are You Going to Dance?	Franz Lehar	Basil Hood	The Count of Luxembourg	1912
Auf Wiedersehn	Sigmund Romberg	Herbert Reynolds	The Blue Paradise	1915
Babes in the Wood	Jerome Kern	Schuyler Greene	Very Good Eddie	1915
Bambalina	Vincent Youmans, Herbert Stothart	Otto Harbach, Oscar Hammerstein II	Wildflower	1923
Because You're You	Victor Herbert	Henry Blossom	The Red Mill	1906
Big Show, The	Jerome Kern	Edgar Allan Woolf	Head Over Heels	1918
Blue Danube Blues	Jerome Kern	Anne Caldwell	Good Morning, Dearie	1921
Bring Me a Rose	Lionel Monckton	Arthur Wimperis, Lionel Monckton	The Arcadians	1910
Bubble, The	Rudolf Friml	Otto Harbach	High Jinks	1913
By the Saskatchewan	Ivan Caryll	C. M. S. McLellan	The Pink Lady	1911
Castle of Dreams	Harry Tierney	Joseph McCarthy	Irene	1919

TITLE	COMPOSER	LYRICIST	SHOW	YEAR
Charleston	James Johnson	Cecil Mack	Runnin' Wild	1923
Chinese Lullaby	Robert Hood Bowers	Robert Hood Bowers	East Is West	1918
Cleopatterer	Jerome Kern	P. G. Wodehouse	Leave It to Jane	1917
Come to the Ball	Lionel Monckton	Adrian Ross	The Quaker Girl	1911
Crickets Are Calling, The	Jerome Kern	P. G. Wodehouse	Leave It to Jane	1917
Crinoline Days	Irving Berlin	Irving Berlin	Music Box Revue	1922
Cuddle Up a Little Closer, Lovey Mine	Karl Hoschna	Otto Harbach	Three Twins	1908
Day Dreams	Heinrich Reinhardt	Harry B. & Robert B. Smith	The Spring Maid	1910
Deep in My Heart, Dear	Sigmund Romberg	Dorothy Donnelly	The Student Prince	1924
Do It Again!	George Gershwin	B. G. DeSylva	The French Doll	1922
Dollar Princess	Leo Fall	George Grossmith, Jr.	The Dollar Princess	1909
Drifting Along with the Tide	George Gershwin	Arthur Jackson	George White's Scandals	1921
Drinking Song	Sigmund Romberg	Dorothy Donnelly	The Student Prince	1924
Drop Me a Line	Efrem Zimbalist	Joseph W. Herbert	Honeydew	1920
Enchanted Train, The	Jerome Kern	P. G. Wodehouse	Sitting Pretty	1924
Every Day Is Ladies' Day with Me	Victor Herbert	Henry Blossom	The Red Mill	1906
Every Little Movement	Karl Hoschna	Otto Harbach	Madame Sherry	1910
Everybody Step	Irving Berlin	Irving Berlin	Music Box Revue	1921
Fascinating Rhythm	George Gershwin	Ira Gershwin	Lady, Be Good	1924
First Rose of Summer	Jerome Kern	Anne Caldwell	She's a Good Fellow	1919
Forty-Five Minutes from Broadway	George M. Cohan	George M. Cohan	Forty-Five Minutes from Broadway	1906
Giannina Mia	Rudolf Friml	Otto Harbach	The Firefly	1912
Give My Regards to Broadway	George M. Cohan	George M. Cohan	Little Johnny Jones	1904
Go, Little Boat	Jerome Kern	P. G. Wodehouse	Miss 1917	1917
Going Up	Louis A. Hirsch	Otto Harbach	Going Up	1917
Golden Days	Sigmund Romberg	Dorothy Donnelly	The Student Prince	1924
Good Morning, Dearie!	Jerome Kern	Anne Caldwell	Good Morning, Dearie	1921
Goodbye Girls, I'm Through	Ivan Caryll	John Golden	Chin-Chin	1914
Half of It, Dearie, Blues, The	George Gershwin	Ira Gershwin	Lady, Be Good	1924
Hang on to Me	George Gershwin	Ira Gershwin	Lady, Be Good	1924
Harrigan	George M. Cohan	George M. Cohan	Fifty Miles from Boston	1908
Has Anybody Here Seen Kelly?	John Charles Moore, C. W. Murphy, William J. McKenna		The Jolly Bachelors	1910
Heidelberg Stein Song	Gustav Luders	Frank Pixley	The Prince of Pilsen	1903

TITLE	COMPOSER	LYRICIST	SHOW	YEAR
Hello, Frisco, Hello	Louis A. Hirsch	Gene Buck	Ziegfeld Follies	1915
High Jinks (Something Seems Tingle-Ingleing)	Rudolf Friml	Otto Harbach	High Jinks	1913
I Can't Do the Sum	Victor Herbert	Glen MacDonough	Babes in Toyland	1903
I Love a Piano	Irving Berlin	Irving Berlin	Stop! Look! Listen!	1915
I Love You	Harry Archer	Harlan Thompson	Little Jessie James	1923
I Love You So	Franz Lehar	Adrian Ross	The Merry Widow	1907
I Might Be Your Once-in-a-While	Victor Herbert	Robert B. Smith	Angel Face	1919
I Never Realized	Cole Porter	Cole Porter	Buddies	1919
I Still Can Dream	Emmerich Kalman	B. G. DeSylva	The Yankee Princess	1921
I Want What I Want when I Want It	Victor Herbert	Henry Blossom	Mlle. Modiste	1905
I Was so Young (You Were so Beautiful)	George Gershwin	Irving Caesar, Al Bryan	Good Morning, Judge	1919
I Wonder Whether	Louis A. Hirsch	P. G. Wodehouse	Oh, My Dear!	1918
If I Told You	Vincent Youmans, Herbert Stothart	Otto Harbach, Oscar Hammerstein II	Wildflower	1923
I'll Build a Stairway to Paradise	George Gershwin	B. G. DeSylva, Arthur Francis (Ira Gershwin)	George White's Scandals	1922
I'm Always Chasing Rainbows	Harry Carroll	Joseph McCarthy	Oh, Look!	1918
I'm Falling in Love with Someone	Victor Herbert	Rida Johnson Young	Naughty Marietta	1910
I'm in Love Again	Cole Porter	Cole Porter	Greenwich Village Follies	1924
I'm Just Wild about Harry	Eubie Blake	Noble Sissle	Shuffle Along	1921
If You Could Care	Herman Darewski	Arthur Wimperis	As You Were	1920
In a Kingdom of Our Own	George M. Cohan	George M. Cohan	The Royal Vagabond	1919
In Love with Love	Jerome Kern	Anne Caldwell	The Stepping Stones	1923
Indian Love Call	Rudolf Friml	Otto Harbach, Oscar Hammerstein II	Rose Marie	1924
Innocent Ingenue Baby	George Gershwin, William Daly	Brian Hooker	Our Nell	1922
Irene	Harry Tierney	Joseph McCarthy	Irene	1919
It Must Be Love	Vincent Youmans	Zelda Sears	Lollipop	1923
It Wasn't Your Fault	Jerome Kern	Herbert Reynolds	Love o' Mike	1917
Italian Street Song	Victor Herbert	Rida Johnson Young	Naughty Marietta	1910
It's Delightful to Be Married	Vincent Scotto	Anna Held	The Parisian Model	1906

TITLE	COMPOSER	LYRICIST	SHOW	YEAR
~~In a Shooting Box in~~ Scotland	T. Lawrason Riggs, Cole Porter		See America First	1916
Jeannette and Her Little Wooden Shoes	Victor Herbert	Robert B. Smith	Sweethearts	1913
Journey's End	Harry Tierney	Joseph McCarthy	Up She Goes	1922
Just a Voice to Call Me, Dear	Emmerich Kalman	P. G. Wodehouse	The Riviera Girl	1917
Ka-Lu-A	Jerome Kern	Anne Caldwell	Good Morning, Dearie	1921
Kiss in the Dark, A	Victor Herbert	B. G. DeSylva	Orange Blossoms	1922
Kiss in Xanadu, A (ballet)	Deems Taylor		Beggar on Horseback	1924
Kiss Me Again	Victor Herbert	Henry Blossom	Mlle. Modiste	1905
Lady of the Evening	Irving Berlin	Irving Berlin	Music Box Revue	1922
Land of "Let's Pretend," The	Jerome Kern	Harry B. Smith	The Girl from Utah	1914
Last Waltz, The	Oscar Straus	Edward Delaney Dunn	The Last Waltz	1921
Learn to Smile	Louis A. Hirsch	Otto Harbach	The O'Brien Girl	1921
Leave It to Jane	Jerome Kern	P. G. Wodehouse	Leave It to Jane	1917
Left All Alone Again Blues	Jerome Kern	Anne Caldwell	The Night Boat	1920
Life's a Tale	Emmerich Kalman	P. G. Wodehouse	The Riviera Girl	1917
Limehouse Blues	Philip Braham	Douglas Furber	Charlot's Revue	1924
Little Girls, Good Bye	Victor Jacobi	William LeBaron	Apple Blossoms	1919
Little Jazz Bird	George Gershwin	Ira Gershwin	Lady, Be Good	1924
Look for the Silver Lining	Jerome Kern	B. G. DeSylva	Sally	1920
Love and the Moon	Jerome Kern	Booth Tarkington	Rose Briar	1922
Love Nest, The	Louis A. Hirsch	Otto Harbach	Mary	1920
Love's Own Sweet Song	Emmerich Kalman	C. C. S. Cushing, E. P. Heath	Sari	1914
Love's Intense in Tents	Richard Rodgers	Lorenz Hart	Poor Little Ritz Girl	1920
Love's Roundelay	Oscar Straus	Joseph W. Herbert	A Waltz Dream	1908
Magic Moments	Leo Fall	Clare Kummer	Madame Pompadour	1924
Man I Love, The*	George Gershwin	Ira Gershwin	Lady, Be Good	1924
Mandy**	Irving Berlin	Irving Berlin	Yip! Yip! Yaphank	1918
March of the Toys	Victor Herbert		Babes in Toyland	1903
Mary's a Grand Old Name	George M. Cohan	George M. Cohan	Forty-Five Minutes from Broadway	1906
Mascot of the Troop, The	Victor Herbert	Henry Blossom	Mlle. Modiste	1905
Maxim's	Franz Lehar	Adrian Ross	The Merry Widow	1907

*Dropped from New York production
**Also in Ziegfeld Follies 1919

TITLE	COMPOSER	LYRICIST	SHOW	YEAR
Message of the Violet, The	Gustav Luders	Frank Pixley	The Prince of Pilsen	1903
M-I-S-S-I-S-S-I-P-P-I	Harry Tierney	Ben Ryan, Bert Hanlon	Hitchy-Koo	1917
Mr. Gallagher and Mr. Shean	Ed Gallagher, Al Shean		Ziegfeld Follies	1922
Moon Song	Jerome Kern	P. G. Wodehouse	Oh, Lady! Lady!!	1918
Moonbeams	Victor Herbert	Henry Blossom	The Red Mill	1906
My Beautiful Lady	Ivan Caryll	C. M. S. McLellan	The Pink Lady	1911
My Dream Girl	Victor Herbert	Rida Johnson Young	The Dream Girl	1924
My Faithful Stradivari	Emmerich Kalman	C. C. S. Cushing, E. P. Heath	Sari	1914
My Hero	Oscar Straus	Stanislaus Stange	The Chocolate Soldier	1909
My Man	Maurice Yvain	Channing Pollock	Ziegfeld Follies	1921
Neapolitan Love Song	Victor Herbert	Henry Blossom	The Princess Pat	1915
Nellie Kelly, I Love You	George M. Cohan	George M. Cohan	Little Nellie Kelly	1922
Nesting Time in Flatbush	Jerome Kern	P. G. Wodehouse	Oh, Boy!	1917
Night Time in Araby	George Gershwin	B. G. DeSylva	George White's Scandals	1924
Nobody but You	George Gershwin	B. G. DeSylva	La La Lucille	1919
Oh, How I Hate to Get Up in the Morning*	Irving Berlin	Irving Berlin	Yip! Yip! Yaphank	1918
Oh, Lady Be Good!	George Gershwin	Ira Gershwin	Lady, Be Good	1924
Oh Me! Oh My!	Vincent Youmans	Arthur Francis (Ira Gershwin)	Two Little Girls in Blue	1921
Old-Fashioned Garden	Cole Porter	Cole Porter	Hitchy-Koo	1919
Old-Fashioned Love	James Johnson	Cecil Mack	Runnin' Wild	1923
Old Fashioned Wife, An	Jerome Kern	P. G. Wodehouse	Oh, Boy!	1917
Once in a Blue Moon	Jerome Kern	Anne Caldwell	The Stepping Stones	1923
Orange Grove in California, An	Irving Berlin	Irving Berlin	Music Box Revue	1923
Pack Up Your Sins and Go to the Devil	Irving Berlin	Irving Berlin	Music Box Revue	1922
Pale Venetian Moon, The	Jerome Kern	Anne Caldwell	The Bunch and Judy	1922
Parade of the Wooden Soldiers	Leon Jessel		Chauve-Souris	1922
Parisian Pierrot	Noel Coward	Noel Coward	Charlot's Revue	1924
Play a Simple Melody	Irving Berlin	Irving Berlin	Watch Your Step	1914
Poor Butterfly	Raymond Hubbell	John Golden	The Big Show	1916
Pretty Girl Is Like a Melody, A	Irving Berlin	Irving Berlin	Ziegfeld Follies	1919
Rackety-Coo	Rudolf Friml	Otto Harbach	Katinka	1915

*Also in "This Is the Army," 1942

TITLE	COMPOSER	LYRICIST	SHOW	YEAR
Raggedy Ann	Jerome Kern	Anne Caldwell	The Stepping Stones	1923
Ragtime Temple Bells	Ivan Caryll	James O'Dea	Chin-Chin	1914
Real American Folk Song, The	George Gershwin	Ira Gershwin	Ladies First	1918
Rice and Shoes	Vincent Youmans	Schuyler Greene, Arthur Francis (Ira Gershwin)	Two Little Girls in Blue	1921
Road to Paradise, The	Sigmund Romberg	Rida Johnson Young	Maytime	1917
Robbers' March	Frederic Norton	Oscar Asche	Chin Chin Chow	1906
Rock-a-Bye Baby	Irving Berlin	Irving Berlin	Music Box Revue	1924
Rose of Washington Square	James F. Hanley	Ballard MacDonald	Ziegfeld Midnight Frolic	1920
Rose Marie	Rudolf Friml	Otto Harbach, Oscar Hammerstein, II	Rose Marie	1924
Same Sort of Girl	Jerome Kern	Harry B. Smith	The Girl from Utah	1914
Saw Mill River Road	Harry Tierney	Joseph McCarthy	Glory	1922
Say It with Music	Irving Berlin	Irving Berlin	Music Box Revue	1921
Say Not Love Is a Dream	Franz Lehar	Basil Hood	The Count of Luxembourg	1912
Second-Hand Rose	James Hanley	Grant Clarke	Ziegfeld Follies	1921
Second Violin, The	Fritz Kreisler	William LeBaron	Apple Blossoms	1919
See America First	Cole Porter	Cole Porter	See America First	1916
Serenade	Sigmund Romberg	Dorothy Donnelly	The Student Prince	1924
Shine on, Harvest Moon	Nora Bayes, Jack Norworth	Jack Norworth	Ziegfeld Follies	1908
Siren's Song, The	Jerome Kern	P. G. Wodehouse	Leave It to Jane	1917
So Am I	George Gershwin	Ira Gershwin	Lady, Be Good	1924
So Long, Mary	George M. Cohan	George M. Cohan	Forty-Five Minutes from Broadway	1906
Some Wonderful Sort of Someone	George Gershwin	Schuyler Greene	Ladies First	1918
Somebody Loves Me	George Gershwin	B. G. DeSylva, Ballard MacDonald	George White's Scandals	1924
Someone Loves You After All	Harry Tierney	Joseph McCarthy	Kid Boots	1923
Song of Love	Sigmund Romberg	Dorothy Donnelly	Blossom Time	1921
South Sea Isles	George Gershwin	Arthur Jackson	George White's Scandals	1921
Streets of New York, The (In Old New York)	Victor Herbert	Henry Blossom	The Red Mill	1906
Swanee	George Gershwin	Irving Caesar	Sinbad	1919
Sweet Lady	Frank Crumit, Dave Zoob	Howard Johnson	Tangerine	1921

TITLE	COMPOSER	LYRICIST	SHOW	YEAR
Sweetest Thing in Life, The	Jerome Kern	B. G. DeSylva	Peter Pan	1924
Sweethearts	Victor Herbert	Robert B. Smith	Sweethearts	1913
Sympathy	Rudolf Friml	Otto Harbach	The Firefly	1912
Take a Little One-Step	Vincent Youmans	Zelda Sears	Lollipop	1924
Teacher, Teacher	Jerome Kern	Anne Caldwell	She's a Good Fellow	1919
Tell Her in the Spring-time	Irving Berlin	Irving Berlin	Music Box Revue	1924
Tell Me, Little Gypsy	Irving Berlin	Irving Berlin	Ziegfeld Follies	1920
Tell Me Pretty Maiden	Leslie Stuart	Owen Hall	Florodora	1900
They Didn't Believe Me	Jerome Kern	Herbert Reynolds	The Girl from Utah	1914
Thine Alone	Victor Herbert	Henry Blossom	Eileen	1917
Throw Me a Rose	Emmerich Kalman	P. G. Wodehouse, M. E. Rourke	Miss Springtime	1916
Tickle Toe, The	Louis A. Hirsch	Otto Harbach	Going Up	1917
Till the Clouds Roll By	Jerome Kern	Jerome Kern, Guy Bolton, P. G. Wodehouse	Oh, Boy!	1917
To the Land of My Own Romance	Victor Herbert	Harry B. Smith	The Enchantress	1911
Toodle-oo	Vincent Youmans	Oscar Hammerstein II, William Cary Duncan	Mary Jane McKane	1923
Totem Tom-Tom	Rudolf Friml	Otto Harbach, Oscar Hammerstein II	Rose Marie	1924
Toyland	Victor Herbert	Glen MacDonough	Babes in Toyland	1903
Tra-La-La	George Gershwin	Arthur Francis (Ira Gershwin)	For Goodness Sake	1922
Tramp! Tramp! Tramp!	Victor Herbert	Rida Johnson Young	Naughty Marietta	1910
Tulip Time	Dave Stamper	Gene Buck	Ziegfeld Follies	1919
Two Little Love Bees	Heinrich Reinhardt	Harry B. & Robert B. Smith	The Spring Maid	1910
Under the Bamboo Tree	Robert Cole	Robert Cole	Sally in our Alley	1902
Vilia	Franz Lehar	Adrian Ross	The Merry Widow	1907
Virginia	George Gershwin	B. G. DeSylva	Sweet Little Devil	1924
Wait Till the Cows Come Home	Ivan Caryll	Anne Caldwell	Jack O'Lantern	1917
Walking Home with Angeline	George Gershwin	Brian Hooker	Our Nell	1922
What Do You Do Sunday, Mary?	Stephen Jones	Irving Caesar	Poppy	1923
When Hearts Are Young	Sigmund Romberg, Alfred Goodman	Cyrus Wood	The Lady in Ermine	1922
When You're Away	Victor Herbert	Henry Blossom	The Only Girl	1914

TITLE	COMPOSER	LYRICIST	SHOW	YEAR
~~Whip Poor Will~~	~~Jerome Kern~~	~~B. G. DeSylva~~	~~Sally~~	~~1920~~
Who Can Tell*	Fritz Kreisler	William LeBaron	Apple Blossoms	1919
Whose Baby Are You?	Jerome Kern	Anne Caldwell	The Night Boat	1920
Wild Rose	Jerome Kern	Clifford Grey	Sally	1920
Wildflower	Vincent Youmans, Herbert Stothart	Otto Harbach, Oscar Hammerstein II	Wildflower	1923
Will You Forget?	Emmerich Kalman	P. G. Wodehouse	The Riviera Girl	1917
Will You Remember?	Sigmund Romberg	Rida Johnson Young	Maytime	1917
Women	Franz Lehar	Adrian Ross	The Merry Widow	1907
Yama-Yama Man, The	Karl Hoschna	George Collin Davis	Three Twins	1908
Yankee Doodle Boy, The	George M. Cohan	George M. Cohan	Little Johnny Jones	1904
You Are Free	Victor Jacobi	William LeBaron	Apple Blossoms	1919
You Can't Fool Your Dreams	Richard Rodgers	Lorenz Hart	Poor Little Ritz Girl	1920
You Found Me and I Found You	Jerome Kern	P. G. Wodehouse	Oh, Lady! Lady!!	1918
You Never Knew About Me	Jerome Kern	P. G. Wodehouse	Oh, Boy!	1917
You Remind Me of My Mother	George M. Cohan	George M. Cohan	Little Nellie Kelly	1922
You Said Something	Jerome Kern	Jerome Kern, P. G. Wodehouse	Have a Heart	1917
You'd Be Surprised	Irving Berlin	Irving Berlin	Ziegfeld Follies	1919
You're a Grand Old Flag	George M. Cohan	George M. Cohan	George Washington, Jr.	1906
You're Here and I'm Here	Jerome Kern	Harry B. Smith	The Marriage Market	1914
You're in Love	Franz Lehar	Adrian Ross	Gypsy Love	1911
Young Man's Fancy, A	Milton Ager	John Murray Anderson, Jack Yellen	What's in a Name?	1922

*Same melody as "Stars in My Eyes" from film "The King Steps Out " 1936 (lyric by Dorothy Fields)

PART TWO

Theatre
Songs
1925-1960

WHO CARES
Copyright 1931 by New World Music Corporation
Used by Permission.

TEA FOR TWO
Copyright 1924 by Harms, Inc.
Used by Permission.

THEATRE
SONGS ☛
1925-1960

MUSICAL COMEDY was, by the mid-twenties, a lively and glamorous part of the American scene. It mirrored, for the most part, those prosperous and tinseled times, and the musical stage was a round of light-hearted songs and happy endings. But at the end of the decade—even before the Wall Street crash and the sobering days that followed—there were signs of a different and more intelligent musical.

A major step was the arrival in 1927 of Jerome Kern and Oscar Hammerstein's *Show Boat*, based on the Edna Ferber novel. It was in its very concept a daring and dramatic undertaking. Characters were three-dimensional, they moved through a relatively complex plot line—and on emotional levels new to the musical stage. There were a half-dozen important and enduring songs, with attractive secondary and thematic music woven into one rich fabric. The work has been performed almost continuously since its premiere, and it was to set authors, composers and lyricists forever searching for more meaningful source material.

The middle years of the twenties were, in other ways, good ones for the musical stage. Richard Rodgers and Lorenz Hart, then almost completely unknown, were asked by the Theatre Guild to write songs for an intimate revue scheduled for two Sunday performances, to raise funds for the Guild Theatre's new tapestries. The show was *The Garrick Gaieties*, and it was obvious that here was a team to listen to. The audience listened—to an extended run of the first show, to a second edition in 1926, and then to two dozen Rodgers and Hart musicals to follow in the years to come.

George and Ira Gershwin were now in full stride, turning out brilliant scores for *Lady, Be Good; Tip-Toes; Oh, Kay!; Funny Face* and *Girl Crazy*. The Gershwin songs, about which so much has been said and written, had, above all, vitality and invention. Some had excitement and drive, others were wonderfully tender and touching. There was also rare musical wit. George Gershwin was to write with distinction in more serious forms — a piano concerto, a tone poem, an opera—but theatre songs were his basic field and his great strength.

The thirties saw fewer musicals produced, but those that found their way to Broadway were distinctly more adult. *Of Thee I Sing*, by George Kaufman, Morrie Ryskind and the Gershwins, satirized the Presidency, the Senate and the Supreme Court, and became the first musical comedy to win a Pulitzer Prize. Equally impressive were several of the decade's revues, notably Moss Hart and Irving Berlin's *As Thousands Cheer*, and *The Band Wagon*, by George Kaufman, Howard Dietz and Arthur Schwartz.

Not every show broke new ground, but clearly the musical theatre was growing up. And further milestones would come. George Gershwin's opera, *Porgy and Bess*, completed just two years before his death, was musical theatre—and theatre music—at its finest. Rodgers and Hart did some innovating of their own in 1940 with *Pal Joey*, based on John O'Hara's short stories. The songs were completely integrated with story and the hero didn't get the girl. Like many another break with convention it was years ahead of its time, and a 1952 revival ran longer than the original production.

By 1941 there had been a complete evolution. *Lady in the Dark,* by Moss Hart, Kurt Weill and Ira Gershwin, was, with its background of psychoanalysis, a completely adult musical play. Then, in 1943, Richard Rodgers and Oscar Hammerstein II formed a significant writing partnership, one that would leave its mark on all musicals to follow. *Oklahoma!, Carousel, South Pacific* and *The King and I* were sensitive, moving and human as musicals had never been before. Every line of lyric and dialogue, every note of music seemed to be in exactly the right place. Through a wide range of subjects, the writing was always of unparalleled integrity. Their collaboration was a theatrical landmark.

The forties and fifties brought other distinguished musicals and scores. These were the years of Cole Porter's *Kiss Me Kate;* of Frank Loesser's *Guys and Dolls*, based on the Damon Runyon stories; of rich Harold Arlen songs for *Bloomer Girl* and *St. Louis Woman;* of Irving Berlin's abundant score for *Annie Get Your Gun*.

The year 1956 should be remembered—theatrically, at any rate—as the year of *My Fair Lady*. Written by Alan Jay Lerner and Frederick Loewe, and based on Shaw's *Pygmalion*, it was musical theatre at its mature, and glamorous, best. More than three million copies of the original cast recording have been sold and the difficulty in obtaining tickets to it became the basis of revue sketches. It was a hit of thunderous proportion. *West Side Story,* a brilliant and deeply moving, yet totally different, kind of musical theatre, arrived a year later, and the audience response was gratifying and significant.

There was perhaps no single season—or even decade—of revolutionary change. But an extraordinary distance had been traveled since the 1927 production of *Show Boat*. Works by O'Neill, Shakespeare, Shaw, Molnar and Sidney Howard were all to find their way to the musical stage, and the audience was ready and receptive. Our theatre music has made its own prominent niche throughout the world; excerpts from *Porgy and Bess, Carousel, Show Boat* and a dozen other shows are performed by major symphony orchestras, to no one's particular surprise.

The songs themselves are apt to have special meanings for us. In fact, some of them have a way of getting nostalgically mixed up with our lives. They take us back to a school dance or a first date or a summer. Undoubtedly, still better musicals will come; but as the new songs appear, the old ones—the good ones, at any rate—won't leave us. The ones we like will go on and on.

THEATRE SONGS 1925—1960

TITLE	COMPOSER	LYRICIST	SHOW	YEAR
About Face	Gerald Marks	Sam Lerner	Hold It!	1948
Abracadabra	Cole Porter	Cole Porter	Mexican Hayride	1944
Ace in the Hole	Cole Porter	Cole Porter	Let's Face It	1941
Acorn in the Meadow	Richard Adler, Jerry Ross		John Murray Ander-son's Almanac	1953
Add a Little Wiggle	Milton Ager	Jack Yellen	Rain or Shine	1928
Adelaide's Lament	Frank Loesser	Frank Loesser	Guys and Dolls	1950
Adorable Julie	Lewis E. Gensler	Owen Murphy, Robert A. Simon	The Gang's All Here	1931
Adorable You	Karl Hajos (based on Chopin)	Harry B. Smith	White Lilacs	1928
After All, It's Spring	Walter Kent	Kim Gannon	Seventeen	1951
After All You're All I'm After	Arthur Schwartz	Edward Heyman	She Loves Me Not	1933
After Graduation Day	Sidney Lippman	Sylvia Dee	Barefoot Boy with Cheek	1947
After You	Cole Porter	Cole Porter	Gay Divorce	1932
Ain' it De Truth?	Harold Arlen	E. Y. Harburg	Jamaica	1957
Ain't Love Wonderful?	Lewis E. Gensler	B. G. DeSylva	Captain Jinks	1925
Ain't Misbehavin'	Thomas (Fats) Waller, Harry Brooks	Andy Razaf	Hot Chocolates	1929
Ain't We Got Love	Eubie Blake	J. Milton Reddie, Cecil Mack	Swing It	1937
Alabama Stomp	James P. Johnson	Henry Creamer	Earl Carroll's Vanities	1926
All Alone Monday	Harry Ruby	Bert Kalmar	The Ramblers	1926
All Around the World	David Baker	David Craig	Phoenix '55	1955
All at Once	Richard Rodgers	Lorenz Hart	Babes in Arms	1937
All at Once You Love Her	Richard Rodgers	Oscar Hammer-stein II	Pipe Dream	1955
All Dark People	Richard Rodgers	Lorenz Hart	Babes in Arms	1937

21

TITLE	COMPOSER	LYRICIST	SHOW	YEAR
All Dressed Up (Spic and Spanish)	Richard Rodgers	Lorenz Hart	Too Many Girls	1939
All 'er Nothin'	Richard Rodgers	Oscar Hammer-stein II	Oklahoma!	1943
All For Love	Allan Roberts	Lester Lee	All for Love	1949
All I Need Is Some-one Like You	Harry Archer	Charles Tobias	Keep It Clean	1929
All I Need Is the Girl	Jule Styne	Stephen Sondheim	Gypsy	1959
All I Want Is Love	Hal Dyson	James Kendis	June Days	1925
All in Fun	Jerome Kern	Oscar Hammer-stein II	Very Warm for May	1939
All I've Got to Get Now Is My Man	Cole Porter	Cole Porter	Panama Hattie	1940
All of These and More	Jerry Bock	Sheldon Harnick	The Body Beautiful	1958
All of You	Cole Porter	Cole Porter	Silk Stockings	1955
All the King's Horses	Alec Wilder	Edward Brandt, Howard Dietz	Three's a Crowd	1930
All the Things You Are	Jerome Kern	Oscar Hammer-stein II	Very Warm for May	1939
All the Time	Harold Levey	Anita Owen	Rainbow Rose	1926
All the Time	Arthur Schwartz	Dorothy Fields	Stars in Your Eyes	1939
All the Time	Jay Livingston	Ray Evans	Oh Captain!	1958
All the Time Is Loving Time	Harold Orlob	Irving Caesar	Talk About Girls	1927
All Through the Night	Cole Porter	Cole Porter	Anything Goes	1934
All You Need Is a Quarter	Jule Styne	Betty Comden, Adolph Green	Do Re Mi	1960
Allez-Vous En, Go Away	Cole Porter	Cole Porter	Can-Can	1953
Almost Like Being in Love	Frederick Loewe	Alan Jay Lerner	Brigadoon	1947
Aloha	Rudolf Friml	J. Keirn Brennan	Luana	1930
Alone (My Lover)	Rudolf Friml	Brian Hooker	The White Eagle	1927
Alone Together	Arthur Schwartz	Howard Dietz	Flying Colors	1932
Alone Too Long	Arthur Schwartz	Dorothy Fields	By the Beautiful Sea	1954
Alone With Only Dreams	Ray Henderson	B. G. DeSylva, Lew Brown	George White's Scandals	1928
Alone With You	G. Romilli	Grace Henry, Jo Trent	Fioretta	1929
Along Came Love	Henry Tobias	Haven Gillespie, Charles Tobias	Earl Carroll's Vanities	1932
Along the Winding Road	Sigmund Romberg	Oscar Hammer-stein II	Sunny River	1941
Along With Me	Harold Rome	Harold Rome	Call Me Mister	1946
Always in my Heart	Ralph Benatzky	Ralph Benatzky	Meet My Sister	1930
Always True to You in My Fashion	Cole Porter	Cole Porter	Kiss Me, Kate	1948

TITLE	COMPOSER	LYRICIST	SHOW	YEAR
Always You	Gerald Marks	Sam Lerner	Hold It!	1948
Amapu	Melville Gideon	Edward Knoblock	The Optimists	1928
America	Leonard Bernstein	Stephen Sondheim	West Side Story	1957
Ameri-Can-Can	Roger Wolfe Kahn	Irving Caesar	Americana	1928
American Eagles	Irving Berlin	Irving Berlin	This Is the Army	1942
American Tune	Ray Henderson	B. G. DeSylva, Lew Brown	George White's Scandals	1928
And Love Was Born	Jerome Kern	Oscar Hammerstein II	Music in the Air	1932
And This Is My Beloved	Robert Wright, George Forrest (based on Borodin)		Kismet	1953
Angel	Peter De Rose	Mitchell Parish	Earl Carroll's Vanities	1940
Angelina*	Cy Coleman	Carolyn Leigh	Wildcat	1960
Animals Are Nice	Lee Wainer	J. B. Rosenberg	New Faces	1942
Ankle Up the Altar With Me	Richard Myers	E. Y. Harburg	Garrick Gaieties	1930
Annina	Rudolf Friml	Rowland Leigh, John Shubert	Music Hath Charms	1934
Another Autumn	Frederick Loewe	Alan Jay Lerner	Paint Your Wagon	1951
Another Case of the Blues	Richard Myers	Johnny Mercer	Tattle Tales	1930
Another Op'nin', Another Show	Cole Porter	Cole Porter	Kiss Me, Kate	1948
Answer Is No, The	Donald Heywood	Donald Heywood	Blackberries	1932
Any Little Fish*	Noel Coward	Noel Coward	The Third Little Show	1931
Any Place I Hang My Hat Is Home	Harold Arlen	Johnny Mercer	St. Louis Woman	1946
Any Time	Clarence Williams, Joe Jordan		Bottomland	1927
Any Way the Wind Blows	Bud Green, Cliff Friend, Sam H. Stept		Shady Lady	1933
Anyone Would Love You	Harold Rome	Harold Rome	Destry Rides Again	1959
Anything Can Happen	Ray Henderson	Jack Yellen	George White's Scandals	1936
Anything Goes	Cole Porter	Cole Porter	Anything Goes	1934
Anything May Happen Any Day	Jerome Kern	Graham John	Ripples	1930
Anything You Can Do	Irving Berlin	Irving Berlin	Annie Get Your Gun	1946
Anything Your Heart Desires	Harry Archer	Walter O'Keefe	Just a Minute	1928
April Face	Ralph Blane	Ralph Blane	Three Wishes for Jamie	1952
April Fool	Richard Rodgers	Lorenz Hart	Garrick Gaieties	1925
April in Paris	Vernon Duke	E. Y. Harburg	Walk a Little Faster	1932
April Snow	Sigmund Romberg	Dorothy Fields	Up in Central Park	1945
Are You Havin' Any Fun?	Sammy Fain	Jack Yellen	George White's Scandals	1939
Are You Love?	Sigmund Romberg	Oscar Hammerstein II	East Wind	1931
Are You Ready, Gyp Watson?	Harold Rome	Harold Rome	Destry Rides Again	1959

*Dropped from New York production

TITLE	COMPOSER	LYRICIST	SHOW	YEAR
Are You Sure?	Meredith Willson	Meredith Willson	The Unsinkable Molly Brown	1950
Armful of Trouble, An*	Jerome Kern	Otto Harbach	Roberta	1933
Armful of You*	Vincent Youmans	Leo Robin, Clifford Grey	Hit the Deck	1927
Army's Made a Man Out of Me, The	Irving Berlin	Irving Berlin	This Is the Army	1942
Art for Art's Sake	Marc Blitzstein	Marc Blitzstein	The Cradle Will Rock	1938
Artificial Flowers	Jerry Bock	Sheldon Harnick	Tenderloin	1960
As Long As I've Got My Mammy	Joseph Meyer, James F. Hanley	B. G. DeSylva	Big Boy	1925
As Long As There's a Mother	Glenn Paxton	Robert Goldman, George Weiss	First Impressions	1959
As Long As We're in Love	Jimmy McHugh	Dorothy Fields	Hello Daddy	1928
As on Through the Seasons We Sail	Cole Porter	Cole Porter	Silk Stockings	1955
As the Girls Go	Jimmy McHugh	Harold Adamson	As the Girls Go	1948
As Time Goes By	Herman Hupfeld	Herman Hupfeld	Everybody's Welcome	1931
Ashes and Fire	Frank Harling	Laurence Stallings	Deep River	1926
Asking for You	Jule Styne	Betty Comden, Adolph Green	Do Re Mi	1960
At Christmastime	Robert Wright, George Forrest (based on Grieg)		Song of Norway	1944
At Last	Henry Tobias	Charles Tobias, Sam Lewis	Earl Carroll's Sketch Book	1935
At Last It's Love	Morgan Lewis	Nancy Hamilton	Two for the Show	1940
At Long Last Love	Cole Porter	Cole Porter	You Never Know	1938
At the Barbecue	Dave Stamper, Harold Levey	Harry A. Steinberg, Eddie Ward	Lovely Lady	1927
At the Check Apron Ball	Bob Merrill	Bob Merrill	New Girl in Town	1957
At the Roxy Music Hall	Richard Rodgers	Lorenz Hart	I Married an Angel	1938
Augusta's Aria	Douglas Moore	John Latouche	The Ballad of Baby Doe	1958
Autumn in New York	Vernon Duke	Vernon Duke	Thumbs Up	1934
Babbitt and the Bromide, The	George Gershwin	Ira Gershwin	Funny Face	1927
Babes in Arms	Richard Rodgers	Lorenz Hart	Babes in Arms	1937
Baby!	George Gershwin	B. G. DeSylva, Ira Gershwin	Tell Me More	1925
Baby	Percy Wenrich	Raymond Peck	Castles in the Air	1926
Baby-Doll Dance	Maury Rubens, Phil Svigals	J. Keirn Brennan, Moe Jaffe	Broadway Nights	1929
Baby, Don't Count on Me	Clay Warnick	Edward Eager	Dream With Music	1944
Baby Mine	Eubie Blake	Andy Razaf	Blackbirds	1930

*Dropped from New York production

TITLE	COMPOSER	LYRICIST	SHOW	YEAR
Baby, Talk to Me	Charles Strouse	Lee Adams	Bye Bye Birdie	1960
Baby Wanna Go Bye-Bye	Lewis E. Gensler	Owen Murphy, Robert A. Simon	The Gang's All Here	1931
Babykins	Oscar Levant	Irving Caesar, Graham John	Ripples	1930
Baby's Awake Now	Richard Rodgers	Lorenz Hart	Spring Is Here	1929
Baby's Baby	David Baker	David Craig	Copper and Brass	1957
Baby's Best Friend, A	Richard Rodgers	Lorenz Hart	She's My Baby	1928
Baby's Blue	Herman Hupfeld	Herman Hupfeld	A La Carte	1927
Bad Timing	Morton Gould	Betty Comden, Adolph Green	Billion Dollar Baby	1945
Bal Petit Bal	Francis Lemarque	Francis Lemarque	New Faces	1952
Balalaika Serenade, The	Franz Steininger (based on Tchaikovsky)	Forman Brown	Music in My Heart	1947
Bali Ha'i	Richard Rodgers	Oscar Hammerstein II	South Pacific	1949
Ballad of the Sad Young Man, The	Tommy Wolf	Fran Landesman	The Nervous Set	1959
Band Started Swinging a Song, The	Cole Porter	Cole Porter	The Seven Lively Arts	1944
Bandanna Babies	Jimmy McHugh	Dorothy Fields	Blackbirds	1928
Bang—The Bell Rang!	Irving Actman	Frank Loesser	The Illustrators' Show	1936
Banjo That Man Joe Plays, The	Cole Porter	Cole Porter	Wake Up and Dream	1929
Barnaby Beach	Morgan Lewis	Nancy Hamilton	Three to Make Ready	1946
Bashful Lover	C. Moulton	Eleanor and Herbert Farjeon	The Two Bouquets	1938
Baubles, Bangles and Beads	Robert Wright, George Forrest (based on Borodin)		Kismet	1953
Be a Mess	Jay Gorney	Walter and Jean Kerr	Touch and Go	1949
Be Good, Be Good, Be Good	James Shelton	James Shelton	Mrs. Patterson	1954
Be Good to Me	Vincent Youmans	Ring Lardner	Smiles	1930
Be Kind to Your Parents	Harold Rome	Harold Rome	Fanny	1954
Be My Guest	Johnny Mercer	Johnny Mercer	Top Banana	1951
Beat Out Dat Rhythm on a Drum	Georges Bizet	Oscar Hammerstein II	Carmen Jones	1943
Beautiful Baby	William B. Friedlander, Con Conrad		Mercenary Mary	1925
Beautiful Baby	James Hanley	B. G. DeSylva	Queen High	1926
Beautiful Girls	Alfred Goodman, J. Fred Coots, Maury Rubens	Clifford Grey	Gay Paree	1926

TITLE	COMPOSER	LYRICIST	SHOW	YEAR
Beautiful Gypsy*	George Gershwin	Ira Gershwin	Rosalie	1928
Bea-u-ti-ful People of Denver	Meredith Willson	Meredith Willson	The Unsinkable Molly Brown	1960
Beauty Is Vanity	Maury Rubens	Clifford Grey	The Great Temptations	1926
Because, Because	George Gershwin	Ira Gershwin	Of Thee I Sing	1931
Because You're Beautiful	Ray Henderson	B. G. DeSylva, Lew Brown	Three Cheers	1928
Begat, The	Burton Lane	E. Y. Harburg	Finian's Rainbow	1947
Begin the Beguine	Cole Porter	Cole Porter	Jubilee	1935
Believe in Me	Arthur Schwartz	Harry B. Smith	The Red Robe	1928
Bells Are Ringing	Jule Styne	Betty Comden, Adolph Green	Bells Are Ringing	1956
Belly Up to the Bar, Boys	Meredith Willson	Meredith Willson	The Unsinkable Molly Brown	1960
Beside the Star of Glory	Karl Hajos (based on Tchaikovsky)	Harry B. Smith	Natja	1925
Bess, You is My Woman	George Gershwin	Ira Gershwin, DuBose Heyward	Porgy and Bess	1935
Best Thing for You, The	Irving Berlin	Irving Berlin	Call Me Madam	1950
Best Things in Life Are Free, The	Ray Henderson	B. G. DeSylva, Lew Brown	Good News	1927
Best Things of All, The	Marc Blitzstein	Marc Blitzstein	Regina	1949
Best Time of Day, The	Gordon Jenkins	Tom Adair	Along Fifth Avenue	1949
Better Be Good to Me	Richard Rodgers	Lorenz Hart	Chee-Chee	1928
Better Times Are Coming	Jimmie Steiger	Dolph Singer	White Lights	1927
Betty Lou	Joe Jordan	Rosamond Johnson	Brown Buddies	1930
Bewitched	Richard Rodgers	Lorenz Hart	Pal Joey	1940
Bianca	Cole Porter	Cole Porter	Kiss Me, Kate	1948
Bidin' My Time	George Gershwin	Ira Gershwin	Girl Crazy	1930
Big Back Yard, The	Sigmund Romberg	Dorothy Fields	Up in Central Park	1945
Big Black Giant, The	Richard Rodgers	Oscar Hammerstein II	Me and Juliet	1953
Big Brass Band from Brazil, The	Bob Hilliard	Carl Sigman	Angel in the Wings	1947
Big "D"	Frank Loesser	Frank Loesser	The Most Happy Fella	1956
Big Four, The	Peter H. Weiss	Peter H. Weiss	All for Love	1949
Big Mole	Kurt Weill	Maxwell Anderson	Lost in the Stars	1949
Big Movie Show in the Sky, The	Robert Emmett Dolan	Johnny Mercer	Texas, Li'l Darlin'	1949
Bigger and Better Than Ever	Cliff Friend	George White	George White's Scandals	1929
Bill	Jerome Kern	P. G. Wodehouse	Show Boat	1927
Bill of Rights, The	Jay Gorney	Henry Myers	Meet the People	1940

*Dropped from New York production

TITLE	COMPOSER	LYRICIST	SHOW	YEAR
Billie	George M. Cohan	George M. Cohan	Billie	1928
Birth of the Blues, The	Ray Henderson	B. G. DeSylva, Lew Brown	George White's Scandals	1926
Bitter Harvest	Raymond Scott	Bernard Hanighen	Lute Song	1946
Black and Blue	Thomas (Fats) Waller	Harry Brooks, Andy Razaf	Hot Chocolates	1929
Black Bottom	Ray Henderson	B. G. DeSylva, Lew Brown	George White's Scandals	1926
Black Swan, The	Gian-Carlo Menotti	Gian-Carlo Menotti	The Medium	1947
Blackberries	Donald Heywood	Donald Heywood	Blackberries	1932
Blade of Mine	George Bagby	Grace Henry	Fioretta	1929
Blah! But Not Blue	Abel Baer	Sam Lewis, Joe Young	Lady Do	1927
Blessings	Victor Young	Stella Unger	Seventh Heaven	1955
Blow a Balloon Up to the Moon	Sammy Fain	Charles Tobias	Hellzapoppin'	1938
Blow, Gabriel, Blow	Cole Porter	Cole Porter	Anything Goes	1934
Blow Hot and Heavy	Philip Charig, Richard Myers	Leo Robin	Allez-Oop	1927
Blow Hot—Blow Cold	Louis Alter	Harry Ruskin, Leighton K. Brill	Ballyhoo	1930
Blow the Blues Away	Werner Janssen	Mann Holiner, J. Keirn Brennan	Boom-Boom	1928
Blowin' the Blues Away	Philip Charig	Ira Gershwin	Americana	1926
Blue Again	Jimmy McHugh	Dorothy Fields	The Vanderbilt Revue	1930
Blue, Blue, Blue	George Gershwin	Ira Gershwin	Let 'Em Eat Cake	1933
Blue Day	Abraham Ellstein	Walter Bullock	Great to be Alive	1950
Blue Eyes	Robert Stolz	Irving Caesar	White Horse Inn	1936
Blue Grass	Arthur Schwartz	Howard Dietz	Inside U. S. A.	1948
Blue Night	Bhumibol-Chakra-band	N. Tong Yai	Michael Todd's Peep Show	1950
Blue Ocean Blues	Richard Rodgers	Lorenz Hart	Present Arms	1928
Blue Room, The	Richard Rodgers	Lorenz Hart	The Girl Friend	1926
Blue Shadows	Louis Alter	Raymond Klages	Earl Carroll's Vanities	1928
Blue Skies	Irving Berlin	Irving Berlin	Betsy	1926
Blue Skies, Gray Skies	George M. Cohan	George M. Cohan	The Merry Malones	1927
Blues	Marc Blitzstein	Marc Blitzstein	Regina	1949
Body and Soul	Johnny Green	Edward Heyman, Robert Sour	Three's a Crowd	1930
Bon Jour	Meredith Willson	Meredith Willson	The Unsinkable Molly Brown	1960
Boomps-A-Daisy	Annette Mills	Annette Mills	Hellzapoppin'	1938
Born and Bred in Old Kentucky	Joseph Meyer, James F. Hanley	B. G. DeSylva	Big Boy	1925
Born Too Late	Vernon Duke	Ogden Nash	The Littlest Revue	1956

TITLE	COMPOSER	LYRICIST	SHOW	YEAR
Boston Beguine	Sheldon Harnick	Sheldon Harnick	New Faces	1952
Boston in the Spring	Richard Lewine	Ted Fetter	The Girl from Wyoming	1938
Bottomland	Clarence Williams, Jo Trent		Bottomland	1927
Bottoms Up	Cliff Friend	George White	George White's Scandals	1929
Boy, Girl, Moon	Dave Stamper	Fred Herendeen	Orchids Preferred	1937
Boy Like You, A	Kurt Weill	Langston Hughes	Street Scene	1947
Boy Most Likely to Succeed, The	Arthur Siegel	June Carroll	New Faces	1956
Boy Named Lem, A	Sam Stept	Lew Brown, Charles Tobias	Yokel Boy	1939
Boy! What Love Has Done to Me!	George Gershwin	Ira Gershwin	Girl Crazy	1930
Boys and Girls Like You and Me*	Richard Rodgers	Oscar Hammerstein II	Oklahoma!	1943
Boys in Gray	Sigmund Romberg	Dorothy Donnelly	My Maryland	1927
Brazilian Nuts	Dorival Caymmi	Al Stillman	Star and Garter	1942
Bread and Butter	Jerome Kern	Anne Caldwell, Otto Harbach	Criss-Cross	1926
Break-Me-Down, The	Harry Archer	Walter O'Keefe	Just a Minute	1928
Breakfast in Bed	Armand Vecsey	P. G. Wodehouse	The Nightingale	1927
Breakfast With You	Milton Ager	Jack Yellen	Rain or Shine	1928
Bride Was Dressed in White, The	Vincent Youmans	Oscar Hammerstein II	Rainbow	1928
Brigadoon	Frederick Loewe	Alan Jay Lerner	Brigadoon	1947
Bring Back Those Minstrel Days	Martin Broones	Ballard MacDonald	Rufus LeMaire's Affairs	1927
Briny Blues, The	Serge Walter	Agnes Morgan	Grand Street Follies	1928
Broadway	Ray Henderson	B. G. DeSylva, Lew Brown	Manhattan Mary	1927
Brother, Can You Spare a Dime?	Jay Gorney	E. Y. Harburg	Americana	1932
Brown	Ford Dabney	Jo Trent	Rang-Tang	1927
Brown Eyes	Rudolf Friml	Otto Harbach, Oscar Hammerstein II	The Wild Rose	1926
Brown Sugar	Donald Heywood	Donald Heywood	Blackberries	1932
Brush Up Your Shakespeare	Cole Porter	Cole Porter	Kiss Me, Kate	1948
Buck in the Bank	Gerald Marks	Sam Lerner	Hold It!	1948
Buckle Down, Winsocki	Hugh Martin	Ralph Blane	Best Foot Forward	1941
Buddie, Beware	Cole Porter	Cole Porter	Anything Goes	1934
Buds Won't Bud*	Harold Arlen	E. Y. Harburg	Hooray For What	1937
Buenos Aires	Leonard Bernstein	Leonard Bernstein	Candide	1956
Bunny, Bunny, Bunny	Harold Rome	Harold Rome	Star and Garter	1942

*Dropped from New York production

TITLE	COMPOSER	LYRICIST	SHOW	YEAR
Bushel and a Peck, A	Frank Loesser	Frank Loesser	Guys and Dolls	1950
But in the Morning, No	Cole Porter	Cole Porter	DuBarry Was a Lady	1939
But Not For Me	George Gershwin	Ira Gershwin	Girl Crazy	1930
But Yours	Bob Merrill	Bob Merrill	Take Me Along	1959
Button Up Your Heart	Jimmy McHugh	Dorothy Fields	The Vanderbilt Revue	1930
Button Up Your Overcoat	Ray Henderson	B. G. DeSylva, Lew Brown	Follow Thru	1928
Buy Yourself a Balloon	Herman Hupfeld	Herman Hupfeld	The Show Is On	1936
By Candlelight	Robert Katscher	Rowland Leigh	You Never Know	1938
By Myself	Arthur Schwartz	Howard Dietz	Between the Devil	1937
By Special Permission of the Copyright Owners, I Love You	Lewis E. Gensler	Owen Murphy, Robert A. Simon	The Gang's All Here	1931
By Strauss	George Gershwin	Ira Gershwin	The Show Is On	1936
By the Beautiful Sea	Arthur Schwartz	Dorothy Fields	By the Beautiful Sea	1954
By the Mississinewah	Cole Porter	Cole Porter	Something for the Boys	1943
By the Sweat of Your Brow	Eubie Blake	J. Milton Reddie, Cecil Mack	Swing It	1937
Bye and Bye	Richard Rodgers	Lorenz Hart	Dearest Enemy	1925
Bye-Bye Babe	Leon DeCosta	Leon DeCosta	The Blonde Sinner	1926
Bye, Bye Baby	Jule Styne	Leo Robin	Gentlemen Prefer Blondes	1949
Cab Song	Emmerich Kalman	George Marion, Jr.	Marinka	1945
Caballero	Noel Coward	Noel Coward	This Year of Grace	1928
Cabin in the Sky	Vernon Duke	John Latouche	Cabin in the Sky	1940
Cakewalk Your Lady	Harold Arlen	Johnny Mercer	St. Louis Woman	1946
California Skies	Harry Ruby	Bert Kalmar	The Ramblers	1926
Calinda, The	Herman Hupfeld	Herman Hupfeld	A La Carte	1927
Call it a Dream	Sigmund Romberg	Oscar Hammerstein II	Sunny River	1941
Call it Applefritters	Richard Stutz	Milton Pascal	Along Fifth Avenue	1949
Call it Love	Abraham Ellstein	Walter Bullock	Great to Be Alive	1950
Call of Broadway, The	Maury Rubens	Jack Osterman, Ted Lewis	Artists and Models	1927
Call of Life, The	Noel Coward	Noel Coward	Bitter Sweet	1929
Call of Love, The	Emmerich Kalman	Harry B. Smith	Countess Maritza	1926
Calliope	Kay Swift	Kay Swift	Paris '90	1952
Camelot	Frederick Loewe	Alan Jay Lerner	Camelot	1960
Can-Can	Cole Porter	Cole Porter	Can-Can	1953
Can This Be Love?	Kay Swift	Paul James	Fine and Dandy	1930
Can You Use Any Money Today?	Irving Berlin	Irving Berlin	Call Me Madam	1950
Can't Help Lovin' Dat Man	Jerome Kern	Oscar Hammerstein II	Show Boat	1927
Can't We Be Friends?	Kay Swift	Paul James	The Little Show	1929

TITLE	COMPOSER	LYRICIST	SHOW	YEAR
Can't We Get Together	Thomas (Fats) Waller, Harry Brooks	Andy Razaf	Hot Chocolates	1929
Can't You Do A Friend a Favor?	Richard Rodgers	Lorenz Hart	A Connecticut Yankee (revival)	1943
Can't You Just See Yourself?	Jule Styne	Sammy Cahn	High Button Shoes	1947
Captain Hook's Waltz	Jule Styne	Betty Comden, Adolph Green	Peter Pan	1954
Careful With My Heart	Senia Pokrass	E. Y. Harburg	Ziegfeld Follies	1934
Carefully Taught	Richard Rodgers	Oscar Hammerstein II	South Pacific	1949
Careless Rhapsody	Richard Rodgers	Lorenz Hart	By Jupiter	1942
Caress Me, Possess Me, Perfume	Moose Charlap	Norman Gimbel	Whoop-up	1958
Carinito	Maria Grever	Raymond Leveen	Viva O'Brien	1941
Carino Mio	Frederick Loewe	Alan Jay Lerner	Paint Your Wagon	1951
Carissima	G. Romilli	Grace Henry	Fioretta	1929
Carlotta	Cole Porter	Cole Porter	Mexican Hayride	1944
Carousel in the Park	Sigmund Romberg	Dorothy Fields	Up in Central Park	1945
Carousel Waltz	Richard Rodgers		Carousel	1945
Carry On, Keep Smiling*	Vincent Youmans	Harold Adamson	Smiles	1930
Catch Our Act at the Met	Jule Styne	Betty Comden, Adolph Green	Two on the Aisle	1951
Caught in the Rain	Henry Sullivan	Howard Dietz	The Little Show	1929
'Cause You Won't Play House	Morgan Lewis	E. Y. Harburg	New Faces	1934
Cavaliers	Rudolf Friml	Rowland Leigh, John Shubert	Music Hath Charms	1934
C'est La Vie	Victor Young	Stella Unger	Seventh Heaven	1955
C'est Magnifique	Cole Porter	Cole Porter	Can-Can	1953
Chain Store Daisy	Harold Rome	Harold Rome	Pins and Needles	1937
Charleston Mad	William B. Friedlander, Con Conrad		Mercenary Mary	1925
Charlie, My Back Door Man	Clarence Todd	Con Conrad, Henry Creamer	Keep Shufflin'	1928
Charm	William Roy	William Roy	Maggie	1953
Charming	Edward Horan	Frederick Herendeen	All the King's Horses	1934
Chatter	Gene Lockhart	Gene Lockhart	Bunk of 1926	1926
Chatterbox, The	Sam Morrison	Dolph Singer	Summer Wives	1936
Cheerful Little Earful	Harry Warren	Ira Gershwin, Billy Rose	Sweet and Low	1930

*Dropped from New York production

TITLE	COMPOSER	LYRICIST	SHOW	YEAR
Cheerio!	Richard Rodgers	Lorenz Hart	Dearest Enemy	1925
Cheerio	Jesse Greer	James J. Walker*	Say When	1928
Cherokee Rose	Frank Harling	Laurence Stallings	Deep River	1926
Cherry Pies Ought to Be You	Cole Porter	Cole Porter	Out of This World	1950
Chick-A-Pen	Meredith Willson	Meredith Willson	The Unsinkable Molly Brown	1960
Child of Erin	Franklin Hauser	Russell Janney	The O'Flynn	1934
Chill in the Air	Frank d'Armond	Will Morrissey	Saluta	1934
China Bogie Man	A. Baldwin Sloane	Harry Cort, George E. Stoddard	China Rose	1925
China Rose	A. Baldwin Sloane	Harry Cort, George E. Stoddard	China Rose	1925
Chinkypin	Marc Blitzstein	Marc Blitzstein	Regina	1949
Chivaree	James P. Johnson	Flournoy Miller	Sugar Hill	1931
Choose Your Flowers	Lucien Denni	Helena Evans	Happy-Go-Lucky	1926
Christine	Sammy Fain	Paul Francis Webster	Christine	1960
Cigarette	H. Maurice Jacquet	William Brady	The Silver Swan	1929
Cigarette!	Ray Henderson	Jack Yellen	George White's Scandals	1936
Cigarettes	Harry Ruby	Bert Kalmar	High Kickers	1941
Cigarettes, Cigars!	Harry Revel	Mack Gordon	Ziegfeld Follies	1931
Cinderella Brown	Jimmy McHugh	Dorothy Fields	Lew Leslie's International Review	1930
Cinderella Girl	Jerome Kern	Anne Caldwell, Otto Harbach	Criss-Cross	1926
Cingalese Girls	Harry Ruby	Bert Kalmar, Otto Harbach	Lucky	1927
Circus Is on Parade, The	Richard Rodgers	Lorenz Hart	Jumbo	1935
City Mouse, Country Mouse	Albert Hague	Arnold B. Horwitt	Plain and Fancy	1955
Civilization	Bob Hilliard	Carl Sigman	Angel in the Wings	1947
Clap Yo' Hands	George Gershwin	Ira Gershwin	Oh, Kay!	1926
Clear Out of this World	Jimmy McHugh	Al Dubin	Keep Off the Grass	1940
Climb Ev'ry Mountain	Richard Rodgers	Oscar Hammerstein II	The Sound of Music	1959
Climb Up the Mountain	Cole Porter	Cole Porter	Out of This World	1950
Climbing Up the Ladder of Love	Jesse Greer	Raymond Klages	Earl Carroll's Vanities	1926
Clorinda	Donald Heywood	Donald Heywood	Africana	1929
Close as Pages in a Book	Sigmund Romberg	Dorothy Fields	Up in Central Park	1945
Close in Your Arms	Ida Hoyt Chamberlain	Ida Hoyt Chamberlain	Enchanted Isle	1927
Close Your Eyes	Alfred Nathan	George Oppenheimer	The Manhatters	1927

Written while Mayor of New York

TITLE	COMPOSER	LYRICIST	SHOW	YEAR
Clutching at Shadows	Alexander Fogarty	Seymour Morris	Cape Cod Follies	1929
Coax Me	Ernest G. Schweikert	Frank Reardon	Rumple	1957
Cockeyed Optimist, A	Richard Rodgers	Oscar Hammerstein II	South Pacific	1949
Cocoanut Sweet	Harold Arlen	E. Y. Harburg	Jamaica	1957
Collegiate	Moe Jaffe	Nat Bonx	Gay Paree	1926
Colonel Buffalo Bill	Irving Berlin	Irving Berlin	Annie Get Your Gun	1946
Colorado Love Call	Rick Besoyan	Rick Besoyan	Little Mary Sunshine	1959
Come Along Sunshine	Harry Tierney	Joseph McCarthy	Cross My Heart	1928
Come Along With Me	Cole Porter	Cole Porter	Can-Can	1953
Come and Tell Me*	Richard Rodgers	Lorenz Hart	Betsy	1926
Come Back, Little Genie	Sammy Fain	E. Y. Harburg	Flahooley	1951
Come Home	Richard Rodgers	Oscar Hammerstein II	Allegro	1947
Come On and Make Whoopee	Werner Janssen	Mann Holiner	Luckee Girl	1928
Come On Home	Donald Heywood	Donald Heywood	Bottomland	1927
Come On In	Cole Porter	Cole Porter	DuBarry Was a Lady	1939
Come Rain or Come Shine	Harold Arlen	Johnny Mercer	St. Louis Woman	1946
Come to Me, Bend to Me	Frederick Loewe	Alan Jay Lerner	Brigadoon	1947
Come to St. Thomas's	George M. Cohan	George M. Cohan	Billie	1928
Come Up and Have a Cup of Coffee	Ray Henderson	Jack Yellen	Ziegfeld Follies	1943
Come West, Little Girl, Come West	Walter Donaldson	Gus Kahn	Whoopee	1928
Comes Love	Sam Stept	Lew Brown, Charles Tobias	Yokel Boy	1939
Comme Ci, Comme Ca	Philip Charig	Irving Caesar	Polly	1929
Company Manners	Will Morrissey	Edmund Joseph	Polly of Hollywood	1927
Confession	Arthur Schwartz	Howard Dietz	The Band Wagon	1931
Consolation	Emmerich Kalman, Herbert Stothart	Otto Harbach, Oscar Hammerstein II	Golden Dawn	1927
Contagious Rhythm	Harold Arlen	Ted Koehler	Earl Carroll's Vanities	1930
Continental Honeymoon	James F. Hanley	Ballard MacDonald	Thumbs Up	1934
Convent Bells Are Ringing	Sigmund Romberg	Harry B. Smith	Princess Flavia	1925
Coo-Coo	Joseph Meyer, Philip Charig	Leo Robin	Just Fancy	1927
Cool	Leonard Bernstein	Stephen Sondheim	West Side Story	1957

*Dropped from New York production

TITLE	COMPOSER	LYRICIST	SHOW	YEAR
Corduroy Road	Cy Coleman	Carolyn Leigh	Wildcat	1960
Cossack Love Song	George Gershwin, Herbert Stothart	Otto Harbach, Oscar Hammerstein II	Song of the Flame	1925
Could Be	Harold Rome	Harold Rome	Wish You Were Here	1952
Could it Be You?	Cole Porter	Cole Porter	Something for the Boys	1943
Could You Use Me?	George Gershwin	Ira Gershwin	Girl Crazy	1930
Count Your Blessings	Cole Porter	Cole Porter	Mexican Hayride	1944
Counting the Sheep	Louis Alter	Max & Nathaniel Lief	Tattle Tales	1930
Cow and a Plough and a Frau, A	Morton Gould	Dorothy Fields	Arms and the Girl	1950
Cradle Will Rock, The	Marc Blitzstein	Marc Blitzstein	The Cradle Will Rock	1938
Crashing the Golden Gate	Jay Gorney	Phil Cohan, E. Y. Harburg	Earl Carroll's Sketch Book	1929
Crazy as a Loon	Jimmy McHugh	Al Dubin	Keep Off the Grass	1940
Crazy Elbows	Richard Rodgers	Lorenz Hart	Present Arms	1928
Crazy Quilt	Harry Warren	Bud Green	Crazy Quilt	1931
Crazy Rhythm	Joseph Meyer, Roger Wolfe Kahn	Irving Caesar	Here's Howe	1928
Croon-Spoon	Marc Blitzstein	Marc Blitzstein	The Cradle Will Rock	1938
Cross Your Fingers	J. Fred Coots	Arthur Swanstrom, Benny Davis	Sons O' Guns	1929
Cross Your Heart	Lewis E. Gensler	B. G. DeSylva	Queen High	1926
Cry Like the Wind	Jule Styne	Betty Comden, Adolph Green	Do Re Mi	1960
Cuckoo-Cheena, The	Alma Sanders	Monte Carlo	Louisiana Lady	1947
Cuddle Up	Gene Lockhart	Gene Lockhart	Bunk of 1926	1926
Cup of Coffee, a Sandwich and You, A	Joseph Meyer	Billy Rose, Al Dubin	Charlot's Revue	1925
Dance Alone With You	George Gershwin	Ira Gershwin	Funny Face	1927
Dance, Little Lady	Noel Coward	Noel Coward	This Year of Grace	1928
Dance, My Darlings	Sigmund Romberg	Oscar Hammerstein II	May Wine	1935
Dance Only With Me	Jule Styne	Betty Comden, Adolph Green	Say, Darling	1958
Dance With Me (Tonight at the Mardi Gras)	Irving Berlin	Irving Berlin	Louisiana Purchase	1940
Dancin' 'Way Your Sin	J. C. Johnson	J. C. Johnson	Brown Buddies	1930
Dancing Girl	Clarence Williams	Spencer Williams	Bottomland	1927
Dancing in the Dark	Arthur Schwartz	Howard Dietz	The Band Wagon	1931
Dancing on the Ceiling*	Richard Rodgers	Lorenz Hart	Simple Simon	1930

*Dropped from New York production

TITLE	COMPOSER	LYRICIST	SHOW	YEAR
Dancing the Devil Away	Harry Ruby	Bert Kalmar, Otto Harbach	Lucky	1927
Dancing Toes	Leon DeCosta	Leon DeCosta	Kosher Kitty Kelly	1925
Danger in the Dark	Jimmy McHugh	Al Dubin	Streets of Paris	1939
Danube So Blue	Johann Strauss	Desmond Carter	The Great Waltz	1934
Daphne	Milton Susskind	Paul Porter, Benjamin H. Burt	Florida Girl	1925
Darky Rhythm	Peter Tinturin	Joe Young	Brown Buddies	1930
Darn Clever, These Chinese	Hoagy Carmichael	Johnny Mercer	Walk With Music	1940
Darn it Baby, That's Love	Joan Edwards	Lynn Duddy	Tickets Please	1950
Darn That Dream	Jimmy Van Heusen	Eddie DeLange	Swingin' the Dream	1939
Dat's Love	Georges Bizet	Oscar Hammerstein II	Carmen Jones	1943
Dawn	Robert Stolz, Herbert Stothart	Otto Harbach, Oscar Hammerstein II	Golden Dawn	1927
Day Before Spring, The	Frederick Loewe	Alan Jay Lerner	The Day Before Spring	1945
Days of Old, The	Oscar Straus	Clare Kummer	Three Waltzes	1937
De-Dum-Dum	Jean Schwartz	Alfred Bryan	A Night in Spain	1927
De Old Clay Road	Frank Harling	Laurence Stallings	Deep River	1926
Dear Eyes That Haunt Me	Emmerich Kalman	Harry B. Smith	The Circus Princess	1927
Dear Home of Mine, Goodbye	Emmerich Kalman	Harry B. Smith	Countess Maritza	1926
Dear Little Café	Noel Coward	Noel Coward	Bitter Sweet	1929
Dear, Oh Dear	Richard Rodgers	Lorenz Hart	Chee-Chee	1928
Deauville	Herman Hupfeld	Herman Hupfeld	The Merry World	1926
Den of Iniquity	Richard Rodgers	Lorenz Hart	Pal Joey	1940
Desert Song, The	Sigmund Romberg	Otto Harbach, Oscar Hammerstein II	The Desert Song	1926
Desire	Sigmund Romberg	Rowland Leigh	My Romance	1948
Devil May Care, The	Ralph Benatzky	Ralph Benatzky	Meet My Sister	1930
Diamonds Are a Girl's Best Friend	Jule Styne	Leo Robin	Gentlemen Prefer Blondes	1949
Diavolo	Richard Rodgers	Lorenz Hart	Jumbo	1935
Did You Close Your Eyes?	Bob Merrill	Bob Merrill	New Girl in Town	1957
Did You Ever Get Stung?	Richard Rodgers	Lorenz Hart	I Married an Angel	1938
Did You Ever Hear the Blues?	David Martin	Langston Hughes	Simply Heavenly	1957
Didn't it?	Cliff Friend	Lew Brown	Piggy	1927
Dig-A Dig-A Doo	Jimmy McHugh	Dorothy Fields	Blackbirds	1928

TITLE	COMPOSER	LYRICIST	SHOW	YEAR
Ding, Dong, Dell	Cliff Friend	Lew Brown	Piggy	1927
Dis-Donc, Dis-Donc	Marguerite Monnot	Julian More, Daniel Heneker, Monte Norman	Irma La Douce	1960
Dis Is de Day	Frank Harling	Laurence Stallings	Deep River	1926
Distant Melody	Jule Styne	Betty Comden, Adolph Green	Peter Pan	1954
Dites-Moi	Richard Rodgers	Oscar Hammerstein II	South Pacific	1949
Dixie	Jimmy McHugh	Dorothy Fields	Blackbirds	1928
Dixie Cinderella	Thomas (Fats) Waller, Harry Brooks	Andy Razaf	Hot Chocolates	1929
Dixie Vagabond	Frank Marcus, Bernard Maltin		Bomboola	1929
Do Do Do	George Gershwin	Ira Gershwin	Oh, Kay!	1926
Do I Hear You Saying?	Richard Rodgers	Lorenz Hart	Present Arms	1928
Do I Love You?	Henri Christiné, E. Ray Goetz	E. Ray Goetz	Naughty Cinderella	1925
Do I Love You?	Cole Porter	Cole Porter	DuBarry Was a Lady	1939
Do It the Hard Way	Richard Rodgers	Lorenz Hart	Pal Joey	1940
Do My Eyes Deceive Me?	Richard Lewine	Ted Fetter	The Fireman's Flame	1937
Do Say You Do	Harry Revel	Mack Gordon, Harold Adamson	Smiling Faces	1932
Do the New York	Ben Oakland	Jack Murray, Barry Trivers	Ziegfeld Follies	1931
Do What You Do!	George Gershwin	Ira Gershwin, Gus Kahn	Show Girl	1929
Do What You Like	Philip Charig	Leo Robin	Shoot the Works	1931
Do What You Wanna Do	Vernon Duke	John Latouche	Cabin in the Sky	1940
Do You?	Robert Russell Bennett	Owen Murphy, Robert A. Simon	Hold Your Horses	1933
Do You Ever Dream of Vienna?	Rick Besoyan	Rick Besoyan	Little Mary Sunshine	1959
Do You Love as I Love?	Joseph Meyer	Irving Caesar	Yes, Yes, Yvette	1927
Do You Love Me?	Richard Rodgers	Lorenz Hart	Garrick Gaieties	1925
Doctor and Ella	Marc Blitzstein	Marc Blitzstein	The Cradle Will Rock	1938
Doin' the Chamberlain	Jimmy McHugh	Al Dubin	Streets of Paris	1939
Doin' the Hot-Cha-Cha	Lester Lee	Lester Lee	Keep It Clean	1929
Doin' the New Low-Down	Jimmy McHugh	Dorothy Fields	Blackbirds	1928
Doin' the Truck	Gerald Dolin	Edward J. Lambert	Smile at Me	1925
Doin' What Comes Naturally	Irving Berlin	Irving Berlin	Annie Get Your Gun	1946
Doing the Reactionary	Harold Rome	Harold Rome	Pins and Needles	1937
Dolce Far Niente	Meredith Willson	Meredith Willson	The Unsinkable Molly Brown	1960

TITLE	COMPOSER	LYRICIST	SHOW	YEAR
~~Don Jose of Far~~ Rockaway	Harold Rome	Harold Rome	Wish You Were Here	1952
Don' Shake My Tree	Raymond Hubbell	Anne Caldwell	Yours Truly	1927
Don't Ask Me Not to Sing*	Jerome Kern	Otto Harbach	The Cat and the Fiddle	1931
Don't be a Woman if You Can	Arthur Schwartz	Ira Gershwin	Park Avenue	1946
Don't Cry	Frank Loesser	Frank Loesser	The Most Happy Fella	1956
Don't Ever Leave Me	Jerome Kern	Oscar Hammerstein II	Sweet Adeline	1929
Don't Fall in Love With Me	Herman Hupfeld	Herman Hupfeld	The Merry World	1926
Don't Forget	James F. Hanley	B. G. DeSylva	Queen High	1926
Don't Forget the Girl From Punxatawney	Jerry Livingston	Mack David	Bright Lights	1943
Don't Hang Your Dreams on a Rainbow	Arnold Johnson	Irving Kahal	Earl Carroll's Sketch Book	1929
Don't Hold Everything	Ray Henderson	B. G. DeSylva, Lew Brown	Hold Everything!	1928
Don't Leave Your Little Blackbird Blue	Joe Jordan, Porter Grainger, Shelton Brooks		Brown Buddies	1930
Don't Let it Get You Down	Burton Lane	E. Y. Harburg	Hold On to Your Hats	1940
Don't Listen to Your Heart	Marianne Brown Waters, Bradford Greene		Right This Way	1938
Don't Look at Me That Way	Cole Porter	Cole Porter	Paris	1928
Don't Look Now	David Baker	David Craig	Copper and Brass	1957
Don't Marry Me	Richard Rodgers	Oscar Hammerstein II	Flower Drum Song	1958
Don't Talk	Morton Gould	Dorothy Fields	Arms and the Girl	1950
Don't Tell Me It's Bad	Ray Henderson	Ted Koehler	Say When	1934
Don't Tell Your Folks	Richard Rodgers	Lorenz Hart	Simple Simon	1930
Don't Throw Me Down	J. Fred Coots	Al Dubin	White Lights	1927
Don't Wait	Arthur Siegel	June Carroll	New Faces	1956
Don't You Cheat	Leon DeCosta	Leon DeCosta	The Blonde Sinner	1926
Doughnuts and Coffee	Sammy Fain	Irving Kahal	Right This Way	1938
Down By the Sea	Richard Rodgers	Lorenz Hart	Present Arms	1928
Down in the Depths (on the Ninetieth Floor)	Cole Porter	Cole Porter	Red, Hot and Blue	1936
Down on MacConnachy Square	Frederick Loewe	Alan Jay Lerner	Brigadoon	1947
Down on the Delta	Alfred Nathan	George Oppenheimer	The Manhatters	1927

*Dropped from New York production. Added to "Roberta"

TITLE	COMPOSER	LYRICIST	SHOW	YEAR
Down the Well	Gerald Marks	Sam Lerner	Hold It!	1948
Down With Love	Harold Arlen	E. Y. Harburg	Hooray for What	1937
Dream a Dream*	Jerome Kern	Otto Harbach, Oscar Hammerstein II	Sunny	1925
Dream Boat	George Bagby	Grace Henry, Jo Trent	Fioretta	1929
Dream Girl	Ida Hoyt Chamberlain	Ida Hoyt Chamberlain	Enchanted Isle	1927
Dream Sweetheart	Harry Tierney	Joseph McCarthy	Cross My Heart	1928
Dreamer With a Penny	Allan Roberts	Lester Lee	All for Love	1949
Dreaming	Henry Souvaine, Con Conrad	J. P. McEvoy	Americana	1926
Dreams Ago	Abraham Ellstein	Walter Bullock	Great to Be Alive	1950
Dreams for Sale	James F. Hanley	Eddie Dowling	Honeymoon Lane	1926
Dreamy Montmartre	Abel Baer	Sam Lewis, Joe Young	Lady Do	1927
Dressed Up for Your Sunday Beau	Joseph Meyer, Philip Charig	Leo Robin	Just Fancy	1927
Drop That Name	Jule Styne	Betty Comden, Adolph Green	Bells Are Ringing	1956
Drugstore Scene	Marc Blitzstein	Marc Blitzstein	The Cradle Will Rock	1938
Drums in My Heart	Vincent Youmans	Edward Heyman	Through the Years	1932
DuBarry, The	Carl Millöcker, Theo Mackeben	Rowland Leigh	The DuBarry	1932
D'Ye Love Me?	Jerome Kern	Otto Harbach, Oscar Hammerstein II	Sunny	1925
Dying Cowboy, The	Richard Lewine	Ted Fetter	The Girl From Wyoming	1938
Eadie Was a Lady	Richard Whiting, Nacio Brown	B. G. DeSylva	Take a Chance	1932
Eagle and Me, The	Harold Arlen	E. Y. Harburg	Bloomer Girl	1944
Earth and the Sky, The	John Rox	John Rox	John Murray Anderson's Almanac	1953
East Wind	Sigmund Romberg	Oscar Hammerstein II	East Wind	1931
Easter Parade	Irving Berlin	Irving Berlin	As Thousands Cheer	1933
Easter Sunday Parade, The	George M. Cohan	George M. Cohan	The Merry Malones	1927
Economics	Kurt Weill	Alan Jay Lerner	Love Life	1948
Edelweiss	Sigmund Romberg	Arthur Wimperis	Louie the 14th	1925
Edelweiss	Richard Rodgers	Oscar Hammerstein II	The Sound of Music	1959

*Dropped from New York production

TITLE	COMPOSER	LYRICIST	SHOW	YEAR
Educate Your Feet	Milton Ager	Jack Yellen	John Murray Anderson's Almanac	1929
Eileen Mavourneen	Henry Sullivan	John Murray Anderson	Thumbs Up	1934
Eleven Levee Street*	Sigmund Romberg	Oscar Hammerstein II	Sunny River	1941
Eleven O'Clock Song, An	Sammy Fain	Dan Shapiro	Ankles Aweigh	1955
Elizabeth	Robert Katscher	Irving Caesar	The Wonder Bar	1931
Elmer's Wedding Day	Sid Kuller, Ray Golden		Meet the People	1940
Embraceable You	George Gershwin	Ira Gershwin	Girl Crazy	1930
Emerald Song, The	Heitor Villa-Lobos	Robert Wright, George Forrest	Magdalena	1948
Empty-Handed Traveler, The	Gian-Carlo Menotti	Gian-Carlo Menotti	The Consul	1950
Engagement Ring, The	Emil Gerstenberger	Howard Johnston	The Lace Petticoat	1927
Evelina	Harold Arlen	E. Y. Harburg	Bloomer Girl	1944
Even As You and I	Sammy Fain	Irving Kahal	Everybody's Welcome	1931
Evening Star	Edward Horan	Frederick Herendeen	All the King's Horses	1934
Everlasting	Jule Styne	Betty Comden, Adolph Green	Two on the Aisle	1951
Every Bit of You	Kenneth Friede, Adrian Samish		Hello, Paris	1930
Every Little Note	Harry Archer	Harlan Thompson	Merry-Merry	1925
Everybody Loves Somebody	Harold Rome	Harold Rome	Wish You Were Here	1952
Everybody's Got a Home But Me	Richard Rodgers	Oscar Hammerstein II	Pipe Dream	1955
Everyone in the World Is Doing the Charleston	Irving Berlin	Irving Berlin	The Cocoanuts	1925
Everything Happens To Me	Hoagy Carmichael	Johnny Mercer	Walk With Music	1940
Everything Is High Yellow Now	Gitz Rice	Paul Porter	Nic Nax of 1926	1926
Everything Reminds Me of You	Eubie Blake	Noble Sissle	Shuffle Along	1933
Everything Will Happen for the Best	Lewis E. Gensler	B. G. DeSylva	Queen High	1926
Everything's Coming Up Roses	Jule Styne	Stephen Sondheim	Gypsy	1959
Ev'ry Boy in Town's My Sweetheart	George M. Cohan	George M. Cohan	Billie	1928
Ev'ry Day a Holiday	Cole Porter	Cole Porter	DuBarry Was a Lady	1939

*Dropped from New York production

TITLE	COMPOSER	LYRICIST	SHOW	YEAR
Ev'ry Little While	Rudolf Friml	P. G. Wodehouse, Clifford Grey	The Three Musketeers	1928
Ev'ry Other Heartbeat	Johnny Green	George Marion, Jr.	Beat the Band	1942
Ev'ry Sunday Afternoon	Richard Rodgers	Lorenz Hart	Higher and Higher	1940
Ev'ry Time	Hugh Martin	Ralph Blane	Best Foot Forward	1941
Ev'ry Time We Say Goodbye	Cole Porter	Cole Porter	The Seven Lively Arts	1944
Ev'rybody Knows I Love Somebody	George Gershwin	Ira Gershwin	Rosalie	1928
Ev'rybody Loves You*	Richard Rodgers	Lorenz Hart	I'd Rather Be Right	1937
Ev'rything I Love	Cole Porter	Cole Porter	Let's Face It	1941
Ev'rything I've Got	Richard Rodgers	Lorenz Hart	By Jupiter	1942
Exactly Like You	Jimmy McHugh	Dorothy Fields	Lew Leslie's International Review	1930
Extra! Extra!	Irving Berlin	Irving Berlin	Miss Liberty	1949
Eyeful of You	J. Fred Coots	Al Dubin	White Lights	1927
Eyes That Haunt Me	Karl Hajos (based on Tchaikovsky)	Harry B. Smith	Natja	1925
Eyes That Love	Sigmund Romberg	Harry B. Smith	The Love Call	1927
Face on the Dime, The	Harold Rome	Harold Rome	Call Me Mister	1946
Fair Land of Dreaming	Edward Kunneke (based on Offenbach)	Harry B. Smith	The Love Song	1925
Fair Warning	Jerry Bock	Sheldon Harnick	The Body Beautiful	1958
Fair Warning	Harold Rome	Harold Rome	Destry Rides Again	1959
Falling in Love	Henry Sullivan	Earle Crooker	The Third Little Show	1931
Falling in Love With Love	Richard Rodgers	Lorenz Hart	The Boys From Syracuse	1938
Falling Off the Wagon	Lewis E. Gensler	E. Y. Harburg	Ballyhoo	1932
Falling Out of Love Can Be Fun	Irving Berlin	Irving Berlin	Miss Liberty	1949
Fancy Forgetting	Sandy Wilson	Sandy Wilson	The Boy Friend	1954
Fancy Our Meeting	Joseph Meyer, Philip Charig	Douglas Furber	Wake Up and Dream	1929
Fanny	Harold Rome	Harold Rome	Fanny	1954
Far Away	Cole Porter	Cole Porter	Leave it to Me	1938
Far Away and Long Ago	Karl Hajos (based on Chopin)	Harry B. Smith	White Lilacs	1928
Faraway Boy	Frank Loesser	Frank Loesser	Greenwillow	1960
Far-Away Love	James P. Johnson	Flournoy Miller	Sugar Hill	1931
Farewell, My Lovely	Arthur Schwartz	Howard Dietz	At Home Abroad	1935
Farewell Song	Douglas Moore	John Latouche	The Ballad of Baby Doe	1958
Farmer and the Cowman, The	Richard Rodgers	Oscar Hammerstein II	Oklahoma!	1943
Farming	Cole Porter	Cole Porter	Let's Face It	1941
Fascinating You	Benee Russell, Charles & Henry Tobias, Vincent Rose		Earl Carroll's Sketch Book	1929

*Dropped from New York production

TITLE	COMPOSER	LYRICIST	SHOW	YEAR
Fatal Fascination	Arthur Schwartz	Howard Dietz	Flying Colors	1932
Father's Day	Jimmy McHugh	Harold Adamson	As the Girls Go	1948
F. D. R. Jones	Harold Rome	Harold Rome	Sing Out the News	1938
Fearfully, Frightful Love	Raymond Hubbell	Anne Caldwell	Yours Truly	1927
Feelin' Good	Owen Murphy	Jack Yellen	Rain or Shine	1928
Feeling I'm Falling	George Gershwin	Ira Gershwin	Treasure Girl	1928
Feeling in Your Heart, A	George M. Cohan	George M. Cohan	The Merry Malones	1927
Feeling Sentimental*	George Gershwin	Ira Gershwin	Show Girl	1929
Feet on the Sidewalk (Head in the Sky)	Sammy Lerner, Gerald Marks		My Dear Public	1943
Fellow and a Girl, A	Jay Gorney	Edward Eliscu	Meet the People	1940
Fellow Needs a Girl, A	Richard Rodgers	Oscar Hammerstein II	Allegro	1947
Feudin' and Fightin'	Burton Lane	Al Dubin, Burton Lane	Laffing Room Only	1944
Fidgety Feet	George Gershwin	Ira Gershwin	Oh, Kay!	1926
Find a Girl	Harry Archer	Harlan Thompson	Twinkle, Twinkle	1926
Find Me a Primitive Man	Cole Porter	Cole Porter	Fifty Million Frenchmen	1929
Fine and Dandy	Kay Swift	Paul James	Fine and Dandy	1930
Fini	Richard Adler, Jerry Ross		John Murray Anderson's Almanac	1953
Fioretta	G. Romilli	G. Romilli	Fioretta	1929
Fireman's Bride, The	Sigmund Romberg	Dorothy Fields	Up in Central Park	1945
Fireworks	Jule Styne	Betty Comden, Adolph Green	Do Re Mi	1960
First Kiss of Love	Percy Wenrich	Raymond Peck	Castles in the Air	1926
First, Last and Only	Harold Levey, Owen Murphy		Rainbow Rose	1926
First Prize at the Fair	Arthur Schwartz	Howard Dietz	Inside U.S.A.	1948
First Thing in the Morning	Donald Heywood	Donald Heywood	Blackberries	1932
First Time I Spoke of You, The	Ernest G. Schweikert	Frank Reardon	Rumple	1957
Five O'Clock Tea	Irving Berlin	Irving Berlin	The Cocoanuts	1925
Five-Step, The	Ray Henderson	B. G. DeSylva, Lew Brown	Manhattan Mary	1927
Fixin' for a Long, Cold Winter	Jack Lawrence, Don Walker		Courtin' Time	1951
Flahooley	Sammy Fain	E. Y. Harburg	Flahooley	1951
Flamenco	Henry Sullivan	Earle Crooker	Thumbs Up	1934
Flattery	Harold Rome	Harold Rome	Wish You Were Here	1952
Flattery	Moose Charlap	Norman Gimbel	Whoop-Up	1958
Flexatone	Alfred Goodman, Maury Rubens, J. Fred Coots	Clifford Grey	Artists and Models	1925
Flings	Bob Merrill	Bob Merrill	New Girl in Town	1957

*Dropped from New York production

TITLE	COMPOSER	LYRICIST	SHOW	YEAR
Floating Thru' the Air	Arthur Schwartz	Henry Myers	The New Yorkers	1927
Florida by the Sea	Irving Berlin	Irving Berlin	The Cocoanuts	1925
Florida, the Moon and You	Rudolf Friml	Gene Buck	No Foolin'	1926
Flotsam and Jetsam	George Kleinsinger	Joe Darion	Shinbone Alley	1957
Flower Waltz, The	Franz Steininger (based on Tchaikovsky)	Forman Brown	Music in My Heart	1947
Fly Butterfly	Ray Henderson	B. G. DeSylva, Lew Brown	George White's Scandals	1925
Follow Me	Frederick Loewe	Alan Jay Lerner	Camelot	1960
Follow the Fold	Frank Loesser	Frank Loesser	Guys and Dolls	1950
Follow the Girls	Philip Charig	Dan Shapiro, Milton Pascal	Follow the Girls	1944
Follow the Sun to the South	Sigmund Romberg	Dorothy Donnelly	My Princess	1927
Follow Thru	Ray Henderson	B. G. DeSylva, Lew Brown	Follow Thru	1929
Follow Your Heart	Albert Hague	Arnold B. Horwitt	Plain and Fancy	1955
Following the Sun Around	Harry Tierney	Joseph McCarthy	Rio Rita	1927
Fond of You	Lewis E. Gensler	B. G. DeSylva	Captain Jinks	1925
Foolish Heart	Kurt Weill	Ogden Nash	One Touch of Venus	1943
Fools Fall in Love	Irving Berlin	Irving Berlin	Louisiana Purchase	1940
For a Girl Like You	Gitz Rice	Joe Goodwin	Nic Nax of 1926	1926
For a Moment of Your Love	Jimmy Van Heusen	Johnny Burke	Carnival in Flanders	1953
For Better or Worse	Michael H. Cleary	Max & Nathaniel Lief	Hey Nonny Nonny!	1932
For No Rhyme or Reason	Cole Porter	Cole Porter	You Never Know	1938
For Someone I Love	Ted Snyder	Benny Davis	Earl Carroll's Sketch Book	1929
For the Life of Me	Arthur Schwartz	Ira Gershwin	Park Avenue	1946
For We Love You Still	Johann Strauss	Desmond Carter	The Great Waltz	1934
Forever and Ever	Milton Ager	Jack Yellen	Rain or Shine	1928
Forget All Your Books	Burton Lane	Howard Dietz	Three's a Crowd	1930
Four Young People	James Shelton	James Shelton	The Straw Hat Revue	1939
Frahngee-Pahnee	Cole Porter	Cole Porter	The Seven Lively Arts	1944
France Will Not Forget	Geoffrey O'Hara	Gordon Johnstone	Half a Widow	1927
Freddy and his Fiddle	Robert Wright, George Forrest (based on Grieg)		Song of Norway	1944
Free*	Irving Berlin	Irving Berlin	Call Me Madam	1950
Free for All	Richard Whiting	Oscar Hammerstein II	Free for All	1931
Free to Love	Sigmund Romberg, Don Walker	Leo Robin	The Girl in Pink Tights	1954

*Dropped from New York production

TITLE	COMPOSER	LYRICIST	SHOW	YEAR
Freedom of the Press, The	Marc Blitzstein	Marc Blitzstein	The Cradle Will Rock	1938
Fresh as a Daisy	Cole Porter	Cole Porter	Panama Hattie	1940
Friendly Enemy	Gerald Marks	Sam Lerner	Hold It!	1948
Friends and Lovers	Maurice Yvain	Max & Nathaniel Lief	Luckee Girl	1928
Friendship	Cole Porter	Cole Porter	DuBarry Was a Lady	1939
From a Prison Cell	Marguerite Monnot	Julian More, Daniel Heneker, Monte Norman	Irma La Douce	1960
From Alpha to Omega	Cole Porter	Cole Porter	You Never Know	1938
From Another World	Richard Rodgers	Lorenz Hart	Higher and Higher	1940
From Morning Till Night	Jacques Belasco	Kay Twomey	The Girl From Nantucket	1945
From Now On	Richard Myers	Edward Eliscu	The Street Singer	1929
From Now On	Cole Porter	Cole Porter	Leave It to Me	1938
From Now Onward	Sigmund Romberg	Rowland Leigh	My Romance	1948
From This Moment On*	Cole Porter	Cole Porter	Out of This World	1950
Fuddle-Dee-Duddle	Sammy Fain	Charles Tobias	Hellzapoppin'	1938
Fugue for Tinhorns	Frank Loesser	Frank Loesser	Guys and Dolls	1950
Fun to be Fooled	Harold Arlen	E. Y. Harburg Ira Gershwin	Life Begins at 8:40	1934
Funnies, The	Irving Berlin	Irving Berlin	As Thousands Cheer	1933
Funny Face	George Gershwin	Ira Gershwin	Funny Face	1927
Funny Heart, A	David Baker	David Craig	Phoenix '55	1955
Funny Old Little Old World	Jay Gorney	Walter & Jean Kerr	Touch and Go	1949
Futuristic Rhythm	Jimmy McHugh	Dorothy Fields	Hello Daddy	1928
Ga-Ga!	Joseph Meyer	Edward Eliscu	Lady Fingers	1929
Ga-Ga	Carl Millöcker, Theo Mackeben	Rowland Leigh	The DuBarry	1932
Game of Love, The	Harold Karr	Matt Dubey	Happy Hunting	1956
Game of Poker, A	Harold Arlen	Johnny Mercer	Saratoga	1959
Garden of Used-To-Be	Jay Gorney	Owen Murphy	Greenwich Village Follies	1925
Gary, Indiana	Meredith Willson	Meredith Willson	The Music Man	1957
Gatekeeper of My Castle	David Martin	Langston Hughes	Simply Heavenly	1957
Gather the Rose	Rudolf Friml	Brian Hooker	The White Eagle	1927
Gazooka, The	Vernon Duke	Ira Gershwin	Ziegfeld Follies	1936
Gee, But It's Good to be Here	Harold Karr	Matt Dubey	Happy Hunting	1956
Gee, Officer Krupke!	Leonard Bernstein	Stephen Sondheim	West Side Story	1957

*Dropped from New York production

TITLE	COMPOSER	LYRICIST	SHOW	YEAR
Gentleman Friend	Richard Lewine	Arnold B. Horwitt	Make Mine Manhattan	1948
Gentleman is a Dope, The	Richard Rodgers	Oscar Hammerstein II	Allegro	1947
Gentlemen Prefer Blondes	Irving Berlin	Irving Berlin	The Cocoanuts	1925
Gentlemen Prefer Blondes	Lewis E. Gensler	B. G. DeSylva	Queen High	1926
Get a Load of This	Harry Archer	Harlan Thompson	Twinkle, Twinkle	1926
Get Away from that Window	Jimmy Johnson	Percy Bradford	Messin' Around	1929
Get Happy	Harold Arlen	Ted Koehler	9:15 Revue	1930
Get Hot Foot	Bud Green, Sam H. Stept		Shady Lady	1933
Get Me to the Church on Time	Frederick Loewe	Alan Jay Lerner	My Fair Lady	1956
Get Out of Town	Cole Porter	Cole Porter	Leave It to Me	1938
Get Your Man	Ray Perkins	Max & Nathaniel Lief	Greenwich Village Follies	1928
Getting to Know You	Richard Rodgers	Oscar Hammerstein II	The King and I	1951
Gideon Briggs, I Love You	Frank Loesser	Frank Loesser	Greenwillow	1960
Gigolette	Franz Lehar	Irving Caesar	Charlot's Revue	1925
Gimme the Shimmy	Harold Rome	Harold Rome	Michael Todd's Peep Show	1950
Girl Friend, The	Richard Rodgers	Lorenz Hart	The Girl Friend	1926
Girl in Your Arms, A	Jay Gorney	Irving Caesar	Sweetheart Time	1926
Girl Is You and the Boy Is Me, The	Ray Henderson	B. G. DeSylva, Lew Brown	George White's Scandals	1926
Girl of the Moment	Kurt Weill	Ira Gershwin	Lady in the Dark	1941
Girl of the Pi Beta Phi, A	Ray Henderson	B. G. DeSylva, Lew Brown	Good News	1927
Girl on the Prow, The	Sigmund Romberg	Oscar Hammerstein II	The New Moon	1928
Girl That I Marry, The	Irving Berlin	Irving Berlin	Annie Get Your Gun	1946
Girl with the Paint on Her Face, The	Irvin Graham	Irvin Graham	Who's Who	1938
Girls	Cole Porter	Cole Porter	Mexican Hayride	1944
Girls and Boys	Richard Lewine	Arnold B. Horwitt	The Girls Against the Boys	1959
Girls and the Gimmies	Percy Wenrich	Raymond Peck	Castles in the Air	1926
Girls 'n Girls 'n Girls	Irvin Graham	Irvin Graham	New Faces	1956
Girls of Summer	Stephen Sondheim	Stephen Sondheim	Girls of Summer	1956
Give a Little, Get a Little	Jule Styne	Betty Comden, Adolph Green	Two on the Aisle	1951
Give a Little Whistle	Cy Coleman	Carolyn Leigh	Wildcat	1960
Give, Baby, Give	Irving Gellers, Otis Spencer	Gladys Shelley	Walk with Music	1940
Give Him the Oo-La-La	Cole Porter	Cole Porter	DuBarry Was a Lady	1939

TITLE	COMPOSER	LYRICIST	SHOW	YEAR
Give it Back to the Indians	Richard Rodgers	Lorenz Hart	Too Many Girls	1939
Give Me a Roll on a Drum	Sigmund Romberg	Irving Caesar	Melody	1933
Give Me One Hour	Rudolf Friml	Brian Hooker	The White Eagle	1927
Give Me Someone	Robert Hood Bowers	Francis DeWitt	Oh, Ernest!	1927
Give Me the Rain	Lester Allen	Henry Creamer	Gay Paree	1926
Give Me the Sunshine	Jimmy Johnson	Con Conrad, Henry Creamer	Keep Shufflin	1928
Give Me Your Tired, Your Poor	Irving Berlin	Emma Lazarus	Miss Liberty	1949
Give Trouble the Air	Louis Alter	Leo Robin	A La Carte	1927
Give Us the Charleston	Ray Henderson	B. G. DeSylva, Lew Brown	George White's Scandals	1925
Give Your Heart a Chance to Sing	Charles Gaynor	Charles Gaynor	Lend an Ear	1948
Give Your Heart in June-Time	Victor Herbert	Clifford Grey, Harold Atteridge	Sky High	1925
Glad to be Unhappy	Richard Rodgers	Lorenz Hart	On Your Toes	1936
Glitter and be Gay	Leonard Bernstein	Richard Wilbur	Candide	1956
Glory! Glory! Glory!	Danton Walker	Danton Walker	Grand Street Follies	1925
Glory of Spring, The	Maury Rubens	J. Keirn Brennan	Music in May	1929
Go Home Ev'ry Once in a While	George M. Cohan	George M. Cohan	Billie	1928
Go One Better	Sam Timberg	Graham John	The Street-Singer	1929
Go South	Richard Myers	Owen Murphy	Greenwich Village Follies	1925
God Is Good to the Irish	George M. Cohan	George M. Cohan	The Merry Malones	1927
God's Country	Harold Arlen	E. Y. Harburg	Hooray for What	1937
God's Green World	Frederick Loewe	Alan Jay Lerner	The Day Before Spring	1945
Goddess of Rain	Thomas (Fats) Waller	Harry Brooks, Andy Razaf	Hot Chocolates	1929
Goin' on a Hayride	Ralph Blane	Ralph Blane	Three Wishes for Jamie	1952
Going Back Home	Robert Stolz	Robert Sour	Mr. Strauss Goes to Boston	1945
Golden Gates of Happiness	J. Fred Coots	Clifford Grey	The Merry World	1926
Goldfish Glide	James Hanley	Eddie Dowling	Sidewalks of New York	1927
Good Boy	Herbert Stothart, Harry Ruby	Bert Kalmar	Good Boy	1928
Good Clean Fun	Jerry Bock	Sheldon Harnick	Tenderloin	1960
Good Evening, Friends	Robert Katscher	Irving Caesar	The Wonder Bar	1931
Good Fellow, Mine	Richard Rodgers	Lorenz Hart	The Girl Friend	1926
Good for You, Bad for Me	Ray Henderson	Lew Brown, B. G. DeSylva	Flying High	1930

TITLE	COMPOSER	LYRICIST	SHOW	YEAR
Good Little Girls*	Vernon Duke	Sammy Cahn	Two's Company	1952
Good Morning	Irving Caesar	Irving Caesar	Yes, Yes, Yvette	1927
Good News	Ray Henderson	B. G. DeSylva, Lew Brown	Good News	1927
Good Night, My Beautiful	Sammy Fain	Jack Yellen	George White's Scandals	1939
Good Old Girl	David Martin	Langston Hughes	Simply Heavenly	1957
Good Pals	Sigmund Romberg	Harry B. Smith	The Love Call	1927
Good Will Movement, The	Cole Porter	Cole Porter	Mexican Hayride	1944
Good-bye Jonah	Arthur Schwartz	Albert Stillman	Virginia	1937
Goodbye, Little Dream, Goodbye	Cole Porter	Cole Porter	Red, Hot and Blue	1936
Goodbye, Old Girl	Richard Adler, Jerry Ross		Damn Yankees	1955
Goodbye to All That	Arthur Schwartz	Ira Gershwin	Park Avenue	1946
Goodness Gracious	Harry Ruby	Bert Kalmar	Top Speed	1929
Goodnight, My Someone	Meredith Willson	Meredith Willson	The Music Man	1957
Goona-Goona	Jerome Moross	John Latouche	The Golden Apple	1954
Goose Never Be a Peacock	Harold Arlen	Johnny Mercer	Saratoga	1959
Got a Bran' New Suit	Arthur Schwartz	Howard Dietz	At Home Abroad	1935
Got a Rainbow	George Gershwin	Ira Gershwin	Treasure Girl	1928
Got Myself Another Jockey Now	Thomas (Fats) Waller	Andy Razaf	Keep Shufflin'	1928
Gotta Go to Town	Harry Warren	Mort Dixon, Joe Young	The Laugh Parade	1931
Gotta See a Man About His Daughter	James F. Hanley	Jean Herbert, Karl Stark	Thumbs Up	1934
Grant Avenue	Richard Rodgers	Oscar Hammerstein II	Flower Drum Song	1958
Gray Goose, The	George Lessner	Miriam Battista, Russell Maloney	Sleepy Hollow	1948
Great Big Bear	Herbert Stothart	Otto Harbach, Oscar Hammerstein II	Song of the Flame	1925
Great Day!	Vincent Youmans	Billy Rose, Edward Eliscu	Great Day!	1929
Great Indoors, The	Cole Porter	Cole Porter	The New Yorkers	1930
Greedy Girl	Marc Blitzstein	Marc Blitzstein	Regina	1949
Green and Blue	Eubie Blake	J. Milton Reddie, Cecil Mack	Swing It	1937
Green Carnation	Noel Coward	Noel Coward	Bitter Sweet	1929
Green Pastures	Eubie Blake	Will Morrissey, Andy Razaf	Blackbirds	1930

*Dropped from New York production. Re-introduced in "The Littlest Revue"

TITLE	COMPOSER	LYRICIST	SHOW	YEAR
Green Up Time	Kurt Weill	Alan Jay Lerner	Love Life	1948
Greenwillow Christmas	Frank Loesser	Frank Loesser	Greenwillow	1960
Growin' Pains	Don Walker	Clay Warnick	Memphis Bound	1945
Growing Pains	Arthur Schwartz	Dorothy Fields	A Tree Grows in Brooklyn	1951
Guess Who I Saw Today?	Murray Grand	Elisse Boyd	New Faces	1952
Gus and Sadie Love Song	Marc Blitzstein	Marc Blitzstein	The Cradle Will Rock	1938
Guys and Dolls	Frank Loesser	Frank Loesser	Guys and Dolls	1950
Gypsy in Me, The	Cole Porter	Cole Porter	Anything Goes	1934
Gypsy Joe	Walter Donaldson	Gus Kahn	Whoopee	1928
Gypsy Song, The	Walter Donaldson	Gus Kahn	Whoopee	1928
Half a Moon	James F. Hanley	Herbert Reynolds, Eddie Dowling	Honeymoon Lane	1926
Half-Caste Woman	Noel Coward	Noel Coward	Ziegfeld Follies	1931
Hallelujah!	Vincent Youmans	Leo Robin, Clifford Grey	Hit the Deck	1927
Ham and Eggs in the Morning	Con Conrad, Abner Silver	Al Dubin	Take the Air	1927
Handbag is Not a Proper Mother, A	Lee Pockriss	Anne Croswell	Ernest in Love	1960
Hang Up!	Arthur Schwartz	Dorothy Fields	By the Beautiful Sea	1954
Hang Your Hat on the Moon	Jean Schwartz	Clifford Grey, William Cary Duncan	Sunny Days	1928
Hangin' Around With You	George Gershwin	Ira Gershwin	Strike Up the Band	1930
Happy	Frank Grey	Earle Crooker, McElbert Moore	Happy	1927
Happy	George M. Cohan	George M. Cohan	Billie	1928
Happy	Nat Reed	Bob Joffe	Brown Buddies	1930
Happy Because I'm in Love	Vincent Youmans	Billy Rose, Edward Eliscu	Great Day!	1929
Happy-Go-Lucky Bird	Harry Ruby	Bert Kalmar	The Five O'Clock Girl	1927
Happy Habit	Arthur Schwartz	Dorothy Fields	By the Beautiful Sea	1954
Happy Heaven of Harlem, The	Cole Porter	Cole Porter	Fifty Million Frenchmen	1929
Happy Hunting Horn	Richard Rodgers	Lorenz Hart	Pal Joey	1940
Happy in Love	Sammy Fain	Jack Yellen	Sons O' Fun	1941
Happy Is the Word	Sammy Fain	Paul Francis Webster	Christine	1960
Happy Melody	Lucien Denni	Gwynne Denni	Happy Go Lucky	1926
Happy Talk	Richard Rodgers	Oscar Hammerstein II	South Pacific	1949
Happy the Day	Jack Waller, Joseph Tunbridge	R. P. Weston, Bert Lee	Tell Her the Truth	1933

TITLE	COMPOSER	LYRICIST	SHOW	YEAR
Harbor of My Heart, The	Vincent Youmans	Leo Robin, Clifford Grey	Hit the Deck	1927
Hark to the Song of the Night	Cole Porter	Cole Porter	Out of This World	1950
Harlem Mania	Donald Heywood	Donald Heywood	Blackberries	1932
Harlem on My Mind	Irving Berlin	Irving Berlin	As Thousands Cheer	1933
Harlem Serenade	George Gershwin	Ira Gershwin, Gus Kahn	Show Girl	1929
Harlem Town	Jimmy Johnson	Percy Bradford	Messin' Around	1929
Has Anybody Seen Our Ship?	Noel Coward	Noel Coward	Tonight at 8:30 (Red Peppers)	1936
Hats Off	Richard Lewine	Ted Fetter	The Girl From Wyoming	1938
Haunted Heart	Arthur Schwartz	Howard Dietz	Inside U. S. A.	1948
Have a Heart	Burton Lane	Harold Adamson	Earl Carroll's Vanities	1931
Have a Little Drinkee	Ned Lehak	Edward Eliscu	Crazy Quilt	1931
Have You Met Delilah?	James Mundy	John Latouche	The Vamp	1955
Have You Met Miss Jones?	Richard Rodgers	Lorenz Hart	I'd Rather Be Right	1937
Hay, Straw	Vincent Youmans	Oscar Hammerstein II	Rainbow	1928
He Is the Type	Jerome Kern	Anne Caldwell	The City Chap	1925
He Just Beats a Tom Tom	Harry Akst	Lew Brown	Calling All Stars	1934
He Knows Where the Rose Is in Bloom	Robert Hood Bowers	Francis DeWitt	Oh, Ernest!	1927
He Loves and She Loves	George Gershwin	Ira Gershwin	Funny Face	1927
He Man	Richard Myers	Leo Robin	Hello, Yourself	1928
He Takes Me Off His Income Tax	Arthur Siegel	June Carroll	New Faces	1952
He Was Too Good to Me*	Richard Rodgers	Lorenz Hart	Simple Simon	1930
He Writes a Song	Edward Kunneke (based on Offenbach)	Harry B. Smith	The Love Song	1925
Headache and a Heartache	Walter Kent	Kim Gannon	Seventeen	1951
Headin' for Harlem	James Hanley	Eddie Dowling	Sidewalks of New York	1927
Headin' for the Bottom	Sammy Fain	Dan Shapiro	Ankles Aweigh	1955
Heart	Richard Adler, Jerry Ross		Damn Yankees	1955
Heart Has Won the Game, The	Glenn Paxton	Robert Goldman, George Weiss	First Impressions	1959
Heart in Hand	Jack Lawrence, Don Walker		Courtin' Time	1951
Heart Is Quicker Than the Eye, The	Richard Rodgers	Lorenz Hart	On Your Toes	1936

*Dropped from New York production

TITLE	COMPOSER	LYRICIST	SHOW	YEAR
Heart of a Rose	J. Fred Coots, Maury Rubens	Clifford Grey	Gay Paree	1926
Heart of Stone	Leroy Anderson	Joan Ford, Jean & Walter Kerr	Goldilocks	1958
Heat Wave	Irving Berlin	Irving Berlin	As Thousands Cheer	1933
Heather on the Hill, The	Frederick Loewe	Alan Jay Lerner	Brigadoon	1947
Heaven Hop	Cole Porter	Cole Porter	Paris	1928
Heaven In My Arms	Jerome Kern	Oscar Hammer-stein, II	Very Warm for May	1939
Heaven on Earth	George Gershwin	Ira Gershwin, Howard Dietz	Oh, Kay!	1926
Heaven on Earth	Jay Gorney	Barry Trivers	Heaven on Earth	1948
Heel and Toe	Philip Charig	Irving Caesar	Polly	1929
Heigh-Ho, Cheerio	Harry Archer	Walter O'Keefe	Just a Minute	1928
Hello, Hello, There	Jule Styne	Betty Comden, Adolph Green	Bells Are Ringing	1956
Hello, My Lover, Goodbye	Johnny Green	Edward Heyman	Here Goes the Bride	1931
Hello 'Tucky	Joseph Meyer, James Hanley	B. G. DeSylva	Big Boy	1925
Hello, Young Lovers	Richard Rodgers	Oscar Hammer-stein II	The King and I	1951
Help Yourself to Happiness	Harry Revel	Harry Richman, Mack Gordon	Ziegfeld Follies	1931
Hence It Don't Make Sense	Cole Porter	Cole Porter	The Seven Lively Arts	1944
Here Am I	Jerome Kern	Oscar Hammer-stein II	Sweet Adeline	1929
Here Am I—Broken Hearted	Ray Henderson	B. G. DeSylva, Lew Brown	Artists and Models	1927
Here and Now	George Lessner	Miriam Battista, Russell Maloney	Sleepy Hollow	1948
Here Comes My Blackbird	Jimmy McHugh	Dorothy Fields	Blackbirds	1928
Here I Go Again	Harry Revel	Arnold B. Horwitt	Are You With It?	1945
Here I'll Stay	Kurt Weill	Alan Jay Lerner	Love Life	1948
Here in My Arms	Richard Rodgers	Lorenz Hart	Dearest Enemy	1925
Here in My Heart	Joseph Meyer	Billy Moll	Jonica	1930
Here in the Dark	Emmerich Kalman, Herbert Stothart	Otto Harbach, Oscar Hammer-stein II	Golden Dawn	1927
Here We Are Again	Bob Merrill	Bob Merrill	New Girl in Town	1957
Here We Are in Love	Ben Oakland	Jack Murray, Barry Trivers	Ziegfeld Follies	1931
Here's a Hand	Richard Rodgers	Lorenz Hart	By Jupiter	1942
Here's a Kiss	Richard Rodgers	Lorenz Hart	Dearest Enemy	1925

TITLE	COMPOSER	LYRICIST	SHOW	YEAR
Here's That Rainy Day	Jimmy Van Heusen	Johnny Burke	Carnival in Flanders	1953
Here's to Dear Old Us	Sammy Fain	Dan Shapiro	Ankles Aweigh	1955
Here's to Night	Henry Sullivan	Edward Eliscu	A Little Racketeer	1932
Here's to the Girl of My Heart	Walter Donaldson	Gus Kahn	Whoopee	1928
Here's to Your Illusions	Sammy Fain	E. Y. Harburg	Flahooley	1951
Hernando's Hideaway	Richard Adler, Jerry Ross		The Pajama Game	1954
He's a Ladies Man	Ray Henderson	B. G. DeSylva, Lew Brown	Good News	1927
He's a Right Guy	Cole Porter	Cole Porter	Something for the Boys	1943
He's in Love	Robert Wright, George Forrest (based on Borodin)		Kismet	1953
He's Mine	Roger Wolfe Kahn	Irving Caesar	Americana	1928
He's Not Worth Your Tears	Harry Warren	Mort Dixon, Billy Rose	Sweet and Low	1930
He's Only Wonderful	Sammy Fain	E. Y. Harburg	Flahooley	1951
Hey, Gal!	Will Irwin	Peter Barry	New Faces	1942
Hey, Good-Lookin'	Cole Porter	Cole Porter	Something for the Boys	1943
Hey, Look Me Over	Cy Coleman	Carolyn Leigh	Wildcat	1960
Hey There	Richard Adler, Jerry Ross		The Pajama Game	1954
High and Low	Arthur Schwartz	Howard Dietz	The Band Wagon	1931
High Hat	George Gershwin	Ira Gershwin	Funny Face	1927
High, High, High	Maury Rubens	J. Keirn Brennan	Music in May	1929
High Shoes	Robert Russell Bennett	Owen Murphy, Robert A. Simon	Hold Your Horses	1933
His and Hers	Sammy Fain	Dan Shapiro	Ankles Aweigh	1955
History Is Made at Night	Harold Rome	Harold Rome	Streets of Paris	1939
Hitch Your Wagon to a Star	Richard Lewine	Ted Fetter	Broadway Show Window	1936
Hittin' the Bottle	Harold Arlen	Ted Koehler	Earl Carroll's Vanities	1930
Hoch, Caroline!	Jack Waller, Joseph Tunbridge	R. P. Weston, Bert Lee	Tell Her the Truth	1933
Hocus-Pocus	James Hanley	Lew Brown	Gay Paree	1926
Hogan's Alley	Henry Souvaine, Jay Gorney	Morrie Ryskind, Howard Dietz	Merry-Go-Round	1927
Hold It!	Gerald Marks	Sam Lerner	Hold It!	1948
Hold Me—Hold Me—Hold Me	Jule Styne	Betty Comden, Adolph Green	Two on the Aisle	1951
Hold That Smile	Ray Henderson	Jack Yellen	Ziegfeld Follies	1943
Hold Your Horses	Robert Russell Bennett	Owen Murphy, Robert A. Simon	Hold Your Horses	1933
Holka-Polka	Will Ortman	Gus Kahn, Raymond B. Egan	Holka-Polka	1925

TITLE	COMPOSER	LYRICIST	SHOW	YEAR
Home for You, A	Rudolf Friml	Brian Hooker	The White Eagle	1927
Home (Is Where the Heart Is)	Jay Gorney	Barry Trivers	Heaven on Earth	1948
Home of My Heart	Will Ortman	Gus Kahn, Raymond B. Egan	Holka-Polka	1925
Home to Harlem	Ray Henderson	Lew Brown	Strike Me Pink	1933
Homeland	Sigmund Romberg	Arthur Wimperis	Louie the 14th	1925
Homework	Irving Berlin	Irving Berlin	Miss Liberty	1949
Honey, Be My Honey-Bee	Maury Rubens, J. Fred Coots	Clifford Grey	The Madcap	1928
Honey Bun	Richard Rodgers	Oscar Hammerstein II	South Pacific	1949
Honey, I'm in Love With You	William B. Friedlander, Con Conrad		Mercenary Mary	1925
Honey in the Honeycomb	Vernon Duke	John Latouche	Cabin in the Sky	1940
Honolulu	Marc Blitzstein	Marc Blitzstein	The Cradle Will Rock	1938
Honor and Glory	Karl Hajos (based on Tchaikovsky)	Harry B. Smith	Natja	1925
Honorable Profession of the Fourth Estate, The*	Irving Berlin	Irving Berlin	Miss Liberty	1949
Hoop De Dingle	Harold Rome	Harold Rome	Destry Rides Again	1959
Hoops	Arthur Schwartz	Howard Dietz	The Band Wagon	1931
Hootin' Owl Trail	Robert Emmett Dolan	Johnny Mercer	Texas, Li'l Darlin'	1949
Horseshoes Are Lucky	Robert Emmett Dolan	Johnny Mercer	Texas, Li'l Darlin'	1949
Hostess With the Mostes' on the Ball, The	Irving Berlin	Irving Berlin	Call Me Madam	1950
Hot!	Lewis E. Gensler	Robert A. Simon	Ups-A-Daisy	1928
Hot Heels	Lee David	Billy Rose, Ballard Mac-Donald	Padlocks	1927
Hot Moonlight	Jay Gorney	E. Y. Harburg	Shoot the Works	1931
Hot Pants	Roger Wolfe Kahn	Irving Caesar	Americana	1928
Hot Sands	Harry Tierney	Joseph McCarthy	Cross My Heart	1928
Hotcha	Ray Henderson	Lew Brown	Hotcha	1932
Hot-Cha Chiquita	Max Rich	Jack Scholl	Keep Moving	1934
Hottentot Potentate, The	Arthur Schwartz	Howard Dietz	At Home Abroad	1935
House Boat on the Styx, The	Alma Sanders	Monte Carlo	The House Boat on the Styx	1928
House of Flowers	Harold Arlen	Truman Capote, Harold Arlen	House of Flowers	1954
House With a Little Red Barn, A	Morgan Lewis	Nancy Hamilton	Two for the Show	1940

*Dropped from New York production

TITLE	COMPOSER	LYRICIST	SHOW	YEAR
How About a Cheer for the Navy	Irving Berlin	Irving Berlin	This Is the Army	1942
How About It?	Jesse Greer	Raymond Klages	Say When	1928
How About It?	Richard Rodgers	Lorenz Hart	America's Sweetheart	1931
How Are Things in Glocca Morra?	Burton Lane	E. Y. Harburg	Finian's Rainbow	1947
How Are You, Lady Love?	Lucien Denni	Gwynne Denni	Happy Go Lucky	1926
How Do You Do It?	Lewis E. Gensler	E. Y. Harburg	Ballyhoo	1932
How Do You Say Goodbye?	Ernest G. Schweik-ert	Frank Reardon	Rumple	1957
How Do You Speak to an Angel?	Jule Styne	Bob Hilliard	Hazel Flagg	1953
How High the Moon	Morgan Lewis	Nancy Hamilton	Two for the Show	1940
How I Could Go For You	Louis Alter	Harry Ruskin, Leighton K. Brill	Ballyhoo	1930
How Long Can Love Keep Laughing?	Harold Rome	Harold Rome	Sing Out the News	1938
How Long Has This Been Going On?	George Gershwin	Ira Gershwin	Rosalie	1928
How Lovely to be a Woman	Charles Strouse	Lee Adams	Bye Bye Birdie	1960
How to Handle a Woman	Frederick Loewe	Alan Jay Lerner	Camelot	1960
How to Win Friends and Influence People	Richard Rodgers	Lorenz Hart	I Married an Angel	1938
How Was I to Know?*	Richard Rodgers	Lorenz Hart	She's My Baby	1928
How Will He Know?	Jule Styne	Betty Comden, Adolph Green	Two on the Aisle	1951
How'd You Like to?	Stephen Jones	Irving Caesar	Yes, Yes, Yvette	1927
How's Chances?	Irving Berlin	Irving Berlin	As Thousands Cheer	1933
How's Your Romance?	Cole Porter	Cole Porter	Gay Divorce	1932
How's Your Uncle?	Jimmy McHugh	Dorothy Fields	Shoot the Works	1931
Huggin' and Muggin'	Eubie Blake	J. Milton Reddie, Cecil Mack	Swing It	1937
Hugs and Kisses	Louis Alter	Raymond Klages	Earl Carroll's Vanities	1926
Huguette Waltz	Rudolf Friml	Brian Hooker	The Vagabond King	1925
Humphrey Bogart Rhumba	Allan Roberts	Lester Lee	All for Love	1949
Humpty-Dumpty	Joseph Meyer, Philip Charig	Leo Robin	Just Fancy	1927
Hundred Million Miracles, A	Richard Rodgers	Oscar Hammer-stein II	Flower Drum Song	1958
Hundred Years From Today, A	Victor Young	Joseph Young, Ned Washington	Blackbirds	1933
Hurry	Murray Grand	Murray Grand, Elisse Boyd	New Faces	1956

*Dropped from New York production

TITLE	COMPOSER	LYRICIST	SHOW	YEAR
Hanky Panky Annabel	Max Ewing	Agnes Morgan	Grand Street Follies	1928
Hussars March	Sigmund Romberg	P. G. Wodehouse	Rosalie	1928
I Ain't Down Yet	Meredith Willson	Meredith Willson	The Unsinkable Molly Brown	1960
I Am Ashamed that Women Are so Simple	Cole Porter	Cole Porter	Kiss Me, Kate	1948
I Am in Love	Cole Porter	Cole Porter	Can-Can	1953
I Am Loved	Cole Porter	Cole Porter	Out of This World	1950
I Am Only Human After All	Vernon Duke	Ira Gershwin, E. Y. Harburg	Garrick Gaieties	1930
I Am So Eager	Jerome Kern	Oscar Hammerstein II	Music in the Air	1932
I Blush*	Richard Rodgers	Lorenz Hart	A Connecticut Yankee	1927
I Built a Dream One Day	Sigmund Romberg	Oscar Hammerstein II	May Wine	1935
I Cain't Say No	Richard Rodgers	Oscar Hammerstein II	Oklahoma!	1943
I Came to Your Room	Richard Addinsell	Clemence Dane	Come of Age	1934
I Can Cook Too	Leonard Bernstein	Betty Comden, Adolph Green	On the Town	1944
I Can Do Wonders With You*	Richard Rodgers	Lorenz Hart	Heads Up	1929
I Can Dream, Can't I?	Sammy Fain	Irving Kahal	Right This Way	1938
I Can Hear it Now	Harold Rome	Harold Rome	Bless You All	1950
I Cannot Live Without Your Love	Ralph Benatzky	Irving Caesar	White Horse Inn	1936
I Can't Afford to Dream	Sam Stept	Lew Brown, Charles Tobias	Yokel Boy	1939
I Can't Believe It's True	Lewis E. Gensler	Robert A. Simon	Ups-A-Daisy	1928
I Can't Believe It's True	Alberta Nichols	Mann Holiner	Angela	1928
I Can't Get Over a Girl Like You	Martin Broones	Harry Ruskin	Rufus LeMaire's Affairs	1927
I Can't Get Started	Vernon Duke	Ira Gershwin	Ziegfeld Follies	1936
I Can't Give You Anything But Love	Jimmy McHugh	Dorothy Fields	Blackbirds	1928
I Can't Remember the Words	Milton Ager, Henry Lodge	Jack Yellen	John Murray Anderson's Almanac	1929
I Come Out of a Dream	Richard Addinsell	Clemence Dane	Come of Age	1934
I Could Be Happy With You	Sandy Wilson	Sandy Wilson	The Boy Friend	1954
I Could Give Up Anything But You	Ray Henderson	B. G. DeSylva, Lew Brown	Follow Thru	1929
I Could Have Danced All Night	Frederick Loewe	Alan Jay Lerner	My Fair Lady	1956

*Dropped from New York production

TITLE	COMPOSER	LYRICIST	SHOW	YEAR
I Could Love a Girl Like You	Dave Stamper, Harold Levey	Cyrus Wood	Lovely Lady	1927
I Could Write a Book	Richard Rodgers	Lorenz Hart	Pal Joey	1940
I Dance Alone	James Shelton	James Shelton	Who's Who	1938
I Dare Not Love You	Sigmund Romberg	Harry B. Smith	Princess Flavia	1925
I Didn't Know What Time It Was	Richard Rodgers	Lorenz Hart	Too Many Girls	1939
I Do	Lewis E. Gensler	B. G. DeSylva	Captain Jinks	1925
I Do! He Doesn't!	Jack Lawrence, Don Walker		Courtin' Time	1951
I Don't Get It	Doris Tauber	Sis Willner	Star and Garter	1942
I Don't Know	Philip Braham	Ronald Jeans	Charlot's Revue	1925
I Don't Know Her Name	Richard Lewine	Arnold B. Horwitt	Make Mine Manhattan	1948
I Don't Love Nobody But You	Jimmy Johnson	Percy Bradford	Messin' Around	1929
I Don't Think I'll End it All Today	Harold Arlen	E. Y. Harburg	Jamaica	1957
I Don't Think I'll Fall in Love Today	George Gershwin	Ira Gershwin	Treasure Girl	1928
I Don't Want Any Labor in My Job	James P. Johnson	Flournoy Miller	Sugar Hill	1931
I Don't Want to Be President	Harry Akst	Lew Brown	Calling All Stars	1934
I Enjoy Being a Girl	Richard Rodgers	Oscar Hammerstein II	Flower Drum Song	1958
I Feel at Home With You	Richard Rodgers	Lorenz Hart	A Connecticut Yankee	1927
I Feel Like I'm Gonna Live Forever	Jule Styne	Bob Hilliard	Hazel Flagg	1953
I Feel Merely Marvelous	Albert Hague	Dorothy Fields	Redhead	1959
I Feel Pretty	Leonard Bernstein	Stephen Sondheim	West Side Story	1957
I Feel Sorry for the Girl	Glenn Paxton	Robert Goldman, George Weiss	First Impressions	1959
I Fell Head Over Heels in Love	Pat Thayer	Donovan Parsons	The Merry World	1926
I Fell in Love With You	Richard Lewine	Arnold B. Horwitt	Make Mine Manhattan	1948
I Found a Friend	Maury Rubens	J. Keirn Brennan	Music in May	1929
I Found a Million Dollar Baby	Harry Warren	Billy Rose, Mort Dixon	Crazy Quilt	1931
I Found a Song	Edward Horan	Frederick Herendeen	All the King's Horses	1934
I Found My Love	Johann Strauss, Jr.	Clare Kummer, Edwin Gilbert	Three Waltzes	1937
I Get a Kick Out of You	Cole Porter	Cole Porter	Anything Goes	1934
I Get Embarrassed	Bob Merrill	Bob Merrill	Take Me Along	1959
I Give My Heart	Carl Millöcker, Theo Mackeben	Rowland Leigh	The DuBarry	1932
I Give Myself Away	Jacques Fray	Edward Eliscu	The Vanderbilt Revue	1930

TITLE	COMPOSER	LYRICIST	SHOW	YEAR
I Got a One Track Mind	Morton Gould	Betty Comden, Adolph Green	Billion Dollar Baby	1945
I Got a Song	Harold Arlen	E. Y. Harburg	Bloomer Girl	1944
I Got Lost in His Arms	Irving Berlin	Irving Berlin	Annie Get Your Gun	1946
I Got Lucky in the Rain	Jimmy McHugh	Harold Adamson	As the Girls Go	1948
I Got Plenty o' Nuttin'	George Gershwin	Ira Gershwin, DuBose Heyward	Porgy and Bess	1935
I Got Rhythm	George Gershwin	Ira Gershwin	Girl Crazy	1930
I Got the Sun in the Morning	Irving Berlin	Irving Berlin	Annie Get Your Gun	1946
I Gotta Have You	Richard Lewine	Arnold B. Horwitt	The Girls Against the Boys	1959
I Gotta Right to Sing the Blues	Harold Arlen	Ted Koehler	Earl Carroll's Vanities	1932
I Guess I'll Have to Change My Plan	Arthur Schwartz	Howard Dietz	The Little Show	1929
I Had Myself a True Love	Harold Arlen	Johnny Mercer	St. Louis Woman	1946
I Happen to Like New York	Cole Porter	Cole Porter	The New Yorkers	1930
I Hate Men	Cole Porter	Cole Porter	Kiss Me, Kate	1948
I Hate Myself (For Falling in Love With You)	Abner Silver, Dave Oppenheim		Brown Buddies	1930
I Hate to Think That You'll Grow Old, Baby	Ray Henderson	Lew Brown	Strike Me Pink	1933
I Hate You, Darling	Cole Porter	Cole Porter	Let's Face It	1941
I Have Dreamed	Richard Rodgers	Oscar Hammerstein II	The King and I	1951
I Have Forgotten You Almost	Gitz Rice	Anna Fitziu	Nic Nax of 1926	1926
I Have Room in My Heart	Frederick Loewe	Earle Crooker	Great Lady	1938
I Have Something Nice For You	Winthrop Cortelyou	Derick Wulff	Kiss Me	1927
I Have to Tell You	Harold Rome	Harold Rome	Fanny	1954
I Haven't Got a Worry in the World	Richard Rodgers	Oscar Hammerstein II	Happy Birthday	1946
I Hear Love Call Me	Karl Hajos (based on Tchaikovsky)	Harry B. Smith	Natja	1925
I Just Couldn't Take It, Baby	Alberta Nichols	Mann Holiner	Blackbirds	1933
I Keep Telling Myself	Arthur Jones	Gen Genovese	Buttrio Square	1952
I Knew I'd Know	Sidney Lippman	Sylvia Dee	Barefoot Boy with Cheek	1947
I Know That You Know	Vincent Youmans	Anne Caldwell	Oh, Please!	1926
I Know You By Heart	Hugh Martin	Ralph Blane	Best Foot Forward	1941

TITLE	COMPOSER	LYRICIST	SHOW	YEAR
I Know Your Kind	Harold Rome	Harold Rome	Destry Rides Again	1959
I Left My Heart at the Stage Door Canteen	Irving Berlin	Irving Berlin	This Is the Army	1942
I Like a Man Around the House	Baldwin Bergersen	Phyllis McGinley	Small Wonder	1948
I Like Ev'rybody	Frank Loesser	Frank Loesser	The Most Happy Fella	1956
I Like the Likes of You	Vernon Duke	E. Y. Harburg	Ziegfeld Follies	1934
I Like the Nose on Your Face	Richard Lewine	Ted Fetter	The Fireman's Flame	1937
I Like to Recognize the Tune	Richard Rodgers	Lorenz Hart	Too Many Girls	1939
I Like You	Harold Rome	Harold Rome	Fanny	1954
I Like You As You Are	Vincent Youmans	Oscar Hammerstein II	Rainbow	1928
I Like Your Face	Arthur Schwartz	Howard Dietz	The Second Little Show	1930
I Live, I Die For You	Sigmund Romberg	Harry B. Smith	The Love Call	1927
I Love a Cop	Jerry Bock	Sheldon Harnick	Fiorello!	1959
I Love a Man in Uniform	Jimmy Monaco	Billy Rose, Ballard Mac-Donald	Harry Delmar's Revels	1927
I Love Louisa	Arthur Schwartz	Howard Dietz	The Band Wagon	1931
I Love Love	Robert Dolan	Walter O'Keefe	Princess Charming	1930
I Love Paris	Cole Porter	Cole Porter	Can-Can	1953
I Love the Moon	Paul A. Rubens, E. Ray Goetz		Naughty Cinderella	1925
I Love the Way We Fell in Love	Sammy Fain	Irving Kahal	Right This Way	1938
I Love You	Cole Porter	Cole Porter	Mexican Hayride	1944
I Love You	Robert Wright, George Forrest (based on Grieg)		Song of Norway	1944
I Love You and I Adore You	Karl Hajos (based on Chopin)	Harry B. Smith	White Lilacs	1928
I Love You and I Like You	Arthur Schwartz	Max & Nathaniel Lief	Grand Street Follies	1929
I Love You, I Adore You	H. Maurice Jacquet	William Brady	The Silver Swan	1929
I Love You More Than Yesterday	Richard Rodgers	Lorenz Hart	Lady Fingers	1929
I Love You, My Darling	Jean Gilbert	George Hirst, Edward Eliscu	Marching By	1932
I Love You So	Maurice Yvain	Max & Nathaniel Lief	Luckee Girl	1928
I Love You This Morning	Frederick Loewe	Alan Jay Lerner	The Day Before Spring	1945
I Loved Him But He Didn't Love Me	Cole Porter	Cole Porter	Wake Up and Dream	1929
I Loved You Once in Silence	Frederick Loewe	Alan Jay Lerner	Camelot	1960

TITLE	COMPOSER	LYRICIST	SHOW	YEAR
I Love You, Porgy	George Gershwin	DuBose Heyward, Ira Gershwin	Porgy and Bess	1935
I Married an Angel	Richard Rodgers	Lorenz Hart	I Married an Angel	1938
I May	Maury Rubens, Kendall Smith	Harry B. Smith	Naughty Riquette	1926
I May Be Wrong (But I Think You're Wonderful)	Henry Sullivan	Harry Ruskin	John Murray Anderson's Almanac	1929
I Mean to Say	George Gershwin	Ira Gershwin	Strike Up the Band	1930
I Mean What I Say	Edward Pola, Eddie Brandt		Woof, Woof	1929
I Met a Girl	Jule Styne	Betty Comden, Adolph Green	Bells Are Ringing	1956
I Might Fall Back on You	Jerome Kern	Oscar Hammerstein II	Show Boat	1927
I Must Be Home by Twelve O'Clock	George Gershwin	Ira Gershwin, Gus Kahn	Show Girl	1929
I Must Have a Dinner Coat	James Shelton	James Shelton	Who's Who	1938
I Must Have That Man	Jimmy McHugh	Dorothy Fields	Blackbirds	1928
I Must Love You	Richard Rodgers	Lorenz Hart	Chee-Chee	1928
I Need a Little Bit— You Need a Little Bit	Cliff Friend	Lew Brown	Piggy	1927
I Need You	Jimmy Johnson	Percy Bradford	Messin' Around	1929
I Need You So	Arthur Schwartz	David Goldberg, Howard Dietz	Grand Street Follies	1929
I Never Has Seen Snow	Harold Arlen	Truman Capote, Harold Arlen	House of Flowers	1954
I Never Know When	Leroy Anderson	Joan Ford, Jean & Walter Kerr	Goldilocks	1958
I Never Meant to Fall in Love	Sammy Fain	Paul Francis Webster	Christine	1960
I Only Know	Morgan Lewis	Nancy Hamilton	One For the Money	1939
I Promise I'll Be Practically True to You	Melville Gideon	Clifford Grey	The Optimists	1928
I Say Hello	Harold Rome	Harold Rome	Destry Rides Again	1959
I Say It's Spinach	Irving Berlin	Irving Berlin	Face the Music	1932
I See Your Face Before Me	Arthur Schwartz	Howard Dietz	Between the Devil	1937
I Sent a Letter to My Love	M. Pinsuti	Eleanor & Herbert Farjeon	The Two Bouquets	1938
I Sing of Love	Cole Porter	Cole Porter	Kiss Me, Kate	1948
I Sit in the Sun	Julian Slade	Dorothy Reynolds, Julian Slade	Salad Days	1958
I Sometimes Wonder	Oscar Straus	Clare Kummer	Three Waltzes	1937

TITLE	COMPOSER	LYRICIST	SHOW	YEAR
I Still Believe in You*	Richard Rodgers	Lorenz Hart	Simple Simon	1930
I Still Get Jealous	Jule Styne	Sammy Cahn	High Button Shoes	1947
I Still See Elisa	Frederick Loewe	Alan Jay Lerner	Paint Your Wagon	1951
I Stumbled Over You	Maury Rubens, Henry Dagand		Hello, Paris	1930
I Stumbled Over You and Fell in Love	Harry Revel	Mack Gordon	Smiling Faces	1932
I Talk to the Trees	Frederick Loewe	Alan Jay Lerner	Paint Your Wagon	1951
I Took Another Look	David Raksin	June Carroll	If the Shoe Fits	1946
I Walk With Music	Hoagy Carmichael	Johnny Mercer	Walk With Music	1940
I Wanna Be Loved by You	Herbert Stothart, Harry Ruby	Bert Kalmar	Good Boy	1928
I Wanna Get Married	Philip Charig	Dan Shapiro, Milton Pascal	Follow the Girls	1944
I Wanna Go to City College	Sammy Fain	George Marion, Jr.	Toplitzky of Notre Dame	1946
I Wanna Go Voom Voom	Cliff Friend	Lew Brown	Piggy	1927
I Want a Lovable Baby	Ray Henderson	B. G. DeSylva, Lew Brown	George White's Scandals	1925
I Want a Man	Vincent Youmans	Oscar Hammerstein II	Rainbow	1928
I Want My Mama	Jararaca & Vincent Paiva	Al Stillman	Earl Carroll's Vanities	1940
I Want Someone	William B. Friedlander	William B. Friedlander	Jonica	1930
I Want the World to Know	Richard Myers	Leo Robin	Hello, Yourself	1928
I Want to Be a War Bride	George Gershwin	Ira Gershwin	Strike Up the Band	1930
I Want to Be Bad	Ray Henderson	B. G. DeSylva, Lew Brown	Follow Thru	1929
I Want to Be Happy	Vincent Youmans	Irving Caesar	No, No, Nanette	1925
I Want to Be With You*	Vincent Youmans	B. G. DeSylva	Take a Chance	1932
I Want to Go Home	Cole Porter	Cole Porter	Leave it to Me	1938
I Want to Live	Sammy Fain	Jack Yellen	Boys and Girls Together	1940
I Was Alone*	Jerome Kern	Oscar Hammerstein II, Otto Harbach	Sunny	1925
I Was Blue	Harry Archer	Harlan Thompson	Merry-Merry	1925
I Watch the Love Parade	Jerome Kern	Otto Harbach	The Cat and the Fiddle	1931
I Went to a Marvelous Party	Noel Coward	Noel Coward	Set to Music	1939
I Whistle a Happy Tune	Richard Rodgers	Oscar Hammerstein II	The King and I	1951
I Wish	David Raksin	June Carroll	If the Shoe Fits	1946

*Dropped from New York production

TITLE	COMPOSER	LYRICIST	SHOW	YEAR
I Wish I Could Laugh at Love	Harry Warren	Mort Dixon, Joe Young	The Laugh Parade	1931
I Wish I Was a Bumble Bee	James Shelton	James Shelton	Mrs. Patterson	1954
I Wish I Were in Love Again	Richard Rodgers	Lorenz Hart	Babes in Arms	1937
I Wish it So	Marc Blitzstein	Marc Blitzstein	Juno	1959
I Wonder What Became of Me*	Harold Arlen	Johnny Mercer	St. Louis Woman	1946
I Wonder What It's Like*	Jerry Bock	Sheldon Harnick	Tenderloin	1960
I Wonder Why	Sigmund Romberg	Dorothy Donnelly	My Princess	1927
I Wonder Why You Wander	Fred Spielman, Arthur Gershwin	Stanley Adams	A Lady Says Yes	1945
I Won't Grow Up	Mark Charlap	Carolyn Leigh	Peter Pan	1954
I Worship You	Cole Porter	Cole Porter	Fifty Million Frenchmen	1929
I Would Die	Bob Merrill	Bob Merrill	Take Me Along	1959
I Would Like to Fondle You	Percy Wenrich	Raymond Peck	Castles in the Air	1926
I Would Love to Have You Love Me	Sammy Lerner, Gerald Marks	Irving Caesar	White Horse Inn	1936
I Wrote a Song For You	Sam Morrison	Dolph Singer, William Dunham	Summer Wives	1936
I'd Be a Fool	Sigmund Romberg	Oscar Hammerstein II	East Wind	1931
I'd Die	Ray Henderson	B. G. DeSylva, Lew Brown	George White's Scandals	1928
I'd Like My Picture Took	Irving Berlin	Irving Berlin	Miss Liberty	1949
I'd Like to Love Them All	Maury Rubens	J. Keirn Brennan	Music in May	1929
I'd Like to Take You Home to Meet My Mother	Robert Russell Bennett	Owen Murphy, Robert A. Simon	Hold Your Horses	1933
I'd Like to Talk About the Weather	Vernon Duke	Ted Fetter	The Lady Comes Across	1942
I'd Like You to Love Me	Ray Henderson	B. G. DeSylva, Lew Brown	Manhattan Mary	1927
I'd Rather Be Right	Richard Rodgers	Lorenz Hart	I'd Rather Be Right	1937
I'd Write a Song	Sigmund Romberg	Irving Caesar	Melody	1933
If Ever I Would Leave You	Frederick Loewe	Alan Jay Lerner	Camelot	1960
If He Really Loves Me	Harold Arlen	Jack Yellen	You Said It	1931
If I Am Dreaming	Carl Millöcker, Theo Mackeben	Rowland Leigh	The DuBarry	1932

*Dropped from New York production

TITLE	COMPOSER	LYRICIST	SHOW	YEAR
If I Had a Lover	Henry Tobias	Billy Rose, Ballard Mac-Donald	Padlocks	1927
If I Had My Druthers	Gene De Paul	Johnny Mercer	Li'l Abner	1956
If I Knew	Meredith Willson	Meredith Willson	The Unsinkable Molly Brown	1960
If I Love Again	Ben Oakland	J. P. Murray	Hold Your Horses	1933
If I Loved You	Richard Rodgers	Oscar Hammerstein II	Carousel	1945
If I Thought I Could Live Without You, I'd Die	Ray Henderson	Lew Brown	George White's Scandals	1931
If I Was a Boy	James Shelton	James Shelton	Mrs. Patterson	1954
If I Were a Bell	Frank Loesser	Frank Loesser	Guys and Dolls	1950
If I Were You	Richard Rodgers	Lorenz Hart	Betsy	1926
If I Were You	Louis Alter	Harry Ruskin, Leighton K. Brill	Ballyhoo	1930
If I Were You, Love	Vincent Youmans	Ring Lardner	Smiles	1930
If It Were Easy to Do	Bob Hilliard	Carl Sigman	Angel in the Wings	1947
If It's a Dream	Victor Young	Stella Unger	Seventh Heaven	1955
If It's Love	Harry Akst	Lew Brown	Calling All Stars	1934
If Love Were All	Noel Coward	Noel Coward	Bitter Sweet	1929
If Only	Sigmund Romberg	Rowland Leigh	My Romance	1948
If That Was Love	Bob Merrill	Bob Merrill	New Girl in Town	1957
If There Is Someone Lovelier Than You	Arthur Schwartz	Howard Dietz	Revenge With Music	1934
If This Isn't Love	Burton Lane	E. Y. Harburg	Finian's Rainbow	1947
If You Can't Get the Love You Want	Vernon Duke	Howard Dietz	Sadie Thompson	1944
If You Cared	Jean Gilbert	Harry Graham	Katja	1926
If You Don't Love Me	Hoagy Carmichael	Paul Webster, Ray Golden	Alive and Kicking	1950
If You Hadn't, But You Did	Jule Styne	Betty Comden, Adolph Green	Two on the Aisle	1951
If You Have Troubles, Laugh Them Away	Lester Lee	Lester Lee	Harry Delmar's Revels	1927
If You Haven't Got a Sweetheart	Arthur Schwartz	Dorothy Fields	A Tree Grows in Brooklyn	1951
If You Haven't Got "It"	Max Ewing	Agnes Morgan	Grand Street Follies	1927
If You Knew Susie	B. G. DeSylva	B. G. DeSylva	Big Boy	1925
If You Know What I Mean	Arthur Schwartz	Theodore Goodwin, Albert Carroll	Grand Street Follies	1926
If You Loved Me Truly	Cole Porter	Cole Porter	Can-Can	1953
If You Smile at Me	Cole Porter	Cole Porter	Around the World	1946

TITLE	COMPOSER	LYRICIST	SHOW	YEAR
If You Were Someone Else	Harold Levey	Owen Murphy	Rainbow Rose	1926
If You Were Someone Else	Arthur Schwartz	Albert Stillman	Virginia	1937
If You Were the Apple	Joseph Meyer	Billy Moll	Jonica	1930
If You'll Be Mine	Hugh Martin	Hugh Martin	Look Ma, I'm Dancin'	1948
If You're in Love, You'll Waltz	Harry Tierney	Joseph McCarthy	Rio Rita	1927
If 'n	Harold Karr	Matt Dubey	Happy Hunting	1956
I'll Admit	Maury Rubens, Henry Dagand		Hello, Paris	1930
I'll Be Hard to Handle	Jerome Kern	Bernard Dougall	Roberta	1933
I'll Be Seeing You	Sammy Fain	Irving Kahal	Right This Way	1938
I'll Be There	Albert Sirmay, Arthur Schwartz	Arthur Swanstrom	Princess Charming	1930
I'll Buy You a Star	Arthur Schwartz	Dorothy Fields	A Tree Grows in Brooklyn	1951
I'll Follow My Secret Heart	Noel Coward	Noel Coward	Conversation Piece	1934
I'll Go Home With Bonnie Jean	Frederick Loewe	Alan Jay Lerner	Brigadoon	1947
I'll Keep on Dreaming	Emmerich Kalman	Harry B. Smith	Countess Maritza	1926
I'll Keep on Dreaming of You	J. Fred Coots	Al Dubin	White Lights	1927
I'll Know	Frank Loesser	Frank Loesser	Guys and Dolls	1950
I'll Know and She'll Know	Harry Ruby	Bert Kalmar	Top Speed	1929
I'll Know Him	Ray Henderson	Lew Brown, B. G. DeSylva	Flying High	1930
I'll Never Leave You	Albert Sirmay, Arthur Schwartz	Arthur Swanstrom	Princess Charming	1930
I'll Never Say No	Meredith Willson	Meredith Willson	The Unsinkable Molly Brown	1960
I'll Pay the Check	Arthur Schwartz	Dorothy Fields	Stars in Your Eyes	1939
I'll Putcha Pitcha in the Papers	Michael Cleary	Max & Nathaniel Lief	The Third Little Show	1931
I'll See You Again	Noel Coward	Noel Coward	Bitter Sweet	1929
I'll Share It All With You	Irving Berlin	Irving Berlin	Annie Get Your Gun	1946
I'll Take an Option on You	Ralph Rainger	Leo Robin	Tattle Tales	1930
I'll Take You to the Country	Maurice Yvain	Max & Nathaniel Lief	Luckee Girl	1928
I'll Tell the Man in the Street	Richard Rodgers	Lorenz Hart	I Married an Angel	1938
Illegitimate Daughter, The	George Gershwin	Ira Gershwin	Of Thee I Sing	1931

TITLE	COMPOSER	LYRICIST	SHOW	YEAR
I'm a Bad, Bad Man	Irving Berlin	Irving Berlin	Annie Get Your Gun	1946
I'm a Fool, Little One	Richard Rodgers	Lorenz Hart	Present Arms	1928
I'm a Funny Dame	Harold Karr	Matt Dubey	Happy Hunting	1956
I'm a Gigolo	Cole Porter	Cole Porter	Wake Up and Dream	1929
I'm a Little Bit Fonder of You*	Irving Caesar	Irving Caesar	Yes, Yes, Yvette	1927
I'm a One Girl Man	George M. Cohan	George M. Cohan	Billie	1928
I'm Afraid	Albert Sirmay	Irving Caesar, Graham John	Ripples	1930
I'm Afraid I'm in Love	Clay Warnick	Edward Eager	Dream With Music	1944
I'm Afraid of the Dark	Richard Addinsell	Clemence Dane	Come of Age	1934
I'm All Alone	A. Baldwin Sloane	Harry Cort, George E. Stoddard	China Rose	1925
I'm Alone	Jerome Kern	Oscar Hammerstein II	Music in the Air	1932
I'm an Indian Too	Irving Berlin	Irving Berlin	Annie Get Your Gun	1946
I'm Back in Circulation	Albert Hague	Dorothy Fields	Redhead	1959
I'm Bringing a Red, Red Rose	Walter Donaldson	Gus Kahn	Whoopee	1928
I'm Coming Virginia	Donald Heywood	Will Cook	Africana	1929
I'm Dreaming While We're Dancing	Gerald Dolin	Edward J. Lambert	Smile at Me	1925
I'm Feelin' Blue ('Cause I Got Nobody)	Jimmy McHugh	Dorothy Fields	Lew Leslie's International Review	1930
I'm Flying	Mark Charlap	Carolyn Leigh	Peter Pan	1954
I'm Flying High	Ray Henderson	Lew Brown, B. G. DeSylva	Flying High	1930
I'm For You	Lee David	J. Keirn Brennan	A Night in Venice	1929
I'm Getting Myself Ready for You	Cole Porter	Cole Porter	The New Yorkers	1930
I'm Getting Tired So I Can Sleep	Irving Berlin	Irving Berlin	This Is the Army	1942
I'm Glad I Waited	Vincent Youmans	Clifford Grey, Harold Adamson	Smiles	1930
I'm Gonna Hang My Hat	Philip Charig	Dan Shapiro, Milton Pascal	Follow the Girls	1944
I'm Gonna Make a Fool Out of April	Victor Young	Edward Heyman	Pardon Our French	1950
I'm Gonna Wash That Man Right Outa My Hair	Richard Rodgers	Oscar Hammerstein II	South Pacific	1949
I'm Head and Heels in Love	Leo Edwards	Irving Caesar	The City Chap	1925

*Dropped from New York production.

TITLE	COMPOSER	LYRICIST	SHOW	YEAR
I'm in Love	Con Conrad	Gus Kahn, Otto Harbach	Kitty's Kisses	1926
I'm in Love	Cole Porter	Cole Porter	Fifty Million Frenchmen	1929
I'm in Love With a Soldier Boy	Cole Porter	Cole Porter	Something For the Boys	1943
I'm in Love With Miss Logan	Ronald Graham	Ronald Graham	New Faces	1952
I'm Just a Little Sparrow	Sammy Fain	Paul Francis Webster	Christine	1960
I'm Leaving the Bad Girls for Good	Dave Stamper	Fred Herendeen	Orchids Preferred	1937
I'm Like a New Broom	Arthur Schwartz	Dorothy Fields	A Tree Grows in Brooklyn	1951
I'm Lost	George Lessner	Ruth Aarons	Sleepy Hollow	1948
I'm Not at All in Love	Richard Adler, Jerry Ross		The Pajama Game	1954
I'm Not Myself Tonight	David Raksin	June Carroll	If the Shoe Fits	1946
I'm Not So Bright	Hugh Martin	Hugh Martin	Look Ma, I'm Dancin'	1948
I'm on My Way	Frederick Loewe	Alan Jay Lerner	Paint Your Wagon	1951
I'm on the Crest of a Wave	Ray Henderson	B. G. DeSylva, Lew Brown	George White's Scandals	1928
I'm on the Lookout	Charles Gaynor	Charles Gaynor	Lend an Ear	1948
I'm One of God's Children	Louis Alter	Oscar Hammerstein II, Harry Ruskin	Ballyhoo	1930
I'm One of Your Admirers	Jimmy Van Heusen	Johnny Burke	Carnival in Flanders	1953
I'm So in Love	Will Irwin	Norman Zeno	Fools Rush In	1934
I'm So Weary of it All	Noel Coward	Noel Coward	Set to Music	1939
I'm Stepping Out With Lulu	Henry Creamer, Jimmy Johnson		A La Carte	1927
I'm Sure of Your Love	Morton Gould	Betty Comden, Adolph Green	Billion Dollar Baby	1945
I'm That Way Over You	J. Fred Coots	Arthur Swanstrom, Benny Davis	Sons o' Guns	1929
I'm the Fellow Who Loves You	Ray Henderson	Jack Yellen	George White's Scandals	1936
I'm the Girl	James Shelton	James Shelton	Dance Me a Song	1950
I'm Tired of Texas	Hugh Martin	Hugh Martin	Look Ma, I'm Dancin'	1948
I'm Unlucky at Gambling	Cole Porter	Cole Porter	Fifty Million Frenchmen	1929
I'm Waiting for a Wonderful Girl	Vincent Youmans	Anne Caldwell	Oh, Please!	1926
I'm Walkin' the Chalk Line	Alberta Nichols	Mann Holiner	Blackbirds	1933
I'm Your Girl	Richard Rodgers	Oscar Hammerstein II	Me and Juliet	1953

TITLE	COMPOSER	LYRICIST	SHOW	YEAR
Imagination	Joseph Meyer, Roger Wolfe Kahn	Irving Caesar	Here's Howe	1928
Imagine My Finding You Here	Ned Lehak	Robert Sour	Sing for Your Supper	1939
In a Great Big Way	Jimmy McHugh	Dorothy Fields	Hello Daddy	1928
In a Little Stucco in the Sticks	Harry Revel	Mack Gordon	Smiling Faces	1932
In a Little Swiss Chalet	Will Irwin	Norman Zeno	White Horse Inn	1936
In a Little While	Will Ortman	Gus Kahn, Raymond B. Egan	Holka-Polka	1925
In a Little While	Mary Rodgers	Marshall Barer	Once Upon a Mattress	1959
In Araby With You	Jerome Kern	Anne Caldwell, Otto Harbach	Criss-Cross	1926
In Armenia	Oscar Straus	Harry B. Smith	Naughty Riquette	1926
In Chi-Chi-Castenango	Jay Gorney	Henry Myers	Meet the People	1940
In Egern on the Tegern See	Jerome Kern	Oscar Hammerstein II	Music in the Air	1932
In Love With Romance	Sigmund Romberg	Rowland Leigh	My Romance	1948
In My Garden	Sigmund Romberg	Irving Caesar	Melody	1933
In My Love Boat	Daisy De Segonzac	Max & Nathaniel Lief	Say When	1928
In My Memoirs	Jimmy McHugh	Al Dubin	Streets of Paris	1939
In My Old Virginia Home (on the River Nile)	Vernon Duke	John Latouche	Cabin in the Sky	1940
In Other Words, Seventeen	Jerome Kern	Oscar Hammerstein II	Very Warm for May	1939
In Our Little Studio	Maurice Yvain, Muriel Pollock	Max & Nathaniel Lief	Luckee Girl	1928
In Paris and in Love	Sigmund Romberg, Don Walker	Leo Robin	The Girl in Pink Tights	1954
In the Dark	William B. Kernell	Dorothy Donnelly	Hello, Lola	1926
In the Heart of the Dark	Jerome Kern	Oscar Hammerstein II	Very Warm for May	1939
In the Merry Month of Maybe	Harry Warren	Ira Gershwin, Billy Rose	Sweet and Low	1930
In the Morning	David Raksin	June Carroll	If the Shoe Fits	1946
In the Shade of the New Apple Tree	Harold Arlen	E. Y. Harburg	Hooray for What	1937
In Times Like These	Ernest G. Schweikert	Frank Reardon	Rumple	1957
Independent	Jule Styne	Betty Comden, Adolph Green	Bells Are Ringing	1956
Inside Looking Out	Henry Sullivan	Edward Eliscu	A Little Racketeer	1932

TITLE	COMPOSER	LYRICIST	SHOW	YEAR
International Rhythm	Jimmy McHugh	Dorothy Fields	Lew Leslie's International Review	1930
Into the Night	Robert Stolz	Robert Sour	Mr. Strauss Goes to Boston	1945
Irma La Douce	Marguerite Monnot	Julian More, Daniel Heneker, Monte Norman	Irma La Douce	1960
Irresistible You	Jimmy Monaco	Billy Rose, Ballard Mac-Donald	Harry Delmar's Revels	1927
Is Everybody Happy Now?	Maury Rubens	Jack Osterman, Ted Lewis	Artists and Models	1927
Is It Any Wonder?	Alma Sanders	Monte Carlo	Oh! Oh! Nurse	1925
Is It Him or Is It Me?	Kurt Weill	Alan Jay Lerner	Love Life	1948
Is It Love?	Oscar Levant	Irving Caesar	Ripples	1930
Is It Possible?	Jimmy McHugh	Al Dubin	Streets of Paris	1939
Is It the Girl?	Cole Porter	Cole Porter	The Seven Lively Arts	1944
Is Izzy Azzy Woz?	Cliff Friend	George White	George White's Scandals	1929
Is Rhythm Necessary?	Sammy Fain	Irving Kahal	Everybody's Welcome	1931
Island in the West Indies	Vernon Duke	Ira Gershwin	Ziegfeld Follies	1936
Isn't It a Pity?	George Gershwin	Ira Gershwin	Pardon My English	1933
Isn't It June?	Ray Henderson	Ted Koehler	Say When	1934
It	Sigmund Romberg	Otto Harbach, Oscar Hammerstein II	The Desert Song	1926
It Ain't Necessarily So	George Gershwin	Ira Gershwin	Porgy and Bess	1935
It All Belongs to Me	Irving Berlin	Irving Berlin	Ziegfeld Follies	1927
It All Depends on You	Ray Henderson	B. G. DeSylva, Lew Brown	Big Boy	1925
It Always Takes Two	Lewis E. Gensler	Owen Murphy, Robert A. Simon	The Gang's All Here	1931
It Doesn't Cost You Anything to Dream	Sigmund Romberg	Dorothy Fields	Up in Central Park	1945
It Doesn't Take a Minute	Albert Hague	Dorothy Fields	Redhead	1959
It Feels Good	Richard Rodgers	Oscar Hammerstein II	Me and Juliet	1953
It Is Love	Edward Kunneke (based on Offenbach)	Harry B. Smith	The Love Song	1925
It Just Had to Happen	Cliff Friend	Lew Brown	Piggy	1927
It Just Occurred to Me	Vernon Duke	Ogden Nash	Two's Company	1952
It Means So Little to You	Richard Myers	Edward Heyman	Here Goes the Bride	1931
It Must Be Fun to Be You	Cole Porter	Cole Porter	Mexican Hayride	1944
It Must Be Heaven	Richard Rodgers	Lorenz Hart	Heads Up	1929
It Must Be Love	Harry Archer	Harlan Thompson	Merry-Merry	1925
It Must Be Me	Leonard Bernstein	Richard Wilbur	Candide	1956

TITLE	COMPOSER	LYRICIST	SHOW	YEAR
It Must Be Religion	Forman Brown	Forman Brown	New Faces	1936
It Must Be Spring	Ralph Blane	Ralph Blane	Three Wishes for Jamie	1952
It Must Have Been the Night	Ray Henderson	Ted Koehler	Say When	1934
It Never Entered My Mind	Richard Rodgers	Lorenz Hart	Higher and Higher	1940
It Never Was You	Kurt Weill	Maxwell Anderson	Knickerbocker Holiday	1938
It Takes a Woman to Take a Man	Jimmy McHugh	Harold Adamson	As the Girls Go	1948
It Was So Nice Having You	Gerald Marks	Sam Lerner	Hold It!	1948
It Was Written in the Stars	Cole Porter	Cole Porter	DuBarry Was a Lady	1939
It Will Be All Right (In a Hundred Years)	Jay Gorney	Walter & Jean Kerr	Touch and Go	1949
It Wonders Me	Albert Hague	Arnold B. Horwitt	Plain and Fancy	1955
It Won't Be Long Now	Ray Henderson	B. G. DeSylva, Lew Brown	Manhattan Mary	1927
It'll Come To You	Irving Berlin	Irving Berlin	Louisiana Purchase	1940
It's a Big, Wide, Wonderful World	John Rox	John Rox	All in Fun	1940
It's a Chemical Reaction, That's All	Cole Porter	Cole Porter	Silk Stockings	1955
It's a Great Little World*	George Gershwin	Ira Gershwin	Tip-Toes	1925
It's a Long Time Till Tomorrow	Abraham Ellstein	Walter Bullock	Great To Be Alive	1950
It's a Lovely Day Today	Irving Berlin	Irving Berlin	Call Me Madam	1950
It's a Lovely Day Tomorrow	Irving Berlin	Irving Berlin	Louisiana Purchase	1940
It's a Lovely Night on the Hudson River	Richard Lewine	Ted Fetter	The Fireman's Flame	1937
It's a Typical Day	Gene De Paul	Johnny Mercer	Li'l Abner	1956
It's a Wishing World	Ralph Blane	Ralph Blane	Three Wishes for Jamie	1952
It's a Wonderful World	Sigmund Romberg	Oscar Hammerstein II	East Wind	1931
It's All Right With Me	Cole Porter	Cole Porter	Can-Can	1953
It's All Yours	Arthur Schwartz	Dorothy Fields	Stars In Your Eyes	1939
It's Always the Way	Emmerich Kalman, Herbert Stothart	Otto Harbach, Oscar Hammerstein II	Golden Dawn	1927
It's an Old Spanish Custom	Jimmy Van Heusen	Johnny Burke	Carnival in Flanders	1953
It's Delightful Down in Chile	Jule Styne	Leo Robin	Gentlemen Prefer Blondes	1949

*Dropped from New York production

TITLE	COMPOSER	LYRICIST	SHOW	YEAR
It's De-Lovely	Cole Porter	Cole Porter	Red, Hot and Blue	1936
It's Different With Me	Harold Arlen	Jack Yellen	You Said It	1931
It's Easy to Say Hello	Cliff Friend	Lew Brown	Piggy	1927
It's Easy to Sing	Julian Slade	Dorothy Reynolds, Julian Slade	Salad Days	1958
It's Every Girl's Ambition	Vincent Youmans	Edward Heyman	Through the Years	1932
It's Good to Be Alive	Bob Merrill	Bob Merrill	New Girl in Town	1957
It's Got to Be Love	Richard Rodgers	Lorenz Hart	On Your Toes	1936
It's Great to Be a Doughboy	Shep Camp	Frank Dupree	Half a Widow	1927
It's Great to Be Alive*	Ray Henderson	Lew Brown	Hotcha	1932
It's Great to Be Alive	Robert Emmett Dolan	Johnny Mercer	Texas, Li'l Darlin'	1949
It's Great to Be in Love	Cliff Friend	Cliff Friend	Earl Carroll's Vanities	1931
It's High Time	Jule Styne	Leo Robin	Gentlemen Prefer Blondes	1949
It's High Time I Got the Low-Down on You	Joseph Meyer	Edward Heyman	New Faces	1936
It's in the Air	Louis Alter	E. Y. Harburg, Billy Rose	Crazy Quilt	1931
It's in the Stars	Michael Cleary	Max & Nathaniel Lief	Shoot the Works	1931
It's Love	Leonard Bernstein	Betty Comden, Adolph Green	Wonderful Town	1953
It's Me	Richard Rodgers	Oscar Hammerstein II	Me and Juliet	1953
It's Me Again	Sam Stept	Lew Brown, Charles Tobias	Yokel Boy	1939
It's More Fun Than a Picnic	Jimmy McHugh	Harold Adamson	As the Girls Go	1948
It's Never Quite the Same	Jay Livingston	Ray Evans	Oh Captain!	1958
It's Never Too Late to Fall in Love	Sandy Wilson	Sandy Wilson	The Boy Friend	1954
It's So Easy to Lose	Hoagy Carmichael	Ted Fetter	The Show Is On	1936
It's the Darndest Thing	Jimmy McHugh	Dorothy Fields	Singin' the Blues	1931
It's the Going Home Together	Jerome Moross	John Latouche	The Golden Apple	1954
It's the Same Old South	Jay Gorney	Edward Eliscu	Meet the People	1940
It's the Second Time You Meet That Matters	Jule Styne	Betty Comden, Adolph Green	Say, Darling	1958
It's Time to Say "Aloha"	Sammy Fain	Charles Tobias	Hellzapoppin'	1938
It's Too Nice a Day to Go to School	Sidney Lippman	Sylvia Dee	Barefoot Boy With Cheek	1947
It's Up to the Band	Irving Berlin	Irving Berlin	Ziegfeld Follies	1927

*Also in "Strike Me Pink."

TITLE	COMPOSER	LYRICIST	SHOW	YEAR
It's You	Meredith Willson	Meredith Willson	The Music Man	1957
It's You I Love	J. Fred Coots	Arthur Swanstrom, Benny Davis	Sons O' Guns	1929
It's You I Want	Paul McGrane	Al Stillman	Who's Who	1938
I've Always Loved You	James Mundy	John Latouche	The Vamp	1955
I've A'ready Started In	Meredith Willson	Meredith Willson	The Unsinkable Molly Brown	1960
I've Come to Wive it Wealthily in Padua	Cole Porter	Cole Porter	Kiss Me, Kate	1948
I've Confessed to the Breeze*	Vincent Youmans	Otto Harbach	No, No, Nanette	1925
I've Gone Nuts Over You	Edward Horan	Frederick Herendeen	All the King's Horses	1934
I've Gone Romantic on You	Harold Arlen	E. Y. Harburg	Hooray For What	1937
I've Got a Bug in My Heart	Jimmy McHugh	Dorothy Fields	Lew Leslie's International Review	1930
I've Got a Cookie Jar But No Cookies	Harry Archer	Walter O'Keefe	Just a Minute	1928
I've Got a Crush on You**	George Gershwin	Ira Gershwin	Treasure Girl	1928
I've Got a Lot to Learn About Life	Tommy Wolf	Fran Landesman	The Nervous Set	1959
I've Got a One Track Mind	Vernon Duke	Howard Dietz	Jackpot	1944
I've Got a Yes Girl	Henry Souvaine, Jay Gorney	Morrie Ryskind, Howard Dietz	Merry-Go-Round	1927
I've Got Five Dollars	Richard Rodgers	Lorenz Hart	America's Sweetheart	1931
I've Got It	Alberta Nichols	Mann Holiner	The Red Robe	1928
I've Got It Again	Ned Lehak	Allan Boretz	Garrick Gaieties	1930
I've Got Me	Jerome Moross	John Latouche	Ballet Ballads	1948
I've Got Somethin'	Harry Ruby	Bert Kalmar	High Kickers	1941
I've Got to Be There	George Gershwin	Ira Gershwin	Pardon My English	1933
I've Got to Get Hot	Ray Henderson	Jack Yellen	George White's Scandals	1936
I've Got You on My Mind	Max Ewing	Max Ewing	Grand Street Follies	1929
I've Got You on My Mind	Cole Porter	Cole Porter	Gay Divorce	1932
I've Gotta Crow	Mark Charlap	Carolyn Leigh	Peter Pan	1954
I've Gotta Keep My Eye on You	Harry Revel	Mack Gordon	Marching By	1932
I've Grown Accustomed to Her Face	Frederick Loewe	Alan Jay Lerner	My Fair Lady	1956
I've Lost My Heart	Morris Hamilton	Grace Henry	The Third Little Show	1931
I've Made a Habit of You	Arthur Schwartz	Howard Dietz	The Little Show	1929
I've Never Been in Love Before	Frank Loesser	Frank Loesser	Guys and Dolls	1950

*Dropped from New York production

**Also in "Strike Up the Band"

TITLE	COMPOSER	LYRICIST	SHOW	YEAR
I've Nothing to Offer	Harry Akst	Lew Brown	Calling All Stars	1934
I've Still Got My Health	Cole Porter	Cole Porter	Panama Hattie	1940
I've Told Ev'ry Little Star	Jerome Kern	Oscar Hammerstein II	Music in the Air	1932
I've Waited for You	Sigmund Romberg	Harry B. Smith	Cherry Blossoms	1927
Jacques De Raque	Jerry Bock, George Weiss, Larry Holofcener		Mr. Wonderful	1956
Jade	Raymond Hubbell	Anne Caldwell	Yours Truly	1927
Je t'Aime Means I Love You	Powers Gouraud	Powers Gouraud	Gay Paree	1926
Je Vous Aime	Arthur L. Beiner	Arthur L. Beiner	Puzzles	1925
Jeannie's Packin' Up	Frederick Loewe	Alan Jay Lerner	Brigadoon	1947
Jenny	Kurt Weill	Ira Gershwin	Lady in the Dark	1941
Jerry, My Soldier Boy	Cole Porter	Cole Porter	Let's Face It	1941
Jersey Walk	James Hanley	Eddie Dowling	Honeymoon Lane	1926
Jig Hop, The	Kay Swift	Paul James	Fine and Dandy	1930
Jimmy	Irving Berlin	Irving Berlin	Ziegfeld Follies	1927
Joe Worker	Marc Blitzstein	Marc Blitzstein	The Cradle Will Rock	1938
Joey, Joey, Joey	Frank Loesser	Frank Loesser	The Most Happy Fella	1956
Johnny-O (Katie-O)	Earl Robinson	Waldo Salt	Sandhog	1954
Johnny One Note	Richard Rodgers	Lorenz Hart	Babes in Arms	1937
Join the Navy!	Vincent Youmans	Leo Robin, Clifford Grey	Hit the Deck	1927
Josephine	Armand Vecsey	Clifford Grey	The Nightingale	1927
Josephine	Cole Porter	Cole Porter	Silk Stockings	1955
Joshua	Frederick Loewe	Alan Jay Lerner	What's Up	1943
Journey's End	Jerome Kern	P. G. Wodehouse	The City Chap	1925
Jubilation T. Cornpone	Gene DePaul	Johnny Mercer	Li'l Abner	1956
Judy, Who D'Ya Love?	Charles Rosoff	Leo Robin	Judy	1927
Jug of Wine, A	Frederick Loewe	Alan Jay Lerner	The Day Before Spring	1945
Julianne	Ida Hoyt Chamberlain	Ida Hoyt Chamberlain	Enchanted Isle	1927
Jumping Jimminy	Niclas Kempner	Graham John	The Street Singer	1929
June	Tom Johnstone	Phil Cook	When You Smile	1925
June Days	Stephen Jones	Clifford Grey, Cyrus Wood	June Days	1925
June Is Bustin' Out All Over	Richard Rodgers	Oscar Hammerstein II	Carousel	1945
Jungle Jingle	Irving Berlin	Irving Berlin	Ziegfeld Follies	1927
Jungle Rose	Ford Dabney	Jo Trent	Rang-Tang	1927
Jupiter Forbid	Richard Rodgers	Lorenz Hart	By Jupiter	1942
Just a Cozy Hide-Away	Ray Henderson	B. G. DeSylva, Lew Brown	Manhattan Mary	1927
Just a Kiss Apart	Jule Styne	Leo Robin	Gentlemen Prefer Blondes	1949

TITLE	COMPOSER	LYRICIST	SHOW	YEAR
Just a Little Bit More	Arthur Schwartz	Dorothy Fields	Stars in Your Eyes	1939
Just a Little Joint With a Juke Box	Hugh Martin	Ralph Blane	Best Foot Forward	1941
Just a Little Love Song	Max Ewing	Max Ewing	Grand Street Follies	1928
Just a Little Smile From You	James Hanley	Eddie Dowling	Sidewalks of New York	1927
Just a Sentimental Tune	Louis Alter	Max & Nathaniel Lief	Tattle Tales	1930
Just Beyond the Rainbow	Harry Revel	Arnold B. Horwitt	Are You With It?	1945
Just Cross the River From Queens	Albert Von Tilzer	Neville Fleeson	Bye, Bye Bonnie	1927
Just For Once	Albert Hague	Dorothy Fields	Redhead	1959
Just for Tonight	Maury Rubens	Clifford Grey	Katja	1926
Just for Tonight	Bronislaw Kaper (based on Chopin)	John Latouche	Polonaise	1945
Just Imagine	Ray Henderson	B. G. DeSylva, Lew Brown	Good News	1927
Just in Time	Jule Styne	Betty Comden, Adolph Green	Bells Are Ringing	1956
Just Like a Man	Vernon Duke	Ogden Nash	Two's Company	1952
Just Like a Wild, Wild Rose	Dave Stamper	Gene Buck	Take the Air	1927
Just Mention Joe	Harry Akst	Lew Brown	Calling All Stars	1934
Just My Luck	Jimmy Van Heusen	Johnny Burke	Nellie Bly	1946
Just My Luck	Jerry Bock	Sheldon Harnick	The Body Beautiful	1958
Just Once Around the Clock	Sigmund Romberg	Oscar Hammerstein II	May Wine	1935
Just One of Those Things	Cole Porter	Cole Porter	Jubilee	1935
Just One Way to Say I Love You	Irving Berlin	Irving Berlin	Miss Liberty	1949
Just Say the Word	Frank D'Armond	Milton Berle	Saluta	1934
Just Suppose	Phil Baker, Maury Rubens	Sid Silvers	Pleasure Bound	1929
Just You and I and the Baby	William B. Friedlander	Con Conrad	Mercenary Mary	1925
Kansas City	Richard Rodgers	Oscar Hammerstein II	Oklahoma!	1943
Kathleen, Mine	Vincent Youmans	Edward Heyman	Through the Years	1932
Katie O'Sullivan	Earl Robinson	Waldo Salt	Sandhog	1954
Katie Went to Haiti	Cole Porter	Cole Porter	DuBarry Was a Lady	1939
Keep A-Hoppin'	Meredith Willson	Meredith Willson	The Unsinkable Molly Brown	1960
Keep 'Em Guessing	James P. Johnson	Flournoy Miller	Sugar Hill	1931

TITLE	COMPOSER	LYRICIST	SHOW	YEAR
Keep It Gay	Richard Rodgers	Oscar Hammer- stein II	Me and Juliet	1953
Keep Smiling at Trouble	Lewis E. Gensler	Al Jolson, B. G. DeSylva	Big Boy	1925
Keep Your Undershirt On	Harry Ruby	Bert Kalmar	Top Speed	1929
Key to My Heart, The	Louis Alter	Ira Gershwin	The Social Register	1931
Keys to Heaven	Richard Rodgers	Lorenz Hart	Garrick Gaieties	1926
Keys to Your Heart	Jimmy McHugh	Dorothy Fields	Lew Leslie's Inter- national Review	1930
Kickin' the Clouds Away	George Gershwin	B. G. DeSylva, Ira Gershwin	Tell Me More	1925
Kickin' the Corn Around	Richard Lewine	Ted Fetter	The Girl From Wyoming	1938
Kids	Charles Strouse	Lee Adams	Bye Bye Birdie	1960
Kiki	Lewis E. Gensler	B. G. DeSylva	Captain Jinks	1925
Kinda Cute	Jay Gorney	E. Y. Harburg	Earl Carroll's Sketch Book	1929
Kinda Like You	Vincent Youmans	Edward Heyman	Through the Years	1932
King Cotton	Giuseppe Verdi	Charles Friedman	My Darlin' Aida	1952
King of the Sword	Robert Stolz, Maury Rubens	J. Keirn Brennan	The Red Robe	1928
Kinkajou, The	Harry Tierney	Joseph McCarthy	Rio Rita	1927
Kiss a Four Leaf Clover	Jerome Kern	Anne Caldwell, Otto Harbach	Criss-Cross	1926
Kiss for Cinderella, A	Richard Rodgers	Lorenz Hart	Present Arms	1928
Kiss in the Moonlight, A	Clarence Gaskill	Clarence Gaskill	Earl Carroll's Vanities	1925
Kiss Me	Winthrop Cortel- you	Derick Wulff	Kiss Me	1927
Kiss Me	Noel Coward	Noel Coward	Bitter Sweet	1929
Kiss Me and Kill Me With Love	Sammy Fain	Dan Shapiro	Ankles Aweigh	1955
Kiss to Remind You, A	Franz Lehar	Edward Eliscu	Frederika	1937
Kisses That You Gave to Me	Will Morrissey	Edmund Joseph	Polly of Hollywood	1927
Kitty's Kisses	Con Conrad	Gus Kahn	Kitty's Kisses	1926
Kling-Kling Bird on the Divi-Divi Tree, The	Cole Porter	Cole Porter	Jubilee	1935
Kosher Kitty Kelly	Leon DeCosta	Leon DeCosta	Kosher Kitty Kelly	1925
K-ra-zy for You	George Gershwin	Ira Gershwin	Treasure Girl	1928
La Fiesta	Sammy Fain	Dan Shapiro	Ankles Aweigh	1955
Lack-A-Day	John Mundy	Edward Eager	The Liar	1950
Lackawanna	Joseph Meyer, James F. Hanley	B. G. DeSylva	Big Boy	1925
Ladies of the Town	Noel Coward	Noel Coward	Bitter Sweet	1929
Ladies Who Sing With a Band, The	Thomas (Fats) Waller	George Marion, Jr.	Early to Bed	1943

TITLE	COMPOSER	LYRICIST	SHOW	YEAR
Lady	Vernon Duke	Ted Fetter	The Lady Comes Across	1942
Lady Do	Abel Baer	Sam Lewis, Joe Young	Lady Do	1927
Lady in Waiting	Leroy Anderson	Joan Ford, Jean & Walter Kerr	Goldilocks	1958
Lady Is a Tramp, The	Richard Rodgers	Lorenz Hart	Babes in Arms	1937
Lady Must Live, A	Richard Rodgers	Lorenz Hart	America's Sweetheart	1931
Lady Needs a Change, A	Arthur Schwartz	Dorothy Fields	Stars in Your Eyes	1939
Lady of My Heart	Milton Susskind	Paul Porter, Benjamin H. Burt	Florida Girl	1925
Lady of the Snow	Harold Levey	Owen Murphy	Greenwich Village Follies	1925
Lady Whippoorwill	Harry Tierney	Joseph McCarthy	Cross My Heart	1928
Lamplight	James Shelton	James Shelton	New Faces	1934
Land of Going to Be, The	E. Ray Goetz, Walter Kollo		Paris	1928
Land of Romance	Percy Wenrich	Raymond Peck	Castles in the Air	1926
Lantern of Love	Percy Wenrich	Raymond Peck	Castles in the Air	1926
Late Love	Jack Urbont	Bruce Geller	Livin' the Life	1957
Latin in Me, The	Sammy Fain	Jack Yellen	Boys and Girls Together	1940
Latin Tune, A Manhattan Moon and You, A	Jimmy McHugh	Al Dubin	Keep Off the Grass	1940
Latins Know How	Irving Berlin	Irving Berlin	Louisiana Purchase	1940
Laugh at Life	Maury Rubens	J. Delany Dunn	The Red Robe	1928
Lazy Afternoon	Jerome Moross	John Latouche	The Golden Apple	1954
Lazy Levee Loungers	Willard Robison	Willard Robison	Garrick Gaieties	1930
Lazy Moon	Leroy Anderson	Joan Ford, Jean & Walter Kerr	Goldilocks	1958
Leader of a Big-Time Band, The	Cole Porter	Cole Porter	Something for the Boys	1943
Leaflets	Marc Blitzstein	Marc Blitzstein	The Cradle Will Rock	1938
Leander	Jean Gilbert	Harry Graham	Katja	1926
Learn to Croon	Harold Arlen	Jack Yellen	You Said It	1931
Learn to Sing a Love Song	Irving Berlin	Irving Berlin	Ziegfeld Follies	1927
Leave It to Katarina	Jara Benes	Irving Caesar	White Horse Inn	1936
Leave Well Enough Alone	Jerry Bock	Sheldon Harnick	The Body Beautiful	1958
Legalize My Name	Harold Arlen	Johnny Mercer	St. Louis Woman	1946
Let 'Em Eat Cake	George Gershwin	Ira Gershwin	Let 'Em Eat Cake	1933
Let It Rain	James Kendis, Hal Dyson		Sky High	1925
Let Me Be Born Again	Victor Young	Joseph Young, Ned Washington	Blackbirds	1933
Let Me Entertain You	Jule Styne	Stephen Sondheim	Gypsy	1959
Let Me Give All My Love to Thee	Vincent Youmans	Oscar Hammerstein II	Rainbow	1928

TITLE	COMPOSER	LYRICIST	SHOW	YEAR
Let Me Hold You in My Arms	Clarence Gaskill	Clarence Gaskill	Keep It Clean	1929
Let Me Weep on Your Shoulder	Joseph Meyer	Edward Eliscu	Lady Fingers	1929
Let Us Gather at the Goal Line	Sammy Fain	George Marion, Jr.	Toplitzky of Notre Dame	1946
Let Your Hair Down With a Bang	Baldwin Bergersen	June Sillman	Who's Who	1938
Let's All Sing the Lard Song	Leslie Sarony	Anne Caldwell	Three Cheers	1928
Let's Ball Awhile	David Martin	Langston Hughes	Simply Heavenly	1957
Let's Be Buddies	Cole Porter	Cole Porter	Panama Hattie	1940
Let's Begin	Jerome Kern	Otto Harbach	Roberta	1933
Let's Call It a Day	Ray Henderson	Lew Brown	Strike Me Pink	1933
Let's Comb Beaches	Johnny Green	George Marion, Jr.	Beat the Band	1942
Let's Do It	Cole Porter	Cole Porter	Paris	1928
Let's Fly Away	Cole Porter	Cole Porter	The New Yorkers	1930
Let's Go Eat Worms in the Garden	Kay Swift	Paul James	Fine and Dandy	1930
Let's Go Too Far	Don Walker	George Marion, Jr.	Allah Be Praised	1944
Let's Have a Love Affair	Sigmund Romberg	Otto Harbach, Oscar Hammerstein II	The Desert Song	1926
Let's Have Another Cup of Coffee	Irving Berlin	Irving Berlin	Face the Music	1932
Let's Hold Hands	Richard Lewine	June Sillman	Fools Rush In	1934
Let's Keep it That Way	Abner Silver	Milton Berle, Ervin Drake	Artists and Models	1943
Let's Kiss and Make Up	George Gershwin	Ira Gershwin	Funny Face	1927
Let's Make Memories Tonight	Sam Stept	Lew Brown, Charles Tobias	Yokel Boy	1939
Let's Merge	J. Fred Coots	Arthur Swanstrom, Benny Davis	Sons O' Guns	1929
Let's Misbehave*	Cole Porter	Cole Porter	Paris	1928
Let's Not Talk About Love	Cole Porter	Cole Porter	Let's Face It	1941
Let's Pretend	Robert Hood Bowers	Francis deWitt	Oh, Ernest!	1927
Let's Run Away and Get Married	Harold Levey, Owen Murphy		Rainbow Rose	1926
Let's Say Goodnight With a Dance	Sammy Fain	Jack Yellen	Sons O' Fun	1941
Let's Sit and Talk About You	Jimmy McHugh	Dorothy Fields	Hello Daddy	1928

*Dropped from New York production

TITLE	COMPOSER	LYRICIST	SHOW	YEAR
Let's Steal a Tune From Offenbach	Jay Gorney	Henry Myers	Meet the People	1940
Let's Step Out	Cole Porter	Cole Porter	Fifty Million Frenchmen	1929
Let's Stroll Along and Sing a Song of Love	Cliff Friend	Lew Brown	Piggy	1927
Let's Swing It	Charles Tobias, Charles Newman, Murray Mencher		Earl Carroll's Sketch Book	1935
Let's Take a Walk Around the Block	Harold Arlen	E. Y. Harburg, Ira Gershwin	Life Begins at 8:40	1934
Let's Take Advantage of Now	Ray Henderson	Ted Koehler	Say When	1934
Let's Take an Old-Fashioned Walk	Irving Berlin	Irving Berlin	Miss Liberty	1949
Letter Song	Douglas Moore	John Latouche	The Ballad of Baby Doe	1958
Lichtenburg	Irving Berlin	Irving Berlin	Call Me Madam	1950
Lida Rose	Meredith Willson	Meredith Willson	The Music Man	1957
Life As a Twosome*	Joseph Meyer, Roger Wolfe Kahn	Irving Caesar	Here's Howe	1928
Life Begins at Sweet Sixteen	Ray Henderson	Jack Yellen	George White's Scandals	1936
Life Could Be So Beautiful	Jerome Moross	Paul Peters, George Sklar	Parade	1935
Life Does a Man a Favor	Jay Livingston	Ray Evans	Oh Captain!	1958
Life Is Just a Bowl of Cherries	Ray Henderson	Lew Brown	George White's Scandals	1931
Life Upon the Wicked Stage	Jerome Kern	Oscar Hammerstein II	Show Boat	1927
Life's a Dance	Harold Arlen	E. Y. Harburg	Hooray for What	1937
Life's a Funny Present From Someone	Vernon Duke	Howard Dietz	Sadie Thompson	1944
Liffey Waltz, The	Marc Blitzstein	Marc Blitzstein	Juno	1959
Like-A-Me, Like-A-You	Frank Grey	McElbert Moore, Frank Grey	The Matinee Girl	1926
Like He Loves Me	Vincent Youmans	Anne Caldwell	Oh, Please!	1926
Like Me Less, Love Me More	Jay Gorney	E. Y. Harburg	Earl Carroll's Sketch Book	1929
Like the Wandering Minstrel	George M. Cohan	George M. Cohan	The Merry Malones	1927
Like You	Emmerich Kalman	Harry B. Smith	The Circus Princess	1927
Like You Do	Harry Ruby	Bert Kalmar	The Ramblers	1926
Lilac Wine	James Shelton	James Shelton	Dance Me a Song	1950
Lily Belle May June	Henry Sullivan	Earle Crooker	Thumbs Up	1934
Lips	Leon DeCosta	Leon DeCosta	The Blonde Sinner	1926

*Also in *Americana (2nd Edition)*

TITLE	COMPOSER	LYRICIST	SHOW	YEAR
Little Birdie Told Me So, A	Richard Rodgers	Lorenz Hart	Peggy Ann	1926
Little Biscuit	Harold Arlen	E. Y. Harburg	Jamaica	1957
Little Bit in Love, A	Leonard Bernstein	Betty Comden, Adolph Green	Wonderful Town	1953
Little Boy Blues, The	Hugh Martin	Hugh Martin	Look Ma, I'm Dancin'	1948
Little Bungalow, A	Irving Berlin	Irving Berlin	The Cocoanuts	1925
Little Change of Atmosphere, A	Cliff Friend	Lew Brown	Piggy	1927
Little Dream That's Coming True	Walter G. Samuels	Morrie Ryskind	Ned Wayburn's Gambols	1929
Little Fish in a Big Pond	Irving Berlin	Irving Berlin	Miss Liberty	1949
Little Girl	Harry Archer	Harlan Thompson	Merry-Merry	1925
Little Girl Blue	Richard Rodgers	Lorenz Hart	Jumbo	1935
Little Girl From Little Rock, A	Jule Styne	Leo Robin	Gentlemen Prefer Blondes	1949
Little Gray House, The	Kurt Weill	Maxwell Anderson	Lost in the Stars	1949
Little Green Snake	Bob Merrill	Bob Merrill	Take Me Along	1959
Little House in Soho, A	Richard Rodgers	Lorenz Hart	She's My Baby	1928
Little Hut in Hoboken, A	Herman Hupfeld	Herman Hupfeld	The Little Show	1929
Little Igloo for Two	Arthur Schwartz	Agnes Morgan	Grand Street Follies	1926
Little Lace Petticoat	Emil Gerstenberger	Carle Carlton	The Lace Petticoat	1927
Little Lacquer Lady	Melville Gideon	Clifford Seyler	The Optimists	1928
Little Lamb	Jule Styne	Stephen Sondheim	Gypsy	1959
Little Mary Sunshine	Rick Besoyan	Rick Besoyan	Little Mary Sunshine	1959
Little Old Lady	Hoagy Carmichael	Stanley Adams	The Show Is On	1936
Little Peach	Sigmund Romberg	Arthur Wimperis	Louie the 14th	1925
Little Rumba Numba, A	Cole Porter	Cole Porter	Let's Face It	1941
Little Skipper from Heaven Above, A	Cole Porter	Cole Porter	Red, Hot and Blue	1936
Little Souvenir, A	Richard Rodgers	Lorenz Hart	Garrick Gaieties	1926
Little Things (Meant So Much to Me)	Harold Rome	Harold Rome	Bless You All	1950
Little Tin Box	Jerry Bock	Sheldon Harnick	Fiorello!	1959
Little White House, The (At the End of Honeymoon Lane)	James Hanley	Eddie Dowling	Honeymoon Lane	1926
Live and Let Live	Cole Porter	Cole Porter	Can-Can	1953
Livin' the Life	Jack Urbont	Bruce Geller	Livin' the Life	1957
Liza	George Gershwin	Ira Gershwin, Gus Kahn	Show Girl	1929
Lizzie Borden	Michael Brown	Michael Brown	New Faces	1952
Lobster Crawl, The	Harry Akst	Benny Davis	Artists and Models	1927
Loneliness of Evening, The*	Richard Rodgers	Oscar Hammerstein II	South Pacific	1949

*Dropped from New York production

TITLE	COMPOSER	LYRICIST	SHOW	YEAR
Lonely Girl, A	Harold Orlob	Irving Caesar	Talk About Girls	1927
Lonely Goatherd, The	Richard Rodgers	Oscar Hammerstein II	The Sound of Music	1959
Lonely Heart	Irving Berlin	Irving Berlin	As Thousands Cheer	1933
Lonely House	Kurt Weill	Langston Hughes	Street Scene	1947
Lonely Road, The	H. Maurice Jacquet	William Brady	The Silver Swan	1929
Lonely Town	Leonard Bernstein	Betty Comden, Adolph Green	On the Town	1944
Lonesome Walls	Jerome Kern	DuBose Heyward	Mamba's Daughters	1939
Long as You Got Your Health	Will Irwin	E. Y. Harburg	The Show Is On	1936
Long Before I Knew You	Jule Styne	Betty Comden, Adolph Green	Bells Are Ringing	1956
Long Island Low Down	Harry Ruby	Bert Kalmar	Animal Crackers	1928
Longing for You	Shep Camp	Frank Dupree	Half a Widow	1927
Look at 'er	Bob Merrill	Bob Merrill	New Girl in Town	1957
Look at the World and Smile	Raymond Hubbell	Anne Caldwell	Yours Truly	1927
Look for a Sky of Blue	Rick Besoyan	Rick Besoyan	Little Mary Sunshine	1959
Look for the Morning Star	David Martin	Langston Hughes	Simply Heavenly	1957
Look to the Rainbow	Burton Lane	E. Y. Harburg	Finian's Rainbow	1947
Look What I Found	Cole Porter	Cole Porter	Around the World	1946
Look Who's Dancing	Arthur Schwartz	Dorothy Fields	A Tree Grows in Brooklyn	1951
Look Who's in Love	Albert Hague	Dorothy Fields	Redhead	1959
Looking at You	Cole Porter	Cole Porter	Wake Up and Dream	1929
Looking for a Boy	George Gershwin	Ira Gershwin	Tip-Toes	1925
Loo-Loo	Vincent Youmans	Leo Robin, Clifford Grey	Hit the Deck	1927
Loose Ankles	Moe Jaffe, Clay Boland, Maury Rubens		A Night in Venice	1929
Lord Done Fixed Up My Soul, The	Irving Berlin	Irving Berlin	Louisiana Purchase	1940
Lordy*	Sigmund Romberg	Oscar Hammerstein II	Sunny River	1941
Lorelei	Frank Grey	Earle Crooker, McElbert Moore	Happy	1927
Lorelei	Noel Coward	Noel Coward	This Year of Grace	1928
Lorelei	George Gershwin	Ira Gershwin	Pardon My English	1933
Lost	Lee Pockriss	Anne Crosswell	Ernest in Love	1960
Lost Horizon	Harry Warren	Jerome Lawrence, Robert E. Lee	Shangri-La	1956
Lost in Loveliness	Sigmund Romberg, Don Walker	Leo Robin	The Girl in Pink Tights	1954

*Dropped from New York production

TITLE	COMPOSER	LYRICIST	SHOW	YEAR
Lost in the Stars	Kurt Weill	Maxwell Anderson	Lost in the Stars	1949
Lost Step, The	Dave Stamper, Harold Levey	Cyrus Wood	Lovely Lady	1927
Lot of Livin' to Do, A	Charles Strouse	Lee Adams	Bye Bye Birdie	1960
Lotus Flower	Raymond Hubbell	Anne Caldwell	Yours Truly	1927
Louisiana	J. Fred Coots, Maury Rubens	McElbert Moore	A Night in Paris	1926
Louisiana Hayride	Arthur Schwartz	Howard Dietz	Flying Colors	1932
Louisiana Purchase	Irving Berlin	Irving Berlin	Louisiana Purchase	1940
Love	Rudolf Friml	Rowland Leigh, John Shubert	Music Hath Charms	1934
Love and I	Baldwin Bergersen	June Sillman	All in Fun	1940
Love, Are You Raising Your Head Again	Lee Wainer	June Carroll	New Faces	1942
Love at Second Sight	Clay Warnick	Edward Eager	Dream With Music	1944
Love at Sundown	Bhumibol-Chakraband, N. Tong Yai		Michael Todd's Peep Show	1950
Love Birds	Kenneth Burton	Clifford Grey	The Great Temptations	1926
Love Birds	Harold Orlob	Irving Caesar	Talk About Girls	1927
Love, Come Take Me	Will Irwin	Norman Zeno	Fools Rush In	1934
Love Comes Only Once in a Lifetime	Harold Stern, Harry Perella	Stella Unger	Three Little Girls	1930
Love Design	Marianne Brown Waters, Bradford Greene		Right This Way	1938
Love Eyes	Moose Charlap	Norman Gimbel	Whoop-Up	1958
Love for Sale!	Rudolf Friml	Brian Hooker	The Vagabond King	1925
Love for Sale	Cole Porter	Cole Porter	The New Yorkers	1930
Love Has Found My Heart	Emmerich Kalman, Al Goodman	Harry B. Smith	Countess Maritza	1926
Love Has Nothing to Do With Looks	Ralph Blane	Charles Lederer	Three Wishes for Jamie	1952
Love Held Lightly	Harold Arlen	Johnny Mercer	Saratoga	1959
Love I Long For, The	Vernon Duke	Howard Dietz	Sadie Thompson	1944
Love in a Home	Gene De Paul	Johnny Mercer	Li'l Abner	1956
Love is a Dancer	Muriel Pollock	Jean Sothern	New Faces	1936
Love Is a Dancing Thing	Arthur Schwartz	Howard Dietz	At Home Abroad	1935
Love Is a Game for Soldiers	Franz Steininger (based on Tchaikovsky)	Forman Brown	Music in My Heart	1947
Love Is a Random Thing	Sammy Fain	George Marion, Jr.	Toplitzky of Notre Dame	1946
Love Is a Simple Thing	Arthur Siegel	June Carroll	New Faces	1952
Love Is a Very Light Thing	Harold Rome	Harold Rome	Fanny	1954
Love Is Free to Everyone	Cliff Friend	George White	George White's Scandals	1929
Love Is Like a Blushing Rose	Albert Von Tilzer	Neville Fleeson	Bye, Bye Bonnie	1927

TITLE	COMPOSER	LYRICIST	SHOW	YEAR
Love Is Like That	Alberta Nichols	Mann Holiner	Angela	1928
Love Is Like That	Ned Lehak	Allen Boretz	Garrick Gaieties	1930
Love Is Sweeping the Country	George Gershwin	Ira Gershwin	Of Thee I Sing	1931
Love Is the Reason	Arthur Schwartz	Dorothy Fields	A Tree Grows in Brooklyn	1951
Love Is the Sun	Rudolf Friml	P. G. Wodehouse, Clifford Grey	The Three Musketeers	1928
Love, It Hurts So Good	Harold Rome	Harold Rome	Alive and Kicking	1950
Love Lasts a Day	Frank Harling	Laurence Stallings	Deep River	1926
Love Letter to Manhattan	Harold Rome	Harold Rome	Bless You All	1950
Love Letters	H. Maurice Jacquet	William Brady	The Silver Swan	1929
Love, Look Away	Richard Rodgers	Oscar Hammerstein II	Flower Drum Song	1958
Love Makes the World Go Round	Richard Lewine	Ted Fetter	Naughty-Naught	1937
Love Me, Don't You?	Rudolf Friml	Otto Harbach, Oscar Hammerstein II	The Wild Rose	1926
Love Me Forever	Harry Warren	Mort Dixon, Joe Young	The Laugh Parade	1931
Love Me More—Love Me Less	Tom Peluso	Ben Bernard	Blackberries	1932
Love Me or Leave Me	Walter Donaldson	Gus Kahn	Whoopee	1928
Love Me Tomorrow	Vernon Duke	John Latouche	Cabin in the Sky	1940
Love Me Tonight	Rudolf Friml	Brian Hooker	The Vagabond King	1925
Love Never Went to College	Richard Rodgers	Lorenz Hart	Too Many Girls	1939
Love Sneaks Up on You	Victor Young	Stella Unger	Seventh Heaven	1955
Love Song	Franz Steininger (based on Tchaikovsky)	Forman Brown	Music in My Heart	1947
Love Song	Kurt Weill	Alan Jay Lerner	Love Life	1948
Love Song, The (Remember Me)	Edward Kunneke (based on Offenbach)	Harry B. Smith	The Love Song	1925
Love Swept Like a Storm	Fred Stamer	Gen Genovese	Buttrio Square	1952
Love Thoughts	Lucien Denni	Gwynne Denni	Happy Go Lucky	1926
Love Tiptoed Through My Heart	Frederick Loewe	Irene Alexander	Petticoat Fever	1935
Love Will Find Out the Way	Glenn Paxton	Robert Goldman, George Weiss	First Impressions	1959
Love Will Find You	Johann Strauss	Desmond Carter	The Great Waltz	1934
Love Will Find You Some Day	Edward Kunneke (based on Offenbach)	Harry B. Smith	The Love Song	1925
Lovelier Than Ever	Frank Loesser	Frank Loesser	Where's Charley?	1948
Lovely Lady	Dave Stamper, Harold Levey	Harry A. Steinberg, Eddie Ward	Lovely Lady	1927

TITLE	COMPOSER	LYRICIST	SHOW	YEAR
Lovely Lady, A	Franklin Hauser	Russell Janney	The O'Flynn	1934
Lovely Laurie*	Jerry Bock	Sheldon Harnick	Tenderloin	1960
Lovely, Lazy Kind of Day, A	Morgan Lewis	Nancy Hamilton	Three to Make Ready	1946
Lover, Come Back to Me	Sigmund Romberg	Oscar Hammerstein II	The New Moon	1928
Love's a Riddle	Jimmy Van Heusen	Eddie De Lange	Swingin' the Dream	1939
Love's Dear Yearning*	Sigmund Romberg	Otto Harbach, Oscar Hammerstein II	The Desert Song	1926
Love's Happy Dream	Walter Kollo	Harry B. Smith	Three Little Girls	1930
Luana	Rudolf Friml	J. Keirn Brennan	Luana	1930
Lucita	Alfred Goodman, Maury Rubens, J. Fred Coots	Clifford Grey	Artists and Models	1925
Luck Be a Lady	Frank Loesser	Frank Loesser	Guys and Dolls	1950
Luckiest Man in the World	George Gershwin	Ira Gershwin	Pardon My English	1933
Lucky	Lee Wainer	Robert Sour	Sing for Your Supper	1939
Lucky Bird	Vincent Youmans	Leo Robin, Clifford Grey	Hit the Deck	1927
Lucky Boy	Irving Berlin	Irving Berlin	The Cocoanuts	1925
Lucky Day	Ray Henderson	B. G. DeSylva, Lew Brown	George White's Scandals	1926
Lucky in Love	Ray Henderson	B. G. DeSylva, Lew Brown	Good News	1927
Lucky Seven	Arthur Schwartz	Howard Dietz	The Second Little Show	1930
Lucky to Be Me	Leonard Bernstein	Betty Comden, Adolph Green	On the Town	1944
Lullaby	Gian-Carlo Menotti	Gian-Carlo Menotti	The Consul	1950
Lullaby of the Plain	Richard Lewine	Ted Fetter	The Girl From Wyoming	1938
Lusty Month of May, The	Frederick Loewe	Alan Jay Lerner	Camelot	1960
Lute Song, The	Raymond Scott	Bernard Hanighen	Lute Song	1946
Ma Belle	Rudolf Friml	P. G. Wodehouse, Clifford Grey	The Three Muskèteers	1928
Ma Mère	Al Jolson, Irving Caesar, Harry Warren		The Wonder Bar	1931
Mack the Knife	Kurt Weill	Marc Blitzstein	The Three Penny Opera	1954
Macumba	Baldwin Bergersen	June Sillman	All In Fun	1940
Mad About the Boy	Noel Coward	Noel Coward	Set to Music	1939
Mad About You	Frank Grey	Earle Crooker, McElbert Moore	Happy	1927

*Dropped from New York production

TITLE	COMPOSER	LYRICIST	SHOW	YEAR
Mad Dogs and English-men	Noel Coward	Noel Coward	The Third Little Show	1931
Mademoiselle in New Rochelle	George Gershwin	Ira Gershwin	Strike Up the Band	1930
Madly in Love	Vernon Duke	Ogden Nash	The Littlest Revue	1956
Magdalena	Heitor Villa-Lobos	Robert Wright, George Forrest	Magdalena	1948
Magic Melody	Maurice Yvain	Max & Nathaniel Lief	Luckee Girl	1928
Magic of Moonlight and Love, The	Karl Hajos (based on Tchaikovsky)	Harry B. Smith	Natja	1925
Magnolia	C. Luckey Roberts	Alex C. Rogers	My Magnolia	1926
Magnolia's Wedding Day	Jimmy McHugh	Dorothy Fields	Blackbirds	1928
Make a Miracle	Frank Loesser	Frank Loesser	Where's Charley?	1948
Make Believe	Jerome Kern	Oscar Hammer-stein II	Show Boat	1927
Make Believe You're Happy	Dave Stamper, Harold Levey	Cyrus Wood	Lovely Lady	1927
Make Believe You're Mine	Oscar Straus	Harry B. Smith	Naughty Riquette	1926
Make it Another Old-Fashioned, Please	Cole Porter	Cole Porter	Panama Hattie	1940
Make Someone Happy	Jule Styne	Betty Comden, Adolph Green	Do Re Mi	1960
Make the Man Love Me	Arthur Schwartz	Dorothy Fields	A Tree Grows in Brooklyn	1951
Making Whoopee	Walter Donaldson	Gus Kahn	Whoopee	1928
Mama's Talkin' Soft*	Jule Styne	Stephen Sondheim	Gypsy	1959
Mamie Is Mimi	Jule Styne	Leo Robin	Gentlemen Prefer Blondes	1949
Man Doesn't Know, A	Richard Adler, Jerry Ross		Damn Yankees	1955
Man I Love Is Here, The	Franklin Hauser	Brian Hooker	The O'Flynn	1934
Man I Used to Be, The	Richard Rodgers	Oscar Hammer-stein II	Pipe Dream	1955
Man in My Life, The	Harold Arlen	Johnny Mercer	Saratoga	1959
Man Never Marries a Wife, A	Jack Lawrence, Don Walker		Courtin' Time	1951
Man With a Dream, A	Victor Young	Stella Unger	Seventh Heaven	1955
Manhattan	Richard Rodgers	Lorenz Hart	Garrick Gaieties	1925
Manhattan Madness	Irving Berlin	Irving Berlin	Face the Music	1932
Manhattan Mary	Ray Henderson	B. G. DeSylva, Lew Brown	Manhattan Mary	1927

*Dropped from New York production

TITLE	COMPOSER	LYRICIST	SHOW	YEAR
Manhattan Walk	Herbert Stothart, Harry Ruby	Bert Kalmar	Good Boy	1928
Manuelo	Richard Lewine	Ted Fetter	The Girl From Wyoming	1938
Many a New Day	Richard Rodgers	Oscar Hammerstein II	Oklahoma!	1943
March of the Musketeers	Rudolf Friml	P. G. Wodehouse, Clifford Grey	The Three Musketeers	1928
March of the Siamese Children	Richard Rodgers		The King and I	1951
March of Time, The	Harold Arlen	Ted Koehler	Earl Carroll's Vanities	1930
Marching By	Gus Edwards	Harry Clark, Guy Robertson	Marching By	1932
Maria	Arthur Schwartz	Howard Dietz	Revenge with Music	1934
Maria	Rudolf Friml	Rowland Leigh, John Shubert	Music Hath Charms	1934
Maria	Cole Porter	Cole Porter	You Never Know	1938
Maria	Leonard Bernstein	Stephen Sondheim	West Side Story	1957
Maria	Richard Rodgers	Oscar Hammerstein II	The Sound of Music	1959
Marian	Walter Donaldson	Ballard MacDonald	Sweetheart Time	1926
Marianne	Sigmund Romberg	Oscar Hammerstein II	The New Moon	1928
Marionettes	Sigmund Romberg	Harry B. Smith	Princess Flavia	1925
Marriage Type Love	Richard Rodgers	Oscar Hammerstein II	Me and Juliet	1953
Marry the Man Today	Frank Loesser	Frank Loesser	Guys and Dolls	1950
Marrying for Love	Irving Berlin	Irving Berlin	Call Me Madam	1950
Mary Dear	James Hanley	Eddie Dowling	Honeymoon Lane	1926
Mary Make Believe	Noel Coward	Noel Coward	This Year of Grace	1928
Matilda	James Shelton	James Shelton	Dance Me a Song	1950
May I Have My Gloves?	Ray Henderson	Jack Yellen	George White's Scandals	1936
May I Suggest Romance?	Frederick Loewe	Earle Crooker	Great Lady	1938
May Moon	Armand Vecsey	Clifford Grey	The Nightingale	1927
Maybe	George Gershwin	Ira Gershwin	Oh, Kay!	1926
Maybe I Should Change My Ways	Duke Ellington	John Latouche	Beggar's Holiday	1946
Maybe I Will	Harold Orlob	Irving Caesar	Talk About Girls	1927
Maybe I'll Baby You	Dave Stamper	Gene Buck	Take the Air	1927
Maybe It's Me	Richard Rodgers	Lorenz Hart	Peggy-Ann	1926
Maybe This Is Love	Ray Henderson	B. G. DeSylva, Lew Brown	Three Cheers	1928
Mayflower	Frank Tours	Clifford Grey	Mayflowers	1925
Me an' My Bundle	Irving Berlin	Irving Berlin	Miss Liberty	1949
Me and Lee	Giuseppe Verdi	Charles Friedman	My Darlin' Aida	1952

TITLE	COMPOSER	LYRICIST	SHOW	YEAR
Me and Love	David Baker	David Craig	Copper and Brass	1957
Me and Marie	Cole Porter	Cole Porter	Jubilee	1935
Me for You	Richard Rodgers	Lorenz Hart	Heads Up	1929
Me for You Forever	Richard Myers	Edward Heyman	Murder at the Vanities	1933
Meet the People	Jay Gorney	Henry Myers	Meet the People	1940
Melodies Within My Heart	Karl Hajos (based on Chopin)	Harry B. Smith	White Lilacs	1928
Melody	Sigmund Romberg	Irving Caesar	Melody	1933
Memories of You	Eubie Blake	Andy Razaf	Blackbirds	1930
Men About Town	Noel Coward	Noel Coward	Tonight at 8:30 (Red Peppers)	1936
Mender of Broken Dreams	John W. Bratton	John W. Bratton	Charlot's Revue	1925
Mercenary Mary	William B. Friedlander, Con Conrad		Mercenary Mary	1925
Messin' Around	Jimmy Johnson	Percy Bradford	Messin' Around	1929
Mexiconga	Sammy Fain	Jack Yellen, Herb Magidson	George White's Scandals	1939
Mia Luna	Puccini	E. Ray Goetz	Naughty Cinderella	1925
Miami	Con Conrad	Al Jolson, B. G. DeSylva	Big Boy	1925
Mickey	Sam Morrison	Dolph Singer	Summer Wives	1936
Midnight Bells	George Gershwin	Otto Harbach, Oscar Hammerstein II	Song of the Flame	1925
Midsummer's Eve	Robert Wright, George Forrest (based on Grieg)		Song of Norway	1944
Military Dancing Drill	George Gershwin	Ira Gershwin	Strike Up the Band	1930
Milky Way	Gene Lockhart	Gene Lockhart	Bunk of 1926	1926
Million Dollars, A	Dave Stamper	Fred Herendeen	Orchids Preferred	1937
Mine	George Gershwin	Ira Gershwin	Let 'Em Eat Cake	1933
Miserable With You	Arthur Schwartz	Howard Dietz	The Band Wagon	1931
Miss Liberty	Irving Berlin	Irving Berlin	Miss Liberty	1949
"Miss You" Kiss, A	Victor Young	Stella Unger	Seventh Heaven	1955
Missouri	Nat Reed	Nat Reed	Brown Buddies	1930
Mister and Missus Fitch	Cole Porter	Cole Porter	Gay Divorce	1932
Mister Snow	Richard Rodgers	Oscar Hammerstein II	Carousel	1945
Moanin' in the Mornin'	Harold Arlen	E. Y. Harburg	Hooray for What	1937
Moanin' Low	Ralph Rainger	Howard Dietz	The Little Show	1929
Modest Little Thing, A	Gene Lockhart	Gene Lockhart	Bunk of 1926	1926
Molly Malone	George M. Cohan	George M. Cohan	The Merry Malones	1927
Molly O'Reilly	Charles Gaynor	Charles Gaynor	Lend an Ear	1948
Moment I Looked in Your Eyes, The	Joan Edwards	Lynn Duddy	Tickets Please	1950
Moment I Saw You, The	Arthur Schwartz	Howard Dietz	Three's a Crowd	1930

TITLE	COMPOSER	LYRICIST	SHOW	YEAR
Moment I Saw You, The	Manning Sherwin	Harold Purcell	Under the Counter	1947
Mon Ami, My Friend	Kurt Weill	Paul Green	Johnny Johnson	1936
Money Isn't Everything	Richard Rodgers	Oscar Hammerstein II	Allegro	1947
Monotonous	Arthur Siegel	June Carroll	New Faces	1952
Month of Sundays, A	Robert Emmett Dolan	Johnny Mercer	Texas, Li'l Darlin'	1949
Montmart'	Cole Porter	Cole Porter	Can-Can	1953
Mood of the Moment	Maria Grever	Raymond Leveen	Viva O'Brien	1941
Moon About Town	Dana Suesse	E. Y. Harburg	Ziegfeld Follies	1934
Moon-Faced, Starry-Eyed	Kurt Weill	Langston Hughes	Street Scene	1947
Moon of My Delight	Richard Rodgers	Lorenz Hart	Chee-Chee	1928
Moonland	Jimmy Van Heusen	Eddie De Lange	Swingin' the Dream	1939
Moonlight and Violins	Charles Tobias, Charles Newman, Murray Mencher		Earl Carroll's Sketch Book	1935
Moonshine Lullaby	Irving Berlin	Irving Berlin	Annie Get Your Gun	1946
More and More	Fred Stamer	Gen Genovese	Buttrio Square	1952
More I Cannot Wish You	Frank Loesser	Frank Loesser	Guys and Dolls	1950
More Love Than Your Love	Arthur Schwartz	Dorothy Fields	By the Beautiful Sea	1954
More Than Ever	Lewis E. Gensler	Owen Murphy, Robert A. Simon	The Gang's All Here	1931
More Than You Know	Vincent Youmans	Billy Rose, Edward Eliscu	Great Day!	1929
More You Hurt Me, The	Harry Warren	Mort Dixon, Joe Young	The Laugh Parade	1931
Morning	Johann Strauss	Desmond Carter	The Great Waltz	1934
Morning Is Midnight*	Richard Rodgers	Lorenz Hart	She's My Baby	1928
Most Beautiful Girl in the World, The	Richard Rodgers	Lorenz Hart	Jumbo	1935
Most Expensive Statue in the World, The	Irving Berlin	Irving Berlin	Miss Liberty	1949
Most Gentlemen Don't Like Love	Cole Porter	Cole Porter	Leave It To Me	1938
Most Happy Fella, The	Frank Loesser	Frank Loesser	The Most Happy Fella	1956
Mother	Sigmund Romberg	Dorothy Donnelly	My Maryland	1927
Mother of the World	Alfred Goodman, Maury Rubens, J. Fred Coots	Clifford Grey	Artists and Models	1925
Mountain Greenery	Richard Rodgers	Lorenz Hart	Garrick Gaieties	1926
Mountain High, Valley Low	Raymond Scott	Bernard Hanighen	Lute Song	1946

*Dropped from New York production

TITLE	COMPOSER	LYRICIST	SHOW	YEAR
Mouse! Mouse!	Muriel Lillie	Hilda Brighten	Charlot's Revue	1925
Mr. Goldstone	Jule Styne	Stephen Sondheim	Gypsy	1959
Mr. Livingstone	Harold Karr	Matt Dubey	Happy Hunting	1956
Mr. Right	Kurt Weill	Alan Jay Lerner	Love Life	1948
Mr. Wonderful	Jerry Bock, George Weiss, Larry Holofcener		Mr. Wonderful	1956
Mrs. Patterson	James Shelton	James Shelton	Mrs. Patterson	1954
Mrs. Sally Adams	Irving Berlin	Irving Berlin	Call Me Madam	1950
Muchacha	Vernon Duke, Jay Gorney	E. Y. Harburg	Shoot the Works	1931
Mu-Cha-Cha	Jule Styne	Betty Comden, Adolph Green	Bells Are Ringing	1956
Mulunghu Tabu	Emmerich Kalman, Herbert Stothart	Otto Harbach, Oscar Hammerstein II	Golden Dawn	1927
Music in My Fingers	Richard Myers	Edward Heyman	Here Goes the Bride	1931
Music in My Heart	Warburton Guilbert	June Sillman	New Faces	1934
Music of a Little Rippling Stream, The	Cliff Friend	Lew Brown	Piggy	1927
Music of Home, The	Frank Loesser	Frank Loesser	Greenwillow	1960
Mutual Admiration Society	Harold Karr	Matt Dubey	Happy Hunting	1956
My Baby Talk Lady	William B. Kernell	Dorothy Donnelly	Hello, Lola	1926
My Baby's Bored	Allan Roberts	Lester Lee	All for Love	1949
My Best Love*	Richard Rodgers	Oscar Hammerstein II	Flower Drum Song	1958
My Bird of Paradise	Rudolf Friml	J. Keirn Brennan	Luana	1930
My Brudder and Me	Richard Lewine	Arnold B. Horwitt	Make Mine Manhattan	1948
My Bus and I	Heitor Villa-Lobos	Robert Wright, George Forrest	Magdalena	1948
My Business Man	David Raksin	June Carroll	If the Shoe Fits	1946
My Bwanna	Emmerich Kalman, Herbert Stothart	Otto Harbach, Oscar Hammerstein II	Golden Dawn	1927
My Castle in Spain	Isham Jones	Isham Jones	By the Way	1925
My Cousin in Milwaukee	George Gershwin	Ira Gershwin	Pardon My English	1933
My Daddy Is a Dandy	James Shelton	James Shelton	Mrs. Patterson	1954
My Darlin' Aida	Giuseppe Verdi	Charles Friedman	My Darlin' Aida	1952
My Darlin' Eileen	Leonard Bernstein	Betty Comden, Adolph Green	Wonderful Town	1953
My Darling	Richard Myers	Edward Heyman	Earl Carroll's Vanities	1932
My Darling, My Darling	Frank Loesser	Frank Loesser	Where's Charley?	1948

*Dropped from New York production

TITLE	COMPOSER	LYRICIST	SHOW	YEAR
My Defenses Are Down	Irving Berlin	Irving Berlin	Annie Get Your Gun	1946
My Fair Lady	George Gershwin	B. G. DeSylva, Ira Gershwin	Tell Me More	1925
My First Love Letter	Sigmund Romberg	Irving Caesar	Louie the 14th	1925
My First Love, My Last Love	Sigmund Romberg	Irving Caesar, Otto Harbach	Nina Rosa	1930
My Funny Valentine	Richard Rodgers	Lorenz Hart	Babes in Arms	1937
My Gal Is Mine Once More	Arthur Schwartz	Howard Dietz	Inside U.S.A.	1948
My Gentle Young Johnny	Jerry Bock	Sheldon Harnick	Tenderloin	1960
My Girl Back Home*	Richard Rodgers	Oscar Hammerstein II	South Pacific	1949
My Girl Is Just Enough Woman For Me	Albert Hague	Dorothy Fields	Redhead	1959
My Handy Man Ain't Handy No More	Eubie Blake	Andy Razaf	Blackbirds	1930
My Heart Belongs to Daddy	Cole Porter	Cole Porter	Leave It to Me	1938
My Heart Is Dancing	Arthur Schwartz	Albert Stillman	Virginia	1937
My Heart Is So Full of You	Frank Loesser	Frank Loesser	The Most Happy Fella	1956
My Heart Is Unemployed	Harold Rome	Harold Rome	Sing Out the News	1938
My Heart Is Yours	Rudolf Friml	Rowland Leigh, John Shubert	Music Hath Charms	1934
My Heart Stood Still	Richard Rodgers	Lorenz Hart	A Connecticut Yankee	1927
My Heart Won't Say Goodbye	Sigmund Romberg, Don Walker	Leo Robin	The Girl in Pink Tights	1954
My Heart's an Open Book	Harden Church	Edward Heyman	Caviar	1934
My Heart's Darlin'	Ralph Blane	Ralph Blane	Three Wishes for Jamie	1942
My Heart's in the Middle of July	Allan Roberts	Lester Lee	All for Love	1949
My Heaven	Alma Sanders	Monte Carlo	The House Boat on the Styx	1928
My Home Is in My Shoes	Johnny Mercer	Johnny Mercer	Top Banana	1951
My House	Leonard Bernstein	Leonard Bernstein	Peter Pan†	1950
My Impression of You	Michael Cleary, Herb Ned Washington	Magidson,	Tattle Tales	1930
My Joe	Georges Bizet	Oscar Hammerstein II	Carmen Jones	1943
My Lady	Frank Crumit	Ben Jerome	Yes, Yes, Yvette	1927
My Lady Love	Alma Sanders	Monte Carlo	Oh! Oh! Nurse	1925
My Last Affair	Haven Johnson	Haven Johnson	New Faces	1936
My Last Love	Frederick Loewe	Alan Jay Lerner	What's Up	1943

*Dropped from New York production; added to film version
†1950 Version

TITLE	COMPOSER	LYRICIST	SHOW	YEAR
My Little Dog Has Ego	Herman Hupfeld	Herman Hupfeld	Dance Me a Song	1950
My Little Lost Girl	Sammy Fain	Paul Francis Webster	Christine	1960
My Lord and Master	Richard Rodgers	Oscar Hammerstein II	The King and I	1951
My Love Carries On	Sam Morrison	Dolph Singer	Summer Wives	1936
My Love Is a Married Man	Frederick Loewe	Alan Jay Lerner	The Day Before Spring	1945
My Love Is Young	Irvin Graham	Bickley Reichner	New Faces	1936
My Lucky Star	Ray Henderson	B. G. DeSylva, Lew Brown	Follow Thru	1929
My Man Is on the Make	Richard Rodgers	Lorenz Hart	Heads Up	1929
My Man's Gone Now	George Gershwin	DuBose Heyward	Porgy and Bess	1935
My Melody Man	Peter De Rose	Charles Tobias, Sidney Clare	Pleasure Bound	1929
My Memory Started With You	Baldwin Bergersen	June Sillman	All In Fun	1940
My Mimosa	Sigmund Romberg	Dorothy Donnelly	My Princess	1927
My Mind's On You	William Roy	William Roy	Maggie	1953
My Miss Mary	Jerry Bock	Sheldon Harnick	Tenderloin	1960
My Mother Told Me Not to Trust a Soldier	Vincent Youmans	Oscar Hammerstein II	Rainbow	1928
My Mother Would Love You	Cole Porter	Cole Porter	Panama Hattie	1940
My One and Only	George Gershwin	Ira Gershwin	Funny Face	1927
My Own	Harry Archer	Harlan Thompson	Merry-Merry	1925
My Own Willow Tree	Sigmund Romberg	Harry B. Smith	Cherry Blossoms	1927
My Palace of Dreams	Rudolf Friml	Rowland Leigh, John Shubert	Music Hath Charms	1934
My Rainbow	Jeanne Hackett	Lester Lee	Harry Delmar's Revels	1927
My Real Ideal	Burton Lane	Sam Lerner	Artists and Models	1930
My Red Letter Day	Vernon Duke	Ira Gershwin	Ziegfeld Follies	1936
My Rhinestone Girl	Irving Berlin	Irving Berlin	Face the Music	1932
My Romance	Richard Rodgers	Lorenz Hart	Jumbo	1935
My Sergeant and I Are Buddies	Irving Berlin	Irving Berlin	This Is the Army	1942
My Ship	Kurt Weill	Ira Gershwin	Lady in the Dark	1941
My Silver Tree	Raymond Hubbell	Anne Caldwell	Three Cheers	1928
My Song	Ray Henderson	Lew Brown	George White's Scandals	1931
My Sweet Hunk O' Trash	James P. Johnson	Flournoy Miller	Sugar Hill	1931
My Sweetheart 'Tis of Thee	Johnny Green	Edward Heyman	Here Goes the Bride	1931
My Sword and I	Rudolf Friml	P. G. Wodehouse, Clifford Grey	The Three Musketeers	1928

TITLE	COMPOSER	LYRICIST	SHOW	YEAR
My Time of Day	Frank Loesser	Frank Loesser	Guys and Dolls	1950
My True Heart	Marc Blitzstein	Marc Blitzstein	Juno	1959
My White Knight	Meredith Willson	Meredith Willson	The Music Man	1957
My Yellow Flower	Jerome Moross	John Latouche	Ballet Ballads	1948
Namely You	Gene De Paul	Johnny Mercer	Li'l Abner	1956
Napoleon	Harold Arlen	E. Y. Harburg	Jamaica	1957
Nature Played an Awful Trick on You	Sammy Fain	Irving Kahal	Everybody's Welcome	1931
Naughty Riquette	Maury Rubens, Kendall Burgess	Harry B. Smith	Naughty Riquette	1926
Near to You	Richard Adler, Jerry Ross		Damn Yankees	1955
Necessity	Burton Lane	E. Y. Harburg	Finian's Rainbow	1947
Neurotic You and Psychopathic Me	Charles Gaynor	Charles Gaynor	Lend an Ear	1948
Never Again	Noel Coward	Noel Coward	Set to Music	1939
Never Before	Moose Charlap	Norman Gimbel	Whoop-Up	1958
Never Give Anything Away	Cole Porter	Cole Porter	Can-Can	1953
Never Had an Education	Sigmund Romberg	Irving Caesar	Melody	1933
Never Never Land	Jule Styne	Betty Comden, Adolph Green	Peter Pan	1954
Never to Leave You Again	Leon DeCosta	Leon DeCosta	Kosher Kitty Kelly	1925
Never Too Late for Love	Harold Rome	Harold Rome	Fanny	1954
Never Wait for Love	David Baker	David Craig	Phoenix '55	1955
Never Will I Marry	Frank Loesser	Frank Loesser	Greenwillow	1960
Never-Land	Leonard Bernstein	Leonard Bernstein	Peter Pan*	1950
Nevermore	Noel Coward	Noel Coward	Conversation Piece	1934
Nevermore	Gerald Marks	Sam Lerner	Hold It!	1948
New Ashmolean Marching Society and Students Conservatory Band, The	Frank Loesser	Frank Loesser	Where's Charley?	1948
New-Fangled Tango, A	Harold Karr	Matt Dubey	Happy Hunting	1956
New Girl in Town	Bob Merrill	Bob Merrill	New Girl in Town	1957
New Kind of Rhythm	Will Morrissey	Edmund Joseph	Polly of Hollywood	1927
New Love	Lewis E. Gensler	B. G. DeSylva	Captain Jinks	1925
New Love Is Old, A	Jerome Kern	Otto Harbach	The Cat and the Fiddle	1931
New Shoes	Will Irwin	June Carroll	New Faces	1942
New Sun in the Sky	Arthur Schwartz	Howard Dietz	The Band Wagon	1931
New York, New York	Leonard Bernstein	Betty Comden, Adolph Green	On the Town	1944
New York Town	Henry Souvaine, Jay Gorney	Morrie Ryskind, Howard Dietz	Merry-Go-Round	1927

*1950 version

TITLE	COMPOSER	LYRICIST	SHOW	YEAR
Next Time I Care, The	Bronislaw Kaper (based on Chopin)	John Latouche	Polonaise	1945
Next Time I Love	Jerry Herman	Jerry Herman	Parade	1960
Next Time it Happens, The	Richard Rodgers	Oscar Hammerstein II	Pipe Dream	1955
Nice Baby!	George Gershwin	Ira Gershwin	Tip-Toes	1925
Nice Girl	Charles Schwab	Henry Myers	Bare Facts	1926
Nickel to My Name, A	Vernon Duke	John Latouche	Banjo Eyes	1941
Nickel Under the Foot	Marc Blitzstein	Marc Blitzstein	The Cradle Will Rock	1938
Nicodemus	Vincent Youmans	Anne Caldwell	Oh, Please!	1926
Nigger Heaven Blues	Alfred Nathan	George Oppenheimer	The Manhatters	1927
Night and Day	Cole Porter	Cole Porter	Gay Divorce	1932
Night of My Nights	Robert Wright, George Forrest (based on Borodin)		Kismet	1953
Night Was All to Blame, The	Alma Sanders	Monte Carlo	Louisiana Lady	1947
Night Was Made For Love, The	Jerome Kern	Otto Harbach	The Cat and the Fiddle	1931
Nightie-Night	George Gershwin	Ira Gershwin	Tip-Toes	1925
Nightingale Song, The	Milton Ager	Jack Yellen	John Murray Anderson's Almanac	1929
Nightingale, The Moon and I, The	Don Walker	Clay Warnick	Memphis Bound	1945
Nina Rosa	Sigmund Romberg	Irving Caesar	Nina Rosa	1930
Nine O'Clock	Bob Merrill	Bob Merrill	Take Me Along	1959
No Foolin'	James Hanley	Gene Buck	No Foolin'	1926
No Lookin' Back	Jay Gorney	Edward Eliscu, Henry Myers	Meet the People	1940
No Lover	Cole Porter	Cole Porter	Out of This World	1950
No More You	Ray Henderson	B. G. DeSylva, Lew Brown	Follow Thru	1929
No, No, Nanette	Vincent Youmans	Otto Harbach	No, No, Nanette	1925
No One Knows	Jerome Kern	Anne Caldwell	The City Chap	1925
No One's Ever Kissed Me	Philip Braham	Ronald Jeans	By the Way	1925
No Other Love	Maury Rubens	J. Keirn Brennan	Music in May	1929
No Other Love	Richard Rodgers	Oscar Hammerstein II	Me and Juliet	1953
No Place Like Home	Roger Wolfe Kahn	Irving Caesar	Americana	1928
No Time for Nothin' But Love	Allan Roberts	Lester Lee	All for Love	1949
No Wonder I'm Blue	Louis Alter	Oscar Hammerstein II	Ballyhoo	1930
No (You Can't Have My Heart)	Dana Suesse	Dana Suesse	You Never Know	1938

TITLE	COMPOSER	LYRICIST	SHOW	YEAR
Nobody Breaks My Heart	Kay Swift	Paul James	Fine and Dandy	1930
Nobody But Fanny	Con Conrad	Al Jolson, B. G. DeSylva	Big Boy	1925
Nobody Else But Me	Jerome Kern	Oscar Hammerstein II	Show Boat (revival)	1946
Nobody Ever Felt Like This Before	Walter Kent	Kim Gannon	Seventeen	1951
Nobody Makes a Pass at Me	Harold Rome	Harold Rome	Pins and Needles	1937
Nobody Told Me	Baldwin Bergersen	Phyllis McGinley	Small Wonder	1948
Nobody Wants Me	Henry Souvaine	Morrie Ryskind	Americana	1926
Nobody's Chasing Me	Cole Porter	Cole Porter	Out of This World	1950
Nobody's Heart	Richard Rodgers	Lorenz Hart	By Jupiter	1942
Nobody's Heart But Mine	Jimmy McHugh	Harold Adamson	As the Girls Go	1948
Normandy	Mary Rodgers	Marshall Barer	Once Upon a Mattress	1959
Northern Blues	Walter Haenschen	Robert A. Simon	Grand Street Follies	1926
Not a Care in the World	Vernon Duke	John Latouche	Banjo Eyes	1941
Not For All the Rice in China	Irving Berlin	Irving Berlin	As Thousands Cheer	1933
Not Like Me	Glenn Paxton	Robert Goldman, George Weiss	First Impressions	1959
Not That I Care	Richard Whiting	Oscar Hammerstein II	Free for All	1931
Nothin' for Nothin'	Morton Gould	Dorothy Fields	Arms and the Girl	1950
Nothing at All	Sammy Fain	Dan Shapiro	Ankles Aweigh	1955
Nothing But Love	Ray Henderson	B. G. DeSylva, Lew Brown	Manhattan Mary	1927
Nothing But You	Richard Rodgers	Lorenz Hart	Higher and Higher	1940
Nothing Could Be Sweeter	Vincent Youmans	Leo Robin, Clifford Grey	Hit the Deck	1927
Nothing Was Ever Like This	Harden Church	Edward Heyman	Caviar	1934
Now	Vernon Duke	Ted Fetter	The Show Is On	1936
Now	Robert Wright, George Forrest (based on Grieg)		Song of Norway	1944
Now I Know	Philip Charig	James Dyrenforth	Nikki	1931
Now Is the Time	Max Rich	Jack Scholl	Keep Moving	1934
Now That I'm Free	Irving Caesar	Irma Hollander	My Dear Public	1943
O Leo	Arthur Schwartz	Howard Dietz	At Home Abroad	1935
Ocarina, The	Irving Berlin	Irving Berlin	Call Me Madam	1950
Ocean Will Never Run Dry, The	Harden Church	Edward Heyman	Caviar	1934
Octopus	Harold Rome	Harold Rome	Fanny	1954
Odle-De-O	Maury Rubens	Clifford Grey	The Madcap	1928

TITLE	COMPOSER	LYRICIST	SHOW	YEAR
Of Thee I Sing	George Gershwin	Ira Gershwin	Of Thee I Sing	1931
Off Again, On Again	Vernon Duke	E. Y. Harburg	Walk a Little Faster	1932
Off Time	Thomas (Fats) Waller, Harry Brooks	Andy Razaf	Hot Chocolates	1929
Oh, Auntie	Sammy Fain	Jack Yellen	Sons O' Fun	1941
Oh, Baby	Cliff Friend	Lew Brown	Piggy	1927
Oh, Baby!	Owen Murphy	Owen Murphy	Rain or Shine	1928
Oh Bess, Oh Where's My Bess?	George Gershwin	Ira Gershwin	Porgy and Bess	1935
Oh! Boy, What a Girl	Wright & Bessinger	Bud Green	Gay Paree	1926
Oh, Daddy	Gitz Rice	Gitz Rice	Nic Nax of 1926	1926
Oh, Diogenes!	Richard Rodgers	Lorenz Hart	The Boys from Syracuse	1938
Oh, Donna Clara	J. Petersburski	Irving Caesar	The Wonder Bar	1931
Oh Gee! Oh Joy!	George Gershwin	P. G. Wodehouse, Ira Gershwin	Rosalie	1928
Oh, Heart of Love	Kurt Weill	Paul Green	Johnny Johnson	1936
Oh How Happy We'll Be	Lewis E. Gensler	Robert A. Simon, Clifford Grey	Ups-A-Daisy	1928
Oh, How I Long to Belong to You	Vincent Youmans	B. G. DeSylva	Take a Chance	1932
Oh, How I Miss You Blues	Lewis E. Gensler	Robert A. Simon, Clifford Grey	Ups-A-Daisy	1928
Oh, How I've Waited for You	Nat D. Ayer	Harry Carlton	By the Way	1925
Oh, How Unfortunate You Mortals Be	Allan Roberts	Lester Lee	All for Love	1949
Oh! How We Love Our Alma Mater	Harry Ruby	Bert Kalmar	The Ramblers	1926
Oh, Kay	George Gershwin	Ira Gershwin, Howard Dietz	Oh, Kay!	1926
Oh, Look at Me!	Julian Slade	Dorothy Reynolds, Julian Slade	Salad Days	1958
Oh, Peggy	Harry Akst	Benny Davis	Artists and Models	1927
Oh, So Nice	George Gershwin	Ira Gershwin	Treasure Girl	1928
Oh, Wasn't it Lovely	Harry Archer	Harlan Thompson	Merry-Merry	1925
Oh, What a Beautiful Mornin'	Richard Rodgers	Oscar Hammerstein II	Oklahoma!	1943
Oh, What a Girl	Tom Johnstone	Phil Cook	When You Smile	1925
Oh You!	Milton Susskind	Paul Porter, Benjamin H. Burt	Florida Girl	1925
Oh, You're a Wonderful Person	Morgan Lewis	Nancy Hamilton	Three to Make Ready	1946
Ohhh! Ahhh!	Johnny Green	Edward Heyman	Here Goes the Bride	1931

TITLE	COMPOSER	LYRICIST	SHOW	YEAR
Ohio	Leonard Bernstein	Betty Comden, Adolph Green	Wonderful Town	1953
O. K. for T. V.	Johnny Mercer	Johnny Mercer	Top Banana	1951
Oklahoma	Richard Rodgers	Oscar Hammerstein II	Oklahoma!	1943
Ol' Man River	Jerome Kern	Oscar Hammerstein II	Show Boat	1927
Old Devil Moon	Burton Lane	E. Y. Harburg	Finian's Rainbow	1947
Old Fashioned Girl	Richard Rodgers	Edith Meiser	Garrick Gaieties	1925
Old Flame Never Dies, An	Arthur Schwartz	Albert Stillman, Laurence Stallings	Virginia	1937
Old Love	Don Walker	Clay Warnick	Memphis Bound	1945
Old Soft Shoe, The	Morgan Lewis	Nancy Hamilton	Three to Make Ready	1946
Oldest Established, The	Frank Loesser	Frank Loesser	Guys and Dolls	1950
On a Desert Island With Thee	Richard Rodgers	Lorenz Hart	A Connecticut Yankee	1927
On a Pony for Two	James F. Hanley	Gene Buck	Take the Air	1927
On a Roof in Manhattan	Irving Berlin	Irving Berlin	Face the Music	1932
On Account of I Love You	Philip Charig	James Dyrenforth	Nikki	1931
On and On and On	George Gershwin	Ira Gershwin	Let 'Em Eat Cake	1933
On Double Fifth Avenue	Abel Baer	Sam Lewis, Joe Young	Lady Do	1927
On Leave for Love	Ann Ronell	Ann Ronell	Count Me In	1942
On My Mind a New Love	Joseph Meyer, Roger Wolfe Kahn	Irving Caesar	Here's Howe	1928
On the Old Park Bench	Jimmy McHugh	Howard Dietz	Keep Off the Grass	1940
On the Rio Grande	Kurt Weill	Paul Green	Johnny Johnson	1936
On the Street Where You Live	Frederick Loewe	Alan Jay Lerner	My Fair Lady	1956
On the Sunny Side of the Street	Jimmy McHugh	Dorothy Fields	Lew Leslie's International Review	1930
On the Wrong Side of the Railroad Track	Duke Ellington	John Latouche	Beggar's Holiday	1946
On With the Dance	Richard Rodgers	Lorenz Hart	Garrick Gaieties	1925
On With the Dance	Philip Charig	Irving Caesar	Polly	1929
On Your Toes	Richard Rodgers	Lorenz Hart	On Your Toes	1936
Once in a Lifetime	Jesse Greer	Raymond Klages	Earl Carroll's Vanities	1928
Once in Love With Amy	Frank Loesser	Frank Loesser	Where's Charley?	1948
Once in September	Armand Vecsey	Clifford Grey	The Nightingale	1927
Once Knew a Fella	Harold Rome	Harold Rome	Destry Rides Again	1959
Once Upon a Time	Morgan Lewis	Nancy Hamilton	One for the Money	1939
Once Upon a Time	Franz Steininger (based on Tchaikovsky)	Forman Brown	Music in My Heart	1947
Once Upon a Time Today	Irving Berlin	Irving Berlin	Call Me Madam	1950

TITLE	COMPOSER	LYRICIST	SHOW	YEAR
One	Franz Lehar	Edward Eliscu	Frederika	1937
One Alone	Sigmund Romberg	Otto Harbach, Oscar Hammerstein II	The Desert Song	1926
One Big Union for Two	Harold Rome	Harold Rome	Pins and Needles	1937
One Boy*	Charles Strouse	Lee Adams	Bye Bye Birdie	1960
One Day We Dance	Cy Coleman	Carolyn Leigh	Wildcat	1960
One Flower Grows Alone in Your Garden	Sigmund Romberg	Otto Harbach, Oscar Hammerstein II	The Desert Song	1926
One Girl, The	Vincent Youmans	Oscar Hammerstein II	Rainbow	1928
One Golden Hour	Rudolf Friml	Otto Harbach, Oscar Hammerstein II	The Wild Rose	1926
One Hand, One Heart	Leonard Bernstein	Stephen Sondheim	West Side Story	1957
One Hour Ahead of the Posse	Philip Charig	Ray Golden, Dave Ormont	Catch a Star	1955
One I'm Looking For, The	Emmerich Kalman	Harry B. Smith	Countess Maritza	1926
One Kind Word	Marc Blitzstein	Marc Blitzstein	Juno	1959
One Kiss	Sigmund Romberg	Oscar Hammerstein II	The New Moon	1928
One Last Kiss	Charles Strouse	Lee Adams	Bye Bye Birdie	1960
One Last Love Song	Emmerich Kalman	George Marion, Jr.	Marinka	1945
One Life to Live	Kurt Weill	Ira Gershwin	Lady in the Dark	1941
One Love	Vincent Youmans	Billy Rose, Edward Eliscu	Great Day	1929
One Love	Harold Arlen	Ted Koehler	Earl Carroll's Vanities	1930
One Moment Alone	Jerome Kern	Otto Harbach	The Cat and the Fiddle	1931
One More Dance	Jerome Kern	Oscar Hammerstein II	Music in the Air	1932
One Night of Love	Maury Rubens	J. Keirn Brennan	A Night in Venice	1929
One O'Clock Baby	Al Jolson	B. G. DeSylva, Lew Brown	Big Boy	1925
One of These Fine Days	Harold Rome	Harold Rome	Sing Out the News	1938
One Second of Sex	Johnny Green	Edward Heyman	Here Goes the Bride	1931
One Step to Heaven	Jesse Greer	Raymond Klages	Say When	1928
One Sunny Day	Jean Schwartz	Clifford Grey, William Cary Duncan	Sunny Days	1928
One Touch of Vienna	Emmerich Kalman	George Marion, Jr.	Marinka	1945
One! Two! Three!	Sonny Burke	Paul Webster, Ray Golden	Alive and Kicking	1950

*Also published as "One Guy"

TITLE	COMPOSER	LYRICIST	SHOW	YEAR
One Way Street	Walter Donaldson	Ballard Mac-Donald	Sweetheart Time	1926
Only a Dream	Edward Kunneke (based on Offenbach)	Harry B. Smith	The Love Song	1925
Only a Rose	Rudolf Friml	Brian Hooker	The Vagabond King	1925
Only Another Boy and Girl	Cole Porter	Cole Porter	The Seven Lively Arts	1944
Only for Americans	Irving Berlin	Irving Berlin	Miss Liberty	1949
Only If You're in Love	Johnny Mercer	Johnny Mercer	Top Banana	1951
Only One	Sigmund Romberg	Harry B. Smith	Princess Flavia	1925
Only One	Frank Grey	McElbert Moore, Frank Grey	The Matinee Girl	1926
Only One for Me, The	Lewis E. Gensler	B. G. DeSylva	Captain Jinks	1925
Only One for Me, The	Harry Akst	Benny Davis	Artists and Models	1927
Ooh, I'm Thinking	Ray Henderson	Lew Brown	Strike Me Pink	1933
Ooh, Maybe It's You	Irving Berlin	Irving Berlin	Ziegfeld Follies	1927
Ooh, Ooh, Ooh, What You Do to Me	Walter Kent	Kim Gannon	Seventeen	1951
Ooh, That Kiss	Harry Warren	Mort Dixon, Joe Young	The Laugh Parade	1931
Ooh! What You Said	Hoagy Carmichael	Johnny Mercer	Walk with Music	1940
Open Book	Joseph Meyer	Edward Eliscu	Lady Fingers	1929
Open Up Your Heart	Vincent Youmans	Billy Rose, Edward Eliscu	Great Day!	1929
Opening Night	Lee Wainer	Robert Sour	Sing for Your Supper	1939
Opposite Sex, The	Michael H. Cleary	Arthur Swanstrom	Sea Legs	1937
Or What Have You?	Morris Hamilton	Grace Henry	The Little Show	1929
Orange Blossom Home	Raymond Hubbell	Anne Caldwell	Three Cheers	1928
Ordinary Couple, An	Richard Rodgers	Oscar Hammerstein II	The Sound of Music	1959
Ordinary Guy	Harold Rome	Harold Rome	Sing Out the News	1938
Oriental Memories	Alfred Goodman, Maury Rubens, J. Fred Coots	Clifford Grey	Artists and Models	1925
Other Fellow's Girl, The	Percy Wenrich	Raymond Peck	Castles in the Air	1926
Our Day of Independence*	Irving Berlin	Irving Berlin	Call Me Madam	1950
Our First Kiss	Sammy Fain	Jack Yellen	George White's Scandals	1939
Our Home	Richard Lewine	Ted Fetter	The Girl From Wyoming	1938
Our Language of Love	Marguerite Monnot	Julian More, Daniel Heneker, Monte Norman	Irma La Douce	1960

*Dropped from New York production

TITLE	COMPOSER	LYRICIST	SHOW	YEAR
Our Last Valse	Oscar Straus	Clare Kummer	Three Waltzes	1937
Our Song	Maria Grever	Raymond Leveen	Viva O'Brien	1941
Our Town	James Shelton	James Shelton	Straw Hat Revue	1939
Ours	Cole Porter	Cole Porter	Red, Hot and Blue	1936
Out in the Open Air	Burton Lane	Howard Dietz, Ted Pola	Three's a Crowd	1930
Out of a Clear Blue Sky	Harold Arlen	Ted Koehler	Earl Carroll's Vanities	1930
Out of the Clear Blue Sky	Vernon Duke	Ogden Nash	Two's Company	1952
Out of Breath	Everett Miller	Johnny Mercer	Garrick Gaieties	1930
Out of My Dreams	Richard Rodgers	Oscar Hammerstein II	Oklahoma!	1943
Out of Sight, Out of Mind	John Mundy	Edward Eager	The Liar	1950
Out of the Blue	Jerome Kern	Oscar Hammerstein II	Sweet Adeline	1929
Out Where the Blues Begin	Jimmy McHugh	Dorothy Fields	Hello Daddy	1928
Outside of That I Love You	Irving Berlin	Irving Berlin	Louisiana Purchase	1940
Over and Over	Hugh Martin	Hugh Martin	Make a Wish	1951
Over and Over Again	Richard Rodgers	Lorenz Hart	Jumbo	1935
Over Here	J. Fred Coots	Arthur Swanstrom, Benny Davis	Sons O' Guns	1929
Overnight	Louis Alter	Billy Rose, Charlotte Kent	Sweet and Low	1930
Ozarks Are Calling Me Home, The	Cole Porter	Cole Porter	Red, Hot and Blue	1936
Pack Up Your Blues and Smile	Peter De Rose, Albert Von Tilzer	Jo Trent	Yes, Yes, Yvette	1927
Palm Beach Walk	Walter G. Samuels	Morrie Ryskind	Ned Wayburn's Gambols	1929
Pango-Pango Maid	Irving Bibo, Fred Phillips		Earl Carroll's Vanities	1925
Panic in Panama, A	Harry Ruby	Bert Kalmar	High Kickers	1941
Papa-De-Da-Da	Spencer Williams, Clarence Todd, Clarence Williams		Blackbirds	1930
Papa, Won't You Dance With Me	Jule Styne	Sammy Cahn	High Button Shoes	1947
Papa's Got a Job	Ned Lehak	Robert Sour, Hector Troy	Sing for Your Supper	1939
Paree, What Did You Do to Me	Cole Porter	Cole Porter	Fifty Million Frenchmen	1929
Paris, France	Hugh Martin	Hugh Martin	Make a Wish	1951
Paris Loves Lovers	Cole Porter	Cole Porter	Silk Stockings	1955
Paris Wakes Up and Smiles	Irving Berlin	Irving Berlin	Miss Liberty	1949

TITLE	COMPOSER	LYRICIST	SHOW	YEAR
Park Avenue Strut	Phil Baker, Maury Rubens	Moe Jaffe, Harold Atteridge	Pleasure Bound	1929
Party's Over, The	Jule Styne	Betty Comden, Adolph Green	Bells Are Ringing	1956
Payador	Sigmund Romberg	Irving Caesar	Nina Rosa	1930
Peace, Brother	Jimmy Van Heusen	Eddie De Lange	Swingin' the Dream	1939
Peace, Sister, Peace	James P. Johnson	Flournoy Miller	Sugar Hill	1931
Penny Candy	Arthur Siegel	June Carroll	New Faces	1952
Penny for Your Thoughts, A	Vernon Duke	E. Y. Harburg	Walk a Little Faster	1932
People Will Say We're in Love	Richard Rodgers	Oscar Hammerstein II	Oklahoma!	1943
Pep	Sigmund Romberg	Arthur Wimperis	Louie the 14th	1925
Perfect Night	Dean Fuller	Marshall Barer	New Faces	1956
Perfection	Lee Pockriss	Anne Croswell	Ernest in Love	1960
Pernambuco	Frank Loesser	Frank Loesser	Where's Charley?	1948
Personality	George M. Cohan	George M. Cohan	Billie	1928
Peter, Peter	Leonard Bernstein	Leonard Bernstein	Peter Pan*	1950
Phil the Fiddler	Richard Lewine	Arnold B. Horwitt	Make Mine Manhattan	1948
Pickin' Cotton	Ray Henderson	B. G. DeSylva, Lew Brown	George White's Scandals	1928
Picture of Me Without You, A	Cole Porter	Cole Porter	Jubilee	1935
Pied Piper of Harlem	Ray Henderson	Jack Yellen	George White's Scandals	1936
Pining	Henry Creamer, Clarence Todd		Keep Shufflin'	1928
Pipe-Dreaming	Cole Porter	Cole Porter	Around the World	1946
Plain We Live	Albert Hague	Arnold B. Horwitt	Plain and Fancy	1955
Plant You Now, Dig You Later	Richard Rodgers	Lorenz Hart	Pal Joey	1940
Play Gypsies, Dance Gypsies	Emmerich Kalman	Harry B. Smith	Countess Maritza	1926
Play Me an Old Time Two-Step	Sam Morrison	Dolph Singer	Summer Wives	1936
Play, Orchestra, Play	Noel Coward	Noel Coward	Tonight at 8:30 (Shadow Play)	1936
Playground in the Sky	James Hanley	Eddie Dowling	Sidewalks of New York	1927
Please Don't Make Me Be Good	Cole Porter	Cole Porter	Fifty Million Frenchmen	1929
Plenty of Pennsylvania	Albert Hague	Arnold B. Horwitt	Plain and Fancy	1955
Po' Lil' Black Chile	Frank Harling	Laurence Stallings	Deep River	1926
Pocketful of Dreams	Harold Rome	Harold Rome	Michael Todd's Peep Show	1950

*1950 Version

TITLE	COMPOSER	LYRICIST	SHOW	YEAR
Polar Bear Strut, The	Arthur Schwartz	Theodore Goodwin	Grand Street Follies	1926
Policeman's Ball, The	Irving Berlin	Irving Berlin	Miss Liberty	1949
Politics and Poker	Jerry Bock	Sheldon Harnick	Fiorello!	1959
Polly	Philip Charig	Irving Caesar	Polly	1929
Pompadour	Sigmund Romberg	Irving Caesar	Melody	1933
Pompanola	Ray Henderson	B. G. DeSylva, Lew Brown	Three Cheers	1928
Ponies on Parade	Clarence Gaskill	Clarence Gaskill	Earl Carroll's Vanities	1925
Pools of Love	Winthrop Cortel-you	Derick Wulff	Kiss Me	1927
Poor As a Church Mouse	Vernon Duke	Howard Dietz	Sadie Thompson	1944
Poor Little Doorstep Baby	Michael Cleary	Max and Nathaniel Lief	Shoot the Works	1931
Poor Little Marie	James F. Hanley	Gene Buck	No Foolin'	1926
Poor Little Rich Girl	Noel Coward	Noel Coward	Charlot's Revue	1925
Poor Pierrot	Harry Archer	Harlan Thompson	Merry-Merry	1925
Poor Pierrot	Jerome Kern	Otto Harbach	The Cat and the Fiddle	1931
Pore Jud	Richard Rodgers	Oscar Hammer-stein II	Oklahoma!	1943
Porgy	Jimmy McHugh	Dorothy Fields	Blackbirds	1928
Poverty Row or Luxury Lane	Gus Edwards	Howard Johnson	Broadway Show Window	1936
Practising Up on You	Philip Charig	Howard Dietz	Three's A Crowd	1930
Pretty Little Stranger	Charles Rosoff	Leo Robin	Judy	1927
Pretty, Petite and Sweet	Harry Archer	Walter O'Keefe	Just a Minute	1928
Pretty to Walk With	Harold Arlen	E. Y. Harburg	Jamaica	1957
Prince Charming	Sigmund Romberg	Dorothy Donnelly	My Princess	1927
Prince Charming	Walter Kollo	Harry B. Smith	Three Little Girls	1930
Princess of Pure Delight, The	Kurt Weill	Ira Gershwin	Lady in the Dark	1941
Promenade Walk, The	Alfred Goodman, Maury Rubens, J. Fred Coots	Clifford Grey	Artists and Models	1925
Promise in Your Eyes, The	James Hanley	B. G. DeSylva	Americana	1926
Promise Me a Rose	Bob Merrill	Bob Merrill	Take Me Along	1959
Proud of You	Johnny Green	George Marion, Jr.	Beat the Band	1942
Pulitzer Prize, The*	Irving Berlin	Irving Berlin	Miss Liberty	1949
Pull Yourself Together	Philip Charig, Richard Myers	Leo Robin	Allez-Oop	1927
Push De Button	Harold Arlen	E. Y. Harburg	Jamaica	1957
Pussy Foot, The	Leroy Anderson	Joan Ford, Jean & Walter Kerr	Goldilocks	1958

*Dropped from New York production

TITLE	COMPOSER	LYRICIST	SHOW	YEAR
Put it Away Till Spring	Peter Nolan	Joshua Titzell	Garrick Gaieties	1930
Put on a Happy Face	Charles Strouse	Lee Adams	Bye Bye Birdie	1960
Put Your Heart in a Song	Ray Henderson	Ted Koehler	Say When	1934
Put Your Mind Right on It	Jimmy Johnson	Percy Bradford	Messin' Around	1929
Put Your Troubles in a Candy Box	J. Fred Coots	Clifford Grey	Mayflowers	1925
Queen Elizabeth	Richard Rodgers	Lorenz Hart	Garrick Gaieties	1926
Queen of My Heart	Rudolf Friml	P. G. Wodehouse, Clifford Grey	The Three Musketeers	1928
Queen of Terre Haute, The	Cole Porter	Cole Porter	Fifty Million Frenchmen	1929
Quelque Chose	Cole Porter	Cole Porter	Paris	1928
Quick Henry, the Flit	Harry Revel	Mack Gordon	Smiling Faces	1932
Quiet Girl, A	Leonard Bernstein	Betty Comden, Adolph Green	Wonderful Town	1953
Quiet Night	Richard Rodgers	Lorenz Hart	On Your Toes	1936
Quittin' Time	John Rox	John Rox	All in Fun	1940
Ragtime Romeo	James Mundy	John Latouche	The Vamp	1955
Rain in My Heart	Louis Alter	Arthur Swanstrom	Ziegfeld Follies	1934
Rain in Spain, The	Frederick Loewe	Alan Jay Lerner	My Fair Lady	1956
Rain on the Sea	Irving Caesar, Sammy Lerner	Gerald Marks	My Dear Public	1943
Rain or Shine	Milton Ager	Jack Yellen	Rain or Shine	1928
Rainbow	Harold Levey	Zelda Sears	Rainbow Rose	1926
Rainbow of Girls	Irving Berlin	Irving Berlin	Ziegfeld Follies	1927
Rainy Day, A	Arthur Schwartz	Howard Dietz	Flying Colors	1932
Raise the Dust	Joseph Meyer	Edward Eliscu	Lady Fingers	1929
Rang-Tang	Ford Dabney	Jo Trent	Rang-Tang	1927
Rangers' Song, The	Harry Tierney	Joseph McCarthy	Rio Rita	1927
Ranger's Song, The	Sigmund Romberg	Harry B. Smith	The Love Call	1927
Raquel	Richard Whiting	Joe Burke	Earl Carroll's Vanities	1928
Reaching for the Moon	Harry Ruby	Bert Kalmar	Top Speed	1929
Reading, Writing and Rhythm	Jimmy McHugh	Al Dubin	Streets of Paris	1939
Real Nice Clambake, A	Richard Rodgers	Oscar Hammerstein II	Carousel	1945
Really and Truly	Jean Schwartz	Clifford Grey, William Cary Duncan	Sunny Days	1928
Reciprocity	Walter Kent	Kim Gannon	Seventeen	1951
Red Ball Express, The	Harold Rome	Harold Rome	Call Me Mister	1946
Red, Hot and Blue	Cole Porter	Cole Porter	Red, Hot and Blue	1936
Red Hot and Blue Rhythm	J. Fred Coots	Arthur Swanstrom, Benny Davis	Sons O' Guns	1929

TITLE	COMPOSER	LYRICIST	SHOW	YEAR
Red Hot Chicago	Ray Henderson	Lew Brown, B. G. DeSylva	Flying High	1930
Red River	Alma Sanders	Monte Carlo	The House Boat on the Styx	1928
Regal Romp	Alberta Nichols	Mann Holiner	Angela	1928
Regency Rakes	Noel Coward	Noel Coward	Conversation Piece	1934
Regimental Song	Rudolf Friml	Brian Hooker	The White Eagle	1927
Relax	Harold Rome	Harold Rome	Wish You Were Here	1952
Remarkable Fellow	Victor Young	Stella Unger	Seventh Heaven	1955
Remember the Night	Frederico Valerio	Elizabeth Miele	Hit the Trail	1954
Remembering You	J. Fred Coots	Clifford Grey	June Days	1925
Rendezvous Time in Paree	Jimmy McHugh	Al Dubin	Streets of Paris	1939
Restless	Joan Edwards	Lynn Duddy	Tickets Please	1950
Restless Heart	Harold Rome	Harold Rome	Fanny	1954
Rhode Island Is Famous for You	Arthur Schwartz	Howard Dietz	Inside U.S.A.	1948
Rhyme for Angela, A	Kurt Weill	Ira Gershwin	The Firebrand of Florence	1945
Rhythm of the Day	Owen Murphy	Donald Lindley	Earl Carroll's Vanities	1925
Rhythm of the Waves	Vincent Rose	Charles & Henry Tobias	Earl Carroll's Sketch Book	1929
Ribbons and Bows	Irving Berlin	Irving Berlin	Ziegfeld Follies	1927
Rich, The	Marc Blitzstein	Marc Blitzstein	The Cradle Will Rock	1938
Rich Man, Poor Man	Richard Rodgers	Lorenz Hart	Spring Is Here	1929
Rich or Poor	Kay Swift	Paul James	Fine and Dandy	1930
Riddle Me This	Lewis E. Gensler	E. Y. Harburg	Ballyhoo	1932
Ridin' High	Cole Porter	Cole Porter	Red, Hot and Blue	1936
Ridin' on the Breeze	Jerome Moross	John Latouche	Ballet Ballads	1948
Ridin' on the Moon	Harold Arlen	Johnny Mercer	St. Louis Woman	1946
Riff Song, The	Sigmund Romberg	Otto Harbach, Oscar Hammer- stein II	The Desert Song	1926
Right As the Rain	Harold Arlen	E. Y. Harburg	Bloomer Girl	1944
Right at the Start of It	Arthur Schwartz	Howard Dietz	Three's a Crowd	1930
Right Finger of My Left Hand, The	Albert Hague	Dorothy Fields	Redhead	1959
Right Man, The	Sam Timberg, Maury Rubens	Moe Jaffe	Broadway Nights	1929
Ring on the Finger	Harold Rome	Harold Rome	Destry Rides Again	1959
Right Out of Heaven	Harry Tierney	Joseph McCarthy	Cross My Heart	1928
Ring the Bell	Jimmy Van Heusen	Johnny Burke	Carnival in Flanders	1953
Rinka Tinka Man	Lew Kessler	June Sillman	Who's Who	1938
Rio Rita	Harry Tierney	Joseph McCarthy	Rio Rita	1927
Rise 'n' Shine	Vincent Youmans	B. G. DeSylva	Take a Chance	1932

TITLE	COMPOSER	LYRICIST	SHOW	YEAR
Rising Star	Franz Lehar	Edward Eliscu	Frederika	1937
River Song, The	Richard Addinsell	Clemence Dane	Come of Age	1934
Road of Dreams, The	Pat Thayer	Donovan Parsons, Clifford Grey	Mayflowers	1925
Rock, Rock, Rock	Jimmy McHugh	Harold Adamson	As the Girls Go	1948
Rockin' in Rhythm	Harold Arlen	Ted Koehler	Earl Carroll's Vanities	1932
Roll, Jordan	Eubie Blake	Andy Razaf	Blackbirds	1930
Romance	Sigmund Romberg	Otto Harbach, Oscar Hammerstein II	The Desert Song	1926
Romance	Rudolf Friml	Rowland Leigh, John Shubert	Music Hath Charms	1934
Romany Rover	J. Fred Coots	Al Dubin	White Lights	1927
Room for Two	Jean Schwartz	Alfred Bryan	A Night in Spain	1927
Room in Bloomsbury, A	Sandy Wilson	Sandy Wilson	The Boy Friend	1954
Room with a View, A	Noel Coward	Noel Coward	This Year of Grace	1928
Rosalie*	George Gershwin	Ira Gershwin	Rosalie	1928
Rose in the Heather	Franz Lehar	Edward Eliscu	Frederika	1937
Rose Is a Rose, A	Harold Rome	Harold Rome	Bless You All	1950
Rose Lovejoy of Paradise Alley	Harold Rome	Harold Rome	Destry Rides Again	1959
Rose of Iran	Winthrop Cortelyou	Derick Wulff	Kiss Me	1927
Rose-Time	Ray Henderson	B. G. DeSylva, Lew Brown	George White's Scandals	1925
Roses of Red	G. Romilli	G. Romilli	Fioretta	1929
Roses Understand	George M. Cohan	George M. Cohan	The Merry Malones	1927
Rosie	Charles Strouse	Lee Adams	Bye Bye Birdie	1960
Roundabout	Vernon Duke	Ogden Nash	Two's Company	1952
Roust-About	Jimmy Johnson	Percy Bradford	Messin' Around	1929
Roustabout's Song	Milton Ager, Owen Murphy	Jack Yellen	Rain or Shine	1928
Rub-A-Dub Your Rabbit's Foot	Frank Marcus, Bernard Maltin		Bomboola	1929
Rub Your Lamp	Cole Porter	Cole Porter	Let's Face It	1941
Rumba Jumps, The	Hoagy Carmichael	Johnny Mercer	Walk With Music	1940
Rumba Rhythm	Jimmy Johnson	Stella Unger	Earl Carroll's Vanities	1930
Run to Me, My Love	Allan Roberts	Lester Lee	All for Love	1949
Russian Blues	Noel Coward	Noel Coward	Charlot's Revue	1925
Sailing at Midnight	Vernon Duke	Howard Dietz	Sadie Thompson	1944
Salaaming the Rajah	Harry Tierney	Joseph McCarthy	Cross My Heart	1928
Salomee	Jule Styne	Bob Hilliard	Hazel Flagg	1953
Sam and Delilah	George Gershwin	Ira Gershwin	Girl Crazy	1930

*Dropped from New York production

TITLE	COMPOSER	LYRICIST	SHOW	YEAR
Same Old Moon	Henry Sullivan	Clifford Orr, John Murray Anderson	John Murray Anderson's Almanac	1929
Same Old Moon, The	Harry Ruby	Bert Kalmar, Otto Harbach	Lucky	1927
Sands of Time	Robert Wright, George Forrest (based on Borodin)		Kismet	1953
Sans Souci	Johnny Mercer	Johnny Mercer	Top Banana	1951
Santo Dinero	Richard Stutz	Milton Pascal	Along Fifth Avenue	1949
Saratoga	Harold Arlen	Johnny Mercer	Saratoga	1959
Satanic Strut	Edward Pola, Eddie Brandt		Woof, Woof	1929
Satan's Li'l Lamb	Harold Arlen	E. Y. Harburg, Johnny Mercer	Americana	1932
Satin and Silk	Cole Porter	Cole Porter	Silk Stockings	1955
Saturday Night in Central Park	Richard Lewine	Arnold B. Horwitt	Make Mine Manhattan	1948
Savage Serenade	Herman Hupfeld	Herman Hupfeld	Murder at the Vanities	1933
Savanna	Harold Arlen	E. Y. Harburg	Jamaica	1957
Savannah Stomp	Walter G. Samuels	Morrie Ryskind	Ned Wayburn's Gambols	1929
Save a Kiss	Leroy Anderson	Joan Ford, Jean & Walter Kerr	Goldilocks	1958
Say	Ray Henderson	Lew Brown	Hotcha	1932
Say, Darling	Jule Styne	Betty Comden, Adolph Green	Say, Darling	1958
Say it Some More	George M. Cohan	George M. Cohan	Billie	1928
Say it with a Solitaire	Jimmie Monaco	Billy Rose, Ballard Mac-Donald	Harry Delmar's Revels	1927
Say So	George Gershwin	P. G. Wodehouse, Ira Gershwin	Rosalie	1928
Say That You Love Me	Richard Myers	Leo Robin	Hello, Yourself	1928
Say the Word	Burton Lane	Harold Adamson	The Third Little Show	1931
Say When	Jesse Greer	Raymond Klages	Say When	1928
Say When	Ray Henderson	Ted Koehler	Say When	1934
Say Yes, Sweetheart	Emmerich Kalman	Harry B. Smith	Countess Maritza	1926
Scratch My Back	Dean Fuller	Marshall Barer	New Faces	1956
Sea Legs	Lewis E. Gensler	B. G. DeSylva	Captain Jinks	1925
Season Ended, The	Michael H. Cleary	Max & Nathaniel Lief	Hey Nonny Nonny!	1932
Second Time in Love	Harry Warren	Jerome Lawrence, Robert E. Lee	Shangri-La	1956
Secret Song	Baldwin Bergersen	George Marion, Jr.	Allah Be Praised	1944
See That You're Born in Texas	Cole Porter	Cole Porter	Something for the Boys	1943

TITLE	COMPOSER	LYRICIST	SHOW	YEAR
~~See the Monkey~~	~~Raymond Scott~~	~~Bernard Hanighen~~	~~Lute Song~~	~~1946~~
Send For Me	Richard Rodgers	Lorenz Hart	Simple Simon	1930
Sensible Thing to Do, The	Jack Lawrence, Don Walker		Courtin' Time	1951
Sentimental Me	Richard Rodgers	Lorenz Hart	Garrick Gaieties	1925
Sentimental Sally	Clarence Gaskill	Billy Rose	Earl Carroll's Vanities	1925
Sentimental Silly	Henry Souvaine, Jay Gorney	Morrie Ryskind, Howard Dietz	Merry-Go-Round	1927
September Song	Kurt Weill	Maxwell Anderson	Knickerbocker Holiday	1938
Serenade Creole	Frank Harling	Laurence Stallings	Deep River	1926
Serenade of Love	Sigmund Romberg	Irving Caesar	Nina Rosa	1930
Set Me Free	Frederico Valerio	Elizabeth Miele	Hit the Trail	1954
Seven Days	Edward Kunneke	Clifford Grey	Mayflowers	1925
Seventeen and Twenty-One*	George Gershwin	Ira Gershwin	Strike Up the Band	1930
Seventy-Six Trombones	Meredith Willson	Meredith Willson	The Music Man	1957
Sevilla	Ray Henderson	B. G. DeSylva, Lew Brown	George White's Scandals	1926
Sh!*	Frederick Loewe	Alan Jay Lerner	Paint Your Wagon	1951
Shady Lady Bird	Hugh Martin	Ralph Blane	Best Foot Forward	1941
Shake Brother	Joseph Meyer, Philip Charig	Leo Robin	Just Fancy	1927
Shake High, Shake Low	Werner Janssen	Mann Holiner, J. Keirn Brennan	Boom-Boom	1929
Shake Well Before Using	Johnny Green	Edward Heyman	Here Goes the Bride	1931
Shaking the Blues Away	Irving Berlin	Irving Berlin	Ziegfeld Follies	1927
Shall I Take My Heart and Go?	Leroy Anderson	Joan Ford, Jean & Walter Kerr	Goldilocks	1958
Shall I Tell Him?	Karl Hajos (based on Tchaikovsky)	Harry B. Smith	Natja	1925
Shall We Dance?	Richard Rodgers	Oscar Hammerstein II	The King and I	1951
Shangri-La	Harry Warren	Jerome Lawrence, Robert E. Lee	Shangri-La	1956
Shauny O'Shay	Hugh Martin	Hugh Martin	Look Ma, I'm Dancin'	1948
Shavian Shivers	Vernon Duke	E. Y. Harburg	Garrick Gaieties	1930
She Could Shake the Maracas	Richard Rodgers	Lorenz Hart	Too Many Girls	1939
She Didn't Say "Yes"	Jerome Kern	Otto Harbach	The Cat and the Fiddle	1931
She Is My Ideal	Ralph Benatzky	Ralph Benatzky	Meet My Sister	1930
She Loves Me Not	Arthur Schwartz	Edward Heyman	She Loves Me Not	1933
She's Got the Lot	Marguerite Monnot	Julian More, Daniel Heneker, Monte Norman	Irma La Douce	1960

*Dropped from New York production

TITLE	COMPOSER	LYRICIST	SHOW	YEAR
She's Just Another Girl	Harold Karr	Matt Dubey	Happy Hunting	1956
She's Such a Comfort to Me	Arthur Schwartz	Max & Nathaniel Lief, Donovan Parsons, Douglas Furber	Wake Up and Dream	1929
Shine on Your Shoes, A	Arthur Schwartz	Howard Dietz	Flying Colors	1932
Ship of Love	Walter G. Samuels	Morrie Ryskind	Ned Wayburn's Gambols	1929
Ship Without a Sail, A	Richard Rodgers	Lorenz Hart	Heads Up	1929
Shoein' the Mare	Harold Arlen	E. Y. Harburg, Ira Gershwin	Life Begins at 8:40	1934
Shoeless Joe from Hannibal, Mo.	Richard Adler, Jerry Ross		Damn Yankees	1955
Shootin' the Pistol	Clarence Williams, Chris Smith		Bottomland	1927
Shopping Around	Harold Rome	Harold Rome	Wish You Were Here	1952
Shortest Day of the Year, The	Richard Rodgers	Lorenz Hart	The Boys from Syracuse	1938
Should I Be Sweet?	Vincent Youmans	B. G. DeSylva	Take a Chance	1932
Should I Tell You I Love You?	Cole Porter	Cole Porter	Around the World	1946
Shout On!	Jimmy Johnson	Percy Bradford	Messin' Around	1929
Show Me	Frederick Loewe	Alan Jay Lerner	My Fair Lady	1956
Show Me the Town*	George Gershwin	Ira Gershwin	Oh, Kay!	1926
Show Off	Albert Selden	Albert Selden	Small Wonder	1948
Show Tune in 2/4 Time	Jerry Herman	Jerry Herman	Parade	1960
Shuffle Your Feet and Roll Along	Jimmy McHugh	Dorothy Fields	Blackbirds	1928
Shy	Mary Rodgers	Marshall Barer	Once Upon a Mattress	1959
Siberia	Cole Porter	Cole Porter	Silk Stockings	1955
Sid Old Kid	Bob Merrill	Bob Merrill	Take Me Along	1959
Side Street Off Broadway	Edgar Fairchild	Henry Myers	The New Yorkers	1927
Sigh By Night	Emmerich Kalman	George Marion, Jr.	Marinka	1945
Signal, The	George Gershwin	Otto Harbach, Oscar Hammerstein II	Song of the Flame	1925
Silk Stockings	Cole Porter	Cole Porter	Silk Stockings	1955
Silver Apron Strings	Max Ewing	Agnes Morgan	Grand Street Follies	1927
Silver Moon	Sigmund Romberg	Dorothy Donnelly	My Maryland	1927
Silver Sails	Harden Church	Edward Heyman	Caviar	1934
Silver Song	Douglas Moore	John Latouche	The Ballad of Baby Doe	1958
Silver Wing	Rudolf Friml	Brian Hooker	The White Eagle	1927
Simple Spanish Maid	Jean Schwartz	Alfred Bryan	A Night in Spain	1927
Simply Heavenly	David Martin	Langston Hughes	Simply Heavenly	1957
Sing**	Richard Rodgers	Lorenz Hart	Betsy	1926
Sing a Little Jingle	Harry Warren	Mort Dixon	Crazy Quilt	1931

*Dropped from New York production

**Also in "Lady Fingers" (1929)

TITLE	COMPOSER	LYRICIST	SHOW	YEAR
Sing a Little Song	Lucien Denni	Gwynne Denni	Happy Go Lucky	1926
Sing a Song in the Rain	Harry Rosenthal	Douglas Furber, Irving Caesar	Polly	1929
Sing, Brothers!	Jack Waller, Joseph Tun-bridge	R. P. Weston, Bert Lee	Tell Her the Truth	1933
Sing, Dance and Smile	Philip Charig	Ben Jerome	Yes, Yes, Yvette	1927
Sing for Your Supper	Richard Rodgers	Lorenz Hart	The Boys from Syracuse	1938
Sing Me a Song with Social Significance	Harold Rome	Harold Rome	Pins and Needles	1937
Sing Me Not a Ballad	Kurt Weill	Ira Gershwin	The Firebrand of Florence	1945
Sing Something Simple	Herman Hupfeld	Herman Hupfeld	The Second Little Show	1930
Sing to Me, Guitar	Cole Porter	Cole Porter	Mexican Hayride	1944
Singin' the Blues	Jimmy McHugh	Dorothy Fields	Singin' the Blues	1931
Singing a Love Song	Richard Rodgers	Lorenz Hart	Chee-Chee	1928
Singing to You	Ben Oakland, Margot Millham	Robert A. Simon	Hold Your Horses	1933
Singing Tree, The	Heitor Villa-Lobos	Robert Wright, George Forrest	Magdalena	1948
Sister Mine	Emmerich Kalman	Harry B. Smith	Countess Maritza	1926
Sit Down You're Rockin' the Boat	Frank Loesser	Frank Loesser	Guys and Dolls	1950
Sittin' in the Sun (Just Wearing a Smile)	Cliff Friend	George White	George White's Scandals	1929
Six O'Clock	Philip Charig	Irving Caesar	Yes. Yes, Yvette	1927
Sixteen Going on Seventeen	Richard Rodgers	Oscar Hammer-stein II	The Sound of Music	1959
Skiddle-De-Skow	Jimmy Johnson	Percy Bradford	Messin' Around	1929
Skip the Build Up	Sammy Fain	Dan Shapiro	Ankles Aweigh	1955
Skipper	Milton Susskind	Paul Porter, Benjamin H. Burt	Florida Girl	1925
Sky City*	Richard Rodgers	Lorenz Hart	Heads Up	1929
Skyscraper Blues	Gordon Jenkins	Tom Adair	Along Fifth Avenue	1949
Slaughter on Tenth Avenue	Richard Rodgers		On Your Toes	1936
Sleep Baby, Don't Cry	Baldwin Bergersen	William Archibald	Carib Song	1945
Sleepin' Bee, A	Harold Arlen	Truman Capote, Harold Arlen	House of Flowers	1954
Sleepy Head	Richard Rodgers	Lorenz Hart	Garrick Gaieties	1926
Sliding Down a Silver Cloud	Lee David	J. Keirn Brennan	A Night in Venice	1929
Slightly Less Than Wonderful	Thomas (Fats) Waller	George Marion, Jr.	Early to Bed	1943

*Dropped from New York production

TITLE	COMPOSER	LYRICIST	SHOW	YEAR
Slightly Perfect	Harry Revel	Arnold B. Horwitt	Are You With It?	1945
Slow Down	Joseph Meyer	Edward Eliscu	Lady Fingers	1929
Slow River	Charles M. Schwab	Henry Myers	The New Yorkers	1927
Slumber Song (Good-Night)	Richard Whiting	Oscar Hammerstein II	Free for All	1931
Small Talk	Richard Adler, Jerry Ross		The Pajama Game	1954
Small World	Jule Styne	Stephen Sondheim	Gypsy	1959
Smellin' of Vanilla (Bamboo Cage)	Harold Arlen	Truman Capote, Harold Arlen	House of Flowers	1954
Smile	Donald Heywood	Donald Heywood	Africana	1929
Smile at Me	Edward J. Lambert	Edward J. Lambert	Smile at Me	1925
Smile, Darn You, Smile	Rudolf Friml	Brian Hooker	The White Eagle	1927
Smoke Gets in Your Eyes	Jerome Kern	Otto Harbach	Roberta	1933
Smokin' Reefers	Arthur Schwartz	Howard Dietz	Flying Colors	1932
Snap Out of It	Harry Akst	Benny Davis	Artists and Models	1927
'S No Use Talking	Jean Schwartz	Clifford Grey, William Cary Duncan	Sunny Days	1928
So Are You!	George Gershwin	Ira Gershwin, Gus Kahn	Show Girl	1929
So Do I	Jean Schwartz	Clifford Grey, William Cary Duncan	Sunny Days	1928
So Do I	Vincent Youmans	B. G. DeSylva	Take a Chance	1932
So Far	Richard Rodgers	Oscar Hammerstein II	Allegro	1947
So in Love	Cole Porter	Cole Porter	Kiss Me, Kate	1948
So Lonesome	Joe Jordan	Rosamond Johnson	Fast and Furious	1931
So Long for Ever So Long	Ray Henderson	Ted Koehler	Say When	1934
So Long to All Our Memories	Maria Grever	Raymond Leveen	Viva O'Brien	1941
So Nonchalant	Vernon Duke	E. Y. Harburg	Walk a Little Faster	1932
So What?	George Gershwin	Ira Gershwin	Pardon My English	1933
Soft in De Moonlight	Frank Harling	Laurence Stallings	Deep River	1926
Soft Lights and Sweet Music	Irving Berlin	Irving Berlin	Face the Music	1932
Softly, As in a Morning Sunrise	Sigmund Romberg	Oscar Hammerstein II	The New Moon	1928
Soldier of Fortune, A	Jean Gilbert	Harry B. Smith	The Red Robe	1928
Soldier of Love	Irving Caesar, Gerald Marks, Sammy Lerner		Thumbs Up	1934
Soliloquy	Richard Rodgers	Oscar Hammerstein II	Carousel	1945
Some Day	Rudolf Friml	Brian Hooker	The Vagabond King	1925
Some Day	Sigmund Romberg	Harry B. Smith	Cherry Blossoms	1927
Some Day I'll Find You	Noel Coward	Noel Coward	Private Lives	1931

TITLE	COMPOSER	LYRICIST	SHOW	YEAR
Some Enchanted Evening	Richard Rodgers	Oscar Hammerstein II	South Pacific	1949
Some Other Time	Leonard Bernstein	Betty Comden, Adolph Green	On the Town	1944
Some People	Jule Styne	Stephen Sondheim	Gypsy	1959
Some Sweet Someone	Herbert Stothart, Harry Ruby	Bert Kalmar	Good Boy	1928
Somebody Else	Raymond Hubbell	Anne Caldwell	Yours Truly	1927
Somebody Like Me	Frank Marcus, Bernard Maltin		Bomboola	1929
Somebody Ought to Be Told	Sigmund Romberg	Oscar Hammerstein II	May Wine	1935
Somebody, Somewhere	Frank Loesser	Frank Loesser	The Most Happy Fella	1956
Somebody's Crazy About You	Owen Murphy, Jay Gorney		Earl Carroll's Vanities	1925
Somehow I've Always Known	Frederico Valerio	Elizabeth Miele	Hit the Trail	1954
Someone	Alfred Goodman, Maury Rubens	Harry B. Smith	Naughty Riquette	1926
Someone	Jack Urbont	Bruce Geller	Livin' the Life	1957
Someone in the Know	Ann Ronell	Ann Ronell	Count Me In	1942
Someone Should Tell Them*	Richard Rodgers	Lorenz Hart	A Connecticut Yankee	1927
Someone to Admire, Someone to Adore	Serge Walter	Agnes Morgan	Grand Street Follies	1928
Someone to Watch Over Me	George Gershwin	Ira Gershwin	Oh, Kay!	1926
Someone's Been Sending Me Flowers	David Baker	Sheldon Harnick	Shoestring Revue	1955
Something for the Boys	Cole Porter	Cole Porter	Something for the Boys	1943
Something Had to Happen	Jerome Kern	Otto Harbach	Roberta	1933
Something I Dreamed Last Night	Sammy Fain	Jack Yellen, Herb Magidson	George White's Scandals	1939
Something New	Howard Blankman	Howard Blankman	By Hex	1956
Something New Is in My Heart	Sigmund Romberg	Oscar Hammerstein II	May Wine	1935
Something Seems to Tell Me	Robert Katscher	Irving Caesar	The Wonder Bar	1931
Something Sort of Grandish	Burton Lane	E. Y. Harburg	Finian's Rainbow	1947
Something Tells Me	Henry Souvaine, Jay Gorney	Morrie Ryskind, Howard Dietz	Merry-Go-Round	1927
Something to Dance About	Irving Berlin	Irving Berlin	Call Me Madam	1950

*Dropped from New York production

TITLE	COMPOSER	LYRICIST	SHOW	YEAR
Something to Live For	Joseph Meyer	Edward Eliscu	Lady Fingers	1929
Something to Remember You By	Arthur Schwartz	Howard Dietz	Three's a Crowd	1930
Something to Tell	Maury Rubens, J. Fred Coots	Clifford Grey	The Madcap	1928
Something Wonderful	Richard Rodgers	Oscar Hammerstein II	The King and I	1951
Something's Always Happening on the River	Jule Styne	Betty Comden, Adolph Green	Say, Darling	1958
Something's Coming	Leonard Bernstein	Stephen Sondheim	West Side Story	1957
Sometimes I'm Happy	Vincent Youmans	Leo Robin, Clifford Grey	Hit the Deck	1927
Somewhere	Leonard Bernstein	Stephen Sondheim	West Side Story	1957
Son of the Sun	Rudolf Friml	J. Keirn Brennan	Luana	1930
Song Is You. The	Jerome Kern	Oscar Hammerstein II	Music in the Air	1932
Song of Harlem, The	Frank Marcus, Bernard Maltin		Bomboola	1929
Song of My Heart	Franklin Hauser	Brian Hooker	The O'Flynn	1934
Song of the Flame	George Gershwin, Herbert Stothart	Otto Harbach, Oscar Hammerstein II	Song of the Flame	1925
Song of the Moonbeams	Vincent Rose	Charles & Henry Tobias	Earl Carroll's Sketch Book	1929
Song of the Setting Sun	Walter Donaldson	Gus Kahn	Whoopee	1928
Song of the Troika	Franz Steininger (based on Tchaikovsky)	Forman Brown	Music in My Heart	1947
Song of the Vagabonds	Rudolf Friml	Brian Hooker	The Vagabond King	1925
Soon	George Gershwin	Ira Gershwin	Strike Up the Band	1930
Soon It's Gonna Rain	Harvey Schmidt	Tom Jones	The Fantasticks	1960
Sorry for Myself	Moose Charlap	Norman Gimbel	Whoop-Up	1958
Sorry That I Strayed Away from You	Jimmy Johnson	Percy Bradford	Messin' Around	1929
Sort O' Lonesome	Herman Hupfeld	Herman Hupfeld	A La Carte	1927
Soul Mates	Alma Sanders	Monte Carlo	The House Boat on the Styx	1928
Sound of Music, The	Richard Rodgers	Oscar Hammerstein II	The Sound of Music	1959
South America, Take it Away	Harold Rome	Harold Rome	Call Me Mister	1946
South American Way	Jimmy McHugh	Al Dubin	Streets of Paris	1939
Spanish Mick, The	Harry Archer	Harlan Thompson	Merry-Merry	1925
Spare a Little Love	Melville Gideon	Clifford Grey	The Optimists	1928
Speak Easy	Lewis E. Gensler	Owen Murphy, Robert A. Simon	The Gang's All Here	1931
Speak Low	Kurt Weill	Ogden Nash	One Touch of Venus	1943
Speaking of Love	Vernon Duke	E. Y. Harburg	Walk a Little Faster	1932

TITLE	COMPOSER	LYRICIST	SHOW	YEAR
Speaking of You	Lewis E. Gensler	Owen Murphy, Robert A. Simon	The Gang's All Here	1931
Spring in Autumn	Will Ortman	Gus Kahn, Raymond B. Egan	Holka-Polka	1925
Spring Is Here	Richard Rodgers	Lorenz Hart	I Married an Angel	1938
Spring Is in the Air	Gus Edwards	Eugene Conrad	Broadway Show Window	1936
Spring Song	Jimmy Van Heusen	Eddie DeLange	Swingin' the Dream	1939
Springtime Cometh, The	Sammy Fain	E. Y. Harburg	Flahooley	1951
Springtime in the Air	Johann Strauss, Sr.	Clare Kummer	Three Waltzes	1937
Stan' Up an' Fight	Georges Bizet	Oscar Hammerstein II	Carmen Jones	1943
Stand Up on Your Feet and Dance	Charles Schwab	Henry Myers	Bare Facts	1926
Standing on the Corner	Frank Loesser	Frank Loesser	The Most Happy Fella	1956
Starlit Hour	Peter De Rose	Mitchell Parish	Earl Carroll's Vanities	1940
Stars Remain, The	Jay Gorney	Henry Myers	Meet the People	1940
Start Stompin'	Charles Rosoff	Leo Robin	Judy	1927
Starting at the Bottom	Kay Swift	Paul James	Fine and Dandy	1930
Stately Homes of England, The	Noel Coward	Noel Coward	Set to Music	1939
Stay East, Young Man	Richard Lewine	Ted Fetter	The Girl from Wyoming	1938
Stay Out of the Kitchen	James P. Johnson	Flournoy Miller	Sugar Hill	1931
Stay Well	Kurt Weill	Maxwell Anderson	Lost in the Stars	1949
Staying Young	Bob Merrill	Bob Merrill	Take Me Along	1959
Steam Heat	Richard Adler, Jerry Ross		The Pajama Game	1954
Steam Is on the Beam, The	Johnny Green	George Marion, Jr.	Beat the Band	1942
Steamboat Days	Clarence Williams	Clarence Williams	Bottomland	1927
Step on the Blues	Con Conrad, Will Donaldson	Otto Harbach	Kitty's Kisses	1926
Step Step Sisters	Harry Archer	Harlan Thompson	Merry-Merry	1925
Stepping Out of the Picture	Harry Akst	Lew Brown	Calling All Stars	1934
Stereophonic Sound	Cole Porter	Cole Porter	Silk Stockings	1955
Still I'd Love You	Ray Henderson	B. G. DeSylva, Lew Brown	Follow Thru	1929
Stolen Kisses	Franz Steininger (based on Tchaikovsky)	Forman Brown	Music in My Heart	1947
Stonewall Moskowitz March	Richard Rodgers	Lorenz Hart	Betsy	1926
Stop, Go!	Maury Rubens, J. Fred Coots	Clifford Grey	The Madcap	1928

TITLE	COMPOSER	LYRICIST	SHOW	YEAR
Store-Bought Suit	Jerome Moross	John Latouche	The Golden Apple	1954
Story of a Carrot, The	Sidney Lippman	Sylvia Dee	Barefoot Boy with Cheek	1947
Story of a Horn, The	Lee Wainer	Robert Sour	Sing for Your Supper	1939
Stouthearted Men	Sigmund Romberg	Oscar Hammer- stein II	The New Moon	1928
Strange Music	Robert Wright, George Forrest (based on Grieg)		Song of Norway	1944
Strange New Look	James Shelton	James Shelton	Dance Me a Song	1950
Stranger	Bronislaw Kaper (based on Chopin)	John Latouche	Polonaise	1945
Stranger, The	George Kleinsinger	Joe Darion	Shinbone Alley	1957
Stranger in Paradise	Robert Wright, George Forrest (based on Borodin)		Kismet	1953
Straw Hat in the Rain	Harry Akst	Lew Brown	Calling All Stars	1934
Strike Me Pink	Ray Henderson	Lew Brown	Strike Me Pink	1933
Strike Up the Band!	George Gershwin	Ira Gershwin	Strike Up the Band	1930
Subway Sun, The	Ray Perkins	Max & Nathaniel Lief	Greenwich Village Follies	1928
Such a Merry Party	Rick Besoyan	Rick Besoyan	Little Mary Sunshine	1959
Such Stuff as Dreams Are Made Of	Sammy Fain	Irving Kahal	Boys and Girls Together	1940
Sudden Thrill, The	Jimmy Van Heusen	Johnny Burke	Carnival in Flanders	1953
Suddenly	Vernon Duke	Billy Rose, E. Y. Harburg	Ziegfeld Follies	1934
Sue Me	Frank Loesser	Frank Loesser	Guys and Dolls	1950
Sugar Plum	Joseph Meyer	B. G. DeSylva	Gay Paree	1926
Sugarfoot	Vernon Duke	Howard Dietz	Jackpot	1944
Suits Me Fine	Hugh Martin	Hugh Martin	Make a Wish	1951
Summer Afternoon	Harold Rome	Harold Rome	Wish You Were Here	1952
Summer Day	Marc Blitzstein	Marc Blitzstein	Regina	1949
Summer Dresses	Harold Rome	Harold Rome	Bless You All	1950
Summer Is A-comin' in*	Vernon Duke	John Latouche	The Lady Comes Across	1942
Summertime	George Gershwin	DuBose Heyward	Porgy and Bess	1935
Summertime Is Summertime	Walter Kent	Kim Gannon	Seventeen	1951
Summertime Love	Frank Loesser	Frank Loesser	Greenwillow	1960
Sun About to Rise, The	Jerome Kern	Oscar Hammer- stein II	Sweet Adeline	1929
Sun Will Shine, The	Arthur Schwartz	Morrie Ryskind	Ned Wayburn's Gambols	1929
Sunday	J. Fred Coots	Clifford Grey	The Merry World	1926
Sunday	Richard Rodgers	Oscar Hammer- stein II	Flower Drum Song	1958
Sunday in the Park	Harold Rome	Harold Rome	Pins and Needles	1937
Sun'll Be Up in the Morning, The	Sammy Fain	Jack Yellen	Boys and Girls Together	1940

*Also in "The Littlest Revue" (1956)

TITLE	COMPOSER	LYRICIST	SHOW	YEAR
Sunny	Jerome Kern	Otto Harbach, Oscar Hammerstein II	Sunny	1925
Sunny Disposish	Philip Charig	Ira Gershwin	Americana	1926
Sunny River	Sigmund Romberg	Oscar Hammerstein II	Sunny River	1941
Sunny Side of You	Frank Grey	Earle Crooker, McElbert Moore	Happy	1927
Sunshine	Jerome Kern	Otto Harbach, Oscar Hammerstein II	Sunny	1925
Sunshine	Jule Styne	Leo Robin	Gentlemen Prefer Blondes	1949
Sunshine Girl	Bob Merrill	Bob Merrill	New Girl in Town	1957
Supper Time	Irving Berlin	Irving Berlin	As Thousands Cheer	1933
Surprise	Jay Livingston	Ray Evans	Oh Captain!	1958
Surrey with the Fringe on Top, The	Richard Rodgers	Oscar Hammerstein II	Oklahoma!	1943
Susan's Dream	Kurt Weill	Alan Jay Lerner	Love Life	1948
Susannah's Squeaking Shoes	Muriel Lillie	Arthur Weigall	Charlot's Revue	1925
Suzie	Jerome Kern	Anne Caldwell	Criss-Cross	1926
Suzy Is a Good Thing	Richard Rodgers	Oscar Hammerstein II	Pipe Dream	1955
Swanee River Melody	Charles Weinberg	Al Wilson	Americana	1926
Swapping Sweet Nothings With You	Robert Russell Bennett	Owen Murphy, Robert A. Simon	Hold Your Horses	1933
Sweet and Hot	Harold Arlen	Jack Yellen	You Said It	1931
Sweet and Low-Down	George Gershwin	Ira Gershwin	Tip-Toes	1925
Sweet Blossoms	M. Pinsuti	Eleanor & Herbert Farjeon	The Two Bouquets	1938
Sweet Fool	Rudolf Friml	Rowland Leigh, John Shubert	Music Hath Charms	1934
Sweet Liar	Herbert Stothart	Irving Caesar	Polly	1929
Sweet Little Stranger	Harry Revel	Mack Gordon	Smiling Faces	1932
Sweet Madness	Victor Young	Ned Washington	Murder at the Vanities	1933
Sweet Music	Arthur Schwartz	Howard Dietz	The Band Wagon	1931
Sweet One	Lewis E. Gensler	Robert A. Simon	Ups-A-Daisy	1928
Sweet Peter	Richard Rodgers	Lorenz Hart	Dearest Enemy	1925
Sweet Savannah Sue	Thomas (Fats) Waller, Harry Brooks	Andy Razaf	Hot Chocolates	1929
Sweet Sixty-Five	Richard Rodgers	Lorenz Hart	I'd Rather Be Right	1937
Sweet So-and-So	Joseph Meyer, Philip Charig	Ira Gershwin	Sweet and Low	1930

TITLE	COMPOSER	LYRICIST	SHOW	YEAR
Sweet Thursday	Richard Rodgers	Oscar Hammer-stein II	Pipe Dream	1955
Sweet William	David Baker	David Craig	Copper and Brass	1957
Sweetenheart	Richard Rodgers	Lorenz Hart	Simple Simon	1930
Sweeter Than You*	Harry Ruby	Bert Kalmar	Twinkle, Twinkle	1926
Sweetheart Time	Joseph Meyer	Irving Caesar	Sweetheart Time	1926
Swing	Leonard Bernstein	Betty Comden, Adolph Green	Wonderful Town	1953
Swing Low, Sweet Harriet	Philip Charig	Dan Shapiro, Milton Pascal	Artists and Models	1943
Swinging on the Gate	William B. Kernell	Dorothy Donnelly	Hello, Lola	1926
Swingy Little Thingy	Bud Green, Sam H. Stept		Shady Lady	1933
'S Wonderful	George Gershwin	Ira Gershwin	Funny Face	1927
Sympathetic Someone	Jerome Kern	Anne Caldwell	The City Chap	1925
Tailspin	Maceo Pinkard	Maceo Pinkard	Change Your Luck	1930
Take a Little Dip	Milton Susskind	Paul Porter, Benjamin H. Burt	Florida Girl	1925
Take a Little Stroll with Me	J. Fred Coots Maury Rubens	Clifford Grey	Mayflowers	1925
Take and Take and Take	Richard Rodgers	Lorenz Hart	I'd Rather Be Right	1937
Take Back Your Mink	Frank Loesser	Frank Loesser	Guys and Dolls	1950
Take Him	Richard Rodgers	Lorenz Hart	Pal Joey	1940
Take It in Your Stride	Irving Berlin	Irving Berlin	Annie Get Your Gun	1946
Take It Slow, Joe	Harold Arlen	E. Y. Harburg	Jamaica	1957
Take Love Easy	Duke Ellington	John Latouche	Beggar's Holiday	1946
Take Me Along	Bob Merrill	Bob Merrill	Take Me Along	1959
Take Me Away	Peter Tinturin	Sidney Clare, Charles Tobias	Earl Carroll's Vanities	1932
Take Me Back to Manhattan	Cole Porter	Cole Porter	The New Yorkers	1930
Take My Heart with You	Fred Spielman, Arthur Gershwin	Stanley Adams	A Lady Says Yes	1945
Take Off the Coat	Harold Rome	Harold Rome	Bless You All	1950
Taking a Chance on Love	Vernon Duke	Ted Fetter, John Latouche	Cabin in the Sky	1940
Taking Off	Philip Charig	James Dyrenforth	Nikki	1931
Taking the Steps to Russia	Cole Porter	Cole Porter	Leave It to Me	1938
Talk About Girls	Stephen Jones	Irving Caesar	Talk About Girls	1927
Talk with Your Heel and Your Toe	Oscar Levant	Irving Caesar	Ripples	1930
Tall Hope	Cy Coleman	Carolyn Leigh	Wildcat	1960
Tampa	Henry Souvaine, Jay Gorney	Morrie Ryskind, Howard Dietz	Merry-Go-Round	1927

*Also in "The Ramblers"

TITLE	COMPOSER	LYRICIST	SHOW	YEAR
Tampico Tap	Albert Von Tilzer	Neville Fleeson	Bye, Bye, Bonnie	1927
Tampico Tune	Frank Marcus, Bernard Maltin		Bomboola	1929
Tango Melody	Irving Berlin	Irving Berlin	The Cocoanuts	1925
Tap Tap, The	Jesse Greer	Billy Rose, Ballard Mac- Donald	Padlocks	1927
Tappin' the Barrel	Victor Young	Joseph Young, Ned Washington	Blackbirds	1933
Tartar Song, The	Richard Rodgers	Lorenz Hart	Chee-Chee	1928
Tea for Two	Vincent Youmans	Irving Caesar	No, No, Nanette	1925
Tea in Chicago	James Shelton	James Shelton	Mrs. Patterson	1954
Teach Me to Dance Like Grandma	Noel Coward	Noel Coward	This Year of Grace	1928
Tee Teedle Tum Di Dum	George M. Cohan	George M. Cohan	The Merry Malones	1927
Teeter Totter Tessie	Morgan Lewis	Nancy Hamilton	One for the Money	1939
Television's Tough on Love	Joan Edwards	Lynn Duddy	Tickets Please	1950
Tell Her	Arthur Siegel	June Carroll	New Faces	1956
Tell Me Again	Shep Camp	Frank Dupree	Half a Widow	1927
Tell Me, Cigarette	Sigmund Romberg	Harry B. Smith	Cherry Blossoms	1927
Tell Me More!	George Gershwin	B. G. DeSylva, Ira Gershwin	Tell Me More	1925
Tell Me Something About Yourself	Michael H. Cleary	Max & Nathaniel Lief	Hey Nonny Nonny!	1932
Tell Me the Story	Morgan Lewis	Nancy Hamilton	Three to Make Ready	1946
Tell the Truth	Ray Henderson	Jack Yellen	George White's Scandals	1936
Temptation Strut	Earl Lindsay, Maury Rubens	Clifford Grey	The Great Temptations	1926
Ten Cents a Dance	Richard Rodgers	Lorenz Hart	Simple Simon	1930
Ten O'Clock Town	Michael H. Cleary	Arthur Swanstrom	Sea Legs	1937
Tender Shepherd	Mark Charlap	Carolyn Leigh	Peter Pan	1954
Terribly Attractive	Arthur Schwartz	Dorothy Fields	Stars in Your Eyes	1939
Texas Stomp	Will Morrissey	Edmund Joseph	Polly of Hollywood	1927
Thank Your Father	Ray Henderson	Lew Brown, B. G. DeSylva	Flying High	1930
That Certain Feeling	George Gershwin	Ira Gershwin	Tip-Toes	1925
That Certain Thing	Edward Pola, Eddie Brandt		Woof, Woof	1929
That Face	Hugh Martin	Hugh Martin	Make a Wish	1951
That Fellow Manuelo	Arthur Schwartz	Howard Dietz	Revenge with Music	1934
That Great Come and Get It Day	Burton Lane	E. Y. Harburg	Finian's Rainbow	1947
That Jungle Jamboree	Thomas (Fats) Waller, Harry Brooks	Andy Razaf	Hot Chocolates	1929
That Lindy Hop	Eubie Blake	Andy Razaf	Blackbirds	1930
That Little Something	Jerome Kern	Bert Kalmar, Harry Ruby	Lucky	1927

TITLE	COMPOSER	LYRICIST	SHOW	YEAR
That Lost Barbershop Chord	George Gershwin	Ira Gershwin	Americana	1926
That Lucky Fellow	Jerome Kern	Oscar Hammer-stein II	Very Warm for May	1939
That Means Nothing to Me!	A. L. Keith, Lee Sterling		Naughty Cinderella	1925
That Moment of Moments	Vernon Duke	Ira Gershwin	Ziegfeld Follies	1936
That Rhythm Man	Thomas (Fats) Waller, Harry Brooks	Andy Razaf	Hot Chocolates	1929
That Russian Winter	Irving Berlin	Irving Berlin	This Is the Army	1942
That Snake Hip Dance	Thomas (Fats) Waller, Harry Brooks	Andy Razaf	Hot Chocolates	1929
That Tired Feeling	Louis Alter	Harry Ruskin, Leighton K. Brill	Ballyhoo	1930
That Was Then	James P. Johnson	Flournoy Miller	Sugar Hill	1931
That's Fine	Jack Waller, Joseph Tunbridge	R. P. Weston, Bert Lee	Tell Her the Truth	1933
That's for Sure	Johnny Mercer	Johnny Mercer	Top Banana	1951
That's Good Enough for Me	Baldwin Bergersen	Virginia Faulkner	All in Fun	1940
That's Good, That's Bad	Sammy Fain	Irving Kahal	Everybody's Welcome	1931
That's Him	Kurt Weill	Ogden Nash	One Touch of Venus	1943
That's How I Know That I'm in Love	Jacques Belasco	Kay Twomey	The Girl from Nantucket	1945
That's How I Love the Blues	Hugh Martin	Ralph Blane	Best Foot Forward	1941
That's Life	Vernon Duke	E. Y. Harburg	Walk a Little Faster	1932
That's Love	Ray Henderson	Lew Brown	George White's Scandals	1931
That's My Fella	Morton Gould	Dorothy Fields	Arms and the Girl	1950
That's Not Cricket	Arthur Schwartz	Howard Dietz	At Home Abroad	1935
That's the Time When I Miss You	Alexander Fogarty	Seymour Morris	Cape Cod Follies	1929
That's the Way it Happens	Richard Rodgers	Oscar Hammer-stein II	Me and Juliet	1953
That's What the Well-dressed Man in Harlem Will Wear	Irving Berlin	Irving Berlin	This Is the Army	1942
That's When a Feller Needs a Friend	William B. Friedlander, Con Conrad		Mercenary Mary	1925
That's Why Darkies Were Born	Ray Henderson	Lew Brown	George White's Scandals	1931
That's Why I Want to Go Home	Alma Sanders	Monte Carlo	Louisiana Lady	1947

TITLE	COMPOSER	LYRICIST	SHOW	YEAR
That's Why We Mis-behave	Alexander Fogarty	Edith Lois, Urana Clarke	Cape Cod Follies	1929
Then	Noel Coward	Noel Coward	Tonight at 8:30 (Shadow Play)	1936
Then I'll Have Time for You	Ray Henderson	B. G. DeSylva, Lew Brown	Follow Thru	1929
There Ain't No Color Line Around the Rainbow	Irving Caesar	Gerald Marks, Sammy Lerner	My Dear Public	1943
There Are Yanks (From the Banks of the Wabash)	Vernon Duke	Howard Dietz	Jackpot	1944
There But for You, Go I	Frederick Loewe	Alan Jay Lerner	Brigadoon	1947
There Can Only Be Only One for Me	Sigmund Romberg	Irving Caesar	Nina Rosa	1930
There Had to Be the Waltz	Frederick Loewe	Earle Crooker	Great Lady	1938
There He Goes, Phileas Fogg	Cole Porter	Cole Porter	Around the World	1946
There I Go Dreaming Again	Ray Henderson	Lew Brown	Hotcha	1932
There Is a Garden in Loveland	Karl Hajos (based on Tchaikovsky)	Harry B. Smith	Natja	1925
There Is Nothin' Like a Dame	Richard Rodgers	Oscar Hammer-stein II	South Pacific	1949
There Is Only One Paris for That	Marguerite Monnot	Julian More, Daniel Heneker, Monte Norman	Irma La Douce	1960
There Must Be Someone For Me	Cole Porter	Cole Porter	Mexican Hayride	1944
There Must Be Some-thin' Better Than Love	Morton Gould	Dorothy Fields	Arms and the Girl	1950
There Once Was a Man	Richard Adler, Jerry Ross		The Pajama Game	1954
There Will Be a Girl	Harry Revel	Mack Gordon	Smiling Faces	1932
There'll Be Love, Life and Laughter	Kurt Weill	Ira Gershwin	The Firebrand of Florence	1945
There's a Boat Dat's Leavin' Soon for New York	George Gershwin	Ira Gershwin	Porgy and Bess	1935
There's a Building Going Up	Sammy Fain	Paul Webster, Ray Golden	Alive and Kicking	1950
There's a Great Day Coming Manana	Burton Lane	E. Y. Harburg	Hold On to Your Hats	1940
There's a Hill Beyond a Hill	Jerome Kern	Oscar Hammer-stein II	Music in the Air	1932
There's a Man in My Life	Thomas (Fats) Waller	George Marion, Jr.	Early to Bed	1943

TITLE	COMPOSER	LYRICIST	SHOW	YEAR
There's a Small Hotel	Richard Rodgers	Lorenz Hart	On Your Toes	1936
There's Always Something Fishy About the French	Noel Coward	Noel Coward	Conversation Piece	1934
There's Got to Be a Wedding	Jimmy Van Heusen	Eddie DeLange	Swingin' the Dream	1939
There's Music in a Kiss	Al Sherman, Al Lewis, Abner Silver		Earl Carroll's Sketch Book	1935
There's No Business Like Show Business	Irving Berlin	Irving Berlin	Annie Get Your Gun	1946
There's No Getting Away From You	Jimmy McHugh	Harold Adamson	As the Girls Go	1948
There's No Holding Me	Arthur Schwartz	Ira Gershwin	Park Avenue	1946
There's No Man Like a Snow Man	Victor Young	Edward Heyman	Pardon Our French	1950
There's No Place Like the Country	Arthur Jones	Gen Genovese	Buttrio Square	1952
There's Nothing Like a Model "T"	Jule Styne	Sammy Cahn	High Button Shoes	1947
There's Nothing New in Old New York	Harry Akst	Benny Davis	Artists and Models	1927
There's Nothing the Matter With Me	Ray Henderson	Lew Brown	Hotcha	1932
There's Nothing Wrong With a Kiss	Oscar Levant	Irving Caesar, Graham John	Ripples	1930
There's Nowhere to Go But Up	Kurt Weill	Maxwell Anderson	Knickerbocker Holiday	1938
There's So Much More	Richard Rodgers	Lorenz Hart	America's Sweetheart	1931
There's Something Spanish in Your Eyes	Cliff Friend	George White	George White's Scandals	1929
These Charming People	George Gershwin	Ira Gershwin	Tip-Toes	1925
They Call the Wind Maria	Frederick Loewe	Alan Jay Lerner	Paint Your Wagon	1951
They Fall in Love	George M. Cohan	George M. Cohan	Billie	1928
They Like Ike	Irving Berlin	Irving Berlin	Call Me Madam	1950
They Say It's Wonderful	Irving Berlin	Irving Berlin	Annie Get Your Gun	1946
They Were You	Harvey Schmidt	Tom Jones	The Fantasticks	1960
They Won't Know Me	Harold Rome	Harold Rome	Wish You Were Here	1952
Thief in the Night	Arthur Schwartz	Howard Dietz	At Home Abroad	1935
Things Are Gonna Hum This Summer	Walter Kent	Kim Gannon	Seventeen	1951
Things That Lovers Say, The	George Lessner	Miriam Battista, Russell Maloney	Sleepy Hollow	1948
Things That Were Made for Love, The	Peter De Rose	Charles Tobias, Irving Kahal	Pleasure Bound	1929

TITLE	COMPOSER	LYRICIST	SHOW	YEAR
Think How Many People Never Find Love	Jule Styne	Bob Hilliard	Hazel Flagg	1953
Thinking of You	Clarence Gaskill	Clarence Gaskill	Earl Carroll's Vanities	1925
Thinking of You	Con Conrad	Gus Kahn	Kitty's Kisses	1926
Thinking of You	Harry Ruby	Bert Kalmar	The Five O'Clock Girl	1927
This Can't Be Love	Richard Rodgers	Lorenz Hart	The Boys from Syracuse	1938
This Funny World	Richard Rodgers	Lorenz Hart	Betsy	1926
This Had Better Be Love	Jay Gorney	Walter & Jean Kerr	Touch and Go	1949
This Is All Very New to Me	Albert Hague	Arnold B. Horwitt	Plain and Fancy	1955
This Is It	Arthur Schwartz	Dorothy Fields	Stars in Your Eyes	1939
This Is My Beloved	Harry Revel	Arnold B. Horwitt	Are You With It?	1945
This Is My Holiday	Frederick Loewe	Alan Jay Lerner	The Day Before Spring	1945
This Is New	Kurt Weill	Ira Gershwin	Lady in the Dark	1941
This Is Not a Song	Vernon Duke	E. Y. Harburg, E. Hartman	Ziegfeld Follies	1934
This Is Our Private Love Song	Irving Caesar	Sammy Lerner	My Dear Public	1943
This Is So Nice	Thomas (Fats) Waller	George Marion, Jr.	Early to Bed	1943
This Is the Army, Mr. Jones	Irving Berlin	Irving Berlin	This Is the Army	1942
This Is the Life	Kurt Weill	Alan Jay Lerner	Love Life	1948
This Is the Missus	Ray Henderson	Lew Brown	George White's Scandals	1931
This Is What I Call Love	Harold Karr	Matt Dubey	Happy Hunting	1956
This Is Where I Came In	Vernon Duke	Ted Fetter	The Lady Comes Across	1942
This Much I Know	Harold Karr	Matt Dubey	Happy Hunting	1956
This Nearly Was Mine	Richard Rodgers	Oscar Hammerstein II	South Pacific	1949
Those Eyes So Tender	Jean Gilbert	Harry Graham	Katja	1926
Those Wonderful Friends	George M. Cohan	George M. Cohan	Billie	1928
Thou Swell	Richard Rodgers	Lorenz Hart	A Connecticut Yankee	1927
Thoughtless	Jerry Livingston	Mack David	Bright Lights	1943
Thousand Islands Song	Bob Hilliard	Carl Sigman	Angel in the Wings	1947
Thousands of Miles	Kurt Weill	Maxwell Anderson	Lost in the Stars	1949
Three "B's." The	Hugh Martin	Ralph Blane	Best Foot Forward	1941
Three Little Maids	Max Ewing	Agnes Morgan	Grand Street Follies	1927
Three Loves	Robert Wright, George Forrest (based on Grieg)		Song of Norway	1944
Three Musketeers	Richard Rodgers	Lorenz Hart	Garrick Gaieties	1925
Three Times a Day	George Gershwin	B. G. DeSylva, Ira Gershwin	Tell Me More	1925
Three White Feathers	Noel Coward	Noel Coward	Set to Music	1939
Thrill Is Gone, The	Ray Henderson	Lew Brown	George White's Scandals	1931

TITLE	COMPOSER	LYRICIST	SHOW	YEAR
Thrill Me	Lewis E. Gensler	E. Y. Harburg	Ballyhoo	1932
Through the Night	Frank Grey	Earle Crooker, McElbert Moore	Happy	1927
Through the Years	Vincent Youmans	Edward Heyman	Through the Years	1932
Ticketyboo	Ann Ronell	Ann Ronell	Count Me In	1942
Tie Your Cares to a Melody	Joseph Meyer	Billy Moll	Jonica	1930
Till I Meet You	H. Maurice Jacquet	William Brady, Alonzo Price	The Silver Swan	1929
Till the Real Thing Comes Along	Alberta Nichols	Mann Holiner, Sammy Cahn	Rhapsody in Black	1931
Till There Was You	Meredith Willson	Meredith Willson	The Music Man	1957
Till Tomorrow	Jerry Bock	Sheldon Harnick	Fiorello!	1959
Tilly of Longacre Square	James F. Hanley	Ballard Mac-Donald	Gay Paree	1926
Time for Jukin'	Walter Kent	Lew Brown, Charles Tobias	Yokel Boy	1939
Time of Your Life	William Provost	Peter K. Smith	Crazy With the Heat	1941
Time on My Hands	Vincent Youmans	Harold Adamson, Mack Gordon	Smiles	1930
Time to Go	Jesse Greer	Stanley Adams	Shady Lady	1933
Time to Sing, The	Harry Ruby	Bert Kalmar	High Kickers	1941
Times Square Dance	Sammy Fain	Jack Yellen	Boys and Girls Together	1940
Ting-A-Ling, The Bells'll Ring	Irving Berlin	Irving Berlin	The Cocoanuts	1925
Tinkle! Tinkle!	Milton Ager	Jack Yellen	John Murray Anderson's Almanac	1929
Tiny Room	Hugh Martin	Hugh Martin	Look Ma, I'm Dancin'	1948
Tired of Love	Del Cleveland	Ted Fetter	The Second Little Show	1930
'Tis Love	Sigmund Romberg	Harry B. Smith	The Love Call	1927
Titina	Léo Daniderff	Bertal-Maubon, E. Ronn	Puzzles	1925
T'morra, T'morra	Harold Arlen	E. Y. Harburg	Bloomer Girl	1944
To Heaven on the Bronx Express	George M. Cohan	George M. Cohan	The Merry Malones	1927
To Keep My Love Alive	Richard Rodgers	Lorenz Hart	A Connecticut Yankee (revival)	1943
To Know You Is to Love You	Ray Henderson	B. G. DeSylva, Lew Brown	Hold Everything!	1928
To Love Is to Live	Johann Strauss, Jr.	Clare Kummer	Three Waltzes	1937
To Love You and to Lose You	Kurt Weill	Edward Heyman	Johnny Johnson	1936
To My Wife	Harold Rome	Harold Rome	Fanny	1954
To Prove My Love	Maria Grever	Raymond Leveen	Viva O'Brien	1941
To the Beat of My Heart	Senia Pokrass	E. Y. Harburg	Ziegfeld Follies	1934

TITLE	COMPOSER	LYRICIST	SHOW	YEAR
To This We're Come	Gian-Carlo Menotti	Gian-Carlo Menotti	The Consul	1950
Toddy's the Drink for Me	(Traditional Air)	Eleanor & Herbert Farjeon	The Two Bouquets	1938
Together Wherever We Go	Jule Styne	Stephen Sondheim	Gypsy	1959
Tokay	Noel Coward	Noel Coward	Bitter Sweet	1929
Tom, Dick or Harry	Cole Porter	Cole Porter	Kiss Me, Kate	1948
Tommy, Tommy	Jerry Bock	Sheldon Harnick	Tenderloin	1960
To-morrow	Cole Porter	Cole Porter	Leave It To Me	1938
Tomorrow Mountain	Duke Ellington	John Latouche	Beggar's Holiday	1946
Tonight	Richard Whiting	Oscar Hammerstein II	Free for All	1931
Tonight	Leonard Bernstein	Stephen Sondheim	West Side Story	1957
Tonight May Never Come Again	Sigmund Romberg	Irving Caesar	Melody	1933
Tonight or Never	Ray Klages, Jack Meskill, Vincent Rose		Earl Carroll's Vanities	1931
Tonight's the Night	Alex Fogarty	June Sillman	New Faces	1936
Too Close for Comfort	Jerry Bock, George Weiss, Larry Holofcener		Mr. Wonderful	1956
Too Darn Hot	Cole Porter	Cole Porter	Kiss Me, Kate	1948
Too Good for the Average Man	Richard Rodgers	Lorenz Hart	On Your Toes	1936
Too Good to Be True	Ray Henderson	B. G. DeSylva, Lew Brown	Hold Everything	1928
Too Many Rings Around Rosie	Vincent Youmans	Irving Caesar	No, No, Nanette	1925
Too Much Work	Richard Addinsell	Clemence Dane	Come of Age	1934
Too, Too Divine	Vernon Duke	E. Y. Harburg	Garrick Gaieties	1930
Tooth and Claw	Duke Ellington	John Latouche	Beggar's Holiday	1946
Top Banana	Johnny Mercer	Johnny Mercer	Top Banana	1951
Torch Parade	Ray Henderson	Ted Koehler	Say When	1934
Torch Song, The	Harry Warren	Mort Dixon, Joe Young	The Laugh Parade	1931
Touch of Your Hand, The	Jerome Kern	Otto Harbach	Roberta	1933
Touched in the Head	Michael H. Cleary	Arthur Swanstrom	Sea Legs	1937
Toujours Gai	George Kleinsinger	Joe Darion	Shinbone Alley	1957
Trailing a Shooting Star	Albert Sirmay, Arthur Schwartz	Arthur Swanstrom	Princess Charming	1930
Train Time	Baldwin Bergersen	June Sillman	Who's Who	1938
Travel the Road of Love	Tommy Wolf	Fran Landesman	The Nervous Set	1959
Treat a Woman Like a Drum	Emmerich Kalman	George Marion, Jr.	Marinka	1945
Treat Me Rough	George Gershwin	Ira Gershwin	Girl Crazy	1930
Tree in the Park, A	Richard Rodgers	Lorenz Hart	Peggy-Ann	1926
Triplets	Arthur Schwartz	Howard Dietz	Between the Devil	1937

TITLE	COMPOSER	LYRICIST	SHOW	YEAR
Tripping the Light Fantastic	Harold Rome	Harold Rome	Wish You Were Here	1952
Trottin' to the Fair	Ralph Blane	Ralph Blane	Three Wishes for Jamie	1952
Trouble Man	Kurt Weill	Maxwell Anderson	Lost in the Stars	1949
Trouble With Women, The	Kurt Weill	Ogden Nash	One Touch of Venus	1943
True Blue	Richard Myers	Leo Robin	Hello, Yourself	1928
True Hearts	Sigmund Romberg	Arthur Wimperis	Louie the 14th	1925
True Love and a Ring	Percy Wenrich	Raymond Peck	Castles in the Air	1926
Try Her Out at Dances	Sigmund Romberg	Oscar Hammerstein II	The New Moon	1928
Try to Forget	Jerome Kern	Otto Harbach	The Cat and the Fiddle	1931
Try to Learn to Love	Noel Coward	Noel Coward	This Year of Grace	1928
Try to Love Me Just As I Am	Jule Styne	Betty Comden, Adolph Green	Say, Darling	1958
Try to Remember	Harvey Schmidt	Tom Jones	The Fantasticks	1960
Tschaikowsky	Kurt Weill	Ira Gershwin	Lady in the Dark	1941
Turn On the Charm	Emmerich Kalman	George Marion, Jr.	Marinka	1945
Turn Out the Light	Nacio Brown, Richard Whiting	B. G. DeSylva	Take a Chance	1932
Turn to Me	Joseph Meyer	Edward Eliscu	Lady Fingers	1929
'Twas a Kiss in the Moonlight	Stephen Jones	Con Conrad, Henry Creamer	Keep Shufflin'	1928
'Twas Not So Long Ago	Jerome Kern	Oscar Hammerstein II	Sweet Adeline	1929
Tweet Tweet	Ray Henderson	B. G. DeSylva, Lew Brown	George White's Scandals	1926
Twelve O'Clock and All Is Well	Philip Charig	Dan Shapiro, Milton Pascal	Follow the Girls	1944
Twice Told Tales	Milton Susskind	Paul Porter, Benjamin H. Burt	Florida Girl	1925
Twilight	Morris Hamilton	Grace Henry	Earl Carroll's Vanities	1926
Twilight Voices	Sigmund Romberg	Harry B. Smith	Princess Flavia	1925
Twinkle in Your Eye, A	Richard Rodgers	Lorenz Hart	I Married an Angel	1938
Twinkle, Twinkle	Harry Archer	Harlan Thompson	Twinkle, Twinkle	1926
Twins	Earl Robinson	Waldo Salt	Sandhog	1954
Two Boys	Ray Henderson	B. G. DeSylva, Lew Brown	Three Cheers	1928
Two By Four	Joseph Meyer	Irving Caesar	Sweetheart Time	1926
Two-Faced Woman	Arthur Schwartz	Howard Dietz	Flying Colors	1932
Two Faces in the Dark	Albert Hague	Dorothy Fields	Redhead	1959
Two Feet in Two Four Time	Harold Arlen	Irving Caesar	George White's Music Hall Varieties	1932
Two Get Together	Will Irwin	Norman Zeno	Fools Rush In	1934
Two in a Taxi	Jimmy McHugh	Howard Dietz	Keep Off the Grass	1940

TITLE	COMPOSER	LYRICIST	SHOW	YEAR
Two Ladies in de Shade of de Banana Tree	Harold Arlen	Truman Capote, Harold Arlen	House of Flowers	1954
Two Little Babes in the Wood	Cole Porter	Cole Porter	Paris	1928
Two Little Bluebirds	Jerome Kern	Otto Harbach, Oscar Hammerstein II	Sunny	1925
Two Little Ships	Armand Vecsey	P. G. Wodehouse	The Nightingale	1927
Two Little Stars	Frank Harling	Laurence Stallings	Deep River	1926
Two Lost Souls	Richard Adler, Jerry Ross		Damn Yankees	1955
Two Loving Arms	Joseph Meyer, Philip Charig	Leo Robin	Just Fancy	1927
Two of Us, The	George M. Cohan	George M. Cohan	Billie	1928
Two Perfect Lovers	Haydn Wood, Joseph Tunbridge, Jack Waller	Dion Titheradge	Artists and Models	1930
Uh-huh, Oh, Yeah!	Jerry Bock	Sheldon Harnick	The Body Beautiful	1958
Uncle Sam's Lullaby	Sam Stept	Lew Brown, Charles Tobias	Yokel Boy	1939
Under the Midsummer Moon	Shep Camp	Harry B. Smith	Half a Widow	1927
Union Label	Jay Gorney	Henry Myers, Edward Eliscu	Meet the People	1940
Union Square	George Gershwin	Ira Gershwin	Let 'Em Eat Cake	1933
Unnecessary Town	Gene dePaul	Johnny Mercer	Li'l Abner	1956
Until You Get Somebody Else	Walter Donaldson	Gus Kahn	Whoopee	1928
Up Among the Chimney Pots	Kay Swift	Paul James	9:15 Revue	1930
Up in the Clouds	Harry Ruby	Bert Kalmar	The Five O'Clock Girl	1927
Ups-A-Daisy	Lewis E. Gensler	Robert A. Simon	Ups-A-Daisy	1928
Ups and Downs	Karl Hajos (based on Tchaikovsky)	Harry B. Smith	Natja	1925
Us on a Bus	Vee Lawnhurst	Tot Seymour	Summer Wives	1936
Use Your Imagination	Cole Porter	Cole Porter	Out of This World	1950
Valencia	Jose Padilla	Clifford Grey	The Great Temptations	1926
Varsity Drag, The	Ray Henderson	B. G. DeSylva, Lew Brown	Good News	1927
Venetian Skies	Milton Susskind	Paul Porter, Benjamin H. Burt	Florida Girl	1925
Venetian Wedding Moon	Alfred Goodman, Maury Rubens, J. Fred Coots	Clifford Grey	Artists and Models	1925
Very Necessary You, The	Jimmy Van Heusen	Johnny Burke	Carnival in Flanders	1953
Very Next Man, The	Jerry Bock	Sheldon Harnick	Fiorello!	1959

TITLE	COMPOSER	LYRICIST	SHOW	YEAR
Very Special Day, A	Richard Rodgers	Oscar Hammerstein II	Me and Juliet	1953
Violins from Nowhere	Sammy Fain	Herb Magidson	Michael Todd's Peep Show	1950
Virginia	Arthur Schwartz	Albert Stillman	Virginia	1937
Visit Panama	Cole Porter	Cole Porter	Panama Hattie	1940
Vivienne	Cole Porter	Cole Porter	Paris	1928
Vodka	George Gershwin, Herbert Stothart	Otto Harbach, Oscar Hammerstein II	Song of the Flame	1925
Waddya Say—We Steal Away	James Hanley	Eddie Dowling	Honeymoon Lane	1926
Wait and See	Sigmund Romberg	Harry B. Smith	Cherry Blossoms	1927
Wait for the Happy Ending	Milton Ager	Jack Yellen	John Murray Anderson's Almanac	1929
Wait for Tomorrow	Bronislaw Kaper (based on Chopin)	John Latouche	Polonaise	1945
Wait Till You See Her	Richard Rodgers	Lorenz Hart	By Jupiter	1942
Waitin' for My Dearie	Frederick Loewe	Alan Jay Lerner	Brigadoon	1947
Waiting	Harry Ruby	Bert Kalmar	Animal Crackers	1928
Wake Up and Dream	Cole Porter	Cole Porter	Wake Up and Dream	1929
Wake Up, Sleepy Moon	Max Rich	Jack Scholl	Keep Moving	1934
Walk Sweet	Harry Warren	Jerome Lawrence, Robert E. Lee	Shangri-La	1956
Walkin' on Air	Harry Revel	Mack Gordon	Fast and Furious	1931
Walking Away Whistling	Frank Loesser	Frank Loesser	Greenwillow	1960
Walking Home with Josie	Jerome Kern	Anne Caldwell	The City Chap	1925
Waltz Divine	Thomas (Fats) Waller, Harry Brooks	Andy Razaf	Hot Chocolates	1929
Waltz Down the Aisle	Cole Porter	Cole Porter	Anything Goes	1934
Waltz I Heard in a Dream, The	Kay Swift	Kay Swift	Paris '90	1952
Waltz of Love, The	Richard Fall	Irving Caesar	White Horse Inn	1936
Waltz Was Born in Vienna, A	Frederick Loewe	Earle Crooker	The Illustrators' Show	1936
Waltzing in the Moonlight	Harry Ruby	Bert Kalmar	High Kickers	1941
Wander Away	Herbert Stothart	Otto Harbach, Oscar Hammerstein II	Song of the Flame	1925
Wandering in Dreamland	Martin Broones, Ballard MacDonald		Rufus LeMaire's Affairs	1927
Wand'rin' Star	Frederick Loewe	Alan Jay Lerner	Paint Your Wagon	1951
Wand'ring Heart	Arthur Schwartz	Howard Dietz	Revenge With Music	1934
Wanna Be Bad	Duke Ellington	John Latouche	Beggar's Holiday	1946
Wanting You	Will Morrissey	Edmund Joseph	Polly of Hollywood	1927

TITLE	COMPOSER	LYRICIST	SHOW	YEAR
Wanting You	Sigmund Romberg	Oscar Hammerstein II	The New Moon	1928
Warm All Over	Frank Loesser	Frank Loesser	The Most Happy Fella	1956
Warm As the Autumn Light	Douglas Moore	John Latouche	The Ballad of Baby Doe	1958
Was I?	Chick Endor	Charlie Farrell	Ziegfeld Follies	1931
Washington Square Dance	Irving Berlin	Irving Berlin	Call Me Madam	1950
Wasn't It Beautiful While It Lasted?	Ray Henderson	Lew Brown, B. G. DeSylva	Flying High	1930
Wasn't It Nice?	Rudolf Friml	Irving Caesar	No Foolin'	1926
Watching the Clouds Roll By	Harry Ruby	Bert Kalmar	Animal Crackers	1928
Way Back in 1939 A.D.	Hoagy Carmichael	Johnny Mercer	Walk With Music	1940
Way Down Blues	George Kleinsinger	Joe Darion	Shinbone Alley	1957
Way It Might Have Been, The	Hugh Martin	Hugh Martin	Look Ma, I'm Dancin'	1948
Way Out in Rainbow Land	Alma Sanders	Monte Carlo	Oh! Oh! Nurse	1925
Way Out West	Richard Rodgers	Lorenz Hart	Babes in Arms	1937
Way to Your Heart, The	Gene Lockhart	Gene Lockhart	Bunk of 1926	1926
We Belong Together	Jerome Kern	Oscar Hammerstein II	Music in the Air	1932
We Can Live on Love	Jimmy McHugh	Al Dubin	Streets of Paris	1939
We Have Sandwiches*	Jay Gorney	Henry Myers	Meet the People	1940
We Kiss in a Shadow	Richard Rodgers	Oscar Hammerstein II	The King and I	1951
We Open in Venice	Cole Porter	Cole Porter	Kiss Me, Kate	1948
We Said We Wouldn't Look Back	Julian Slade	Dorothy Reynolds, Julian Slade	Salad Days	1958
We Should Care	Irving Berlin	Irving Berlin	The Cocoanuts	1925
We Two	Emmerich Kalman, Herbert Stothart	Otto Harbach, Oscar Hammerstein II	Golden Dawn	1927
We Two Shall Meet Again	Emmerich Kalman	Harry B. Smith	The Circus Princess	1927
We Were a Wow	Harry Archer	Harlan Thompson	Merry-Merry	1925
We Were Dancing	Noel Coward	Noel Coward	Tonight at 8:30 (We Were Dancing)	1936
We Won't Charleston	Harry Ruby	Bert Kalmar	The Ramblers	1926
We Won't Let It Happen Here	Teddy Hall	Don George	Hellzapoppin'	1938
Wear Your Sunday Smile	Charles Rosoff	Leo Robin	Judy	1927
Wee Toy	Milton Susskind	Paul Porter, Benjamin H. Burt	Florida Girl	1925

*Dropped from New York production

TITLE	COMPOSER	LYRICIST	SHOW	YEAR
Weep No More	Gordon Jenkins	Tom Adair	Along Fifth Avenue	1949
Weep No More, My Baby	Johnny Green	Edward Heyman	Murder at the Vanities	1933
Welcome Home	Harold Rome	Harold Rome	Fanny	1954
We'll Be the Same	Richard Rodgers	Lorenz Hart	America's Sweetheart	1931
We'll Build a Brand New Bamboo Bungalow	A. Baldwin Sloane	Harry Cort, George E. Stoddard	China Rose	1925
We'll Get Along	Muriel Pollock	Max & Nathaniel Lief	Pleasure Bound	1929
We'll Go Away Together	Kurt Weill	Langston Hughes	Street Scene	1947
We'll Have a Kingdom	Rudolf Friml	Otto Harbach, Oscar Hammerstein II	The Wild Rose	1926
We'll Have a New Home in the Mornin'	Willard Robison	J. Russel Robinson, Gene Buck	Take the Air	1927
We'll Have Our Good Days	Harry Tierney	Joseph McCarthy	Cross My Heart	1928
We'll Just Be Two Commuters	Harry Archer	Walter O'Keefe	Just a Minute	1928
Well, Did You Evah?*	Cole Porter	Cole Porter	DuBarry Was a Lady	1939
Wells Fargo Wagon	Meredith Willson	Meredith Willson	The Music Man	1957
Wendy	Jule Styne	Betty Comden, Adolph Green	Peter Pan	1954
We're Having a Baby	Vernon Duke	Harold Adamson	Banjo Eyes	1941
Were Thine That Special Face	Cole Porter	Cole Porter	Kiss Me, Kate	1948
We're Not Children	Jay Livingston	Ray Evans	Oh Captain!	1958
West Point Song	Sigmund Romberg	P. G. Wodehouse	Rosalie	1928
West Wind	Kurt Weill	Ogden Nash	One Touch of Venus	1943
What a Case I've Got on You	Arthur Schwartz	Howard Dietz	The Second Little Show	1930
What a Day!	Abraham Ellstein	Walter Bullock	Great to Be Alive	1950
What a Dummy Love Has Made of Me	Will Irwin	Norman Zeno	The Show Is On	1936
What a Girl	Werner Janssen	Mann Holiner, J. Keirn Brennan	Boom-Boom	1929
What a Life	Harry Archer	Harlan Thompson	Merry-Merry	1925
What a Wonderful World	Arthur Schwartz	Howard Dietz	At Home Abroad	1935
What a World This Would Be	Ray Henderson	B. G. DeSylva, Lew Brown	George White's Scandals	1925
What Are We Here For?	George Gershwin	Ira Gershwin	Treasure Girl	1928
What Are You Going to Do About Love?	Dave Stamper	Fred Herendeen	Orchids Preferred	1937
What Can Be Sweeter?	Philip Charig	Irving Caesar	Polly	1929
What Can You Say in a Love Song?	Harold Arlen	E. Y. Harburg, Ira Gershwin	Life Begins at 8:40	1934

*Also in film "High Society"

TITLE	COMPOSER	LYRICIST	SHOW	YEAR
What Chance Have I With Love?	Irving Berlin	Irving Berlin	Louisiana Purchase	1940
What Could I Do?	Werner Janssen	Mann Holiner, J. Keirn Brennan	Boom-Boom	1929
What Did Della Wear?	Arthur Schwartz	Agnes Morgan, Albert Carroll	Grand Street Follies	1929
What Do I Care?	Sigmund Romberg	Harry B. Smith	Princess Flavia	1925
What Do I Have to Do to Get My Picture in the Paper?*	Irving Berlin	Irving Berlin	Miss Liberty	1949
What Do the Simple Folk Do?	Frederick Loewe	Alan Jay Lerner	Camelot	1960
What Do We Care	Harold Arlen	Jack Yellen	You Said It	1931
What Do You Think I Am?	Hugh Martin	Ralph Blane	Best Foot Forward	1941
What Does He Look Like?	Irving Berlin	Irving Berlin	This Is the Army	1942
What D'Ya Say?	Jesse Greer	Raymond Klages	The Circus Princess	1927
What D'Ya Say?	Ray Henderson	B. G. DeSylva, Lew Brown	George White's Scandals	1928
What Every Woman Knows	William Roy	William Roy	Maggie	1953
What Good Does It Do?	Harold Arlen	E. Y. Harburg	Jamaica	1957
What Good Is Love	Harold Rome	Harold Rome	Pins and Needles	1937
What Good Would the Moon Be?	Kurt Weill	Langston Hughes	Street Scene	1947
What Happened?	Vernon Duke	Howard Dietz	Jackpot	1944
What I Mean to Say	Moose Charlap	Norman Gimbel	Whoop-Up	1958
What I Was Warned About	Hugh Martin	Hugh Martin	Make a Wish	1951
What Is a Man?	Richard Rodgers	Lorenz Hart	Pal Joey	1940
What Is Love?	Howard Blankman	Howard Blankman	By Hex	1956
What Is That Tune?	Cole Porter	Cole Porter	You Never Know	1938
What Is the Good?	Lew Kessler	Clifford Grey	Ned Wayburn's Gambols	1929
What Is There to Say?	Vernon Duke	E. Y. Harburg	Ziegfeld Follies	1934
What Is This Thing Called Love?	Cole Porter	Cole Porter	Wake Up and Dream	1929
What Shall I Do?	Cole Porter	Cole Porter	You Never Know	1938
What Takes My Fancy	Cy Coleman	Carolyn Leigh	Wildcat	1960
What Will It Be?	Marc Blitzstein	Marc Blitzstein	Regina	1949
What Would I Care?	Harry Ruby	Bert Kalmar	Top Speed	1929
Whatever Lola Wants (Lola Gets)	Richard Adler, Jerry Ross		Damn Yankees	1955
What'll They Think of Next?	Hoagy Carmichael	Johnny Mercer	Walk With Music	1940

*Dropped from New York production

TITLE	COMPOSER	LYRICIST	SHOW	YEAR
What's a Girl Supposed to Do	Robert Stolz	Robert Sour	Mr. Strauss Goes to Boston	1945
What's in a Name?	John Mundy	Edward Eager	The Liar	1950
What's Keeping My Prince Charming?	Alberta Nichols	Mann Holiner	Rhapsody in Black	1931
What's My Fatal Charm?	Frederico Valerio	Elizabeth Miele	Hit the Trail	1954
What's New at the Zoo?	Jule Styne	Betty Comden, Adolph Green	Do Re Mi	1960
What's the Reason?	Maury Rubens	Harold Atteridge	Greenwich Village Follies	1928
What's the Use?	Leonard Bernstein	Richard Wilbur	Candide	1956
What's the Use of Talking	Richard Rodgers	Lorenz Hart	Garrick Gaieties	1926
What's the Use of Wond'rin'	Richard Rodgers	Oscar Hammerstein II	Carousel	1945
When	Cliff Friend	Lew Brown	Piggy	1927
When a Fellow Meets a Flapper on Broadway	Philip Charig	Irving Caesar	Polly	1929
When Did I Fall in Love?	Jerry Bock	Sheldon Harnick	Fiorello!	1959
When Do We Dance?	George Gershwin	Ira Gershwin	Tip-Toes	1925
When Does This Feeling Go Away?	Hugh Martin	Hugh Martin	Make a Wish	1951
When Evening Shadows Fall	Jay Gorney, Irving Caesar, Owen Murphy		Greenwich Village Follies	1925
When I Fall in Love	Albert Selden	Albert Selden	Small Wonder	1948
When I Go on the Stage	Richard Rodgers	Lorenz Hart	She's My Baby	1928
When I Make a Million for You	Lucien Denni	Helena Evans	Happy Go Lucky	1926
When I March with April in May	Clarence Williams, Spencer Williams		Bottomland	1927
When I Walk with You	Duke Ellington	John Latouche	Beggar's Holiday	1946
When I Was a Little Cuckoo	Cole Porter	Cole Porter	The Seven Lively Arts	1944
When I'm in a Quiet Mood	David Martin	Langston Hughes	Simply Heavenly	1957
When I'm Not Near the Girl I Love	Burton Lane	E. Y. Harburg	Finian's Rainbow	1947
When Love Beckoned (in 52nd Street)	Cole Porter	Cole Porter	DuBarry Was a Lady	1939
When Love Comes Swingin' Along	Ray Henderson	Ted Koehler	Say When	1934
When Love Comes Your Way	Cole Porter	Cole Porter	Jubilee	1935
When Love Is Near	Will Ortman	Gus Kahn, Raymond B. Egan	Holka-Polka	1925
When Love's in the Air	Jean Gilbert	Harry Graham	Katja	1926
When McGregor Sings Off Key	Sammy Fain	Charles Tobias	Hellzapoppin'	1938

TITLE	COMPOSER	LYRICIST	SHOW	YEAR
When My Baby Goes to Town	Cole Porter	Cole Porter	Something for the Boys	1943
When Romance Is Gone	Percy Wenrich	Raymond Peck	Castles in the Air	1926
When Someone You Love Loves You	Charles Gaynor	Charles Gaynor	Lend an Ear	1948
When the Bo-Tree Blossoms Again	Jerome Kern	Bert Kalmar, Harry Ruby	Lucky	1927
When the Boys Come Home	Harold Arlen	E. Y. Harburg	Bloomer Girl	1944
When the Children Are Asleep	Richard Rodgers	Oscar Hammerstein II	Carousel	1945
When the Idle Poor Become the Idle Rich	Burton Lane	E. Y. Harburg	Finian's Rainbow	1947
When the Only One Meets the Only One	Percy Wenrich	Raymond Peck	Castles in the Air	1926
When the Sea Is All Around Us	David Baker	Sheldon Harnick	Shoestring Revue	1955
When the Spring Is in the Air	Jerome Kern	Oscar Hammerstein II	Music in the Air	1932
When the Sun Kissed the Rose Goodbye	Gitz Rice	Paul Porter	Nic Nax of 1926	1926
When the Tall Man Talks	Moose Charlap	Norman Gimbel	Whoop-Up	1958
When We Meet Again	Harold Rome	Harold Rome	Call Me Mister	1946
When We Were Young	Jerome Moross	John Latouche	The Golden Apple	1954
When We're in Love	Richard Lewine	Ted Fetter	Naughty-Naught (revival)	1946
When You Are Close to Me	Alma Sanders	Monte Carlo	Louisiana Lady	1947
When You Live on an Island	Vernon Duke	Howard Dietz	Sadie Thompson	1944
When You Look in Your Looking Glass	Paul Mann, Stephen Weiss	Sam Lewis	Hellzapoppin'	1938
When You Love Only One	Arthur Schwartz	Howard Dietz	Revenge with Music	1934
When You Smile	Tom Johnstone	Phil Cook	When You Smile	1925
When You Walk in the Room	Sigmund Romberg	Dorothy Fields	Up in Central Park	1945
When You Were Sweet Sixteen	James Hanley	Eddie Dowling	Sidewalks of New York	1927
When Your Boy Becomes a Man	Richard Whiting	Oscar Hammerstein II	Free For All	1931
When You're Eighteen	Sidney Lippman	Sylvia Dee	Barefoot Boy With Cheek	1947
When Yuba Plays the Rumba on His Tuba	Herman Hupfeld	Herman Hupfeld	The Third Little Show	1931
Where Can I Go from You?	Baldwin Bergersen	S. K. Russell	All In Fun	1940
Where Did the Night Go?	Harold Rome	Harold Rome	Wish You Were Here	1952

TITLE	COMPOSER	LYRICIST	SHOW	YEAR
Where Did We Go? Out	Richard Lewine	Arnold B. Horwitt	The Girls Against The Boys	1959
Where Do I Go from Here?*	Jerry Bock	Sheldon Harnick	Fiorello!	1959
Where Have We Met Before?	Vernon Duke	E. Y. Harburg	Walk a Little Faster	1932
Where Have You Been?	Cole Porter	Cole Porter	The New Yorkers	1930
Where Have You Been All My Life?	Philip Charig, Richard Myers	Leo Robin	Allez-Oop	1927
"Where Has My Hubby Gone" Blues	Vincent Youmans	Irving Caesar	No, No, Nanette	1925
Where Is That Someone for Me?	Victor Young	Stella Unger	Seventh Heaven	1955
Where Is the Life That Late I Led?	Cole Porter	Cole Porter	Kiss Me, Kate	1948
Where, Oh Where	Cole Porter	Cole Porter	Out of This World	1950
Where, Oh Where Can I Find Love?	Jesse Greer	Stanley Adams	Shady Lady	1933
Where or When	Richard Rodgers	Lorenz Hart	Babes In Arms	1937
Where the Morning Glories Twine	Martin Broones	Ballard MacDonald	Rufus LeMaire's Affairs	1927
Where We Can Be in Love	Leon DeCosta	Leon DeCosta	Kosher Kitty Kelly	1925
Where Were You— Where Was I?	George M. Cohan	George M. Cohan	Billie	1928
Where You Are	Philip Charig	Dan Shapiro, Milton Pascal	Follow The Girls	1944
Where You Are	Raymond Scott	Bernard Hanighen	Lute Song	1946
Where You Go I Go	George Gershwin	Ira Gershwin	Pardon My English	1933
Where Your Name Is Carved with Mine	Ray Henderson	B. G. DeSylva, Lew Brown	George White's Scandals	1928
Wherever They Fly the Flag of England	Cole Porter	Cole Porter	Around The World	1946
Wherever You Are	James Hanley	Eddie Dowling	Sidewalks of New York	1927
Where's Charley?	Frank Loesser	Frank Loesser	Where's Charley?	1948
Where's My Happy Ending?	Harry Revel	Mack Gordon, Harold Adamson	Fast and Furious	1931
Where's That Rainbow?	Richard Rodgers	Lorenz Hart	Peggy-Ann	1926
Where's the Boy? Here's the Girl!	George Gershwin	Ira Gershwin	Treasure Girl	1928
Which?	Cole Porter	Cole Porter	Paris	1928
While There's a Song to Sing	Franz Steininger (based on Tchaikovsky)	Forman Brown	Music in My Heart	1947
While You Are Young	Harold Arlen	Jack Yellen	You Said It	1931
While You Love Me	Johann Strauss	Desmond Carter	The Great Waltz	1934

*Dropped from New York production

TITLE	COMPOSER	LYRICIST	SHOW	YEAR
~~Whiling My Time Away~~	~~Henry Sullivan~~	~~Edward Eliscu~~	~~A Little Racketeer~~	~~1932~~
Whip, The	Emmerich Kalman, Herbert Stothart	Otto Harbach, Oscar Hammerstein II	Golden Dawn	1927
Whispering Song	Leon DeCosta	Leon DeCosta	The Blonde Sinner	1926
Whispering Trees	Maury Rubens, J. Fred Coots	Herbert Reynolds	The Merry World	1926
Whistle*	Harry Ruby	Bert Kalmar	The Ramblers	1926
Whistle Away Your Blues	Richard Myers	Leo Robin	Greenwich Village Follies	1925
Whistling for a Kiss	Richard Myers	E. Y. Harburg, Johnny Mercer	Americana	1932
White Horse Inn	Ralph Benatzky	Irving Caesar	White Horse Inn	1936
White Lilacs	Karl Hajos	Harry B. Smith	White Lilacs	1928
White Rose—Red Rose	Raoul Moretti	Clifford Grey	The Great Temptations	1926
White Sails	Vivian Ellis	Irving Caesar	White Horse Inn	1936
White Witch, The	Arthur Siegel	June Carroll	New Faces	1956
Who?	Jerome Kern	Otto Harbach, Oscar Hammerstein II	Sunny	1925
Who Am I?	Leonard Bernstein	Leonard Bernstein	Peter Pan†	1950
Who Am I That You Should Care for Me?**	Vincent Youmans	Gus Kahn	Rainbow	1928
Who Am I Thinking of?	A. Baldwin Sloane	Harry Cort, George E. Stoddard	China Rose	1925
Who Are You?	Dede Meyer	Dede Meyer	She Shall Have Music	1959
Who Cares?	Emmerich Kalman	Harry B. Smith	The Circus Princess	1927
Who Cares?	Haydn Wood, Joseph Tunbridge, Jack Waller	Dion Titheradge	Artists and Models	1930
Who Cares?	George Gershwin	Ira Gershwin	Of Thee I Sing	1931
Who Did? You Did	Harry Ruby	Bert Kalmar	The Five O'Clock Girl	1927
Who Do You Love?	Fred Rich, Hugo Frey, Raymond Klages		Earl Carroll's Vanities	1926
Who Do You Love, I Hope	Irving Berlin	Irving Berlin	Annie Get Your Gun	1946
Who Hit Me?	Charles Gaynor	Charles Gaynor	Lend an Ear	1948
Who Is It Always There?	John Addison	John Cranko	Cranks	1956
Who Knows?	Robert Stolz	Robert Sour	Mr. Strauss Goes to Boston	1945
Who Loves You As I Do?	Joseph Meyer	Irving Caesar	Sweetheart Time	1926
Who Said There Is No Santa Claus?	Sammy Fain	E. Y. Harburg	Flahooley	1951

*Also in "Twinkle, Twinkle"
†1950 version
**Dropped from New York production

TITLE	COMPOSER	LYRICIST	SHOW	YEAR
Who Was Chasing Paul Revere?	Joseph Meyer, James F. Hanley	B. G. DeSylva	Big Boy	1925
Who Would Have Dreamed?	Cole Porter	Cole Porter	Panama Hattie	1940
Whoopsie!	Richard Rodgers	Lorenz Hart	She's My Baby	1928
Who's Been Listening to My Heart?	Harry Ruby	Bert Kalmar	Animal Crackers	1928
Who's Goin' to Get You?	Milton Ager	Jack Yellen	Rain or Shine	1928
Who's Got the Pain?	Richard Adler, Jerry Ross		Damn Yankees	1955
Who's the Boy?	Ray Perkins	Max & Nathaniel Lief	Greenwich Village Follies	1928
Whosis-Whatsis, The	Ray Henderson	B. G. DeSylva, Lew Brown	George White's Scandals	1925
Why?	J. Fred Coots	Arthur Swanstrom, Benny Davis	Sons O' Guns	1929
Why Ain't We Free?	Giuseppe Verdi	Charles Friedman	My Darlin' Aida	1952
Why Be Afraid to Dance?	Harold Rome	Harold Rome	Fanny	1954
Why Can't I?	Richard Rodgers	Lorenz Hart	Spring Is Here	1929
Why Can't It Happen Again?	Michel Emer	Sammy Gallop	All For Love	1949
Why Can't This Night Last Forever?	Frederick Loewe	Earle Crooker	Great Lady	1938
Why Can't You Behave?	Cole Porter	Cole Porter	Kiss Me, Kate	1948
Why Did You Do It?	Arthur Schwartz	Howard Dietz	Between the Devil	1937
Why Did You Kiss My Heart Awake?	Franz Lehar	Edward Eliscu	Frederika	1937
Why Didn't You Tell Me?	Edward Pola, Eddie Brandt		Woof, Woof	1929
Why Do I?	Richard Rodgers	Lorenz Hart	The Girl Friend	1926
Why Do I Love You?	George Gershwin	B. G. DeSylva, Ira Gershwin	Tell Me More	1925
Why Do I Love You?	Jerome Kern	Oscar Hammerstein II	Show Boat	1927
Why Do You Roll Those Eyes?	Philip Charig	Morrie Ryskind	Americana	1926
Why Do You Suppose?	Richard Rodgers	Lorenz Hart	Heads Up	1929
Why Do You Tease Me?	Muriel Pollock	Max & Nathaniel Lief	Pleasure Bound	1929
Why Do You Want to Know Why?	Irving Berlin	Irving Berlin	The Cocoanuts	1925
Why Does It Have to Be You?	James Mundy	John Latouche	The Vamp	1955
Why Don't We?	Maury Rubens, Sam Timberg	Moe Jaffe	Broadway Nights	1929
Why Is Love?	J. Fred Coots	Clifford Grey	June Days	1925

TITLE	COMPOSER	LYRICIST	SHOW	YEAR
Why Must We Always Be Dreaming?	Sigmund Romberg	P. G. Wodehouse	Rosalie	1928
Why, Oh Why?*	Vincent Youmans	Leo Robin, Clifford Grey	Hit the Deck	1927
Why Should We Be Wasting Time?	J. Fred Coots, Maury Rubens	Eddie Conrad, McElbert Moore	A Night in Paris	1926
Why Shouldn't I?	Cole Porter	Cole Porter	Jubilee	1935
Why Was I Born?	Jerome Kern	Oscar Hammerstein II	Sweet Adeline	1929
Why Wouldn't I Do?	Ivor Novello	Desmond Carter	Wake Up and Dream	1929
Wicked Man, A	Lee Pockriss	Anne Croswell	Ernest in Love	1960
Wild About You	Irving Berlin	Irving Berlin	Louisiana Purchase	1940
Wild Rose	Rudolf Friml	Otto Harbach, Oscar Hammerstein II	The Wild Rose	1926
Will You Remember Me?	Kurt Weill	Maxwell Anderson	Knickerbocker Holiday	1938
Will You Remember? Will You Forget?	Lewis E. Gensler	Robert A. Simon, Clifford Grey	Ups-A-Daisy	1928
Willow Song	Douglas Moore	John Latouche	The Ballad of Baby Doe	1958
Willow Tree	Thomas (Fats) Waller	Andy Razaf	Keep Shufflin'	1928
Windflowers	Jerome Moross	John Latouche	The Golden Apple	1954
Wine from My Slipper	Irvin Graham	Irvin Graham	Crazy With the Heat	1941
Wings	Dave Stamper	Gene Buck	Take the Air	1927
Wintergreen for President	George Gershwin	Ira Gershwin	Of Thee I Sing	1931
Wish	Ernest G. Schweikert	Frank Reardon	Rumple	1957
Wish Me Luck	Jay Gorney	Walter & Jean Kerr	Touch and Go	1949
Wish You Were Here	Harold Rome	Harold Rome	Wish You Were Here	1952
Wishbone Song, The	Jack Lawrence, Don Walker		Courtin' Time	1951
With a Family Reputation	Irving Berlin	Irving Berlin	The Cocoanuts	1925
With a Little Bit of Luck	Frederick Loewe	Alan Jay Lerner	My Fair Lady	1956
With a Song in My Heart	Richard Rodgers	Lorenz Hart	Spring Is Here	1929
With a Twist of the Wrist	Irvin Graham	Irvin Graham	Crazy With the Heat	1941
With All My Heart	Johann Strauss	Desmond Carter	The Great Waltz	1934
With My Head in the Clouds	Irving Berlin	Irving Berlin	This Is the Army	1942
Without a Caress	Fred Spielman, Arthur Gershwin	Stanley Adams	A Lady Says Yes	1945
Without a Song	Vincent Youmans	Billy Rose, Edward Eliscu	Great Day	1929
Without Love	Ray Henderson	Lew Brown, B. G. DeSylva	Flying High	1930
Without Love	Cole Porter	Cole Porter	Silk Stockings	1955

*Originally published as "Nothing Could Be Sweeter"

TITLE	COMPOSER	LYRICIST	SHOW	YEAR
Without the One You Love	Werner Janssen	Gitz Rice	Nic Nax of 1926	1926
Without Your Love	Carl Millöcker	Theo Mackeben, Rowland Leigh	The DuBarry	1932
Wolf Time	Sammy Fain	George Marion, Jr.	Toplitzky of Notre Dame	1946
Woman Is a Rascal	Baldwin Bergersen	William Archibald	Carib Song	1945
Woman Is a Sometime Thing, A	George Gershwin	DuBose Heyward	Porgy and Bess	1935
Woman of the Year, The	Ann Ronell	Ann Ronell	Count Me In	1942
Woman Wouldn't Be a Woman, A	George Kleinsinger	Joe Darion	Shinbone Alley	1957
Woman's Prerogative, A	Harold Arlen	Johnny Mercer	St. Louis Woman	1946
Wonderful Guy, A	Richard Rodgers	Oscar Hammerstein II	South Pacific	1949
Wonderful Yesterday	Tom Johnstone	Phil Cook	When You Smile	1925
Wondering Who	Alexander Fogarty	George Fitch	Cape Cod Follies	1929
Won't I Do?	Edward Pola, Eddie Brandt		Woof, Woof	1929
Won't You Marry Me?	Sigmund Romberg	Dorothy Donnelly	My Maryland	1927
Words Without Music	Vernon Duke	Ira Gershwin	Ziegfeld Follies	1936
World Is in My Arms, The	Burton Lane	E. Y. Harburg	Hold On to Your Hats	1940
World Is Mine, The	George Gershwin	Ira Gershwin	Funny Face	1927
World Is Your Balloon, The	Sammy Fain	E. Y. Harburg	Flahooley	1951
World of Strangers, A	Sammy Fain	Paul Webster, Ray Golden	Alive and Kicking	1950
World Weary	Noel Coward	Noel Coward	This Year of Grace	1928
Would You Be So Kindly	Burton Lane	E. Y. Harburg	Hold On to Your Hats	1940
Would You Let Me Know?	John Addison	John Cranko	Cranks	1956
Would You Like to Take a Walk?	Harry Warren	Mort Dixon, Billy Rose	Sweet and Low	1930
Would'ja for a Big Red Apple?	Henry Souvaine	Everett Miller, Johnny Mercer	Americana	1932
Wouldn't It Be Loverly?	Frederick Loewe	Alan Jay Lerner	My Fair Lady	1956
Wouldn't That Be Wonderful?	Herman Hupfeld	Herman Hupfeld	Hey Nonny Nonny!	1932
Wow-Ooh-Wolf	Cole Porter	Cole Porter	The Seven Lively Arts	1944
Wrapped Up in You	Ben Oakland	Jack Murray, Barry Trivers	Ziegfeld Follies	1931
Wrong Note Rag, The	Leonard Bernstein	Betty Comden, Adolph Green	Wonderful Town	1953
Wunderbar	Cole Porter	Cole Porter	Kiss Me, Kate	1948
Ya Got Me	Leonard Bernstein	Betty Comden, Adolph Green	On the Town	1944
Yaller	Charles Schwab	Richard Myers	Three's a Crowd	1930

TITLE	COMPOSER	LYRICIST	SHOW	YEAR
Yankee Doodle Rhythm*	George Gershwin	Ira Gershwin	Rosalie	1928
Yankee Father in the Yankee Home, The	George M. Cohan	George M. Cohan	The Merry Malones	1927
Yes Or No	Sigmund Romberg	Harry B. Smith	Princess Flavia	1925
Yes Or No	Edward Kunneke (based on Offenbach)	Harry B. Smith	The Love Song	1925
Yes, Sir, I've Made a Date	Lee Wainer	J. B. Rosenberg	New Faces	1942
Yesterday I Loved You	Mary Rodgers	Marshall Barer	Once Upon a Mattress	1959
Yesterdays	Jerome Kern	Otto Harbach	Roberta	1933
Yip-Ahoy	Harold Rome	Harold Rome	Sing Out the News	1938
Yodel Blues, The	Robert Emmett Dolan	Johnny Mercer	Texas, Li'l Darlin'	1949
You	Albert Sirmay, Arthur Schwartz	Arthur Swanstrom	Princess Charming	1930
You Ain't So Hot	Jerome Moross	Paul Peters, George Sklar	Parade	1935
You Always Love the Same Girl	Richard Rodgers	Lorenz Hart	A Connecticut Yankee (revival)	1943
You and I Are Passersby	Jean Gilbert	Harry B. Smith	The Red Robe	1928
You and I Know	Arthur Schwartz	Albert Stillman, Laurence Stallings	Virginia	1937
You and I Love You and Me	Albert Von Tilzer	Neville Fleeson	Bye, Bye Bonnie	1927
You and the Night and the Music	Arthur Schwartz	Howard Dietz	Revenge With Music	1934
You Are Beautiful	Richard Rodgers	Oscar Hammerstein II	Flower Drum Song	1958
You Are Love	Jerome Kern	Oscar Hammerstein II	Show Boat	1927
You Are Mine Evermore	Emmerich Kalman	Harry B. Smith	The Circus Princess	1927
You Are My Downfall	Sammy Fain	George Marion, Jr.	Toplitzky of Notre Dame	1946
You Are My Only Romance	Frank Black	Gladys Shelley	The Duchess Misbehaves	1946
You Are My Woman	Sigmund Romberg	Oscar Hammerstein II	East Wind	1931
You Are Never Away	Richard Rodgers	Oscar Hammerstein II	Allegro	1947
You Are Romance	Phil Charig	Dan Shapiro, Milton Pascal	Artists and Models	1943
You Are So Lovely and I'm So Lonely	Richard Rodgers	Lorenz Hart	Something Gay	1935
You Are the Song	Sigmund Romberg	Irving Caesar	Melody	1933

*Dropped from New York production

TITLE	COMPOSER	LYRICIST	SHOW	YEAR
You Are You	George Gershwin, Herbert Stothart	Otto Harbach, Oscar Hammerstein II	Song of the Flame	1925
You Become Me	William Roy	William Roy	Maggie	1953
You Better Go Now	Irvin Graham	Bickley Reichner	New Faces	1936
You Came Along	Joseph Meyer, Philip Charig	Leo Robin	Just Fancy	1927
You Can Dance with Any Girl at All	Vincent Youmans	Irving Caesar	No, No, Nanette	1925
You Can Have Him	Irving Berlin	Irving Berlin	Miss Liberty	1949
You Can Make My Life a Bed of Roses	Ray Henderson	Lew Brown	Hotcha!	1932
You Can't Brush Me Off	Irving Berlin	Irving Berlin	Louisiana Purchase	1940
You Can't Get a Man With a Gun	Irving Berlin	Irving Berlin	Annie Get Your Gun	1946
You Can't Lose a Broken Heart	James P. Johnson	Flournoy Miller	Sugar Hill	1931
You Can't Make Love	Lee Pockriss	Anne Croswell	Ernest in Love	1960
You Can't Put Catsup on the Moon	Sammy Fain	Irving Kahal	Boys and Girls Together	1940
You Can't Stop Me From Lovin' You	Alberta Nichols	Mann Holiner	Rhapsody in Black	1931
You Can't Take It With You	Joan Edwards	Lynn Duddy	Tickets Please	1950
You Can't Walk Back From an Aeroplane	Irving Bibo, William B. Friedlander		Footlights	1927
You Do Something to Me	Cole Porter	Cole Porter	Fifty Million Frenchmen	1929
You Don't Know Him	Jay Livingston	Ray Evans	Oh Captain!	1958
You Don't Know Paree	Cole Porter	Cole Porter	Fifty Million Frenchmen	1929
You Don't Remind Me*	Cole Porter	Cole Porter	Out of This World	1950
You Forgot Your Gloves	Ned Lehak	Edward Eliscu	The Third Little Show	1931
You Have Cast Your Shadow on the Sea	Richard Rodgers	Lorenz Hart	The Boys from Syracuse	1938
You Have Everything	Arthur Schwartz	Howard Dietz	Between the Devil	1937
You Have Me—I Have You	Harold Levey	Owen Murphy	Greenwich Village Follies	1925
You Haven't Changed at All	Frederick Loewe	Alan Jay Lerner	The Day Before Spring	1945
You Irritate Me So	Cole Porter	Cole Porter	Let's Face It	1941
You Kissed Me	Morton Gould	Dorothy Fields	Arms and the Girl	1950
You Know, I Know	Harry Archer	Harlan Thompson	Twinkle, Twinkle	1926
You Lost Your Opportunity	Charles Schwab	Henry Myers	Garrick Gaieties-3rd edition	1930

*Dropped from New York production

TITLE	COMPOSER	LYRICIST	SHOW	YEAR
You May Not Love Me	Jimmy Van Heusen	Johnny Burke	Nellie Bly	1946
You Might As Well Pretend	Morgan Lewis	Ted Fetter, Edward Eliscu	The Third Little Show	1931
You Might Have Known I Loved You	Niclas Kempner	Graham John	The Street Singer	1929
You Must Come Over Blues	Lewis E. Gensler	B. G. DeSylva, Ira Gershwin	Captain Jinks	1925
You Mustn't Kick It Around	Richard Rodgers	Lorenz Hart	Pal Joey	1940
You Never Know	Cole Porter	Cole Porter	You Never Know	1938
You Never Know What Hit You	Harold Rome	Harold Rome	Bless You All	1950
You Never Say Yes	Richard Rodgers	Lorenz Hart	Spring Is Here	1929
You, Or Nobody!	Irving Caesar	Irving Caesar	Yes, Yes, Yvette	1927
You Said It	Harold Arlen	Jack Yellen	You Said It	1931
You Say the Nicest Things, Baby	Jimmy McHugh	Harold Adamson	As the Girls Go	1948
You Say You Care	Jule Styne	Leo Robin	Gentlemen Prefer Blondes	1949
You Should Be Set to Music	Irvin Graham	Irvin Graham	Crazy With the Heat	1941
You Smiled at Me	Harry Ruby	Bert Kalmar	The Ramblers	1926
You Took Advantage of Me	Richard Rodgers	Lorenz Hart	Present Arms	1928
You Took Me by Surprise	Vernon Duke	Ted Fetter	The Lady Comes Across	1942
You Took Posession of Me	Gerald Marks	Sam Lerner	Hold It!	1948
You Walked Out	David Baker	David Craig	Copper and Brass	1957
You Wanted Me— I Wanted You*	Harold Arlen	Ted Koehler	9:15 Revue	1930
You Wash and I'll Dry	Frederick Loewe	Alan Jay Lerner	What's Up	1943
You Were There	Noel Coward	Noel Coward	Tonight at 8:30 (Shadow Play)	1936
You Will, Won't You?	Jerome Kern	Anne Caldwell	Criss-Cross	1926
You Wouldn't Fool Me, Would You?	Ray Henderson	B. G. DeSylva, Lew Brown	Follow Thru	1929
You'll Do	Harold Arlen	Jack Yellen	You Said It	1931
You'll Kill 'Em	Harry Archer	Walter O'Keefe	Just A Minute	1928
You'll Know That It's Me	Philip Charig	Dan Shapiro, Milton Pascal	Artists and Models	1943
You'll Never Get Away from Me	Jule Styne	Stephen Sondheim	Gypsy	1959
You'll Never Know	Lewis E. Gensler	B. G. DeSylva	Queen High	1926

*Dropped from New York production

TITLE	COMPOSER	LYRICIST	SHOW	YEAR
You'll Never Walk Alone	Richard Rodgers	Oscar Hammer-stein II	Carousel	1945
Young and Foolish	Albert Hague	Arnold B. Horwitt	Plain and Fancy	1955
Young Black Joe	Roger Wolfe Kahn	Irving Caesar	Americana (2nd edition)	1928
Young Ideas	Charles Tobias, Charles Newman, Murray Mencher		Earl Carroll's Sketch Book	1935
Young Man in Love	Sigmund Romberg	Oscar Hammer-stein II	East Wind	1931
Younger Than Springtime	Richard Rodgers	Oscar Hammer-stein II	South Pacific	1949
Your Broadway and Mine	Maury Rubens	Moe Jaffe	Broadway Nights	1929
Your Disposition Is Mine	Jimmy McHugh	Dorothy Fields	Hello Daddy	1928
Your Eyes	Rudolf Friml	P. G. Wodehouse, Clifford Grey	The Three Musketeers	1928
Your Face Is So Familiar	Alex Fogarty	Edwin Gilbert	New Faces	1936
Your Fatal Fascination	Jacques Belasco	Kay Twomey	The Girl From Nan-tucket	1945
Your Good Morning	Jerry Herman	Jerry Herman	Parade	1960
Your Hand in Mine	Jerry Herman	Jerry Herman	Parade	1960
Your Land and My Land	Sigmund Romberg	Dorothy Donnelly	My Maryland	1927
Your Love I Crave	Jimmy Johnson	Percy Bradford	Messin' Around	1929
Your Mother's Son-in-law	Alberta Nichols	Mann Holiner	Blackbirds	1933
Your Smiles, Your Tears	Sigmund Romberg	Irving Caesar	Nina Rosa	1930
You're a Bad Influence	Cole Porter	Cole Porter	Red, Hot and Blue	1936
You're a Builder Upper	Harold Arlen	E. Y. Harburg, Ira Gershwin	Life Begins at 8:40	1934
You're a Magician	Gerald Dolin	Edward J. Lambert	Smile at Me	1925
You're an Old Smoothie	Richard Whiting, Nacio Brown	B. G. DeSylva	Take a Chance	1932
You're Devastating	Jerome Kern	Otto Harbach	Roberta	1933
You're Everywhere	Vincent Youmans	Edward Heyman	Through the Years	1932
You're Far Away from Home*	Cy Coleman	Carolyn Leigh	Wildcat	1960
You're Far from Wonderful	Vernon Duke	Ogden Nash	The Littlest Revue	1956
You're Far Too Near to Me	Kurt Weill	Ira Gershwin	The Firebrand of Florence	1945
You're Gonna Dance With Me, Willie	Jule Styne	Bob Hilliard	Hazel Flagg	1953
You're in Love	Cole Porter	Cole Porter	Gay Divorce	1932
You're Just in Love	Irving Berlin	Irving Berlin	Call Me Madam	1950

*Dropped from New York production

TITLE	COMPOSER	LYRICIST	SHOW	YEAR
You're Lonely and I'm Lonely	Irving Berlin	Irving Berlin	Louisiana Purchase	1940
You're Lucky to Me	Eubie Blake	Andy Razaf	Blackbirds	1930
You're More Than a Name and Address	Fred Spielman, Arthur Gershwin	Stanley Adams	A Lady Says Yes	1945
You're My Everything	Harry Warren	Mort Dixon, Joe Young	The Laugh Parade	1931
You're My Friend, Ain'tcha?	Bob Merrill	Bob Merrill	New Girl in Town	1957
You're My Girl	Jule Styne	Sammy Cahn	High Button Shoes	1947
You're My Relaxation	Charles Schwab	Robert Sour	New Faces	1934
You're on My Mind	Harry Ruby	Bert Kalmar	High Kickers	1941
You're One in a Million	Harden Church	Edward Heyman	Caviar	1934
You're Perf	Philip Charig	Dan Shapiro, Milton Pascal	Follow the Girls	1944
You're Perfect	Joseph Meyer	Edward Eliscu	Lady Fingers	1929
You're So Much a Part of Me	Richard Adler, Jerry Ross		John Murray Anderson's Almanac	1953
You're So Near (So Near and Yet So Far)	Jay Gorney	Barry Trivers	Heaven on Earth	1948
You're So Right for Me	Jay Livingston	Ray Evans	Oh Captain!	1958
You're the Cream in My Coffee	Ray Henderson	B. G. DeSylva, Lew Brown	Hold Everything!	1928
You're the First Cup of Coffee	Jay Gorney	Barry Trivers	Heaven on Earth	1948
You're the One	Harry Archer	Harlan Thompson	Merry-Merry	1925
You're the One	Arthur Schwartz	Otto Harbach	Good Boy	1928
You're the Only One	Clarence Williams, Len Gray		Bottomland	1927
You're the Sunrise	Arthur Schwartz	Howard Dietz	The Second Little Show	1930
You're the Top	Cole Porter	Cole Porter	Anything Goes	1934
You're What I Need	Richard Rodgers	Lorenz Hart	She's My Baby	1928
Yours Sincerely	Richard Rodgers	Lorenz Hart	Spring Is Here	1929
Yours Truly	Raymond Hubbell	Anne Caldwell	Yours Truly	1927
You've Come Home	Cy Coleman	Carolyn Leigh	Wildcat	1960
You've Got a Hold on Me	Frederick Loewe	Alan Jay Lerner	What's Up	1943
You've Got a Lease on My Heart	Sammy Fain	Irving Kahal	Everybody's Welcome	1931
You've Got a Way With You	Richard Myers	Leo Robin	Hello, Yourself	1928
You've Got It All	Ann Ronell	Ann Ronell	Count Me In	1942
You've Got Me Up a Tree	Alberta Nichols	Mann Holiner	Angela	1928
You've Got Something	Cole Porter	Cole Porter	Red, Hot and Blue	1936
You've Got That Thing	Cole Porter	Cole Porter	Fifty Million Frenchmen	1929
You've Got to Dance	Elsie Janis	Elsie Janis	Puzzles	1925

TITLE	COMPOSER	LYRICIST	SHOW	YEAR
You've Got to Know Just How to Make Love	Alma Sanders	Monte Carlo	The House Boat on the Styx	1928
You've Made Me Happy Today!	Niclas Kempner	Graham John	The Street Singer	1929
Zigeuner	Noel Coward	Noel Coward	Bitter Sweet	1929
Zim-Zam-Zee	Richard Lewine	Ted Fetter	Naughty-Naught	1937
Zing! Went the Strings of My Heart	James F. Hanley	James F. Hanley	Thumbs Up	1934

PART THREE

Motion Picture Songs

By Theatre Composers and Lyricists

MOTION
PICTURE
SONGS

IT WAS INEVITABLE that as the screen learned to talk, it would also learn to sing. Music had always accompanied motion pictures, from the tinny piano of the early "flickers" to the lush symphonic scores written to accompany the last of the silent spectacles.

When the talkie came along there was an initial torrent of lavish and overproduced screen musicals. There were songs, lots of them, but they were all but lost among staircases, waterfalls and huge dance routines. Finally, the accent on heavy productions lessened and there evolved a more intimate form of musical picture, one in which the songs themselves were featured—often starred.

It was then that the theatre composers and lyricists were summoned. By the end of the twenties—and through the thirties—there was a brisk traffic of Broadway writers between the East and West Coasts. In the advance guard was the team of **DeSylva, Brown** and Henderson, who turned out a half-dozen bright and popular songs for the Charles Farrell-Janet Gaynor picture *Sunny Side Up*. Soon Romberg, Kern, Hammerstein, the Gershwins, Rodgers and Hart, Porter and Berlin were all busily involved at the various studios. The result was that the quality of film songs went soaring skyward.

From Rodgers and Hart's *Love Me Tonight*, through the memorable Astaire-Rogers musicals, with scores by Berlin, Kern and the Gershwins, to Lerner and Loewe's *Gigi*, there has been a continuing flow of vital and rich picture songs by theatre composers and lyricists. A great many of them have become perennial favorites, those blue chips that the music industry affectionately calls "standards."

It is for such songs as these, and others which have the unmistakable sound of the stage, that this section is included. No attempt is made to list *all* good picture songs—a formidable undertaking in itself. These are, rather, motion-picture songs by established Broadway writers, songs that are, in every sense, "theatre" songs.

MOTION PICTURE SONGS
By Theatre Composers and Lyricists

TITLE	COMPOSER	LYRICIST	FILM	YEAR
Ac-cent-tchu-ate the Positive	Harold Arlen	Johnny Mercer	Here Come the Waves	1944
Adelaide	Frank Loesser	Frank Loesser	Guys and Dolls	1955
All at Once	Kurt Weill	Ira Gershwin	Where Do We Go From Here?	1945
All I Owe Ioway	Richard Rodgers	Oscar Hammerstein II	State Fair	1945
All Through the Day	Jerome Kern	Oscar Hammerstein II	Centennial Summer	1946
Amarillo	Richard Rodgers	Lorenz Hart	They Met in Argentina	1941
Andiamo	Harold Arlen	Dorothy Fields	Mr. Imperium	1951
Any Moment Now	Jerome Kern	E. Y. Harburg	Can't Help Singing	1944
Anywhere I Wander	Frank Loesser	Frank Loesser	Hans Christian Andersen	1951
Are You My Love?	Richard Rodgers	Lorenz Hart	Dancing Pirate	1936
Baby, It's Cold Outside	Frank Loesser	Frank Loesser	Neptune's Daughter	1949
Back Bay Polka, The	George Gershwin	Ira Gershwin	The Shocking Miss Pilgrim	1946
Bad in Every Man, The	Richard Rodgers	Lorenz Hart	Manhattan Melodrama	1934
Be a Clown	Cole Porter	Cole Porter	The Pirate	1948
Beginner's Luck	George Gershwin	Ira Gershwin	Shall We Dance	1937
Better Luck Next Time	Irving Berlin	Irving Berlin	Easter Parade	1948
Blah-Blah-Blah	George Gershwin	Ira Gershwin	Delicious	1931
Blue Moon*	Richard Rodgers	Lorenz Hart		1933
Blues in the Night	Harold Arlen	Johnny Mercer	Blues in the Night	1941
Bojangles of Harlem	Jerome Kern	Dorothy Fields	Swing Time	1936
Boy Next Door, The	Hugh Martin	Ralph Blane	Meet Me in St. Louis	1944
Boys in the Backroom, The	Frederick Hollander	Frank Loesser	Destry Rides Again	1939
Ca c'est l'amour	Cole Porter	Cole Porter	Les Girls	1957
Californ-i-ay	Jerome Kern	E. Y. Harburg	Can't Help Singing	1944

*Originally written as "Prayer" for "Hollywood Revue of 1933"

TITLE	COMPOSER	LYRICIST	SHOW	YEAR
Can I Forget You	Jerome Kern	Oscar Hammerstein II	High, Wide and Handsome	1937
Can't Help Singing	Jerome Kern	E. Y. Harburg	Can't Help Singing	1944
Carioca	Vincent Youmans	Edward Eliscu, Gus Kahn	Flying Down to Rio	1933
Change Partners	Irving Berlin	Irving Berlin	Carefree	1938
Changing My Tune	George Gershwin	Ira Gershwin	The Shocking Miss Pilgrim	1946
Cheek to Cheek	Irving Berlin	Irving Berlin	Top Hat	1935
Close	Cole Porter	Cole Porter	Rosalie	1937
Come to Me	Ray Henderson	B. G. DeSylva, Lew Brown	Indiscreet	1931
Continental, The*	Con Conrad	Herb Magidson	The Gay Divorcee	1934
Couple of Swells, A	Irving Berlin	Irving Berlin	Easter Parade	1948
Cuban Love Song	Jimmy McHugh, Herbert Stothart	Dorothy Fields	Cuban Love Song	1931
Dearly Beloved	Jerome Kern	Johnny Mercer	You Were Never Lovelier	1942
Delishious	George Gershwin	Ira Gershwin	Delicious	1931
Ding Dong! The Witch Is Dead	Harold Arlen	E. Y. Harburg	The Wizard of Oz	1939
Dissertation on the State of Bliss	Harold Arlen	Ira Gershwin	The Country Girl	1954
Donkey Serenade, The**	Rudolf Friml, Herbert Stothart	Robert Wright, George Forrest	The Firefly	1937
Don't Fence Me In	Cole Porter	Cole Porter	Hollywood Canteen	1944
Down by the River	Richard Rodgers	Lorenz Hart	Mississippi	1935
Dream Dancing	Cole Porter	Cole Porter	You'll Never Get Rich	1941
Dreamer, The	Arthur Schwartz	Frank Loesser	Thank Your Lucky Stars	1943
Easy to Love	Cole Porter	Cole Porter	Born to Dance	1936
Everything I Have is Yours	Burton Lane	Harold Adamson	Dancing Lady	1933
Fancy Free	Harold Arlen	Johnny Mercer	The Petty Girl	1950
Farewell, Amanda	Cole Porter	Cole Porter	Adam's Rib	1949
Fated to be Mated	Cole Porter	Cole Porter	Silk Stockings	1957
Fella with an Umbrella, A	Irving Berlin	Irving Berlin	Easter Parade	1948
Fine Romance, A	Jerome Kern	Dorothy Fields	Swing Time	1936
Flying Down to Rio	Vincent Youmans	Edward Eliscu, Gus Kahn	Flying Down to Rio	1933
Foggy Day, A	George Gershwin	Ira Gershwin	A Damsel in Distress	1937
Folks Who Live on the Hill, The	Jerome Kern	Oscar Hammerstein II	High, Wide and Handsome	1937

*Academy Award Winner
**Based on Friml's "Chanson"

TITLE	COMPOSER	LYRICIST	SHOW	YEAR
For You, For Me, For Evermore	George Gershwin	Ira Gershwin	The Shocking Miss Pilgrim	1946
French Lesson, The	Roger Edens	Betty Comden, Adolph Green	Good News	1947
Gal in Calico, A	Arthur Schwartz	Leo Robin	The Time, The Place and The Girl	1946
Get Thee Behind Me Satan	Irving Berlin	Irving Berlin	Follow the Fleet	1936
Gigi*	Frederick Loewe	Alan Jay Lerner	Gigi	1958
Girl on the Police Gazette, The	Irving Berlin	Irving Berlin	On the Avenue	1937
Give Her a Kiss	Richard Rodgers	Lorenz Hart	The Phantom President	1932
Go Home and Tell Your Mother	Jimmy McHugh	Dorothy Fields	Love in the Rough	1930
Good Night, Good Neighbor	Arthur Schwartz	Frank Loesser	Thank Your Lucky Stars	1943
Gotta Have Me Go With You	Harold Arlen	Ira Gershwin	A Star is Born	1954
Hallelujah, I'm a Bum	Richard Rodgers	Lorenz Hart	Hallelujah, I'm a Bum	1933
Happiness is a Thing Called Joe	Harold Arlen	E. Y. Harburg	Cabin in the Sky	1943
Have Yourself a Merry Little Christmas	Hugh Martin	Ralph Blane	Meet Me in St. Louis	1944
Heavenly Party, A	Jerome Kern	Dorothy Fields	The Joy of Living	1938
Here's What I'm Here For	Harold Arlen	Ira Gershwin	A Star is Born	1954
Hey, Babe, Hey	Cole Porter	Cole Porter	Born to Dance	1936
High, Wide and Handsome	Jerome Kern	Oscar Hammerstein II	High, Wide and Handsome	1937
Hit the Road to Dreamland	Harold Arlen	Johnny Mercer	Star Spangled Rhythm	1942
Hollywood Party	Richard Rodgers	Lorenz Hart	Hollywood Party	1934
Hooray for Love	Harold Arlen	Leo Robin	Casbah	1948
How About You	Burton Lane	Ralph Freed	Babes on Broadway	1941
How Can You Forget?	Richard Rodgers	Lorenz Hart	Fools for Scandal	1938
How Could You Believe Me When I Said I Loved You	Burton Lane	Alan Jay Lerner	Royal Wedding	1951
How Sweet You Are	Arthur Schwartz	Frank Loesser	Thank Your Lucky Stars	1943
I Bring a Love Song	Sigmund Romberg	Oscar Hammerstein II	Viennese Nights	1930
I Can't Be Bothered Now	George Gershwin	Ira Gershwin	A Damsel in Distress	1937

*Academy Award Winner

TITLE	COMPOSER	LYRICIST	SHOW	YEAR
I Concentrate on You	Cole Porter	Cole Porter	Broadway Melody of 1940	1939
I Don't Want to Walk Without You	Jule Styne	Frank Loesser	Sweater Girl	1942
I Dream Too Much	Jerome Kern	Dorothy Fields	I Dream Too Much	1935
I Feel a Song Comin' on	Jimmy McHugh	Dorothy Fields, George Oppenheimer	Every Night at Eight	1935
I Got Love	Jerome Kern	Dorothy Fields	I Dream Too Much	1935
I Have the Room Above	Jerome Kern	Oscar Hammerstein II	Show Boat	1936
I Love to Rhyme	George Gershwin	Ira Gershwin	Goldwyn Follies	1938
I Love You, Samantha	Cole Porter	Cole Porter	High Society	1956
I Love You So Much	Harry Ruby	Bert Kalmar	The Cuckoos	1930
I Mean to Say "I Love You"	Erich Wolfgang Korngold	Oscar Hammerstein II	Give Us This Night	1936
I Still Suits Me	Jerome Kern	Oscar Hammerstein II	Show Boat	1936
I Used to be Color Blind	Irving Berlin	Irving Berlin	Carefree	1938
I Was Doing All Right	George Gershwin	Ira Gershwin	Goldwyn Follies	1938
I Won't Dance	Jerome Kern	Dorothy Fields, Oscar Hammerstein II´ Otto Harbach, Jimmy McHugh	Roberta	1935
If I Had a Talking Picture of You	Ray Henderson	B. G. DeSylva, Lew Brown	Sunny Side Up	1929
If I Only Had a Brain	Harold Arlen	E. Y. Harburg	The Wizard of Oz	1939
I'll Take Romance	Ben Oakland	Oscar Hammerstein II	I'll Take Romance	1937
I'll Walk Alone	Jule Styne	Sammy Cahn	Follow the Boys	1944
I'm a Dreamer (Aren't We All)	Ray Henderson	B. G. DeSylva, Lew Brown	Sunny Side Up	1929
I'm Glad I'm Not Young Any More	Frederick Loewe	Alan Jay Lerner	Gigi	1958
I'm in the Mood for Love	Jimmy McHugh	Dorothy Fields	Every Night at Eight	1935
I'm Old Fashioned	Jerome Kern	Johnny Mercer	You Were Never Lovelier	1942
I'm Putting All My Eggs in One Basket	Irving Berlin	Irving Berlin	Follow the Fleet	1936
I'm Shooting High	Jimmy McHugh	Ted Koehler	King of Burlesque	1935
I'm the Echo	Jerome Kern	Dorothy Fields	I Dream Too Much	1935
In Love in Vain	Jerome Kern	Leo Robin	Centennial Summer	1946
In Our United State	Burton Lane	Ira Gershwin	Give a Girl a Break	1953
In the Still of the Night	Cole Porter	Cole Porter	Rosalie	1937
Inchworm	Frank Loesser	Frank Loesser	Hans Christian Andersen	1951

TITLE	COMPOSER	LYRICIST	SHOW	YEAR
Isn't It Kinda Fun	Richard Rodgers	Oscar Hammerstein II	State Fair	1945
Isn't It Romantic	Richard Rodgers	Lorenz Hart	Love Me Tonight	1932
Isn't This a Lovely Day	Irving Berlin	Irving Berlin	Top Hat	1935
It Might As Well Be Spring*	Richard Rodgers	Oscar Hammerstein II	State Fair	1945
It's a Grand Night for Singing	Richard Rodgers	Oscar Hammerstein II	State Fair	1945
It's a Most Unusual Day	Jimmy McHugh	Harold Adamson	A Date with Judy	1948
It's a New World	Harold Arlen	Ira Gershwin	A Star Is Born	1954
It's Easy to Remember	Richard Rodgers	Lorenz Hart	Mississippi	1935
It's Magic	Jule Styne	Sammy Cahn	Romance on the High Seas	1948
It's Only a Paper Moon	Harold Arlen	E. Y. Harburg, Billy Rose	Take a Chance	1933
I've Got My Eyes on You	Cole Porter	Cole Porter	Broadway Melody of 1940	1939
I've Got My Love to Keep Me Warm	Irving Berlin	Irving Berlin	On the Avenue	1937
I've Got You Under My Skin	Cole Porter	Cole Porter	Born to Dance	1936
Jockey on the Carrousel, The	Jerome Kern	Dorothy Fields	I Dream Too Much	1935
Jolly Tar and the Milk Maid, The	George Gershwin	Ira Gershwin	A Damsel in Distress	1937
Just Let Me Look at You	Jerome Kern	Dorothy Fields	The Joy of Living	1938
Keepin' Myself for You	Vincent Youmans	Sidney Clare	Hit the Deck	1929
Lady's in Love with You, The	Burton Lane	Frank Loesser	Some Like It Hot	1939
Last Time I Saw Paris, The*	Jerome Kern	Oscar Hammerstein, II	Lady, Be Good	1941
Les Girls	Cole Porter	Cole Porter	Les Girls	1957
Let Yourself Go	Irving Berlin	Irving Berlin	Follow the Fleet	1936
Let's Call the Whole Thing Off	George Gershwin	Ira Gershwin	Shall We Dance	1937
Let's Face the Music and Dance	Irving Berlin	Irving Berlin	Follow the Fleet	1936
Let's Fall in Love	Harold Arlen	Ted Koehler	Let's Fall in Love	1934
Let's Take the Long Way Home	Harold Arlen	Johnny Mercer	Here Come the Waves	1944
Like Ordinary People Do	Richard Rodgers	Lorenz Hart	The Hot Heiress	1931

*Academy Award Winner

TITLE	COMPOSER	LYRICIST	SHOW	YEAR
Little One	Cole Porter	Cole Porter	High Society	1956
Long Ago and Far Away	Jerome Kern	Ira Gershwin	Cover Girl	1944
Lost in a Fog	Jimmy McHugh	Dorothy Fields	Have a Heart	1934
Love	Hugh Martin	Ralph Blane	Ziegfeld Follies	1946
Love Is Here to Stay	George Gershwin	Ira Gershwin	Goldwyn Follies	1938
Love Is Just Around the Corner	Lewis E. Gensler	Leo Robin	Here Is My Heart	1934
Love Is Like a Song	Vincent Youmans	J. Russel Robinson, George Waggner	What a Widow!	1930
Love Is Love Anywhere	Harold Arlen	Ted Koehler	Let's Fall in Love	1934
Love Me Tonight	Richard Rodgers	Lorenz Hart	Love Me Tonight	1932
Love of My Life	Cole Porter	Cole Porter	The Pirate	1948
Love Walked In	George Gershwin	Ira Gershwin	Goldwyn Follies	1938
Lovely to Look at	Jerome Kern	Dorothy Fields, Jimmy McHugh	Roberta	1935
Lovely Way to Spend an Evening, A	Jimmy McHugh	Harold Adamson	Higher and Higher	1943
Lover	Richard Rodgers	Lorenz Hart	Love Me Tonight	1932
Lover of My Dreams* (Mirabelle Waltz)	Noel Coward	Noel Coward	Cavalcade	1932
Lydia, the Tattooed Lady	Harold Arlen	E. Y. Harburg	At the Circus	1939
Mack the Black	Cole Porter	Cole Porter	The Pirate	1948
Madly in Love	Fritz Kreisler	Dorothy Fields	The King Steps Out	1936
Make Way for Tomorrow	Jerome Kern	Ira Gershwin	Cover Girl	1944
Man That Got Away, The	Harold Arlen	Ira Gershwin	A Star Is Born	1954
Merry Old Land of Oz, The	Harold Arlen	E. Y. Harburg	The Wizard of Oz	1939
Merry Widow Waltz†	Franz Lehar	Lorenz Hart	The Merry Widow	1934
Mimi	Richard Rodgers	Lorenz Hart	Love Me Tonight	1932
Mind if I Make Love to You?	Cole Porter	Cole Porter	High Society	1956
Mist Is Over the Moon, A	Ben Oakland	Oscar Hammerstein II	The Lady Objects	1938
More and More	Jerome Kern	E. Y. Harburg	Can't Help Singing	1944
Music Makes Me	Vincent Youmans	Gus Kahn, Edward Eliscu	Flying Down to Rio	1933
My Dancing Lady	Jimmy McHugh	Dorothy Fields	Dancing Lady	1933

*Originally in London Stage Production
†New lyric for film version

TITLE	COMPOSER	LYRICIST	SHOW	YEAR
My Girl Back Home	Richard Rodgers	Oscar Hammerstein II	South Pacific	1958
My One and Only Highland Fling	Harry Warren	Ira Gershwin	The Barkleys of Broadway	1949
My Shining Hour	Harold Arlen	Johnny Mercer	The Sky's the Limit	1943
Never Gonna Dance	Jerome Kern	Dorothy Fields	Swing Time	1936
Nice Work if You Can Get It	George Gershwin	Ira Gershwin	A Damsel in Distress	1937
Night Is Young, The	Sigmund Romberg	Oscar Hammerstein II	The Night Is Young	1935
Night They Invented Champagne, The	Frederick Loewe	Alan Jay Lerner	Gigi	1958
Nina	Cole Porter	Cole Porter	The Pirate	1948
Nina, the Pinta, the Santa Maria, The	Kurt Weill	Ira Gershwin	Where Do We Go from Here?	1945
No Strings	Irving Berlin	Irving Berlin	Top Hat	1935
No Two People	Frank Loesser	Frank Loesser	Hans Christian Andersen	1951
Now I Know	Harold Arlen	Ted Koehler	Up in Arms	1944
Now You Has Jazz	Cole Porter	Cole Porter	High Society	1956
Oh, But I Do!	Arthur Schwartz	Leo Robin	The Time, the Place and the Girl	1946
One for My Baby	Harold Arlen	Johnny Mercer	The Sky's the Limit	1943
Orchids in the Moonlight	Vincent Youmans	Edward Eliscu, Gus Kahn	Flying Down to Rio	1933
Our Song	Jerome Kern	Dorothy Fields	When You're in Love	1937
Out of This World	Harold Arlen	Johnny Mercer	Out of This World	1945
Over the Rainbow*	Harold Arlen	E. Y. Harburg	The Wizard of Oz	1939
Parisians, The	Frederick Loewe	Alan Jay Lerner	Gigi	1958
Piccolino, The	Irving Berlin	Irving Berlin	Top Hat	1935
Pick Yourself Up	Jerome Kern	Dorothy Fields	Swing Time	1936
Poor Apache, The	Richard Rodgers	Lorenz Hart	Love Me Tonight	1932
Promenade (Walking the Dog)	George Gershwin		Shall We Dance	1937
Puttin' on the Ritz	Irving Berlin	Irving Berlin	Puttin' on the Ritz	1929
Rainy Night in Rio, A	Arthur Schwartz	Leo Robin	The Time, the Place and the Girl	1946
Reckless	Jerome Kern	Oscar Hammerstein II	Reckless	1935
Remind Me	Jerome Kern	Dorothy Fields	One Night in the Tropics	1940
Rhythm of the Day	Richard Rodgers	Lorenz Hart	Dancing Lady	1933
Ritz Roll and Rock	Cole Porter	Cole Porter	Silk Stockings	1957

*Academy Award Winner

TITLE	COMPOSER	LYRICIST	SHOW	YEAR
~~Reading~~	~~Cole Porter~~	~~Cole Porter~~	~~Rosalie~~	~~1937~~
Say a Prayer for Me Tonight	Frederick Loewe	Alan Jay Lerner	Gigi	1958
Say "Oui" Cherie	Vincent Youmans	J. Russel Robinson. George Waggner	What a Widow!	1930
Sayonara	Irving Berlin	Irving Berlin	Sayonara	1957
Seal It with a Kiss	Arthur Schwartz	Edward Heyman	That Girl from Paris	1936
Search Is Through, The	Harold Arlen	Ira Gershwin	The Country Girl	1954
Serenade to the Stars, A	Jimmy McHugh	Harold Adamson	Mad About Music	1938
Shall We Dance	George Gershwin	Ira Gershwin	Shall We Dance	1937
She Is Not Thinking of Me (Waltz at Maxim's)	Frederick Loewe	Alan Jay Lerner	Gigi	1958
Shoes with Wings On	Harry Warren	Ira Gershwin	The Barkleys of Broadway	1949
Simpatica	Richard Rodgers	Lorenz Hart	They Met in Argentina	1941
Sing My Heart	Harold Arlen	Ted Koehler	Love Affair	1939
Slap That Bass	George Gershwin	Ira Gershwin	Shall We Dance	1937
Slumming on Park Avenue	Irving Berlin	Irving Berlin	On the Avenue	1937
So Near and Yet So Far	Cole Porter	Cole Porter	You'll Never Get Rich	1941
Something's Got to Give	Johnny Mercer	Johnny Mercer	Daddy Long Legs	1955
Sonny Boy	Ray Henderson	B. G. DeSylva, Lew Brown, Al Jolson	The Singing Fool	1928
Soon	Richard Rodgers	Lorenz Hart	Mississippi	1935
Spring Again	Vernon Duke	Ira Gershwin	Goldwyn Follies	1938
Spring Has Sprung	Arthur Schwartz	Dorothy Fields	Excuse My Dust	1951
Spring Will Be a Little Late This Year	Frank Loesser	Frank Loesser	Christmas Holiday	1944
Stars in My Eyes*	Fritz Kreisler	Dorothy Fields	The King Steps Out	1936
Steppin' Out with My Baby	Irving Berlin	Irving Berlin	Easter Parade	1948
Stiff Upper Lip	George Gershwin	Ira Gershwin	A Damsel in Distress	1937
Sunny Side Up	Ray Henderson	B. G. DeSylva, Lew Brown	Sunny Side Up	1929
Sure Thing	Jerome Kern	Ira Gershwin	Cover Girl	1944
Tess's Torch Song	Harold Arlen	Ted Koehler	Up in Arms	1944
Thank Heaven for Little Girls	Frederick Loewe	Alan Jay Lerner	Gigi	1958
Thank You for a Lovely Evening	Jimmy McHugh	Dorothy Fields	Have a Heart	1934
That Old Black Magic	Harold Arlen	Johnny Mercer	Star Spangled Rhythm	1942

*Same melody as "Who Can Tell" from operetta "Apple Blossoms" 1919 (lyric by William LeBaron)

TITLE	COMPOSER	LYRICIST	SHOW	YEAR
That Week in Paris	Ben Oakland	Oscar Hammer-stein II	The Lady Objects	1938
That's Entertainment	Arthur Schwartz	Howard Dietz	The Band Wagon	1953
That's for Me	Richard Rodgers	Oscar Hammer-stein II	State Fair	1945
That's Love	Richard Rodgers	Lorenz Hart	Nana	1934
There's a Boy in Harlem	Richard Rodgers	Lorenz Hart	Fools for Scandal	1938
They All Fall in Love	Cole Porter	Cole Porter	The Battle of Paris	1929
They All Laughed	George Gershwin	Ira Gershwin	Shall We Dance	1937
They Can't Take That Away from Me	George Gershwin	Ira Gershwin	Shall We Dance	1937
They're Either Too Young or Too Old	Arthur Schwartz	Frank Loesser	Thank Your Lucky Stars	1943
Things Are Looking Up	George Gershwin	Ira Gershwin	A Damsel in Distress	1937
This Time the Dream's on Me	Harold Arlen	Johnny Mercer	Blues in the Night	1941
This Year's Kisses	Irving Berlin	Irving Berlin	On the Avenue	1937
Three Coins in the Fountain**	Jule Styne	Sammy Cahn	Three Coins in the Fountain	1954
Three Little Words	Bert Kalmar	Harry Ruby	Check and Double Check	1930
Thumbelina	Frank Loesser	Frank Loesser	Hans Christian Andersen	1951
Too Late Now	Burton Lane	Alan Jay Lerner	Royal Wedding	1951
Top Hat, White Tie and Tails	Irving Berlin	Irving Berlin	Top Hat	1935
Trolley Song, The	Hugh Martin	Ralph Blane	Meet Me in St. Louis	1944
True Love	Cole Porter	Cole Porter	High Society	1956
Turn on the Heat	Ray Henderson	B. G. DeSylva, Lew Brown	Sunny Side Up	1929
Twentieth Century Blues*	Noel Coward	Noel Coward	Cavalcade	1932
Up With the Lark	Jerome Kern	Leo Robin	Centennial Summer	1946
Vilia†	Franz Lehar	Lorenz Hart	The Merry Widow	1934
Waltz in Swingtime, The	Jerome Kern	Dorothy Fields	Swing Time	1936
Waltzing in the Clouds	Robert Stolz	Gus Kahn	Spring Parade	1940
Way You Look Tonight, The**	Jerome Kern	Dorothy Fields	Swing Time	1936
We Saw the Sea	Irving Berlin	Irving Berlin	Follow the Fleet	1936
We Were So Young	Jerome Kern	Oscar Hammer-stein II	Sweet Adeline	1934
We Will Always Be Sweethearts	Oscar Straus	Leo Robin	One Hour with You	1932
Wedding in the Spring	Jerome Kern	Johnny Mercer	You Were Never Lovelier	1942
We're Off to See the Wizard	Harold Arlen	E. Y. Harburg	The Wizard of Oz	1939

Originally in London stage production
**Academy Award Winner*
†*New lyric for film version*

TITLE	COMPOSER	LYRICIST	SHOW	YEAR
West Wind	Vincent Youmans	J. Russel Robinson	Song of the West	1930
What's Good About Goodbye?	Harold Arlen	Leo Robin	Casbah	1948
What's Good About Good-Night?	Jerome Kern	Dorothy Fields	The Joy of Living	1938
When I Grow Too Old to Dream	Sigmund Romberg	Oscar Hammer- stein II	The Night Is Young	1935
When I'm Looking at You	Herbert Stothart	Clifford Grey	The Rogue Song	1930
When You're in the Room	Ben Oakland	Oscar Hammer- stein II	The Lady Objects	1938
White Christmas*	Irving Berlin	Irving Berlin	Holiday Inn	1942
White Dove, The**	Franz Lehar, Herbert Stothart	Clifford Grey	The Rogue Song	1930
Who Are You?	Richard Rodgers	Lorenz Hart	The Boys from Syracuse	1940
Who Wants to be a Millionaire?	Cole Porter	Cole Porter	High Society	1956
Will You Marry Me Tomorrow, Maria?	Jerome Kern	Oscar Hammer- stein II	High, Wide and Handsome	1937
Wishing (Will Make It So)	B. G. DeSylva	B. G. DeSylva	Love Affair	1939
Woman in Love, A	Frank Loesser	Frank Loesser	Guys and Dolls	1955
Wonderful Copenhagen	Frank Loesser	Frank Loesser	Hans Christian Andersen	1951
You and Your Kiss	Jerome Kern	Dorothy Fields	One Night in the Tropics	1940
You Are Too Beautiful	Richard Rodgers	Lorenz Hart	Hallelujah, I'm a Bum	1933
You Can Do No Wrong	Cole Porter	Cole Porter	The Pirate	1948
You Couldn't Be Cuter	Jerome Kern	Dorothy Fields	The Joy of Living	1938
You Were Never Lovelier	Jerome Kern	Johnny Mercer	You Were Never Lovelier	1942
You Will Remember Vienna	Sigmund Romberg	Oscar Hammer- stein II	Viennese Nights	1930
You'd Be Hard to Replace	Harry Warren	Ira Gershwin	The Barkleys of Broadway	1949
You'd Be So Nice to Come Home to	Cole Porter	Cole Porter	Something to Shout About	1942
You're a Sweetheart	Jimmy McHugh	Harold Adamson	You're a Sweetheart	1937
You're Always in My Arms	Harry Tierney	Joseph McCarthy	Rio Rita	1929
You're Laughing at Me	Irving Berlin	Irving Berlin	On the Avenue	1937
You're Nearer	Richard Rodgers	Lorenz Hart	Too Many Girls	1940
You're Sensational	Cole Porter	Cole Porter	High Society	1956
You're the Cats	Richard Rodgers	Lorenz Hart	The Hot Heiress	1931
You're the One	Vincent Youmans	J. Russel Robinson, George Waggner	What a Widow!	1930
You've Got What Gets Me	George Gershwin	Ira Gershwin	Girl Crazy	1932

*Academy Award Winner
**Same melody as "You're in Love" from operetta "Gypsy Love" (1911)

PART FOUR

Show
Chronology
1925-1960

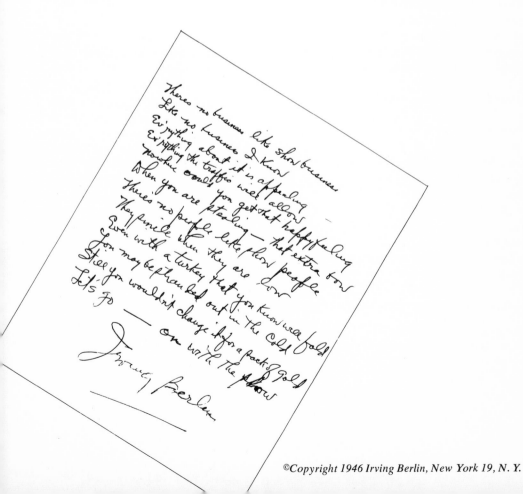

SHOW CHRONOLOGY 1925-1960
Date Below Each Show Indicates New York Première

BIG BOY
January 7, 1925

As Long as I've Got My Mammy
*Music by Joseph Meyer, James Hanley, words
by B. G. DeSylva*

Born and Bred in Old Kentucky
*Music by Joseph Meyer, James Hanley, words
by B. G. DeSylva*

Hello Tucky
*Music by Joseph Meyer, James Hanley, words
by B. G. DeSylva*

If You Knew Susie
Music and words by B. G. DeSylva

It All Depends on You
*Music by Ray Henderson, words by B. G.
DeSylva, Lew Brown*

Keep Smiling at Trouble
*Music by Lewis E. Gensler, words by Al Jolson,
B. G. DeSylva*

Lackawanna
*Music by Joseph Meyer, James Hanley, words
by B. G. DeSylva*

Miami
*Music by Con Conrad, words by Al Jolson, B. G.
DeSylva*

Nobody but Fanny
*Music by Con Conrad, words by Al Jolson, B. G.
DeSylva*

One O'Clock Baby
*Music by Al Jolson, words by B. G. DeSylva,
Lew Brown*

Who Was Chasing Paul Revere?
*Music by Joseph Meyer, James Hanley, words
by B. G. DeSylva*

THE LOVE SONG
January 13, 1925

MUSIC BY EDWARD KUNNEKE (BASED ON
OFFENBACH)
WORDS BY HARRY B. SMITH

Fair Land of Dreaming
He Writes a Song
It Is Love
Love Song, The (Remember Me)
Love Will Find You Some Day
Only a Dream
Yes or No

CHINA ROSE
January 19, 1925

MUSIC BY A. BALDWIN SLOANE
WORDS BY HARRY CORT, GEORGE E. STODDARD

China Bogie Man
China Rose
I'm All Alone
We'll Build a Brand New Bamboo Bungalow
Who Am I Thinking of?

PUZZLES OF 1925
February 2, 1925

Je Vous Aime
Music and words by Arthur L. Beiner

153

PUZZLES OF 1925 (*continued*)

~~Titi~~

Music by Léo Daniderff, words by Bertal-Maubon, E. Ronn

You've Got to Dance
Music and words by Elsie Janis

NATJA
February 16, 1925

MUSIC BY KARL HAJOS (BASED ON TCHAIKOVSKY)
WORDS BY HARRY B. SMITH

Beside the Star of Glory
Eyes That Haunt Me
Honor and Glory
I Hear Love Call Me
Magic of Moonlight and Love, The
Shall I Tell Him?
There Is a Garden in Loveland
Ups and Downs

SKY HIGH
March 2, 1925

Give Your Heart in June-Time
Music by Victor Herbert, words by Clifford Grey, Harold Atteridge
Let It Rain
Music and words by James Kendis, Hal Dyson

LOUIE THE 14th
March 3, 1925

MUSIC BY SIGMUND ROMBERG
WORDS BY ARTHUR WIMPERIS

Edelweiss
Words by Clifford Grey
Homeland
Little Peach
My First Love Letter
Words by Irving Caesar
Pep
True Hearts

*TELL ME MORE

~~April 13, 1925~~

MUSIC BY GEORGE GERSHWIN
WORDS BY B. G. DeSYLVA, IRA GERSHWIN

Baby!
Kickin' the Clouds Away
My Fair Lady
Tell Me More!
Three Times a Day
Why Do I Love You?

MERCENARY MARY
April 13, 1925

MUSIC BY CON CONRAD
WORDS BY WILLIAM B. FRIEDLANDER

Beautiful Baby
Charleston Mad
Honey, I'm in Love with You
Just You and I and the Baby
Mercenary Mary
That's When a Feller Needs a Friend

THE GARRICK GAIETIES
May 17, 1925

MUSIC BY RICHARD RODGERS
LYRICS BY LORENZ HART

April Fool
Do You Love Me?
Manhattan
Old Fashioned Girl
Words by Edith Meiser
On with the Dance
Sentimental Me
Three Musketeers

KOSHER KITTY KELLY
June 15, 1925

MUSIC AND WORDS BY LEON DECOSTA

Dancing Toes
Kosher Kitty Kelly

*Original out-of-town title "My Fair Lady"

Never to Leave You Again
Where We Can Be in Love

GRAND STREET FOLLIES OF 1925
June 18, 1925

Glory! Glory! Glory!
Music and words by Danton Walker

GEORGE WHITE'S SCANDALS (7th Edition)
June 22, 1925

MUSIC BY RAY HENDERSON
WORDS BY B. G. DeSYLVA, LEW BROWN

Fly Butterfly
Give Us the Charleston
I Want a Lovable Baby
Rose-Time
What a World This Would Be
Whosis-Whatsis, The

ARTISTS AND MODELS
June 24, 1925

MUSIC BY ALFRED GOODMAN,.MAURY RUBENS,
   J. FRED COOTS
WORDS BY CLIFFORD GREY

Flexatone
Lucita
Mother of the World
Oriental Memories
Promenade Walk, The
Venetian Wedding Moon

EARL CARROLL'S VANITIES
July 6, 1925

Kiss in the Moonlight, A
Music and words by Clarence Gaskill
Pango-Pango Maid
Music and words by Irving Bibo, Fred Phillips
Ponies on Parade
Music and words by Clarence Gaskill
Rhythm of the Day
*Music by Owen Murphy, words by Donald
Lindley*

Sentimental Sally
Music by Clarence Gaskill, words by Billy Rose
Somebody's Crazy About You
Music and words by Owen Murphy, Jay Gorney
Thinking of You
Music and words by Clarence Gaskill

JUNE DAYS
August 6, 1925

All I Want Is Love
Music by Hal Dyson, words by James Kendis
June Days
*Music by Stephen Jones, words by Clifford
Grey, Cyrus Wood*
Remembering You
Music by J. Fred Coots, words by Clifford Grey
Why Is Love?
Music by J. Fred Coots, words by Clifford Grey

SMILE AT ME
August 23, 1925

MUSIC BY GERALD DOLIN
WORDS BY EDWARD J. LAMBERT

Doin' the Truck
I'm Dreaming While We're Dancing
Smile at Me
Music and words by Edward J. Lambert
You're a Magician

*CAPTAIN JINKS
September 8, 1925

MUSIC BY LEWIS E. GENSLER
WORDS BY B. G. DeSYLVA

Ain't Love Wonderful?
Fond of You
I Do
Kiki
New Love
Only One for Me, The

*Based on play "Captain Jinks of the Horse Marines" by Clyde
Fitch*

CAPTAIN JINKS (*continued*)

~~Sea Legs~~

You Must Come Over Blues
  Words by B. G. DeSylva and Ira Gershwin

NO, NO, NANETTE
September 16, 1925

MUSIC BY VINCENT YOUMANS
WORDS BY IRVING CAESAR, OTTO HARBACH

I Want to Be Happy
  Words by Irving Caesar

*I've Confessed to the Breeze
  Words by Otto Harbach

No, No, Nanette
  Words by Otto Harbach

Tea for Two
  Words by Irving Caesar

Too Many Rings Around Rosie
  Words by Irving Caesar

You Can Dance with Any Girl at All
  Words by Irving Caesar

"Where Has My Hubby Gone" Blues
  Words by Irving Caesar

DEAREST ENEMY
September 18, 1925

MUSIC BY RICHARD RODGERS
WORDS BY LORENZ HART

Bye and Bye
Cheerio!
Here in My Arms
Here's a Kiss
Sweet Peter

†THE VAGABOND KING
September 21, 1925

MUSIC BY RUDOLF FRIML
WORDS BY BRIAN HOOKER

Huguette Waltz
Love for Sale!

Dropped from New York production
†*Based on play "If I Were King" by Justin Huntly McCarthy*

Love Me Tonight
~~Only a Rose~~
Some Day
Song of the Vagabonds

SUNNY
September 22, 1925

MUSIC BY JEROME KERN
WORDS BY OSCAR HAMMERSTEIN II, OTTO HARBACH

D'Ye Love Me
*Dream a Dream
*I Was Alone
Sunny
Sunshine
Two Little Bluebirds
Who?

MERRY-MERRY
September 24, 1925

MUSIC BY HARRY ARCHER
WORDS BY HARLAN THOMPSON

Every Little Note
I Was Blue
It Must Be Love
Little Girl
My Own
Oh, Wasn't It Lovely
Poor Pierrot
Spanish Mick, The
Step Step Sisters
We Were a Wow
What a Life
You're the One

WHEN YOU SMILE
October 5, 1925

MUSIC BY TOM JOHNSTONE
WORDS BY PHIL COOK

June
Oh, What a Girl
When You Smile
Wonderful Yesterday

HOLKA-POLKA
October 14, 1925

MUSIC BY WILL ORTMAN
WORDS BY GUS KAHN, RAYMOND B. EGAN

Holka-Polka
Home of My Heart
In a Little While
Spring in Autumn
When Love Is Near

THE CITY CHAP
October 26, 1925

MUSIC BY JEROME KERN
WORDS BY ANNE CALDWELL

He Is the Type
I'm Head and Heels in Love
   Music by Leo Edwards, words by Irving Caesar
Journey's End
   Words by P. G. Wodehouse
No One Knows
Sympathetic Someone
Walking Home with Josie

*PRINCESS FLAVIA
November 2, 1925

MUSIC BY SIGMUND ROMBERG
WORDS BY HARRY B. SMITH

Convent Bells Are Ringing
I Dare Not Love You
Marionettes
Only One
Twilight Voices
What Do I Care?
Yes or No

FLORIDA GIRL
November 2, 1925

MUSIC BY MILTON SUSSKIND
WORDS BY PAUL PORTER,
  BENJAMIN HAPGOOD BURT

Daphne
Lady of My Heart
Oh, You!

*Based on novel "The Prisoner of Zenda" by Anthony Hope

Skipper
Take a Little Dip
Twice Told Tales
Venetian Skies
Wee Toy

NAUGHTY CINDERELLA
November 9, 1925

Do I Love You?
   Music by Henri Christiné, E. Ray Goetz, words
   by E. Ray Goetz
I Love the Moon
   Music and words by Paul A. Rubens,
   E. Ray Goetz
Mia Luna
   Music by Puccini, words by E. Ray Goetz
That Means Nothing to Me!
   Music and words by A. L. Keith, Lee Sterling

CHARLOT'S REVUE OF 1926
November 10, 1925

Cup of Coffee, A Sandwich and You, A
   Music by Joseph Meyer, words by Billy Rose,
   Al Dubin
Gigolette
   Music by Franz Lehar, words by Irving Caesar
I Don't Know
   Music by Philip Braham, words by Ronald Jeans
Mender of Broken Dreams
   Music and words by John W. Bratton
Mouse! Mouse!
   Music by Muriel Lillie, words by Hilda Brighten
Poor Little Rich Girl
   Music and words by Noel Coward
Russian Blues
   Music and words by Noel Coward
Susannah's Squeaking Shoes
   Music by Muriel Lillie, words by Arthur Weigall

MAYFLOWERS
November 24, 1925

Mayflower
   Music by Frank Tours, words by Clifford Grey
Put Your Troubles in a Candy Box
   Music by J. Fred Coots, words by Clifford Grey

MAYFLOWERS (continued)

Road of Dreams, The
  Music by Pat Thayer, words by Donovan
  Parsons, Clifford Grey

Seven Days
  Music by Edward Kunneke, words by Clifford
  Grey

Take a Little Stroll with Me
  Music by J. Fred Coots, Maury Rubens, words
  by Clifford Grey

OH! OH! NURSE
December 7, 1925

MUSIC BY ALMA SANDERS
WORDS BY MONTE CARLO

Is It Any Wonder?
My Lady Love
Way Out in Rainbow Land

THE COCOANUTS
December 8, 1925

MUSIC AND WORDS BY IRVING BERLIN

Everyone in the World Is Doing the Charleston
Five O'Clock Tea
Florida by the Sea
Gentlemen Prefer Blondes
Little Bungalow, A
Lucky Boy
Tango Melody
Ting-A-Ling, The Bells'll Ring
We Should Care
Why Do You Want to Know Why?
With a Family Reputation

GREENWICH VILLAGE FOLLIES
December 24, 1925

Garden of Used-to-Be
  Music by Jay Gorney, words by Owen Murphy

Go South
  Music by Richard Myers, words by Owen
  Murphy

Lady of the Snow
  Music by Harold Levey, words by Owen Murphy

When Evening Shadows Fall
  Music and words by Jay Gorney, Irving Caesar,
  Owen Murphy

Whistle Away Your Blues
  Music by Richard Myers, words by Leo Robin

You Have Me—I Have You
  Music by Harold Levey, words by Owen Murphy

TIP-TOES
December 28, 1925

MUSIC BY GEORGE GERSHWIN
WORDS BY IRA GERSHWIN

*It's a Great Little World
Looking for a Boy
Nice Baby!
Nightie-Night
Sweet and Low-Down
That Certain Feeling
These Charming People
When Do We Dance?

BY THE WAY
December 28, 1925

My Castle in Spain
  Music and words by Isham Jones

No One's Ever Kissed Me
  Music by Philip Braham, words by Ronald Jeans

Oh, How I've Waited for You
  Music by Nat D. Ayer, words by Harry Carlton

SONG OF THE FLAME
December 30, 1925

MUSIC BY GEORGE GERSHWIN AND HERBERT
  STOTHART
WORDS BY OTTO HARBACH, OSCAR
  HAMMERSTEIN II

Cossack Love Song
Great Big Bear
  Music by Herbert Stothart

Midnight Bells
  Music by George Gershwin

*Dropped from New York production

Signal, The
Music by George Gershwin
Song of the Flame
Vodka
Wander Away
Music by Herbert Stothart
You Are You

A NIGHT IN PARIS
January 5, 1926

Louisiana
Music by J. Fred Coots, Maury Rubens, words by McElbert Moore
Why Should We Be Wasting Time?
Music by J. Fred Coots, Maury Rubens, Alfred Goodman, words by Eddie Conrad, McElbert Moore

*HELLO, LOLA
January 12, 1926

MUSIC BY WILLIAM B. KERNELL
WORDS BY DOROTHY DONNELLY

In the Dark
My Baby Talk Lady
Swinging on the Gate

SWEETHEART TIME
January 19, 1926

Girl in Your Arms, A
Music by Jay Gorney, words by Irving Caesar
Marian
Music by Walter Donaldson, words by Ballard MacDonald
One Way Street
Music by Walter Donaldson, words by Ballard MacDonald
Sweetheart Time
Music by Joseph Meyer, words by Irving Caesar
Two By Four
Music by Joseph Meyer, words by Irving Caesar
Who Loves You as I Do?
Music by Joseph Meyer, words by Irving Caesar

Based on novel and play "Seventeen" by Booth Tarkington

THE MATINEE GIRL
February 1, 1926

MUSIC BY FRANK GREY
WORDS BY McELBERT MOORE AND FRANK GREY

Like-a-Me, Like-a-You
Only One

BUNK OF 1926
February 16, 1926

MUSIC AND WORDS BY GENE LOCKHART

Chatter
Cuddle Up
Milky Way
Modest Little Thing, A
Way to Your Heart, The

RAINBOW ROSE
March 16, 1926

All the Time
Music and words by Harold Levey, Anita Owen
First, Last and Only
Music and words by Harold Levey, Owen Murphy
If You Were Someone Else
Music and words by Harold Levey, Owen Murphy
Let's Run Away and Get Married
Music and words by Harold Levey, Owen Murphy
Rainbow
Music by Harold Levey, words by Zelda Sears

THE GIRL FRIEND
March 17, 1926

MUSIC BY RICHARD RODGERS
WORDS BY LORENZ HART

Blue Room, The
Girl Friend, The
Good Fellow, Mine
Why Do I?

KITTY'S KISSES
May 6, 1926

MUSIC BY CON CONRAD
WORDS BY GUS KAHN

I'm in Love
  Words by Gus Kahn, Otto Harbach
Kitty's Kisses
Step on the Blues
  Music by Con Conrad, Will Donaldson, words by Otto Harbach
Thinking of You

THE GARRICK GAIETIES (Second Edition)
May 10, 1926

MUSIC BY RICHARD RODGERS
WORDS BY LORENZ HART

Keys to Heaven
Little Souvenir
Mountain Greenery
Queen Elizabeth
Sleepy Head
What's the Use of Talking

THE GREAT TEMPTATIONS
May 18, 1926

Beauty Is Vanity
  Music by Maury Rubens, words by Clifford Grey
Love Birds
  Music by Kenneth Burton, words by Clifford Grey
Temptation Strut
  Music by Earl Lindsay, Maury Rubens, words by Clifford Grey
Valencia
  Music by José Padilla, words by Clifford Grey
White Rose—Red Rose
  Music by Raoul Moretti, words by Clifford Grey

THE MERRY WORLD
June 8, 1926

Deauville
  Music and words by Herman Hupfeld

Don't Fall in Love with Me
  Music and words by Herman Hupfeld
Golden Gates of Happiness
  Music by J. Fred Coots, words by Clifford Grey
I Fell Head Over Heels in Love
  Music by Pat Thayer, words by Donovan Parsons
Sunday
  Music by J. Fred Coots, words by Clifford Grey
Whispering Trees
  Music by Maury Rubens, J. Fred Coots, words by Herbert Reynolds

GEORGE WHITE'S SCANDALS (8th Edition)
June 14, 1926

MUSIC BY RAY HENDERSON
WORDS BY B. G. DeSYLVA, LEW BROWN

Birth of the Blues, The
Black Bottom
Girl Is You and the Boy Is Me, The
Lucky Day
Sevilla
Tweet Tweet

GRAND STREET FOLLIES OF 1926
June 15, 1926

If You Know What I Mean
  Music by Arthur Schwartz, words by Theodore Goodwin, Albert Carroll
Little Igloo for Two
  Music by Arthur Schwartz, words by Agnes Morgan
Northern Blues
  Music by Walter Haenschen, words by Robert A. Simon
Polar Bear Strut
  Music by Arthur Schwartz, words by Theodore Goodwin

NO FOOLIN'
June 24, 1926

Florida, the Moon and You
  Music by Rudolf Friml, words by Gene Buck

No Foolin'
Music by James Hanley, words by Gene Buck

Poor Little Marie
Music by James Hanley, words by Gene Buck

Wasn't It Nice?
Music by Rudolf Friml, words by Irving Caesar

MY MAGNOLIA
July 8, 1926

MUSIC BY LUCKEY ROBERTS
WORDS BY ALEX C. ROGERS

Magnolia

THE BLONDE SINNER
July 14, 1926

MUSIC AND WORDS BY LEON DECOSTA

Bye-Bye Babe
Don't You Cheat
Lips
Whispering Song

BARE FACTS OF 1926
July 16, 1926

MUSIC BY CHARLES M. SCHWAB
WORDS BY HENRY MYERS

Nice Girl
Stand Up on Your Feet and Dance

AMERICANA (First Edition)
July 26, 1926

Blowin' the Blues Away
Music by Philip Charig, words by Ira Gershwin

Dreaming
Music by Henry Souvaine, Con Conrad, words by J. P. McEvoy

Nobody Wants Me
Music by Henry Souvaine, words by Morrie Ryskind

Promise in Your Eyes, The
Music by James Hanley, words by B. G. DeSylva

Sunny Disposish
Music by Philip Charig, words by Ira Gershwin

Swanee River Melody
Music by Charles Weinberg, words by Al Wilson

That Lost Barbershop Chord
Music by George Gershwin, words by Ira Gershwin

Why Do Ya Roll Those Eyes?
Music by Philip Charig, words by Morrie Ryskind

NIC NAX OF 1926
August 2, 1926

MUSIC BY GITZ RICE

Everything Is High Yellow Now
Words by Paul Porter

For a Girl Like You
Words by Joe Goodwin

I Have Forgotten You Almost
Words by Anna Fitziu

Oh, Daddy
Words by Gitz Rice

When the Sun Kissed the Rose Goodbye
Words by Paul Porter

Without the One You Love
Music by Werner Janssen, words by Gitz Rice

EARL CARROLL'S VANITIES
August 24, 1926

Alabama Stomp
Music by James P. Johnson, words by Henry Creamer

Climbing Up the Ladder of Love
Music by Jesse Greer, words by Raymond Klages

Hugs and Kisses
Music by Louis Alter, words by Raymond Klages

Twilight
Music by Morris Hamilton, words by Grace Henry

Who Do You Love?
Music and words by Fred Rich, Hugo Frey, Raymond Klages

CASTLES IN THE AIR
September 6, 1926

MUSIC BY PERCY WENRICH
WORDS BY RAYMOND PECK

Baby
First Kiss of Love
Girls and the Gimmies
I Would Like to Fondle You
Land of Romance
Lantern of Love
Other Fellow's Girl, The
True Love and a Ring
When Romance Is Gone
When the Only One Meets the Only One

QUEEN HIGH
September 8, 1926

MUSIC BY LEWIS E. GENSLER
WORDS BY B. G. DeSYLVA

Beautiful Baby
  Music by James Hanley
Cross Your Heart
Don't Forget
Everything Will Happen for the Best
Gentlemen Prefer Blondes
You'll Never Know

NAUGHTY RIQUETTE
September 13, 1926

WORDS BY HARRY B. SMITH

I May
  Music by Maury Rubens, Kendall Burgess
In Armenia
  Music by Oscar Straus
Make Believe You're Mine
  Music by Oscar Straus
Naughty Riquette
  Music by Maury Rubens, Kendall Burgess
Someone
  Music by Alfred Goodman, Maury Rubens

COUNTESS MARITZA

MUSIC BY EMMERICH KALMAN
WORDS BY HARRY B. SMITH

Call of Love, The
Dear Home of Mine, Goodbye
I'll Keep on Dreaming
Love Has Found My Heart
  Music by Emmerich Kalman, Alfred Goodman
One I'm Looking for, The
Play Gypsies, Dance Gypsies
Say Yes, Sweetheart
Sister Mine

THE RAMBLERS
September 20, 1926

MUSIC BY HARRY RUBY
WORDS BY BERT KALMAR

All Alone Monday
California Skies
Like You Do
Oh! How We Love Our Alma Mater
Sweeter Than You
We Won't Charleston
You Smiled at Me

HONEYMOON LANE
September 20, 1926

MUSIC BY JAMES HANLEY
WORDS BY EDDIE DOWLING

Dreams for Sale
Half a Moon
  Words by Eddie Dowling, Herbert Reynolds
Jersey Walk
Little White House, The (At the End of Honeymoon Lane)
Mary Dear
Waddya Say—We Steal Away

HAPPY GO LUCKY
September 30, 1926

MUSIC BY LUCIEN DENNI
WORDS BY GWYNNE DENNI

Choose Your Flowers
  Words by Helena Evans

Happy Melody
How Are You, Lady Love
Love Thoughts
Sing a Little Song
When I Make a Million for You
Words by Helena Evans

DEEP RIVER
October 4, 1926

MUSIC BY FRANK HARLING
WORDS BY LAURENCE STALLINGS

Ashes and Fire
Cherokee Rose
De Old Clay Road
Dis Is de Day
Love Lasts a Day
Po' Lil' Black Chile
Serenade Creole
Soft in de Moonlight
Two Little Stars

CRISS-CROSS
October 12, 1926

MUSIC BY JEROME KERN
WORDS BY ANNE CALDWELL, OTTO HARBACH

Bread and Butter
Cinderella Girl
In Araby With You
Kiss a Four Leaf Clover
Suzie
Words by Anne Caldwell
You Will, Won't You?

KATJA
October 18, 1926

MUSIC BY JEAN GILBERT
WORDS BY HARRY GRAHAM

If You Cared
Just for Tonight
Music by Maury Rubens, words by
Clifford Grey
Leander
Those Eyes So Tender
When Love's in the Air

THE WILD ROSE
October 20, 1926

MUSIC BY RUDOLF FRIML
WORDS BY OTTO HARBACH, OSCAR
HAMMERSTEIN II

Brown Eyes
Love Me, Don't You?
One Golden Hour
We'll Have a Kingdom
Wild Rose

OH, KAY!
November 8, 1926

MUSIC BY GEORGE GERSHWIN
WORDS BY IRA GERSHWIN

Clap Yo' Hands
Do Do Do
Fidgety Feet
Heaven on Earth
Words by Ira Gershwin, Howard Dietz
Maybe
Oh, Kay
*Show Me the Town
Someone to Watch Over Me

GAY PAREE
November 9, 1926

Beautiful Girls
Music by Alfred Goodman, J. Fred Coots,
Maury Rubens; words by Clifford Grey
Collegiate
Music by Moe Jaffe, words by Nat Bonx
Give Me the Rain
Music by Lester Allen, words by Henry
Creamer
Heart of a Rose
Music by J. Fred Coots, Maury Rubens, words
by Clifford Grey
Hocus-Pocus
Music by James Hanley, words by Lew Brown
"Je t'Aime" Means I Love You
Music and words by Powers Gouraud

*Dropped from New York production

GAY PAREE (*continued*)

~~Oh, Boy, What a Girl~~
   *Music by Wright & Bessinger, words by Bud
   Green*

Sugar Plum
   *Music by Joseph Meyer, words by B. G.
   DeSylva*

Tilly of Longacre Square
   *Music by James Hanley, words by Ballard
   MacDonald*

TWINKLE, TWINKLE
November 16, 1926

MUSIC BY HARRY ARCHER
WORDS BY HARLAN THOMPSON

Find a Girl
Get a Load of This
*Sweeter Than You
   Music by Harry Ruby, words by Bert Kalmar
Twinkle, Twinkle
You Know, I Know
Whistle
   Music by Harry Ruby, words by Bert Kalmar

THE DESERT SONG
November 30, 1926

MUSIC BY SIGMUND ROMBERG
WORDS BY OTTO HARBACH, OSCAR
   HAMMERSTEIN II

Desert Song, The
"It"
Let's Have a Love Affair
Love's Dear Yearning
One Alone
One Flower Grows Alone in Your Garden
Riff Song, The
Romance

OH, PLEASE!
December 17, 1926

MUSIC BY VINCENT YOUMANS
WORDS BY ANNE CALDWELL

I Know That You Know
I'm Waiting for a Wonderful Girl

*Also in "The Ramblers"

Like He Loves Me
~~Nicodemus~~

PEGGY-ANN
December 27, 1926

MUSIC BY RICHARD RODGERS
WORDS BY LORENZ HART

Little Birdie Told Me So, A
Maybe It's Me
Tree in the Park, A
Where's That Rainbow?

BETSY
December 28, 1926

MUSIC BY RICHARD RODGERS
WORDS BY LORENZ HART

Blue Skies
   Music and words by Irving Berlin
**Come and Tell Me
If I Were You
Sing
Stonewall Moskowitz March
This Funny World

THE NIGHTINGALE
January 3, 1927

MUSIC BY ARMAND VECSEY

Breakfast in Bed
   Words by P. G. Wodehouse
Josephine
   Words by Clifford Grey
May Moon
   Words by P. G. Wodehouse
Once in September
   Words by Clifford Grey
Two Little Ships
   Words by P. G. Wodehouse

**Dropped from New York production

THE LACE PETTICOAT
January 4, 1927

MUSIC BY EMIL GERSTENBERGER

Engagement Ring, The
 Words by Howard Johnston
Little Lace Petticoat
 Words by Carle Carlton

PIGGY
January 11, 1927

MUSIC BY CLIFF FRIEND
WORDS BY LEW BROWN

Didn't It?
Ding, Dong, Dell
I Need a Little Bit—You Need a Little Bit
I Wanna Go Voom Voom
It Just Had to Happen
It's Easy to Say Hello
Let's Stroll Along and Sing a Song of Love
Little Change of Atmosphere, A
Music of a Little Rippling Stream, The
Oh, Baby
When

BYE BYE, BONNIE
January 13, 1927

MUSIC BY ALBERT VON TILZER
WORDS BY NEVILLE FLEESON

Just Cross the River from Queens
Love Is Like a Blushing Rose
Tampico Tap
You and I Love You and Me

YOURS TRULY
January 25, 1927

MUSIC BY RAYMOND HUBBELL
LYRICS BY ANNE CALDWELL

Don' Shake My Tree
Fearfully, Frightful Love
Jade
Look at the World and Smile

Lotus Flower
Somebody Else
Yours Truly

RIO RITA
February 2, 1927

MUSIC BY HARRY TIERNEY
WORDS BY JOSEPH McCARTHY

Following the Sun Around
If You're in Love, You'll Waltz
Kinkajou, The
Rangers' Song, The
Rio Rita

JUDY
February 8, 1927

MUSIC BY CHARLES ROSOFF
WORDS BY LEO ROBIN

Judy, Who D'Ya Love?
Pretty Little Stranger
Start Stompin'
Wear Your Sunday Smile

POLLY OF HOLLYWOOD
February 21, 1927

MUSIC BY WILL MORRISSEY
WORDS BY EDMUND JOSEPH

Company Manners
Kisses that You Gave to Me, The
New Kind of Rhythm
Texas Stomp
Wanting You

THE NEW YORKERS
March 10, 1927

Floating thru' the Air
 Music by Arthur Schwartz, words by Henry Myers
Side Street Off Broadway, A
 Music by Edgar Fairchild, words by Henry Myers

THE NEW YORKERS (*continued*)

Slow River
   Music by Charles M. Schwab, words by Henry Myers

LUCKY
March 22, 1927

Cingalese Girls
   Music by Harry Ruby, words by Bert Kalmar, Otto Harbach

Dancing the Devil Away
   Music by Harry Ruby, words by Bert Kalmar, Otto Harbach

Same Old Moon, The
   Music by Harry Ruby, words by Bert Kalmar, Otto Harbach

That Little Something
   Music by Jerome Kern, words by Bert Kalmar, Harry Ruby

When the Bo-Tree Blossoms Again
   Music by Jerome Kern, words by Bert Kalmar, Harry Ruby

RUFUS LEMAIRE'S AFFAIRS
March 28, 1927

MUSIC BY MARTIN BROONES

Bring Back Those Minstrel Days
   Words by Ballard MacDonald

I Can't Get Over a Girl Like You
   Words by Harry Ruskin

Wandering in Dreamland
   Music and words by Martin Broones, Ballard MacDonald

Where the Morning Glories Twine
   Words by Ballard MacDonald

CHERRY BLOSSOMS
March 28, 1927

MUSIC BY SIGMUND ROMBERG
WORDS BY HARRY B. SMITH

I've Waited for You
My Own Willow Tree

Some Day
Tell Me, Cigarette
Wait and See

LADY DO
April 18, 1927

MUSIC BY ABEL BAER
WORDS BY SAM LEWIS, JOE YOUNG

Blah! but Not Blue
Dreamy Montmartre
Lady Do
On Double Fifth Avenue

HIT THE DECK!
April 25, 1927

MUSIC BY VINCENT YOUMANS
WORDS BY LEO ROBIN, CLIFFORD GREY

*Armful of You
Hallelujah!
Harbor of My Heart, The
Join the Navy!
Loo-Loo
Lucky Bird
Sometimes I'm Happy
**Why, Oh Why?

THE CIRCUS PRINCESS
April 25, 1927

MUSIC BY EMMERICH KALMAN
WORDS BY HARRY B. SMITH

Dear Eyes That Haunt Me
Like You
We Two Shall Meet Again
What D'Ya Say?
   Music by Jesse Greer, words by Raymond Klages

Who Cares?
You Are Mine Evermore

*Dropped from New York production
**Originally published as "Nothing Could Be Sweeter"

A NIGHT IN SPAIN
May 3, 1927

MUSIC BY JEAN SCHWARTZ
WORDS BY ALFRED BRYAN

De-dum-dum
Room for Two
Simple Spanish Maid

*OH, ERNEST!
May 9, 1927

MUSIC BY ROBERT HOOD BOWERS
WORDS BY FRANCIS DE WITT

Give Me Someone
He Knows Where the Rose Is in Bloom
Let's Pretend

GRAND STREET FOLLIES OF 1927
May 19, 1927

MUSIC BY MAX EWING
WORDS BY AGNES MORGAN

If You Haven't Got "It"
Silver Apron Strings
Three Little Maids

MERRY-GO-ROUND
May 31, 1927

MUSIC BY HENRY SOUVAINE, JAY GORNEY
WORDS BY MORRIE RYSKIND, HOWARD DIETZ

Hogan's Alley
I've Got a Yes Girl
Sentimental Silly
New York Town
Something Tells Me
Tampa

TALK ABOUT GIRLS
June 14, 1927

MUSIC BY HAROLD ORLOB
WORDS BY IRVING CAESAR

All the Time Is Loving Time
Lonely Girl, A

Based on Play "The Importance of Being Earnest" by Oscar Wilde

Love Birds
Maybe I Will
Talk About Girls
   Music by Stephen Jones

BOTTOMLAND
June 27, 1927

Any Time
   Music and words by Clarence Williams, Jo Jordan

Bottomland
   Music and words by Clarence Williams, Jc Trent

Come on Home
   Music and words by Donald Heywood

Dancing Girl
   Music and words by Clarence Williams, Spencer Williams

Shootin' the Pistol
   Music and words by Clarence Williams, Chris Smith

Steamboat Days
   Music and words by Clarence Williams

When I March with April in May
   Music and words by Clarence Williams, Spencer Williams

You're the Only One
   Music and words by Clarence Williams, Len Gray

PADLOCKS OF 1927
July 5, 1927

Hot Heels
   Music by Lee David, words by Billy Rose, Ballard MacDonald

If I Had a Lover
   Music by Henry Tobias, words by Billy Rose, Ballard MacDonald

Tap Tap, The
   Music by Jesse Greer, words by Billy Rose, Ballard MacDonald

RANG-TANG
July 12, 1927

MUSIC BY FORD DABNEY
WORDS BY JO TRENT

Brown
Jungle Rose
Rang-tang

KISS ME
July 18, 1927

MUSIC BY WINTHROP CORTELYOU
WORDS BY DERICK WULFF

I Have Something Nice for You
Kiss Me
Pools of Love
Rose of Iran

ALLEZ-OOP
August 2, 1927

MUSIC BY PHILIP CHARIG, RICHARD MYERS
WORDS BY LEO ROBIN

Blow Hot and Heavy
Pull Yourself Together
Where Have You Been All My Life?

THE MANHATTERS
August 3, 1927

MUSIC BY ALFRED NATHAN
WORDS BY GEORGE OPPENHEIMER

Close Your Eyes
Down on the Delta
Nigger Heaven Blues

ZIEGFELD FOLLIES OF 1927
August 16, 1927

MUSIC AND WORDS BY IRVING BERLIN

It All Belongs to Me
It's Up to the Band
Jimmy
Jungle Jingle
Learn to Sing a Love Song
Ooh, Maybe It's You

Rainbow of Girls
Ribbons and Bows
Shaking the Blues Away

A LA CARTE
August 17, 1927

Baby's Blue
   Music and words by Herman Hupfeld
Calinda, The
   Music and words by Herman Hupfeld
Give Trouble the Air
   Music by Louis Alter, words by Leo Robin
I'm Stepping Out with Lulu
   Music and words by Henry Creamer,
   Jimmy Johnson
Sort o' Lonesome
   Music and words by Herman Hupfeld

FOOTLIGHTS
August 19, 1927

MUSIC AND WORDS BY IRVING BIBO, WILLIAM B.
FRIEDLANDER

You Can't Walk Back from an Aeroplane

GOOD NEWS
September 6, 1927

MUSIC BY RAY HENDERSON
WORDS BY B. G. DeSYLVA, LEW BROWN

Best Things in Life Are Free, The
Girl of the Pi Beta Phi, A
Good News
He's a Ladies Man
Just Imagine
Lucky in Love
Varsity Drag, The

HALF A WIDOW
September 12, 1927

MUSIC BY SHEP CAMP

France Will Not Forget
   Music and words by Geoffrey O'Hara, Gordon
   Johnstone

It's Great to Be a Doughboy
Words by Frank Dupree

Longing for You
Words by Frank Dupree

Tell Me Again
Words by Frank Dupree

Under the Midsummer Moon
Words by Harry B. Smith

*MY MARYLAND
September 12, 1927

MUSIC BY SIGMUND ROMBERG
WORDS BY DOROTHY DONNELLY

Boys in Gray
Mother
Silver Moon
Won't You Marry Me
Your Land and My Land

ENCHANTED ISLE
September 19, 1927

MUSIC AND WORDS BY IDA HOYT CHAMBERLAIN

Close in Your Arms
Dream Girl
Julianne

THE MERRY MALONES
September 26, 1927

MUSIC AND WORDS BY GEORGE M. COHAN

Blue Skies, Gray Skies
Easter Sunday Parade, The
Feeling in Your Heart, A
God Is Good to the Irish
Like the Wandering Minstrel
Molly Malone
Roses Understand
Tee Teedle Tum Di Dum
To Heaven on the Bronx Express
Yankee Father in the Yankee Home, The

Based on Play "Barbara Frietchie" by Clyde Fitch

MANHATTAN MARY
September 26, 1927

MUSIC BY RAY HENDERSON
WORDS BY B. G. DeSYLVA, LEW BROWN

Broadway
Five-Step, The
I'd Like You to Love Me
It Won't Be Long Now
Just a Cozy Hide-away
Manhattan Mary
Nothing but Love

SIDEWALKS OF NEW YORK
October 3, 1927

MUSIC BY JAMES HANLEY
WORDS BY EDDIE DOWLING

Goldfish Glide
Headin' for Harlem
Just a Little Smile from You
Playground in the Sky
When You Were Sweet Sixteen
Wherever You Are

YES, YES, YVETTE
October 3, 1927

Do You Love as I Love?
Music by Joseph Meyer, words by Irving Caesar

How'd You Like To?
Music by Stephen Jones, words by Irving Caesar

*I'm a Little Bit Fonder of You
Music and words by Irving Caesar

My Lady
Music and words by Frank Crumit, Ben Jerome

Pack up Your Blues and Smile
Music by Peter DeRose, Albert Von Tilzer, words by Jo Trent

Sing, Dance and Smile
Music by Philip Charig, words by Ben Jerome

Six O'Clock
Music by Philip Charig, Words by Irving Caesar

You, or Nobody!
Music and words by Irving Caesar

Dropped from New York production

MY PRINCESS
October 6, 1927

MUSIC BY SIGMUND ROMBERG
WORDS BY DOROTHY DONNELLY

Follow the Sun to the South
I Wonder Why
My Mimosa
Prince Charming

THE FIVE O'CLOCK GIRL
October 10, 1927

MUSIC BY HARRY RUBY
WORDS BY BERT KALMAR

Happy-Go-Lucky Bird
Thinking of You
Up in the Clouds
Who Did? You Did

WHITE LIGHTS
October 11, 1927

MUSIC BY J. FRED COOTS
WORDS BY AL DUBIN

Better Times Are Coming
  *Music by Jimmie Steiger, words by Dolph
  Singer*
Don't Throw Me Down
Eyeful of You
I'll Keep On Dreaming of You
Romany Rover

JUST FANCY
October 11, 1927

MUSIC BY JOSEPH MEYER, PHILIP CHARIG
WORDS BY LEO ROBIN

Coo-Coo
Dressed Up for Your Sunday Beau
Humpty-Dumpty
Shake Brother
Two Loving Arms
You Came Along

THE LOVE CALL
October 24, 1927

MUSIC BY SIGMUND ROMBERG
WORDS BY HARRY B. SMITH

Eyes That Love
Good Pals
I Live, I Die for You
Ranger's Song, The
'Tis Love

*A CONNECTICUT YANKEE
November 3, 1927

MUSIC BY RICHARD RODGERS
WORDS BY LORENZ HART

**I Blush
I Feel at Home with You
My Heart Stood Still
On a Desert Island with Thee
**Someone Should Tell Them
Thou Swell

ARTISTS AND MODELS
November 15, 1927

Call of Broadway, The
  *Music by Maury Rubens, words by Jack Oster-
  man, Ted Lewis*
Here Am I—Broken Hearted
  *Music by Ray Henderson, words by B. G. De-
  Sylva, Lew Brown*
Is Everybody Happy Now?
  *Music by Maury Rubens, words by Jack Oster-
  man, Ted Lewis*
Lobster Crawl, The
  Music by Harry Akst, words by Benny Davis
Oh, Peggy
  Music by Harry Akst, words by Benny Davis
Only One For Me, The
  Music by Harry Akst, words by Benny Davis
Snap Out of It
  Music by Harry Akst, words by Benny Davis
There's Nothing New in Old New York
  Music by Harry Akst, words by Benny Davis

*Based on novel by Mark Twain
**Dropped from New York production

FUNNY FACE
November 22, 1927

MUSIC BY GEORGE GERSHWIN
WORDS BY IRA GERSHWIN

Babbitt and the Bromide, The
Dance Alone with You
Funny Face
He Loves and She Loves
High Hat
Let's Kiss and Make Up
My One and Only
'S Wonderful
World Is Mine, The

TAKE THE AIR
November 27, 1927

Ham and Eggs in the Morning
   Music by Con Conrad, Abner Silver, words by Al Dubin
Just Like a Wild, Wild Rose
   Music by Dave Stamper, words by Gene Buck
Maybe I'll Baby You
   Music by Dave Stamper, words by Gene Buck
On a Pony for Two
   Music by James F. Hanley, words by Gene Buck
We'll Have a New Home in the Mornin'
   Music by Willard Robison, words by J. Russel Robinson, Gene Buck
Wings
   Music by Dave Stamper, words by Gene Buck

HARRY DELMAR'S REVELS
November 28, 1927

I Love a Man in Uniform
   Music by Jimmie Monaco, words by Billy Rose, Ballard MacDonald
If You Have Troubles Laugh Them Away
   Music and words by Lester Lee
Irresistible You
   Music by Jimmie Monaco, words by Billy Rose, Ballard MacDonald

My Rainbow
   Music by Jeanne Hackett, words by Lester Lee
Say it with a Solitaire
   Music by Jimmie Monaco, words by Billy Rose, Ballard MacDonald

GOLDEN DAWN
November 30, 1927

MUSIC BY EMMERICH KALMAN, HERBERT STOTHART
WORDS BY OTTO HARBACH, OSCAR HAMMERSTEIN II

Consolation
Dawn
   Music by Robert Stolz, Herbert Stothart
Here in the Dark
It's Always the Way
Mulunghu Tabu
My Bwanna
We Two
Whip, The

HAPPY
December 5, 1927

MUSIC BY FRANK GREY
WORDS BY EARLE CROOKER, MC ELBERT MOORE

Happy
Lorelei
Mad about You
Sunny Side of You
Through the Night

*THE WHITE EAGLE
December 26, 1927

MUSIC BY RUDOLF FRIML
WORDS BY BRIAN HOOKER

Alone (My Lover)
Gather the Rose
Give Me One Hour
Home for You, A
Regimental Song
Silver Wing
Smile, Darn You, Smile

Based on play "The Squaw Man" by Edwin-Milton Royle

‡ **SHOW BOAT**
December 27, 1927

Whoopsie!
You're What I Need

MUSIC BY JEROME KERN
WORDS BY OSCAR HAMMERSTEIN II

Bill
Words by P. G. Wodehouse
Can't Help Lovin' Dat Man
I Might Fall Back on You
Life upon the Wicked Stage
Make Believe
**Nobody Else but Me
Ol' Man River
Why Do I Love You?
You Are Love

LOVELY LADY
December 29, 1927

MUSIC BY DAVE STAMPER AND HAROLD LEVEY

At the Barbecue
Words by Harry A. Steinberg, Eddie Ward
I Could Love a Girl Like You
Words by Cyrus Wood
Lost Step, The
Words by Cyrus Wood
Lovely Lady
Words by Harry A. Steinberg, Eddie Ward
Make Believe You're Happy
Words by Cyrus Wood

SHE'S MY BABY
January 3, 1928

MUSIC BY RICHARD RODGERS
WORDS BY LORENZ HART

Baby's Best Friend, A
*How Was I To Know?
Little House in Soho, A
*Morning Is Midnight
When I Go on the Stage

†*Based on the Edna Ferber novel*
***From 1946 revival*
**Dropped from New York production*

ROSALIE
January 10, 1928

*Beautiful Gypsy
Music by George Gershwin, words by Ira Gershwin
Ev'rybody Knows I Love Somebody
Music by George Gershwin, words by Ira Gershwin
How Long Has This Been Going On?
Music by George Gershwin, words by Ira Gershwin
Hussars March
Music by Sigmund Romberg, words by P. G. Wodehouse
Oh Gee! Oh Joy!
Music by George Gershwin, words by Ira Gershwin, P. G. Wodehouse
*Rosalie
Music by George Gershwin, words by Ira Gershwin
Say So!
Music by George Gershwin, words by P. G. wodehouse, Ira Gershwin
West Point Song
Music by Sigmund Romberg, words by P. G. Wodehouse
Why Must We Always Be Dreaming?
Music by Sigmund Romberg, words by P. G. Wodehouse
*Yankee Doodle Rhythm
Music by George Gershwin, words by Ira Gershwin

THE OPTIMISTS
January 30, 1928

MUSIC BY MELVILLE GIDEON

Amapu
Words by Edward Knoblock

I Promise I'll Be Practically True to You
Words by Clifford Grey

Little Lacquer Lady
Words by Clifford Seyler

Spare a Little Love
Words by Clifford Grey

THE MADCAP
January 31, 1928

MUSIC BY MAURY RUBENS, J. FRED COOTS
WORDS BY CLIFFORD GREY

Honey, Be My Honey-Bee
Odle-De-O
Music by Maury Rubens

Something to Tell
Stop, Go!

SUNNY DAYS
February 8, 1928

MUSIC BY JEAN SCHWARTZ
WORDS BY CLIFFORD GREY, WILLIAM CARY DUN-
CAN

Hang Your Hat on the Moon
One Sunny Day
Really and Truly
'S No Use Talking
So Do I

RAIN OR SHINE
February 9, 1928

MUSIC BY MILTON AGER
LYRICS BY JACK YELLEN

Add a Little Wiggle
Breakfast with You
Feelin' Good
Music by Owen Murphy

Forever and Ever
Oh, Baby!
Music and words by Owen Murphy

Rain Or Shine
Roustabout's Song
Music by Milton Ager, Owen Murphy

Who's Goin' to Get You?

KEEP SHUFFLIN'
February 27, 1928

Charlie, My Back Door Man
*Music by Clarence Todd, words by Con Conrad,
Henry Creamer*

Give Me the Sunshine
*Music by Jimmy Johnson, words by Con Con-
rad, Henry Creamer*

Got Myself Another Jockey Now
*Music by Thomas (Fats) Waller, words by Andy
Razaf*

Pining
*Music and words by Henry Creamer, Clarence
Todd*

'Twas a Kiss in the Moonlight
*Music by Stephen Jones, words by Con Conrad,
Henry Creamer*

Willow Tree
*Music by Thomas (Fats) Waller, words by Andy
Razaf*

*THE THREE MUSKETEERS
March 13, 1928

MUSIC BY RUDOLF FRIML
WORDS BY P. G. WODEHOUSE, CLIFFORD GREY

Ev'ry Little While
Love Is the Sun
Ma Belle
March of the Musketeers
My Sword and I
Queen of My Heart
Your Eyes

GREENWICH VILLAGE FOLLIES
April 9, 1928

Get Your Man
*Music by Ray Perkins, words by Max and
Nathaniel Lief*

Subway Sun, The
*Music by Ray Perkins, words by Max and
Nathaniel Lief*

*Based on the Alexandre Dumas novel

GREENWICH VILLAGE FOLLIES (continued)

What's the Reason?
Music by Maury Rubens, words by Harold
Atteridge

Who's the Boy?
Music by Ray Perkins, words by Max and
Nathaniel Lief

PRESENT ARMS
April 26, 1928

MUSIC BY RICHARD RODGERS
WORDS BY LORENZ HART

Blue Ocean Blues
Crazy Elbows
Do I Hear You Saying?
Down By the Sea
I'm a Fool, Little One
Kiss for Cinderella, A
You Took Advantage of Me

HERE'S HOWE
May 1, 1928

MUSIC BY JOSEPH MEYER, ROGER WOLFE KAHN
WORDS BY IRVING CAESAR

Crazy Rhythm
Imagination
*Life as a Twosome
On My Mind a New Love

BLACKBIRDS OF 1928
May 9, 1928

MUSIC BY JIMMY McHUGH
WORDS BY DOROTHY FIELDS

Bandanna Babies
Dig-a Dig-a Doo
Dixie
Doin' the New Low-Down
Here Comes My Blackbird
I Can't Give You Anything but Love
I Must Have That Man
Magnolia's Wedding Day
Porgy
Shuffle Your Feet and Roll Along

Also in "Americana," 2nd edition

GRAND STREET FOLLIES OF 1928
May 28, 1928

Briny Blues
Music by Serge Walter, words by Agnes Morgan
Husky Dusky Annabel
Music by Max Ewing, words by Agnes Morgan
Just a Little Love Song
Music and words by Max Ewing
Someone to Admire, Someone to Adore
Music by Serge Walter, words by Agnes Morgan

SAY WHEN
June 26, 1928

MUSIC BY JESSE GREER
WORDS BY RAYMOND KLAGES

Cheerio
Words by James J. Walker
How About It?
In My Love Boat
Music by Daisy De Segonzac, words by Max
and Nathaniel Lief
One Step to Heaven
Say When

GEORGE WHITE'S SCANDALS (9th Edition)
July 2, 1928

MUSIC BY RAY HENDERSON
WORDS BY B. G. DeSYLVA, LEW BROWN

Alone with Only Dreams
American Tune
I'd Die
I'm on the Crest of a Wave
Pickin' Cotton
What D'Ya Say?
Where Your Name Is Carved with Mine

EARL CARROLL'S VANITIES
August 6, 1928

Blue Shadows
Music by Louis Alter, words by Ray Klages
Once in a Lifetime
Music by Jesse Greer, words by Ray Klages
Raquel
Music by Richard Whiting, words by Joe Burke

GOOD BOY
September 5, 1928

MUSIC BY HARRY RUBY, HERBERT STOTHART
WORDS BY BERT KALMAR

Good Boy
I Wanna Be Loved by You
Manhattan Walk
Some Sweet Someone
You're the One
   Music by Arthur Schwartz, words by Otto Harbach

WHITE LILACS
September 10, 1928

MUSIC BY KARL HAJOS (BASED ON CHOPIN)
WORDS BY HARRY B. SMITH

Adorable You
Far Away and Long Ago
I Love You and I Adore You
Melodies Within My Heart
White Lilacs

LUCKEE GIRL
September 15, 1928

MUSIC BY MAURICE YVAIN
WORDS BY MAX AND NATHANIEL LIEF

Come On and Make Whoopee
   Music by Werner Janssen, words by Mann Holiner
Friends and Lovers
I Love You So
I'll Take You to the Country
In Our Little Studio
   Music by Maurice Yvain, Muriel Pollock
Magic Melody

CROSS MY HEART
September 17, 1928

MUSIC BY HARRY TIERNEY
LYRICS BY JOSEPH McCARTHY

Come Along Sunshine
Dream Sweetheart
Hot Sands

Lady Whippoorwill
Right Out of Heaven
Salaaming the Rajah
We'll Have Our Good Days

THE NEW MOON
September 19, 1928

MUSIC BY SIGMUND ROMBERG
WORDS BY OSCAR HAMMERSTEIN II

Girl on the Prow, The
Lover, Come Back to Me
Marianne
One Kiss
Softly, as in a Morning Sunrise
Stouthearted Men
Try Her Out at Dances
Wanting You

CHEE-CHEE
September 25, 1928

MUSIC BY RICHARD RODGERS
WORDS BY LORENZ HART

Better Be Good to Me
Dear, Oh Dear
I Must Love You
Moon of My Delight
Singing a Love Song
Tartar Song, The

BILLIE
October 1, 1928

MUSIC AND WORDS BY GEORGE M. COHAN

Billie
Come to St. Thomas's
Ev'ry Boy in Town's My Sweetheart
Go Home Ev'ry Once in a While
Happy
I'm a One Girl Man
Personality
Say It Some More
Two of Us, The
They Fall in Love
Those Wonderful Friends
Where Were You—Where Was I?

JUST A MINUTE
October 8, 1928

MUSIC BY HARRY ARCHER
WORDS BY WALTER O'KEEFE

Anything Your Heart Desires
Break-Me-Down, The
Heigh-Ho Cheerio
I've Got a Cookie Jar but No Cookies
Pretty, Petite and Sweet
We'll Just Be Two Commuters
You'll Kill 'Em

PARIS
October 8, 1928

MUSIC AND WORDS BY COLE PORTER

Don't Look at Me That Way
Heaven Hop
Land of Going To Be, The
   Music and words by E. Ray Goetz, Walter Kollo
Let's Do It
*Let's Misbehave
Quelque Chose
Two Little Babes in the Wood
Vivienne
Which?

UPS-A-DAISY
October 8, 1928

MUSIC BY LEWIS E. GENSLER
WORDS BY ROBERT A. SIMON

Hot!
I Can't Believe It's True
Oh, How Happy We'll Be
   Words by Robert A. Simon, Clifford Grey
Oh, How I Miss You Blues!
   Words by Robert A. Simon, Clifford Grey
Sweet One
Ups-A-Daisy!
Will You Remember? Will You Forget?
   Words by Robert A. Simon, Clifford Grey

*Dropped from New York production

HOLD EVERYTHING!
October 10, 1928

MUSIC BY RAY HENDERSON
WORDS BY B. G. DeSYLVA, LEW BROWN

Don't Hold Everything
To Know You Is to Love You
Too Good to Be True
You're the Cream in My Coffee

THREE CHEERS
October 15, 1928

MUSIC BY RAY HENDERSON
WORDS BY B. G. DeSYLVA, LEW BROWN

Because You're Beautiful
Let's All Sing the Lard Song
   Music by Leslie Sarony, words by Anne Caldwell
Maybe This Is Love
My Silver Tree
   Music by Raymond Hubbell, words by Anne Caldwell
Orange Blossom Home
   Music by Raymond Hubbell, words by Anne Caldwell
Pompanola
Two Boys

ANIMAL CRACKERS
October 23, 1928

MUSIC BY HARRY RUBY
WORDS BY BERT KALMAR

Long Island Low Down
Waiting
Watching the Clouds Roll By
Who's Been Listening to My Heart?

AMERICANA (2nd Edition)
October 30, 1928

MUSIC BY ROGER WOLFE KAHN
WORDS BY IRVING CAESAR

Ameri-can-can
He's Mine

Hot Pants
Life as a Twosome
No Place Like Home
Young Black Joe

HELLO, YOURSELF
October 30, 1928

MUSIC BY RICHARD MYERS
WORDS BY LEO ROBIN

He Man
I Want the World to Know
Say That You Love Me
True Blue
You've Got a Way with You

THIS YEAR OF GRACE
November 7, 1928

MUSIC AND WORDS BY NOEL COWARD

Caballero
Dance, Little Lady
Lorelei
Mary Make Believe
Room with a View, A
Teach Me to Dance Like Grandma
Try to Learn to Love
World Weary

TREASURE GIRL
November 8, 1928

MUSIC BY GEORGE GERSHWIN
WORDS BY IRA GERSHWIN

Feeling I'm Falling
Got a Rainbow
I Don't Think I'll Fall in Love Today
† I've Got a Crush on You
K-ra-zy For You
Oh, So Nice
What Are We Here For?
Where's the Boy? Here's the Girl!

†Also in ''Strike Up The Band ''

RAINBOW
November 21, 1928

MUSIC BY VINCENT YOUMANS
WORDS BY OSCAR HAMMERSTEIN II

Bride Was Dressed in White, The
Hay, Straw
I Like You as You Are
I Want a Man
Let Me Give All My Love to Thee
My Mother Told Me Not to Trust a Soldier
One Girl, The
*Who Am I that You Should Care for Me?
  Words by Gus Kahn

ANGELA
December 3, 1928

MUSIC BY ALBERTA NICHOLS
WORDS BY MANN HOLINER

I Can't Believe It's True
Love Is Like That
Regal Romp
You've Got Me up a Tree

**WHOOPEE
December 4, 1928

MUSIC BY WALTER DONALDSON
WORDS BY GUS KAHN

Come West, Little Girl, Come West
Gypsy Joe
Gypsy Song, The
Here's to the Girl of My Heart
I'm Bringing a Red, Red Rose
Love Me or Leave Me
Making Whoopee
Song of the Setting Sun
Until You Get Somebody Else

THE HOUSEBOAT ON THE STYX
December 25, 1928

MUSIC BY ALMA SANDERS
WORDS BY MONTE CARLO

House Boat on the Styx, The
My Heaven

*Dropped from New York production
**Based on play ''The Nervous Wreck'' by Owen Davis

THE HOUSEBOAT ON THE STYX (continued)

Red River
Soul Mates
You've Got to Know Just How to Make Love

THE RED ROBE
December 25, 1928

Believe in Me
Music by Arthur Schwartz, words by Harry B. Smith
I've Got It
Music by Alberta Nichols, words by Mann Holiner
King of the Sword
Music by Robert Stolz, Maury Rubens, words by J. Keirn Brennan
Laugh at Life
Music by Maury Rubens, words by J. Delany Dunn
Soldier of Fortune, A
Music by Jean Gilbert, words by Harry B. Smith
You and I Are Passersby
Music by Jean Gilbert, words by Harry B. Smith

HELLO DADDY
December 26, 1928

MUSIC BY JIMMY McHUGH
WORDS BY DOROTHY FIELDS

As Long As We're in Love
Futuristic Rhythm
In a Great Big Way
Let's Sit and Talk about You
Out Where the Blues Begin
Your Disposition Is Mine

POLLY
January 8, 1929

MUSIC BY PHILIP CHARIG
WORDS BY IRVING CAESAR

Comme ci, Comme ca
Heel and Toe

On with the Dance
Polly

Sing a Song in the Rain
Music by Harry Rosenthal, words by Douglas Furber, Irving Caesar
Sweet Liar
Music by Herbert Stothart, words by Irving Caesar
What Can Be Sweeter?
When a Fellow Meets a Flapper on Broadway

FOLLOW THRU
January 9, 1929

MUSIC BY RAY HENDERSON
WORDS BY B. G. DeSYLVA, LEW BROWN

Button Up Your Overcoat
Follow Thru
I Could Give Up Anything but You
I Want to Be Bad
My Lucky Star
No More You
Still I'd Love You
Then I'll Have Time for You
You Wouldn't Fool Me, Would You?

NED WAYBURN'S GAMBOLS
January 15, 1929

MUSIC BY WALTER G. SAMUELS
WORDS BY MORRIE RYSKIND

Little Dream That's Coming True
Palm Beach Walk
Savannah Stomp
Ship of Love
Sun Will Shine, The
Music by Arthur Schwartz
What Is the Good
Music by Lew Kessler, words by Clifford Grey

BOOM-BOOM
January 28, 1929

MUSIC BY WERNER JANSSEN
WORDS BY MANN HOLINER, J. KEIRN BRENNAN

Blow the Blues Away
Shake High, Shake Low

What a Girl
What Could I Do?

LADY FINGERS
January 31, 1929

MUSIC BY JOSEPH MEYER
WORDS BY EDWARD ELISCU

Ga-Ga!
I Love You More than Yesterday
  Music by Richard Rodgers, words by Lorenz Hart
Let Me Weep on Your Shoulder
Open Book
Raise the Dust
Sing
  Music by Richard Rodgers, words by Lorenz Hart
Slow Down
Something to Live For
Turn to Me
You're Perfect

FIORETTA
February 5, 1929

Alone with You
  Music by G. Romilli, words by Grace Henry, Jo Trent
Blade of Mine
  Music by George Bagby, words by Grace Henry
Carissima
  Music by G. Romilli, words by Grace Henry
Dream Boat
  Music by George Bagby, words by Grace Henry, Jo Trent
Fioretta
  Music and words by G. Romilli
Roses of Red
  Music and words by G. Romilli

PLEASURE BOUND
February 18, 1929

Just Suppose
  Music by Phil Baker, Maury Rubens, words by Sid Silvers, Moe Jaffe

My Melody Man
  Music by Peter DeRose, words by Charles Tobias, Sidney Clare
Park Avenue Strut
  Music by Phil Baker, Maury Rubens, words by Moe Jaffe, Harold Atteridge
Things That Were Made for Love, The
  Music by Peter DeRose, words by Charles Tobias, Irving Kahal
We'll Get Along
  Music by Muriel Pollock, words by Max and Nathaniel Lief
Why Do You Tease Me?
  Music by Muriel Pollock, words by Max and Nathaniel Lief

SPRING IS HERE
March 11, 1929

MUSIC BY RICHARD RODGERS
WORDS BY LORENZ HART

Baby's Awake Now
Rich Man, Poor Man
Why Can't I?
With a Song in My Heart
You Never Say Yes
Yours Sincerely

MUSIC IN MAY
April 1, 1929

MUSIC BY MAURY RUBENS
WORDS BY J. KEIRN BRENNAN

Glory of Spring, The
High, High, High
I Found a Friend
I'd Like to Love Them All
No Other Love

MESSIN' AROUND
April 22, 1929

MUSIC BY JIMMY JOHNSON
WORDS BY PERCY BRADFORD

Get Away from That Window
Harlem Town

MESSIN' AROUND (*continued*)

I Need You

Messin' Around

Put Your Mind Right on It

Roust-About

Shout On!

Skiddle-de-Skow

Sorry that I Strayed Away from You

Your Love I Crave

THE LITTLE SHOW (**First Edition**)
April 30, 1929

Can't We Be Friends?
Music by Kay Swift, words by Paul James

Caught in the Rain
Music by Henry Sullivan, words by Howard Dietz

I Guess I'll Have to Change My Plan
Music by Arthur Schwartz, words by Howard Dietz

I've Made a Habit of You
Music by Arthur Schwartz, words by Howard Dietz

Little Hut in Hoboken, A
Music and words by Herman Hupfeld

Moanin' Low
Music by Ralph Rainger, words by Howard Dietz

Or What Have You?
Music by Morris Hamilton, words by Grace Henry

GRAND STREET FOLLIES OF 1929
May 1, 1929

I Love You and I Like You
Music by Arthur Schwartz, words by Max and Nathaniel Lief

I Need You So
Music by Arthur Schwartz, words by David Goldberg, Howard Dietz

I've Got You on My Mind
Music and words by Max Ewing

What Did Della Wear?
Music by Arthur Schwartz, words by A. Morgan, Albert Carroll

A NIGHT IN VENICE
May 21, 1929

I'm for You
Music by Lee David, words by J. Keirn Brennan

Loose Ankles
Music and words by Moe Jaffe, Clay Boland, Maury Rubens

One Night of Love
Music by Maury Rubens, words by J. Keirn Brennan

Sliding Down a Silver Cloud
Music by Lee David, words by J. Keirn Brennan

KEEP IT CLEAN
June 24, 1929

All I Need Is Someone Like You
Music by Harry Archer, words by Charles Tobias

Doin' the Hot-cha-cha
Music and words by Lester Lee

Let Me Hold You in My Arms
Music and words by Clarence Gaskill

BOMBOOLA
June 26, 1929

MUSIC AND WORDS BY FRANK MARCUS AND BERNARD MALTIN

Dixie Vagabond

Rub-A-Dub Your Rabbit's Foot

Somebody Like Me

Song of Harlem, The

Tampico Tune

HOT CHOCOLATES
June 29, 1929

MUSIC BY THOMAS (FATS) WALLER, HARRY BROOKS
WORDS BY ANDY RAZAF

Ain't Misbehavin'

Black and Blue

Can't We Get Together
Dixie Cinderella
Goddess of Rain
Off Time
Sweet Savannah Sue
That Jungle Jamboree
That Rhythm Man
That Snake Hip Dance
Waltz Divine

EARL CARROLL'S SKETCH BOOK
July 1, 1929

Crashing the Golden Gate
*Music by Jay Gorney, Phil Cohan, words by
E. Y. Harburg*
Don't Hang Your Dreams on a Rainbow
Music by Arnold Johnson, words by Irving Kahal
Fascinating You
*Music and words by Benee Russell, Charles and
Henry Tobias, Vincent Rose*
For Someone I Love
Music by Ted Snyder, words by Benny Davis
Kinda Cute
Music by Jay Gorney, words by E. Y. Harburg
Like Me Less, Love Me More
Music by Jay Gorney, words by E. Y. Harburg
Rhythm of the Waves
*Music by Vincent Rose, words by Charles and
Harry Tobias*
Song of the Moonbeams
*Music by Vincent Rose, words by Charles and
Harry Tobias*

*SHOW GIRL
July 2, 1929

MUSIC BY GEORGE GERSHWIN
WORDS BY IRA GERSHWIN AND GUS KAHN

Do What You Do!
**Feeling Sentimental
Harlem Serenade
I Must Be Home by Twelve O'Clock
Liza
So Are You!

*Based on novel of same title by J. P. McEvoy
**Dropped from New York production

AFRICANA
July 11, 1929

MUSIC AND WORDS BY DONALD HEYWOOD

Clorinda
I'm Coming Virginia
Words by Will Cook and Donald Heywood
Smile

BROADWAY NIGHTS
July 15, 1929

Baby-Doll Dance
*Music by Maury Rubens, Phil Svigals, words by
J. Keirn Brennan, Moe Jaffe*
Right Man, The
*Music by Sam Timberg, Maury Rubens, words
by Moe Jaffe*
Why Don't We?
*Music by Maury Rubens, Sam Timberg, words
by Moe Jaffe*
Your Broadway and Mine
Music by Maury Rubens, words by Moe Jaffe

JOHN MURRAY ANDERSON'S ALMANAC
August 14, 1929

Educate Your Feet
Music by Milton Ager, words by Jack Yellen
I Can't Remember the Words
*Music by Milton Ager, Henry Lodge, words by
Jack Yellen*
I May Be Wrong (But I Think You're Wonderful)
*Music by Henry Sullivan, words by Harry Rus-
kin*
Nightingale Song, The
Music by Milton Ager, words by Jack Yellen
Same Old Moon
*Music by Henry Sullivan, words by Clifford
Orr, John Murray Anderson*
Tinkle! Tinkle!
Music by Milton Ager, words by Jack Yellen
Wait for the Happy Ending
Music by Milton Ager, words by Jack Yellen

SWEET ADELINE
September 3, 1929

MUSIC BY JEROME KERN
WORDS BY OSCAR HAMMERSTEIN II

Don't Ever Leave Me
Here Am I
Out of the Blue
Sun About to Rise, The
'Twas Not So Long Ago
Why Was I Born?

THE STREET SINGER
September 17, 1929

MUSIC BY NICLAS KEMPNER
WORDS BY GRAHAM JOHN

From Now On
  *Music by Richard Myers, words by Edward
  Eliscu*
Go One Better
  Music by Sam Timberg
Jumping Jimminy
You Might Have Known I Loved You
  *Music and words by Niclas Kempner, Graham
  John*
You've Made Me Happy Today!

CAPE COD FOLLIES
September 18, 1929

MUSIC BY ALEXANDER FOGARTY

Clutching at Shadows
  Words by Seymour Morris
That's the Time When I Miss You
  Words by Seymour Morris
That's Why We Misbehave
  Words by Edith Lois, Urana Clarke
Wondering Who
  Words by George Fitch

GEORGE WHITE'S SCANDALS (10th Edition)
September 23, 1929

MUSIC AND WORDS BY CLIFF FRIEND, GEORGE
  WHITE

Bottoms Up
Bigger and Better than Ever

Is Izzy Azzy Woz?
Love Is Free to Everyone
Sittin' in the Sun (Just Wearing a Smile)
There's Something Spanish in Your Eyes

GREAT DAY!
October 17, 1929

MUSIC BY VINCENT YOUMANS
WORDS BY WILLIAM (BILLY) ROSE, EDWARD
  ELISCU

Great Day!
Happy Because I'm in Love
More Than You Know
One Love
Open Up Your Heart
Without a Song

BITTER SWEET
November 5, 1929

MUSIC AND WORDS BY NOEL COWARD

Call of Life, The
Dear Little Café
Green Carnation
I'll See You Again
If Love Were All
Kiss Me
Ladies of the Town
Tokay
Zigeuner

HEADS UP!
November 11, 1929

MUSIC BY RICHARD RODGERS
WORDS BY LORENZ HART

*I Can Do Wonders With You
It Must Be Heaven
Me for You
My Man Is on the Make
Ship Without a Sail, A
*Sky City
Why Do You Suppose?

*Dropped from New York production

SONS O' GUNS
November 26, 1929

MUSIC BY J. FRED COOTS
WORDS BY ARTHUR SWANSTROM AND BENNY
   DAVIS

Cross Your Fingers
I'm That Way Over You
It's You I Love
Let's Merge
Over Here
Red Hot and Blue Rhythm
Why?

FIFTY MILLION FRENCHMEN
November 27, 1929

MUSIC AND WORDS BY COLE PORTER

Find Me a Primitive Man
Happy Heaven of Harlem, The
I Worship You
I'm in Love
I'm Unlucky at Gambling
Let's Step Out
Paree, What Did You Do to Me?
Please Don't Make Me Be Good
Queen of Terre Haute, The
You Do Something to Me
You Don't Know Paree
You've Got That Thing

THE SILVER SWAN
November 27, 1929

MUSIC BY H. MAURICE JACQUET
WORDS BY WILLIAM BRADY

Cigarette
I Love You, I Adore You
Lonely Road, The
Love Letters
Till I Meet You
   Words by William Brady, Alonzo Price

TOP SPEED
December 25, 1929

MUSIC BY HARRY RUBY
WORDS BY BERT KALMAR

Goodness Gracious
I'll Know and She'll Know

Keep Your Undershirt On
Reaching for the Moon
What Would I Care?

WOOF, WOOF
December 25, 1929

MUSIC AND WORDS BY EDWARD POLA, EDDIE
   BRANDT

I Mean What I Say
Satanic Strut
That Certain Thing
Why Didn't You Tell Me?
Won't I Do?

WAKE UP AND DREAM
December 30, 1929

MUSIC AND WORDS BY COLE PORTER

Banjo That Man Joe Plays, The
Fancy Our Meeting
   Music by Joseph Meyer, Philip Charig, words
   by Douglas Furber
I Loved Him But He Didn't Love Me
I'm a Gigolo
Looking at You
She's Such a Comfort to Me
   Music by Arthur Schwartz, words by Douglas
   Furber, Max and Nathaniel Lief, Donovan Par-
   sons
Wake Up and Dream
What Is This Thing Called Love?
Why Wouldn't I Do?
   Music by Ivor Novello, words by Ivor Novello,
   Desmond Carter

STRIKE UP THE BAND
January 14, 1930

MUSIC BY GEORGE GERSHWIN
WORDS BY IRA GERSHWIN

Hangin' Around with You
I Mean to Say
I Want to Be a War Bride
†I've Got a Crush on You

†Also in "Treasure Girl"

STRIKE UP THE BAND (*continued*)

Military Dancing Drill
*Seventeen and Twenty-one
Soon
Strike Up the Band!

9:15 REVUE
February 11, 1930

Get Happy
    Music by Harold Arlen, words by Ted Koehler

Up Among the Chimney Pots
    Music by Kay Swift, words by Paul James

You Wanted Me—I Wanted You
    Music by Harold Arlen, words by Ted Koehler

RIPPLES
February 11, 1930

MUSIC BY OSCAR LEVANT
WORDS BY IRVING CAESAR, GRAHAM JOHN

Anything May Happen Any Day
    Music by Jerome Kern, words by Graham John

Babykins
I'm Afraid
    Music by Albert Sirmay

Is It Love?
    Words by Irving Caesar

Talk with Your Heel and Your Toe
    Words by Irving Caesar

There's Nothing Wrong with a Kiss

SIMPLE SIMON
February 18, 1930

MUSIC BY RICHARD RODGERS
WORDS BY LORENZ HART

*Dancing on the Ceiling
Don't Tell Your Folks
*He Was Too Good to Me
*I Still Believe in You
Send for Me
Sweetenheart
Ten Cents a Dance

Dropped from N. Y. production

LEW LESLIE'S INTERNATIONAL REVIEW
February 25, 1930

MUSIC BY JIMMY McHUGH
WORDS BY DOROTHY FIELDS

Cinderella Brown
Exactly Like You
I'm Feelin' Blue ('Cause I Got Nobody)
International Rhythm
I've Got a Bug in My Heart
Keys to Your Heart
On the Sunny Side of the Street

FLYING HIGH
March 3, 1930

MUSIC BY RAY HENDERSON
WORDS BY LEW BROWN, B. G. DeSYLVA

Good for You—Bad for Me
I'll Know Him
I'm Flying High
Red Hot Chicago
Thank Your Father
Wasn't It Beautiful While It Lasted?
Without Love

JONICA
April 7, 1930

MUSIC BY JOSEPH MEYER
WORDS BY BILLY MOLL

Here in My Heart
I Want Someone
    Music and words by William B. Friedlander
If You Were the Apple
Tie Your Cares to a Melody

THREE LITTLE GIRLS
April 14, 1930

Love Comes Only Once in a Lifetime
    *Music by Harold Stern, Harry Perella, words by
    Stella Unger*
Love's Happy Dream
    *Music by Walter Kollo, words by Harry B.
    Smith*

Prince Charming
Music by Walter Kollo, words by Harry B. Smith

TATTLE TALES
June 1, 1930

Another Case of the Blues
Music by Richard Myers, words by Johnny Mercer

Counting the Sheep
Music by Louis Alter, words by Max and Nathaniel Lief

I'll Take an Option on You
Music by Ralph Rainger, words by Leo Robin

Just a Sentimental Tune
Music by Louis Alter, words by Max and Nathaniel Lief

My Impression of You
Music and words by Michael Cleary, Herb Magidson, Ned Washington

THE GARRICK GAIETIES (Third Edition)
June 4, 1930

Ankle Up the Altar with Me
Music by Richard Myers, words by E. Y. Harburg

I Am Only Human After All
Music by Vernon Duke, words by Ira Gershwin, E. Y. Harburg

I've Got It Again
Music by Ned Lehak, words by Allen Boretz

Lazy Levee Loungers
Music and words by Willard Robison

Love Is Like That
Music by Ned Lehak, words by Allen Boretz

Out of Breath
Music by Everett Miller, words by Johnny Mercer

Put It Away Till Spring
Music by Peter Nolan, words by Joshua Titzell

Shavian Shivers
Music by Vernon Duke, words by E. Y. Harburg

Too, Too Divine
Music by Vernon Duke, words by E. Y. Harburg

You Lost Your Opportunity
Music by Charles M. Schwab, words by Henry Myers

CHANGE YOUR LUCK
June 6, 1930

Tailspin
Music and words by Maceo Pinkard

ARTISTS AND MODELS
June 10, 1930

My Real Ideal
Music by Burton Lane, words by Samuel Lerner

Two Perfect Lovers
Music by Burton Lane, words by Samuel Lerner

Who Cares?
Music by Haydn Wood, Joseph Tunbridge, Jack Waller, words by Dion Titheradge

EARL CARROLL'S VANITIES (8th Edition)
July 1, 1930

MUSIC BY HAROLD ARLEN
WORDS BY TED KOEHLER

Contagious Rhythm
Hittin' the Bottle
March of Time, The
One Love
Out of a Clear Blue Sky
Rumba Rhythm
Music by Jimmy Johnson, words by Stella Unger

THE SECOND LITTLE SHOW
September 2, 1930

MUSIC BY ARTHUR SCHWARTZ
WORDS BY HOWARD DIETZ

I Like Your Face
Lucky Seven
Sing Something Simple
Music and words by Herman Hupfeld

THE SECOND LITTLE SHOW (continued)

Music by Del Cleveland, words by Ted Fetter

What a Case I've Got on You

You're the Sunrise

*LUANA
September 17, 1930

MUSIC BY RUDOLF FRIML
WORDS BY J. KEIRN BRENNAN

Aloha

Luana

My Bird of Paradise

Son of the Sun

NINA ROSA
September 20, 1930

MUSIC BY SIGMUND ROMBERG
WORDS BY IRVING CAESAR

My First Love, My Last Love
Words by Irving Caesar, Otto Harbach

Nina Rosa

Payador

Serenade of Love

There Can Only Be Only One for Me

Your Smiles, Your Tears

FINE AND DANDY
September 23, 1930

MUSIC BY KAY SWIFT
WORDS BY PAUL JAMES

Can This Be Love?

Fine and Dandy

Jig Hop, The

Let's Go Eat Worms in the Garden

Nobody Breaks My Heart

Rich or Poor

Starting at the Bottom

Based on play "The Bird of Paradise" by Richard Walton Tully

BROWN BUDDIES
October 7, 1930

Betty Lou
Music by Joe Jordan, words by Rosamond Johnson

Dancin' 'Way Your Sin
Music and words by J. C. Johnson

Darky Rhythm
Music by Peter Tinturin, words by Joe Young

Don't Leave Your Little Blackbird Blue
Music and words by Joe Jordan, Porter Grainger, Shelton Brooks

Happy
Music by Nat Reed, words by Bob Joffe

I Hate Myself (For Falling in Love with You)
Music and words by Abner Silver, Dave Oppenheim

Missouri
Music and words by Nat Reed

PRINCESS CHARMING
October 13, 1930

MUSIC BY ALBERT SIRMAY AND ARTHUR SCHWARTZ
WORDS BY ARTHUR SWANSTROM

I Love Love
Music by Robert Dolan, words by Walter O'Keefe

I'll Be There

I'll Never Leave You

Trailing a Shooting Star

You

GIRL CRAZY
October 14, 1930

MUSIC BY GEORGE GERSHWIN
WORDS BY IRA GERSHWIN

Bidin' My Time

Boy! What Love Has Done to Me!

But Not for Me

Could You Use Me?

Embraceable You

I Got Rhythm

Sam and Delilah

Treat Me Rough

THREE'S A CROWD
October 15, 1930

All the King's Horses
  Music by Alec Wilder, words by Edward Brandt,
  Howard Dietz

Body and Soul
  Music by Johnny Green, words by Edward Hey-
  man, Robert Sour

Forget All Your Books
  Music by Burton Lane, words by Howard Dietz

Moment I Saw You, The
  Music by Arthur Schwartz, words by Howard
  Dietz

Out in the Open Air
  Music by Burton Lane, words by Howard Dietz,
  Ted Pola

Practising Up on You
  Music by Philip Charig, words by Howard Dietz

Right at the Start of It
  Music by Arthur Schwartz, words by Howard
  Dietz

Something to Remember You By
  Music by Arthur Schwartz, words by Howard
  Dietz

Yaller
  Music by Charles M. Schwab, words by Richard
  Myers

BLACKBIRDS OF 1930
October 22, 1930

MUSIC BY EUBIE BLAKE
WORDS BY ANDY RAZAF

Baby Mine
Green Pastures
  Words by Will Morrissey, Andy Razaf

Memories of You
My Handy Man Ain't Handy No More
Papa-De-Da-Da
  Music and words by Spencer Williams, Clarence
  Todd, Clarence Williams

Roll Jordan
That Lindy Hop
You're Lucky to Me

THE VANDERBILT REVUE
November 5, 1930

MUSIC BY JIMMY McHUGH
WORDS BY DOROTHY FIELDS

Blue Again
Button Up Your Heart
I Give Myself Away
  Music by Jacques Fray, words by Edward
  Eliscu

HELLO, PARIS
November 15, 1930

Every Bit of You
  Music and words by Kenneth Friede, Adrian
  Samish

I Stumbled over You
  Music and words by Maury Rubens, Henry
  Dagand

I'll Admit
  Music and words by Maury Rubens, Henry
  Dagand

SWEET AND LOW
November 17, 1930

MUSIC BY HARRY WARREN

Cheerful Little Earful
  Words by Ira Gershwin, Billy Rose

He's Not Worth Your Tears
  Words by Mort Dixon, Billy Rose

In the Merry Month of Maybe
  Words by Ira Gershwin, Billy Rose

Overnight
  Music by Louis Alter, words by Billy Rose,
  Charlotte Kent

Sweet So-and-So
  Music by Joseph Meyer, Philip Charig, words
  by Ira Gershwin

Would You Like to Take a Walk?
  Words by Mort Dixon, Billy Rose

SMILES
November 18, 1930

MUSIC BY VINCENT YOUMANS

Be Good to Me
  Words by Ring Lardner
*Carry On, Keep Smiling
  Words by Harold Adamson
If I Were You, Love
  Words by Ring Lardner
I'm Glad I Waited
  Words by Clifford Grey, Harold Adamson
Time on My Hands
  Words by Harold Adamson, Mack Gordon

THE NEW YORKERS
December 8, 1930

MUSIC AND WORDS BY COLE PORTER

Great Indoors, The
I Happen to Like New York
I'm Getting Myself Ready for You
Let's Fly Away
Love for Sale
Take Me Back to Manhattan
Where Have You Been?

BALLYHOO
December 22, 1930

MUSIC BY LOUIS ALTER
WORDS BY HARRY RUSKIN, LEIGHTON K. BRILL

Blow Hot—Blow Cold
How I Could Go for You
I'm One of God's Children
  Words by Oscar Hammerstein II, Harry Ruskin
If I Were You
No Wonder I'm Blue
  Words by Oscar Hammerstein II
That Tired Feeling

*Dropped from New York production

MEET MY SISTER
December 30, 1930

MUSIC AND WORDS BY RALPH BENATZKY

Always in My Heart
Devil May Care, The
She Is My Ideal

YOU SAID IT
January 19, 1931

MUSIC BY HAROLD ARLEN
WORDS BY JACK YELLEN

If He Really Loves Me
It's Different with Me
Learn to Croon
Sweet and Hot
What Do We Care
While You Are Young
You Said It
You'll Do

PRIVATE LIVES
January 27, 1931

Some Day I'll Find You
  Music and words by Noel Coward

AMERICA'S SWEETHEART
February 10, 1931

MUSIC BY RICHARD RODGERS
WORDS BY LORENZ HART

How About It?
I've Got Five Dollars
Lady Must Live, A
There's So Much More
We'll Be the Same

THE GANG'S ALL HERE
February 18, 1931

MUSIC BY LEWIS E. GENSLER
WORDS BY OWEN MURPHY, ROBERT A. SIMON

Adorable Julie
Baby Wanna Go Bye-Bye

By Special Permission of the Copyright Owners,
  I Love You
It Always Takes Two
More than Ever
Speak Easy
Speaking of You

THE WONDER BAR
March 17, 1931

MUSIC BY ROBERT KATSCHER
WORDS BY IRVING CAESAR

Elizabeth
Good Evening, Friends
Ma Mère
  *Music and words by Al Jolson, Irving Caesar,
  Harry Warren*
Oh, Donna Clara
  Music by J. Petersburski
Something Seems to Tell Me

RHAPSODY IN BLACK
May 4, 1931

MUSIC BY ALBERTA NICHOLS
WORDS BY MANN HOLINER

Till the Real Thing Comes Along
  *Music and words by Alberta Nichols, Mann
  Holiner, Sammy Cahn*
What's Keeping My Prince Charming?
You Can't Stop Me from Lovin' You

CRAZY QUILT
May 19, 1931

Crazy Quilt
  Music by Harry Warren, words by Bud Green
Have a Little Drinkee
  Music by Ned Lehak, words by Edward Eliscu
I Found a Million Dollar Baby
  *Music by Harry Warren, words by Billy Rose,
  Mort Dixon*

It's in the Air
  *Music by Louis Alter, words by E. Y. Harburg,
  Billy Rose*
Sing a Little Jingle
  Music by Harry Warren, words by Mort Dixon

THE THIRD LITTLE SHOW
June 1, 1931

*Any Little Fish
  Music and words by Noel Coward
Falling in Love
  *Music by Henry Sullivan, words by Earle
  Crooker*
I'll Putcha Pitcha in the Papers
  *Music by Michael Cleary, words by Max and
  Nathaniel Lief*
I've Lost My Heart
  *Music by Morris Hamilton, words by Grace
  Henry*
Mad Dogs and Englishmen
  Music and words by Noel Coward
Say the Word
  *Music by Burton Lane, words by Harold
  Adamson*
When Yuba Plays the Rumba on His Tuba
  Music and words by Herman Hupfeld
You Forgot Your Gloves
  Music by Ned Lehak, words by Edward Eliscu
You Might as Well Pretend
  *Music by William (Morgan) Lewis, Jr., words
  by Ted Fetter, Edward Eliscu*

THE BAND WAGON
June 3, 1931

MUSIC BY ARTHUR SCHWARTZ
WORDS BY HOWARD DIETZ

Confession
Dancing in the Dark
High and Low
Hoops
I Love Louisa
Miserable with You
New Sun in the Sky
Sweet Music

Dropped from New York production

ZIEGFELD FOLLIES OF 1931
July 1, 1931

Cigarettes, Cigars!
Music by Harry Revel, words by Mack Gordon

Do the New York
Music by Ben Oakland, words by Jack Murray,
Barry Trivers

Half-Caste Woman
Music and words by Noel Coward

Help Yourself to Happiness
Music by Harry Revel, words by Harry Rich-
man, Mack Gordon

Here We Are in Love
Music by Ben Oakland, words by Jack Murray,
Barry Trivers

Was I?
Music by Chick Endor, words by Charlie Farrell

Wrapped Up in You
Music by Ben Oakland, words by Jack Murray,
Barry Trivers

SHOOT THE WORKS
July 21, 1931

Do What You Like
Music by Philip Charig, words by Leo Robin

Hot Moonlight
Music by Jay Gorney, words by E. Y. Harburg

How's Your Uncle?
Music by Jimmy McHugh, words by Dorothy
Fields

It's In the Stars
Music by Michael Cleary, words by Max and
Nathaniel Lief

Muchacha
Music by Vernon Duke, Jay Gorney, words by
E. Y. Harburg

Poor Little Doorstep Baby
Music by Michael Cleary, words by Max and
Nathaniel Lief

EARL CARROLL'S VANITIES (9th Edition)
August 27, 1931

Have a Heart
Music by Burton Lane, words by Harold
Adamson

It's Great to Be in Love
Music and words by Cliff Friend

Tonight or Never
Music and words by Jack Meskill, Raymond
Klages, Vincent Rose

FREE FOR ALL
September 8, 1931

MUSIC BY RICHARD A. WHITING
WORDS BY OSCAR HAMMERSTEIN II

Free for All
Not That I Care
Slumber Song (Good Night)
Tonight
When Your Boy Becomes a Man

GEORGE WHITE'S SCANDALS (11th Edition)
September 14, 1931

MUSIC BY RAY HENDERSON
WORDS BY LEW BROWN

If I Thought I Could Live Without You I'd Die
Life is Just a Bowl of Cherries
My Song
That's Love
That's Why Darkies Were Born
This Is the Missus
Thrill Is Gone, The

FAST AND FURIOUS
September 15, 1931

So Lonesome
Music by Joe Jordan, words by Rosamond
Johnson

Walkin' on Air
Music by Harry Revel, words by Mack Gordon

Where's My Happy Ending?
Music by Harry Revel, words by Mack Gordon,
Harold Adamson

SINGIN' THE BLUES
September 16, 1931

MUSIC BY JIMMY McHUGH
WORDS BY DOROTHY FIELDS

It's the Darndest Thing
Singin' the Blues

NIKKI
September 29, 1931

MUSIC BY PHILIP CHARIG
WORDS BY JAMES DYRENFORTH

Now I Know
On Account of I Love You
Taking Off

EVERYBODY'S WELCOME
October 13, 1931

As Time Goes By
  Music and words by Herman Hupfeld
Even as You and I
  Music by Sammy Fain, words by Irving Kahal
Is Rhythm Necessary
  Music by Sammy Fain, words by Irving Kahal
Nature Played an Awful Trick on You
  *Music by Manning Sherwin, words by Arthur
  Lippmann, Milton Pascal*
That's Good, That's Bad
  Music by Sammy Fain, words by Irving Kahal
You've Got a Lease on My Heart
  Music by Sammy Fain, words by Irving Kahal

THE CAT AND THE FIDDLE
October 15, 1931

MUSIC BY JEROME KERN
WORDS BY OTTO HARBACH

*Don't Ask Me Not to Sing
I Watch the Love Parade
New Love Is Old, A
Night Was Made for Love, The
One Moment Alone
Poor Pierrot
She Didn't Say "Yes"
Try to Forget

EAST WIND
October 27, 1931

MUSIC BY SIGMUND ROMBERG
WORDS BY OSCAR HAMMERSTEIN II

Are You Love?
East Wind

Dropped from New York production

I'd Be a Fool
It's a Wonderful World
You Are My Woman
Young Man in Love

THE LAUGH PARADE
November 2, 1931

MUSIC BY HARRY WARREN
WORDS BY MORT DIXON, JOE YOUNG

Gotta Go to Town
I Wish I Could Laugh at Love
Love Me Forever
More You Hurt Me, The
Ooh, That Kiss
Torch Song, The
You're My Everything

HERE GOES THE BRIDE
November 3, 1931

MUSIC BY JOHNNY GREEN
WORDS BY EDWARD HEYMAN

Hello, My Lover, Good-bye
It Means So Little to You
  Music by Richard Myers
Music in My Fingers
  Music by Richard Myers
My Sweetheart 'Tis of Thee
Ohhh! Ahhh!
One Second of Sex
Shake Well Before Using

THE SOCIAL REGISTER
  (Play with one song)
November 9, 1931

Key to My Heart, The
  Music by Louis Alter, words by Ira Gershwin

SUGAR HILL
December 25, 1931

MUSIC BY JAMES P. JOHNSON
WORDS BY FLOURNOY MILLER

Chivaree
Far-Away Love

SUGAR HILL (*continued*)

~~I Don't Want Any Labor in My Job~~

Keep 'Em Guessing
My Sweet Hunk o' Trash
Peace, Sister, Peace
Stay Out of the Kitchen
That Was Then
You Can't Lose a Broken Heart

OF THEE I SING
December 26, 1931

MUSIC BY GEORGE GERSHWIN
WORDS BY IRA GERSHWIN

Because, Because
Illegitimate Daughter, The
Love Is Sweeping the Country
Of Thee I Sing
Who Cares?
Wintergreen for President

A LITTLE RACKETEER
January 18, 1932

MUSIC BY HENRY SULLIVAN
WORDS BY EDWARD ELISCU

Here's To Night
Inside Looking Out
Whiling My Time Away

*THROUGH THE YEARS
January 28, 1932

MUSIC BY VINCENT YOUMANS
WORDS BY EDWARD HEYMAN

Drums in My Heart
It's Every Girl's Ambition
Kathleen Mine
Kinda Like You
Through the Years
You're Everywhere

*Based on play "Smilin' Through" by Jane Cowl and Jane
Murfin.

FACE THE MUSIC
February 17, 1932

~~MUSIC AND WORDS BY IRVING BERLIN~~

I Say It's Spinach
Let's Have Another Cup of Coffee
Manhattan Madness
My Rhinestone Girl
On a Roof in Manhattan
Soft Lights and Sweet Music

MARCHING BY
March 3, 1932

I Love You, My Darling
    *Music by Jean Gilbert, words by George Hirst,
    Edward Eliscu*
I've Gotta Keep My Eye on You
    Music by Harry Revel, words by Mack Gordon
Marching By
    *Music by Gus Edwards, words by Harry Clark,
    Guy Robertson*

HOT-CHA!
March 8, 1932

MUSIC BY RAY HENDERSON
WORDS BY LEW BROWN

Hot-cha
It's Great to Be Alive!
Say
There I Go Dreaming Again
There's Nothing the Matter with Me
You Can Make My Life a Bed of Roses

BLACKBERRIES OF 1932
April 4, 1932

MUSIC AND WORDS BY DONALD HEYWOOD

Answer Is No, The
Blackberries
Brown Sugar
First Thing in the Morning
Harlem Mania
Love Me More—Love Me Less
    Music by Tom Peluso, words by Ben Bernard

HEY NONNY NONNY!
June 6, 1932

MUSIC BY MICHAEL H. CLEARY
WORDS BY MAX AND NATHANIEL LIEF

For Better or Worse
Season Ended, The
Tell Me Something About Yourself
Wouldn't That Be Wonderful
  Music and words by Herman Hupfeld

SMILING FACES
August 30, 1932

MUSIC BY HARRY REVEL
WORDS BY MACK GORDON

Do Say You Do
I Stumbled Over You and Fell in Love
In a Little Stucco in the Sticks
Quick Henry, the Flit
Sweet Little Stranger
There Will Be a Girl

BALLYHOO OF '32
September 6, 1932

MUSIC BY LEWIS E. GENSLER
WORDS BY E. Y. HARBURG

Falling off the Wagon
How Do You Do It?
Riddle Me This
Thrill Me

FLYING COLORS
September 15, 1932

MUSIC BY ARTHUR SCHWARTZ
WORDS BY HOWARD DIETZ

Alone Together
Fatal Fascination
Louisiana Hayride
Rainy Day, A
Shine on Your Shoes, A
Smokin' Reefers
Two-Faced Woman

EARL CARROLL'S VANITIES
September 27, 1932

Along Came Love
  Music by Henry Tobias, words by Haven Gillespie, Charles Tobias
I Gotta Right to Sing the Blues
  Music by Harold Arlen, words by Ted Koehler
My Darling
  Music by Richard Myers, words by Edward Heyman
Rockin' in Rhythm
  Music by Harold Arlen, words by Ted Koehler
Take Me Away
  Music by Peter Tinturin, words by Sidney Clare, Charles Tobias

AMERICANA (3rd Edition)
October 5, 1932

Brother, Can You Spare a Dime?
  Music by Jay Gorney, words by E. Y. Harburg
Satan's Li'l Lamb
  Music by Harold Arlen, words by E. Y. Harburg, Johnny Mercer
Whistling for a Kiss
  Music by Richard Myers, words by E. Y. Harburg, Johnny Mercer
Would'ja for a Big Red Apple
  Music by Henry Souvaine, words by Everett Miller, Johnny Mercer

MUSIC IN THE AIR
November 8, 1932

MUSIC BY JEROME KERN
WORDS BY OSCAR HAMMERSTEIN II

And Love Was Born
I Am So Eager
I'm Alone
In Egern on the Tegern See
I've Told Every Little Star
One More Dance
Song Is You, The
There's a Hill Beyond a Hill
We Belong Together
When the Spring Is in the Air

THE DUBARRY
November 22, 1932

MUSIC BY CARL MILLÖCKER (revised by Theo
   Mackeben)
WORDS BY ROWLAND LEIGH

Dubarry, The
Ga-Ga
I Give My Heart
If I Am Dreaming
Without Your Love

GEORGE WHITE'S MUSIC HALL
   VARIETIES
November 22, 1932

MUSIC BY HAROLD ARLEN
WORDS BY IRVING CAESAR

Two Feet in Two Four Time

TAKE A CHANCE
November 26, 1932

MUSIC BY VINCENT YOUMANS, NACIO BROWN,
   RICHARD A. WHITING
WORDS BY B. G. DeSYLVA

Eadie Was a Lady
   Music by Richard A. Whiting, Nacio Brown

*I Want to Be with You
   Music by Vincent Youmans

Oh, How I Long to Belong to You
   Music by Vincent Youmans

Rise 'n Shine
   Music by Vincent Youmans

Should I Be Sweet?
   Music by Vincent Youmans

So Do I
   Music by Vincent Youmans

Turn Out the Light
   Music by Richard A. Whiting, Nacio Brown

You're an Old Smoothie
   Music by Richard A. Whiting, Nacio Brown

Dropped from New York production

GAY DIVORCE
November 29, 1932

MUSIC AND WORDS BY COLE PORTER

After You
How's Your Romance?
I've Got You on My Mind
Mister and Missus Fitch
Night and Day
You're in Love

WALK A LITTLE FASTER
December 7, 1932

MUSIC BY VERNON DUKE
WORDS BY E. Y. HARBURG

April in Paris
Off Again, On Again
Penny for Your Thoughts, A
So Nonchalant
Speaking of Love
That's Life
Where Have We Met Before?

SHUFFLE ALONG OF 1933
December 26, 1932

MUSIC BY EUBIE BLAKE
WORDS BY NOBLE SISSLE

Everything Reminds Me of You

PARDON MY ENGLISH
January 20, 1933

MUSIC BY GEORGE GERSHWIN
WORDS BY IRA GERSHWIN

Isn't It a Pity?
I've Got to Be There
Lorelei
Luckiest Man in the World
My Cousin in Milwaukee
So What?
Where You Go I Go

MELODY
February 14, 1933

MUSIC BY SIGMUND ROMBERG
WORDS BY IRVING CAESAR

Give Me a Roll on a Drum
I'd Write a Song
In My Garden
Melody
Never Had an Education
Pompadour
Tonight May Never Come Again
You Are the Song

STRIKE ME PINK
March 4, 1933

MUSIC BY RAY HENDERSON
WORDS BY LEW BROWN

Home to Harlem
I Hate to Think that You'll Grow Old, Baby
It's Great to Be Alive
Let's Call It a Day
Ooh, I'm Thinking
Strike Me Pink

SHADY LADY
July 5, 1933

Any Way the Wind Blows
  Music and words by Bud Green, Cliff Friend,
  Sam H. Stept
Get Hot Foot
  Music and words by Bud Green, Sam H. Stept
Swingy Little Thingy
  Music and words by Bud Green, Sam H. Stept
Time to Go
  Music by Jesse Greer, Words by Stanley Adams
Where, Oh Where Can I Find Love
  Music by Jesse Greer, words by Stanley Adams

MURDER AT THE VANITIES
September 8, 1933

Me For You Forever
  Music by Richard Myers, words by Edward
  Heyman

Savage Serenade
  Music and words by Herman Hupfeld
Sweet Madness
  Music by Victor Young, words by Ned
  Washington
Weep No More, My Baby
  Music by Johnny Green, words by Edward
  Heyman

HOLD YOUR HORSES
September 25, 1933

MUSIC BY ROBERT RUSSELL BENNETT
WORDS BY OWEN MURPHY, ROBERT A. SIMON

Do You?
High Shoes
Hold Your Horses
I'd Like to Take You Home to Meet My Mother
If I Love Again
  Music by Ben Oakland, words by J. P. Murray
Singing To You
  Music and words by Ben Oakland, Margot
  Millham, Robert A. Simon
Swapping Sweet Nothings With You

AS THOUSANDS CHEER
September 30, 1933

MUSIC AND WORDS BY IRVING BERLIN

Easter Parade
Funnies, The
Harlem on My Mind
Heat Wave
How's Chances?
Lonely Heart
Not For All the Rice in China
Supper Time

LET 'EM EAT CAKE
October 21, 1933

MUSIC BY GEORGE GERSHWIN
WORDS BY IRA GERSHWIN

Blue, Blue, Blue
Let'Em Eat Cake

LET' EM EAT CAKE (*continued*)

On and On and On
Union Square

TELL HER THE TRUTH
October 28, 1933

MUSIC BY JACK WALLER, JOSEPH TUNBRIDGE
WORDS BY R. P. WESTON, BERT LEE

Happy the Day
Hoch, Caroline!
Sing, Brothers!
That's Fine

†ROBERTA
November 18, 1933

MUSIC BY JEROME KERN
WORDS BY OTTO HARBACH

*Armful of Trouble, An
I'll Be Hard to Handle
   Words by Bernard Dougall
Let's Begin
Smoke Gets in Your Eyes
Something Had to Happen
Touch of Your Hand, The
Yesterdays
You're Devastating

SHE LOVES ME NOT
November 20, 1933

MUSIC BY ARTHUR SCHWARTZ
WORDS BY EDWARD HEYMAN

After All, You're All I'm After
She Loves Me Not

BLACKBIRDS OF 1934
December 2, 1933

Hundred Years From Today, A
   Music by Victor Young, words by Joseph Young,
   Ned Washington

†*Based on novel "Gowns by Roberta" by Alice Duer Miller*
Dropped from New York production

I Just Couldn't Take It, Baby
   Music by Alberta Nichols, words by Mann
   Holiner
I'm Walkin' the Chalk Line
   Music by Alberta Nichols, words by Mann
   Holiner
Let Me Be Born Again
   Music by Victor Young, words by Joseph Young,
   Ned Washington
Tappin' the Barrel
   Music by Victor Young, words by Joseph Young,
   Ned Washington
Your Mother's Son-in-Law
   Music by Alberta Nichols, words by Mann
   Holiner

ZIEGFELD FOLLIES OF 1934
January 4, 1934

MUSIC BY VERNON DUKE
WORDS BY E. Y. HARBURG

Careful With My Heart
   Music by Senia Pokrass
I Like the Likes of You
Moon About Town
   Music by Dana Suesse
Rain in My Heart
   Music by Louis Alter, words by Arthur
   Swanstrom
Suddenly
   Words by E. Y. Harburg, Billy Rose
This Is Not a Song
   Words by E. Y. Harburg, E. Hartman
To the Beat of My Heart
   Music by Senia Pokrass
What Is There to Say?

COME OF AGE
January 12, 1934

MUSIC BY RICHARD ADDINSELL
WORDS BY CLEMENCE DANE

I Came to Your Room
I Come Out of a Dream

I'm Afraid of the Dark
River Song, The
Too Much Work

ALL THE KING'S HORSES
January 30, 1934

MUSIC BY EDWARD HORAN
WORDS BY FREDERICK HERENDEEN

Charming
Evening Star
I Found a Song
I've Gone Nuts Over You

NEW FACES
March 15, 1934

'Cause You Won't Play House
  Music by Morgan Lewis, words by E. Y. Harburg
Lamplight
  Music and words by James Shelton
Music in My Heart
  Music by Warburton Guilbert, words by June Sillman
You're My Relaxation
  Music by Charles M. Schwab, words by Robert Sour

CAVIAR
June 7, 1934

MUSIC BY HARDEN CHURCH
WORDS BY EDWARD HEYMAN

My Heart's an Open Book
Nothing Was Ever Like This
Ocean Will Never Run Dry, The
Silver Sails
You're One in a Million

KEEP MOVING
August 23, 1934

MUSIC BY MAX RICH
WORDS BY JACK SCHOLL

Hot-Cha Chiquita
Now Is the Time
Wake Up, Sleepy Moon

LIFE BEGINS AT 8:40
August 27, 1934

MUSIC BY HAROLD ARLEN
WORDS BY E. Y. HARBURG, IRA GERSHWIN

Fun to Be Fooled
Let's Take a Walk Around the Block
Shoein' the Mare
What Can You Say in a Love Song?
You're a Builder Upper

SALUTA
August 28, 1934

MUSIC BY FRANK D'ARMOND

Chill in the Air
  Words by Will Morrissey
Just Say the Word
  Words by Milton Berle

THE GREAT WALTZ
September 22, 1934

MUSIC BY JOHANN STRAUSS
WORDS BY DESMOND CARTER

Danube So Blue
For We Love You Still
Love Will Find You
Morning
While You Love Me
With All My Heart

CONVERSATION PIECE
October 23, 1934

MUSIC AND WORDS BY NOEL COWARD

I'll Follow My Secret Heart
Nevermore
Regency Rakes
There's Always Something Fishy About the French

SAY WHEN
November 8, 1934

MUSIC BY RAY HENDERSON
WORDS BY TED KOEHLER

Don't Tell Me It's Bad
Isn't It June?

SAY WHEN (*continued*)

It Must Have Been the Night

Let's Take Advantage of Now

Put Your Heart in a Song

Say When

So Long For Ever So Long

Torch Parade

When Love Comes Swingin' Along

ANYTHING GOES
November 20, 1934

MUSIC AND WORDS BY COLE PORTER

All Through the Night

Anything Goes

Blow, Gabriel, Blow

Buddie, Beware

Gypsy In Me, The

I Get a Kick Out of You

Waltz Down the Aisle

You're the Top

*REVENGE WITH MUSIC
November 28, 1934

MUSIC BY ARTHUR SCHWARTZ
WORDS BY HOWARD DIETZ

If There Is Someone Lovelier Than You

Maria

That Fellow Manuelo

Wand'ring Heart

When You Love Only One

You and the Night and the Music

CALLING ALL STARS
December 13, 1934

MUSIC BY HARRY AKST
WORDS BY LEW BROWN

He Just Beats a Tom Tom

I Don't Want to Be President

If It's Love

I've Nothing to Offer

Just Mention Joe

Stepping Out of the Picture

Straw Hat in the Rain

Based on novel "The Three-Cornered Hat" by Pedro de Alarcón

FOOLS RUSH IN
December 25, 1934

I'm So in Love
Music by Will Irwin, words by Norman Zeno

Let's Hold Hands
Music by Richard Lewine, words by June Sillman

Love, Come Take Me
Music by Will Irwin, words by Norman Zeno

Two Get Together
Music by Will Irwin, words by Norman Zeno

THUMBS UP
December 27, 1934

Autumn in New York
Music and words by Vernon Duke

Continental Honeymoon
Music by James Hanley, words by Ballard MacDonald

Eileen Mavourneen
Music by Henry Sullivan, words by John Murray Anderson

Flamenco
Music by Henry Sullivan, words by Earle Crooker

Gotta See a Man About His Daughter
Music by James Hanley, words by Jean Herbert, Karl Stark

Lily Belle May June
Music by Henry Sullivan, words by Earle Crooker

Soldier of Love
Music and words by Irving Caesar, Gerald Marks, Sammy Lerner

Zing! Went the Strings of My Heart
Music and words by James Hanley

THE O'FLYNN
December 27, 1934

MUSIC BY FRANKLIN HAUSER

Child of Erin
Words by Russell Janney

Lovely Lady, A
Words by Russell Janney

Man I Love Is Here, The
Words by Brian Hooker

Song of My Heart
Words by Brian Hooker

MUSIC HATH CHARMS
December 29, 1934

MUSIC BY RUDOLF FRIML
WORDS BY ROWLAND LEIGH, JOHN SHUBERT

Annina
Cavaliers
Love
Maria
My Heart Is Yours
My Palace of Dreams
Romance
Sweet Fool

PETTICOAT FEVER
(Play with one song)
March 4, 1935

Love Tiptoed Through My Heart
Music by Frederick Loewe, words by Irene Alexander

SOMETHING GAY
(Play with one song)
April 29, 1935

You Are So Lovely and I'm So Lonely
Music by Richard Rodgers, words by Lorenz Hart

PARADE
May 20, 1935

MUSIC BY JEROME MOROSS
WORDS BY PAUL PETERS AND GEORGE SKLAR

Life Could Be So Beautiful
You Ain't So Hot

EARL CARROLL'S SKETCH BOOK
June 4, 1935

At Last
Music by Henry Tobias, words by Charles Tobias, Sam Lewis

Let's Swing It
Music and words by Charles Tobias, Charles Newman, Murray Mencher

Moonlight and Violins
Music and words by Charles Tobias, Charles Newman, Murray Mencher

There's Music in a Kiss
Music and words by Al Sherman, Al Lewis, Abner Silver

Young Ideas
Music and words by Charles Tobias, Charles Newman, Murray Mencher

AT HOME ABROAD
September 19, 1935

MUSIC BY ARTHUR SCHWARTZ
WORDS BY HOWARD DIETZ

Farewell, My Lovely
Got a Bran' New Suit
Hottentot Potentate, The
Love Is a Dancing Thing
O Leo
That's Not Cricket
Thief in the Night
What a Wonderful World

*PORGY AND BESS
October 10, 1935

MUSIC BY GEORGE GERSHWIN

Bess, You Is My Woman
Words by Ira Gershwin, DuBose Heyward

I Got Plenty o' Nuttin'
Words by Ira Gershwin, DuBose Heyward

I Loves You, Porgy
Words by Ira Gershwin, DuBose Heyward

It Ain't Necessarily So
Words by Ira Gershwin

My Man's Gone Now
Words by DuBose Heyward

Oh Bess, Oh Where's My Bess?
Words by Ira Gershwin

Summertime
Words by DuBose Heyward

Based on play "Porgy" by DuBose and Dorothy Heyward

PORGY AND BESS (*continued*)

~~There's a Boat Dat's Leavin' Soon For New York~~

   Words by Ira Gershwin

Woman Is a Sometime Thing, A
   Words by DuBose Heyward

JUBILEE
October 12, 1935

MUSIC AND WORDS BY COLE PORTER

Begin the Beguine
Just One of Those Things
Kling-Kling Bird on the Divi-Divi Tree, The
Me and Marie
Picture of Me Without You, A
When Love Comes Your Way
Why Shouldn't I?

JUMBO
November 16, 1935

MUSIC BY RICHARD RODGERS
WORDS BY LORENZ HART

Circus Is on Parade, The
Diavolo
Little Girl Blue
Most Beautiful Girl in the World, The
My Romance
Over and Over Again

MAY WINE
December 5, 1935

MUSIC BY SIGMUND ROMBERG
WORDS BY OSCAR HAMMERSTEIN II

Dance, My Darlings
I Built a Dream One Day
Just Once Around the Clock
Somebody Ought to Be Told
Something New Is in My Heart

GEORGE WHITE'S SCANDALS OF 1936
December 25, 1935

MUSIC BY RAY HENDERSON
WORDS BY JACK YELLEN

Anything Can Happen
Cigarette

I'm the Fellow Who Loves You
I've Got to Get Hot
Life Begins at Sweet Sixteen
May I Have My Gloves?
Pied Piper of Harlem
Tell the Truth

THE ILLUSTRATORS' SHOW
January 22, 1936

Bang-the Bell Rang!
   Music by Irving Actman, words by Frank Loesser

Waltz Was Born in Vienna, A
   Music by Frederick Loewe, words by Earle Crooker

ZIEGFELD FOLLIES OF 1936
January 30, 1936

MUSIC BY VERNON DUKE
WORDS BY IRA GERSHWIN

Gazooka, The
I Can't Get Started
Island in the West Indies
My Red Letter Day
That Moment of Moments
Words Without Music

ON YOUR TOES
April 11, 1936

MUSIC BY RICHARD RODGERS
WORDS BY LORENZ HART

Glad to Be Unhappy
Heart Is Quicker Than the Eye, The
It's Got to Be Love
On Your Toes
Quiet Night
Slaughter on Tenth Avenue
There's a Small Hotel
Too Good for the Average Man

BROADWAY SHOW WINDOW
April 12, 1936

Hitch Your Wagon to a Star
   Music by Richard Lewine, words by Ted Fetter

Poverty Row or Luxury Lane
Music by Gus Edwards, words by Howard Johnson

Spring Is in the Air
Music by Gus Edwards, words by Eugene Conrad

SUMMER WIVES
April 13, 1936

MUSIC BY SAM MORRISON
WORDS BY DOLPH SINGER

Chatterbox, The
I Wrote a Song For You
Words by Dolph Singer, William Dunham
Mickey
My Love Carries On
Play Me an Old Time Two-Step
Us on a Bus
Music by Vee Lawnhurst, words by Tot Seymour

NEW FACES OF 1936
May 19, 1936

It Must Be Religion
Music and words by Forman Brown

It's High Time I Got the Low-Down on You
Music by Joseph Meyer, words by Edward Heyman

Love Is a Dancer
Music by Muriel Pollock, words by Jean Sothern

My Last Affair
Music and words by Haven Johnson

My Love Is Young
Music by Irvin Graham, words by Bickley Reichner

Tonight's the Night
Music by Alex Fogarty, words by June Sillman

You Better Go Now
Music by Irvin Graham, words by Bickley Reichner

Your Face Is So Familiar
Music by Alex Fogarty, words by Edwin Gilbert

WHITE HORSE INN
October 1, 1936

WORDS BY IRVING CAESAR

Blue Eyes
Music by Robert Stolz

I Cannot Live Without Your Love
Music by Ralph Benatzky

I Would Love to Have You Love Me
Music by Sammy Lerner, Gerald Marks

In a Little Swiss Chalet
Music by Will Irwin, words by Norman Zeno

Leave it to Katarina
Music by Jara Benes

Waltz of Love
Music by Richard Fall

White Horse Inn
Music by Ralph Benatzky

White Sails
Music by Vivian Ellis

RED, HOT AND BLUE
October 29, 1936

MUSIC AND WORDS BY COLE PORTER

Down in the Depths (On the Ninetieth Floor)
Goodbye, Little Dream, Goodbye
It's De-Lovely
Little Skipper From Heaven Above, A
Ours
Ozarks Are Calling Me Home, The
Red, Hot and Blue
Ridin' High
You're a Bad Influence
You've Got Something

JOHNNY JOHNSON
November 19, 1936

MUSIC BY KURT WEILL
WORDS BY PAUL GREEN

Mon Ami, My Friend
Oh, Heart of Love
On the Rio Grande
To Love You and to Lose You
Words by Edward Heyman

TONIGHT AT 8:30
November 24, 1936

MUSIC AND WORDS BY NOEL COWARD

from RED PEPPERS
Has Anybody Seen Our Ship?
Men About Town

from SHADOW PLAY
Play, Orchestra, Play!
Then
You Were There

from WE WERE DANCING
We Were Dancing

THE SHOW IS ON
December 25, 1936

Buy Yourself a Balloon
  Music and words by Herman Hupfeld
By Strauss
  *Music by George Gershwin, words by Ira
  Gershwin*
It's So Easy to Lose
  *Music by Hoagy Carmichael, words by Ted
  Fetter*
Little Old Lady
  *Music by Hoagy Carmichael, words by Stanley
  Adams*
Long As You Got Your Health
  Music by Will Irwin, words by E. Y. Harburg
Now
  Music by Vernon Duke, words by Ted Fetter
What a Dummy Love Has Made of Me
  Music by Will Irwin, words by Norman Zeno

NAUGHTY-NAUGHT
January 23, 1937

MUSIC BY RICHARD LEWINE
WORDS BY TED FETTER

Love Makes the World Go Round
When We're in Love (from *1946* revival)
Zim-Zam-Zee

FREDERIKA
February 4, 1937

MUSIC BY FRANZ LEHAR
WORDS BY EDWARD ELISCU

Kiss to Remind You, A
One
Rising Star
Rose in the Heather
Why Did You Kiss My Heart Awake?

BABES IN ARMS
April 14, 1937

MUSIC BY RICHARD RODGERS
WORDS BY LORENZ HART

All at Once
All Dark People
Babes in Arms
I Wish I Were in Love Again
Johnny One Note
Lady Is a Tramp, The
My Funny Valentine
Way Out West
Where or When

ORCHIDS PREFERRED
May 11, 1937

MUSIC BY DAVE STAMPER
WORDS BY FRED HERENDEEN

Boy, Girl, Moon
I'm Leaving the Bad Girls for Good
Million Dollars, A
What Are You Going to Do About Love?

SEA LEGS
May 18, 1937

MUSIC BY MICHAEL H. CLEARY
WORDS BY ARTHUR SWANSTROM

Opposite Sex, The
Ten O'Clock Town
Touched in the Head

SWING IT
July 22, 1937

MUSIC BY EUBIE BLAKE
WORDS BY J. MILTON REDDIE, CECIL MACK

Ain't We Got Love
By the Sweat of Your Brow
Green and Blue
Huggin' and Muggin'

VIRGINIA
September 2, 1937

MUSIC BY ARTHUR SCHWARTZ
WORDS BY ALBERT STILLMAN

Good-bye Jonah
If You Were Someone Else
My Heart Is Dancing
Old Flame Never Dies, An
    Words by Albert Stillman, Laurence Stallings
Virginia
You and I Know
    Words by Albert Stillman, Laurence Stallings

THE FIREMAN'S FLAME
October 9, 1937

MUSIC BY RICHARD LEWINE
WORDS BY TED FETTER

Do My Eyes Deceive Me?
I Like the Nose on Your Face
It's a Lovely Night on the Hudson River

I'D RATHER BE RIGHT
November 2, 1937

MUSIC BY RICHARD RODGERS
WORDS BY LORENZ HART
*Everybody Loves You
Have You Met Miss Jones?
I'd Rather Be Right
Sweet Sixty-five
Take and Take and Take

Dropped from New York production

PINS & NEEDLES
November 27, 1937

MUSIC AND WORDS BY HAROLD ROME

Chain Store Daisy
Doing the Reactionary
Nobody Makes a Pass at Me
One Big Union for Two
Sing Me a Song with Social Significance
Sunday in the Park
What Good Is Love

HOORAY FOR WHAT
December 1, 1937

MUSIC BY HAROLD ARLEN
WORDS BY E. Y. HARBURG

Buds Won't Bud
Down With Love
God's Country
In the Shade of the New Apple Tree
I've Gone Romantic on You
Life's a Dance
Moanin' in the Mornin'

BETWEEN THE DEVIL
December 22, 1937

MUSIC BY ARTHUR SCHWARTZ
WORDS BY HOWARD DIETZ

By Myself
I See Your Face Before Me
Triplets
Why Did You Do It?
You Have Everything

THREE WALTZES
December 25, 1937

Days of Old, The
    *Music by Oscar Straus, words by Clare
    Kummer*
I Found My Love
    *Music by Johann Strauss, Jr., words by Clare
    Kummer, Edwin Gilbert*

THREE WALTZES (continued)

I Sometimes Wonder
Music by Oscar Straus, words by Clare
Kummer

Our Last Valse
Music by Oscar Straus, words by Clare
Kummer

Springtime in the Air
Music by Johann Strauss, Sr., words by
Clare Kummer

To Love Is to Live
Music by Johann Strauss, Jr., words by
Clare Kummer

THE CRADLE WILL ROCK
January 3, 1938

MUSIC AND WORDS BY MARC BLITZSTEIN

Art for Art's Sake
Cradle Will Rock, The
Croon-Spoon
Doctor and Ella
Drugstore Scene
Freedom of the Press, The
Gus and Sadie Love Song
Honolulu
Joe Worker
Leaflets
Nickel Under the Foot
Rich, The

RIGHT THIS WAY
January 4, 1938

MUSIC BY SAMMY FAIN
WORDS BY IRVING KAHAL

Don't Listen To Your Heart
Music and words by Marianne Brown Waters,
Bradford Greene

Doughnuts and Coffee
I Can Dream, Can't I?
I Love the Way We Fell in Love
I'll Be Seeing You
Love Design
Music and words by Marianne Brown Waters,
Bradford Greene

WHO'S WHO
March 1, 1938

Girl With the Paint on Her Face, The
Music and words by Irvin Graham

I Dance Alone
Music and words by James Shelton

I Must Have a Dinner Coat
Music and words by James Shelton

It's You I Want
Music by Paul McGrane, words by Al
Stillman

Let Your Hair Down With a Bang
Music by Baldwin Bergersen, words by June
Sillman

Rinka Tinka Man
Music by Lew Kessler, words by June Sillman

Train Time
Music by Baldwin Bergersen, words by June
Sillman

I MARRIED AN ANGEL
May 11, 1938

MUSIC BY RICHARD RODGERS
WORDS BY LORENZ HART

At the Roxy Music Hall
Did You Ever Get Stung?
How to Win Friends and Influence People
I Married an Angel
I'll Tell the Man in the Street
Spring Is Here
Twinkle in Your Eye, A

THE TWO BOUQUETS
May 31, 1938

WORDS BY ELEANOR AND HERBERT FARJEON

Bashful Lover
Music by C. Moulton

I Sent a Letter to My Love
Music by M. Pinsuti

Sweet Blossoms
Music by M. Pinsuti

Toddy's the Drink for Me
Traditional air

YOU NEVER KNOW
September 21, 1938

MUSIC AND WORDS BY COLE PORTER

At Long Last Love
By Candlelight
   Music by Robert Katscher, words by Rowland
   Leigh
For No Rhyme or Reason
From Alpha to Omega
Maria
No (You Can't Have My Heart)
   Music and words by Dana Suesse
What Is That Tune?
What Shall I Do?
You Never Know

HELLZAPOPPIN'
September 22, 1938

MUSIC BY SAMMY FAIN
WORDS BY CHARLES TOBIAS

Blow a Balloon Up To The Moon
Boomps-A-Daisy
   Music and words by Annette Mills
Fuddle-Dee-Duddle
It's Time To Say "Aloha"
We Won't Let It Happen Here
   Music by Teddy Hall, words by Don George
When McGregor Sings Off Key
When You Look in Your Looking Glass
   Music by Paul Mann, Stephen Weiss, words
   by Sam Lewis

SING OUT THE NEWS
September 24, 1938

MUSIC AND WORDS BY HAROLD ROME

F. D. R. Jones
How Long Can Love Keep Laughing?
My Heart Is Unemployed
One of These Fine Days
Ordinary Guy
Yip-Ahoy

KNICKERBOCKER HOLIDAY
October 19, 1938

MUSIC BY KURT WEILL
WORDS BY MAXWELL ANDERSON

It Never Was You
September Song
There's Nowhere to Go But Up
Will You Remember Me?

THE GIRL FROM WYOMING
October 29, 1938

MUSIC BY RICHARD LEWINE
WORDS BY TED FETTER

Boston in the Spring
Dying Cowboy, The
Hats Off
Kickin' the Corn Around
Lullaby of the Plain
Manuelo
Our Home
Stay East, Young Man

*LEAVE IT TO ME
November 9, 1938

MUSIC AND WORDS BY COLE PORTER

Far Away
From Now On
Get Out of Town
I Want to Go Home
Most Gentlemen Don't Like Love
My Heart Belongs to Daddy
Taking the Steps to Russia
To-morrow

**THE BOYS FROM SYRACUSE
November 23, 1938

MUSIC BY RICHARD RODGERS
WORDS BY LORENZ HART

Falling in Love with Love
Oh, Diogenes!

Based on play "Clear All Wires" by Samuel and Bella
   Spewack
**Based on "The Comedy of Errors" by William Shakespeare*

THE BOYS FROM SYRACUSE (*continued*)

Shortest Day of the Year, The
Sing for Your Supper
This Can't Be Love
You Have Cast Your Shadow on the Sea

GREAT LADY
December 1, 1938

MUSIC BY FREDERICK LOEWE
WORDS BY EARLE CROOKER

I Have Room in My Heart
May I Suggest Romance?
There Had to Be the Waltz
Why Can't This Night Last Forever?

MAMBA'S DAUGHTERS
(Play with one song)
January 3, 1939

Lonesome Walls
Music by Jerome Kern, words by DuBose Heyward

SET TO MUSIC
January 18, 1939

MUSIC AND WORDS BY NOEL COWARD

I Went to a Marvelous Party
I'm So Weary of It All
Mad About the Boy
Never Again
Stately Homes of England, The
Three White Feathers

ONE FOR THE MONEY
February 4, 1939

MUSIC BY MORGAN LEWIS
WORDS BY NANCY HAMILTON

I Only Know
Once Upon a Time
Teeter Totter Tessie

STARS IN YOUR EYES
February 9, 1939

MUSIC BY ARTHUR SCHWARTZ
WORDS BY DOROTHY FIELDS

All the Time
I'll Pay the Check
It's All Yours
Just a Little Bit More
Lady Needs a Change, A
Terribly Attractive
This Is It

SING FOR YOUR SUPPER
April 24, 1939

Imagine My Finding You Here
Music by Ned Lehak, words by Robert Sour
Lucky
Music by Lee Wainer, words by Robert Sour
Opening Night
Music by Lee Wainer, words by Robert Sour
Papa's Got a Job
Music by Ned Lehak, words by Robert Sour, Hector Troy
Story of a Horn, The
Music by Lee Wainer, words by Robert Sour

STREETS OF PARIS
June 19, 1939

MUSIC BY JIMMY McHUGH
WORDS BY AL DUBIN

Danger in the Dark
Doin' the Chamberlain
History Is Made at Night
Music and words by Harold Rome
*In My Memories
Is It Possible?
Reading, Writing and Rhythm
Rendezvous Time in Paree
South American Way
We Can Live on Love

Dropped from New York production

YOKEL BOY
July 6, 1939

MUSIC BY SAM STEPT
WORDS BY LEW BROWN, CHARLES TOBIAS

Boy Named Lem, A
Comes Love
I Can't Afford to Dream
It's Me Again
Let's Make Memories Tonight
Time for Jukin'
   Music by Walter Kent
Uncle Sam's Lullaby

GEORGE WHITE'S SCANDALS OF 1939
August 28, 1939

MUSIC BY SAMMY FAIN
WORDS BY JACK YELLEN

Are You Havin' Any Fun?
Good Night, My Beautiful
Our First Kiss
Mexiconga
   Words by Jack Yellen, Herb Magidson
Something I Dreamed Last Night
   Words by Jack Yellen, Herb Magidson

THE STRAW HAT REVUE
September 29, 1939

MUSIC AND WORDS BY JAMES SHELTON

Four Young People
Our Town

TOO MANY GIRLS
October 18, 1939

MUSIC BY RICHARD RODGERS
WORDS BY LORENZ HART

All Dressed Up (Spic and Spanish)
Give It Back to the Indians
I Didn't Know What Time It Was
I Like to Recognize the Tune
Love Never Went to College
She Could Shake the Maracas

VERY WARM FOR MAY
November 17, 1939

MUSIC BY JEROME KERN
WORDS BY OSCAR HAMMERSTEIN II

All In Fun
All the Things You Are
Heaven in My Arms
In Other Words, Seventeen
In the Heart of the Dark
That Lucky Fellow

SWINGIN' THE DREAM
November 29, 1939

MUSIC BY JIMMY VAN HEUSEN
WORDS BY EDDIE DE LANGE

Darn That Dream
Love's a Riddle
Moonland
Peace, Brother
Spring Song
There's Got to Be a Wedding

DU BARRY WAS A LADY
December 6, 1939

MUSIC AND WORDS BY COLE PORTER

But in the Morning, No
Come On In
Do I Love You?
Ev'ry Day a Holiday
Friendship
Give Him the Oo-La-La
It Was Written in the Stars
Katie Went to Haiti
Well, Did You Evah?
When Love Beckoned (in Fifty-second Street)

EARL CARROLL'S VANITIES
January 13, 1940

Angel
   Music by Peter De Rose, words by Mitchell Parish

EARL CARROLL'S VANITIES (continued)

I Want My Mama
Music by Jararaca and Vincent Paiva, words by Al Stillman

Starlit Hour
Music by Peter De Rose, words by Mitchell Parish

TWO FOR THE SHOW
February 8, 1940

MUSIC BY MORGAN LEWIS
WORDS BY NANCY HAMILTON

At Last It's Love
House with a Little Red Barn, A
How High the Moon

HIGHER AND HIGHER
April 4, 1940

MUSIC BY RICHARD RODGERS
WORDS BY LORENZ HART

Ev'ry Sunday Afternoon
From Another World
It Never Entered My Mind
Nothing But You

KEEP OFF THE GRASS
May 23, 1940

MUSIC BY JIMMY McHUGH
WORDS BY AL DUBIN

Clear Out of This World
Crazy As a Loon
Latin Tune, a Manhattan Moon and You, A
On the Old Park Bench
Words by Howard Dietz
Two in a Taxi
Words by Howard Dietz

LOUISIANA PURCHASE
May 28, 1940

MUSIC AND WORDS BY IRVING BERLIN

Dance with Me (Tonight at the Mardi Gras)
Fools Fall in Love

It'll Come to You
It's a Lovely Day Tomorrow
Latins Know How
Lord Done Fixed Up My Soul, The
Louisiana Purchase
Outside of That I Love You
What Chance Have I with Love?
Wild About You
You Can't Brush Me Off
You're Lonely and I'm Lonely

WALK WITH MUSIC
June 4, 1940

MUSIC BY HOAGY CARMICHAEL
WORDS BY JOHNNY MERCER

Darn Clever, These Chinese
Everything Happens to Me
Give, Baby, Give
Music by Irving Gellers, Otis Spencer, words by Gladys Shelley
I Walk with Music
Ooh! What You Said
Rumba Jumps, The
Way Back in 1939 A.D.
What'll They Think of Next?

HOLD ON TO YOUR HATS
September 11, 1940

MUSIC BY BURTON LANE
WORDS BY E. Y. HARBURG

Don't Let It Get You Down
There's a Great Day Coming Manana
World Is in My Arms, The
Would You Be So Kindly

BOYS AND GIRLS TOGETHER
October 1, 1940

MUSIC BY SAMMY FAIN
WORDS BY IRVING KAHAL, JACK YELLEN

I Want to Live
Words by Jack Yellen
Latin in Me, The
Words by Jack Yellen

Such Stuff As Dreams Are Made Of
Words by Irving Kahal

Sun'll Be Up in the Morning, The
Words by Jack Yellen

Times Square Dance
Words by Jack Yellen

You Can't Put Catsup on the Moon
Words by Irving Kahal

CABIN IN THE SKY
October 25, 1940

MUSIC BY VERNON DUKE
WORDS BY JOHN LATOUCHE

Cabin in the Sky
Do What You Wanna Do
Honey in the Honeycomb
In My Old Virginia Home (on the River Nile)
Love Me Tomorrow
Taking a Chance on Love
   Words by John Latouche, Ted Fetter

PANAMA HATTIE
October 30, 1940

MUSIC AND WORDS BY COLE PORTER

All I've Got to Get Now Is My Man
Fresh As a Daisy
I've Still Got My Health
Let's Be Buddies
Make It Another Old Fashioned, Please
My Mother Would Love You
Visit Panama
Who Would Have Dreamed?

*PAL JOEY
December 25, 1940

MUSIC BY RICHARD RODGERS
WORDS BY LORENZ HART

Bewitched
Den of Iniquity
Do It the Hard Way

*Based on short stories by John O'Hara

Happy Hunting Horn
I Could Write a Book
Plant You Now, Dig You Later
Take Him
What Is a Man?
You Mustn't Kick It Around

MEET THE PEOPLE
December 25, 1940

MUSIC BY JAY GORNEY

Bill of Rights, The
   Words by Henry Myers

Elmer's Wedding Day
   Music and words by Sid Kuller, Ray Golden

Fellow and a Girl, A
   Words by Edward Eliscu

In Chi-Chi-Castenango
   Words by Henry Myers

It's the Same Old South
   Words by Edward Eliscu

Let's Steal a Tune from Offenbach
   Words by Henry Myers

Meet the People
   Words by Henry Myers

No Lookin' Back
   Words by Henry Myers, Edward Eliscu

Stars Remain, The
   Words by Henry Myers

Union Label
   Words by Henry Myers, Edward Eliscu

**We Have Sandwiches
   Words by Henry Myers

ALL IN FUN
December 27, 1940

It's a Big, Wide Wonderful World
   Music and words by John Rox

Love and I
   Music by Baldwin Bergersen, words by June Sillman

**Dropped from New York production

ALL IN FUN (*continued*)

Macumba
Music by Baldwin Bergersen, words by June Sillman

My Memory Started with You
Music by Baldwin Bergersen, words by June Sillman

Quittin' Time
Music and words by John Rox

That's Good Enough for Me
Music by Baldwin Bergersen, words by Virginia Faulkner

Where Can I Go From You?
Music by Baldwin Bergersen, words by S. K. Russell

CRAZY WITH THE HEAT
January 14, 1941

Time of Your Life, The
Music by William Provost, words by Peter K. Smith

Wine from My Slipper
Music and words by Irvin Graham

With a Twist of the Wrist
Music and words by Irvin Graham

You Should Be Set to Music
Music and words by Irvin Graham

LADY IN THE DARK
January 23, 1941

MUSIC BY KURT WEILL
WORDS BY IRA GERSHWIN

Girl of the Moment
Jenny
My Ship
One Life to Live
Princess of Pure Delight, The
This Is New
Tschaikowsky

BEST FOOT FORWARD
October 1, 1941

MUSIC BY HUGH MARTIN
WORDS BY RALPH BLANE

Buckle Down, Winsocki
Ev'ry Time

I Know You by Heart
Just a Little Joint with a Juke Box
Shady Lady Bird
That's How I Love the Blues
Three "B's", The
What Do You Think I Am?

VIVA O'BRIEN
October 9, 1941

MUSIC BY MARIA GREVER
WORDS BY RAYMOND LEVEEN

Carinito
Mood of the Moment
Our Song
So Long to All Our Memories
To Prove My Love

*LET'S FACE IT
October 29, 1941

MUSIC AND WORDS BY COLE PORTER

Ace in the Hole
Ev'rything I Love
Farming˜
I Hate You Darling
Jerry, My Soldier Boy
Let's Not Talk About Love
Little Rumba Numba, A
Rub Your Lamp
You Irritate Me So

HIGH KICKERS
October 31, 1941

MUSIC BY HARRY RUBY
WORDS BY BERT KALMAR

Cigarettes
I've Got Somethin'
Panic in Panama, A
Time to Sing, The
Waltzing in the Moonlight
You're On My Mind

*Based on play "The Cradle Snatchers" by Norma Mitchell and Russell Medcraft

SONS O' FUN
December 1, 1941

MUSIC BY SAMMY FAIN
WORDS BY JACK YELLEN

Happy in Love
Let's Say Goodnight with a Dance
Oh, Auntie

SUNNY RIVER
December 4, 1941

MUSIC BY SIGMUND ROMBERG
WORDS BY OSCAR HAMMERSTEIN II

Along the Winding Road
Call It a Dream
*Eleven Levee Street
*Lordy
Sunny River

**BANJO EYES
December 25, 1941

MUSIC BY VERNON DUKE
WORDS BY JOHN LATOUCHE

Nickel to My Name, A
Not a Care in the World
We're Having a Baby
   Words by Harold Adamson

THE LADY COMES ACROSS
January 9, 1942

MUSIC BY VERNON DUKE
WORDS BY TED FETTER

I'd Like to Talk About the Weather
Lady
Summer Is A-Comin' In
   Words by John Latouche
This Is Where I Came In
You Took Me by Surprise

*Dropped from New York production
**Based on play "Three Men on a Horse" by John Cecil Holm
   and George Abbott*

BY JUPITER
June 2, 1942

MUSIC BY RICHARD RODGERS
WORDS BY LORENZ HART

Careless Rhapsody
Ev'rything I've Got
Here's a Hand
Jupiter Forbid
Nobody's Heart
Wait Till You See Her

STAR AND GARTER
June 24, 1942

Brazilian Nuts
   Music by Dorival Caymmi, words by Al Stillman
Bunny, Bunny, Bunny
   Music and words by Harold Rome
I Don't Get It
   Music by Doris Tauber, words by Sis Willner

THIS IS THE ARMY
July 4, 1942

MUSIC AND WORDS BY IRVING BERLIN

American Eagles
Army's Made a Man Out of Me, The
How About A Cheer for the Navy
I Left My Heart at the Stage Door Canteen
I'm Getting Tired So I Can Sleep
My Sergeant and I Are Buddies
That Russian Winter
That's What the Well Dressed Man in Harlem
   Will Wear
This Is the Army, Mr. Jones
What Does He Look Like?
With My Head in the Clouds

COUNT ME IN
October 8, 1942

MUSIC AND WORDS BY ANN RONELL

On Leave for Love
Someone in the Know
Ticketyboo

COUNT ME IN (*continued*)

Woman of the Year, The
You've Got It All

BEAT THE BAND
October 14, 1942

MUSIC BY JOHNNY GREEN
WORDS BY GEORGE MARION, JR.

Ev'ry Other Heartbeat
Let's Comb Beaches
Proud of You
Steam Is on the Beam, The

NEW FACES OF 1943
December 22, 1942

Animals Are Nice
  Music by Lee Wainer, words by J. B. Rosenberg
Hey, Gal!
  Music by Will Irwin, words by Peter Barry
Love, Are You Raising Your Head Again?
  Music by Lee Wainer, words by June Carroll
New Shoes
  Music by Will Irwin, words by June Carroll
Yes, Sir, I've Made a Date
  Music by Lee Wainer, words by J. B. Rosenberg

SOMETHING FOR THE BOYS
January 7, 1943

MUSIC AND WORDS BY COLE PORTER

By the Mississinewah
Could It Be You?
He's a Right Guy
Hey, Good-Lookin'
I'm in Love with a Soldier Boy
Leader of a Big-Time Band, The
See That You're Born in Texas
Something for the Boys
When My Baby Goes to Town

*OKLAHOMA!
March 31, 1943

MUSIC BY RICHARD RODGERS
WORDS BY OSCAR HAMMERSTEIN II

All 'er Nothin'
**Boys and Girls Like You and Me
Farmer and the Cowman, The
I Cain't Say No
Kansas City
Many a New Day
Oh, What a Beautiful Mornin'
Oklahoma
Out of My Dreams
People Will Say We're In Love
Pore Jud
Surrey with the Fringe on Top, The

ZIEGFELD FOLLIES
April 1, 1943

MUSIC BY RAY HENDERSON
WORDS BY JACK YELLEN

Come Up and Have a Cup of Coffee
Hold that Smile

EARLY TO BED
June 17, 1943

MUSIC BY THOMAS (FATS) WALLER
WORDS BY GEORGE MARION, JR.

Ladies Who Sing with a Band, The
Slightly Less Than Wonderful
There's a Man in My Life
This Is So Nice

MY DEAR PUBLIC
September 9, 1943

Feet on the Sidewalk (Head in the Sky)
  Music and words by Sammy Lerner, Gerald Marks

**Based on play "Green Grow the Lilacs" by Lynn Riggs*
***Dropped from New York production*

Now That I'm Free
*Music by Irving Caesar, words by Irma Hol-
lander*

Rain on the Sea
*Music by Irving Caesar, Sammy Lerner, words
by Gerald Marks*

There Ain't No Color Line Around the Rainbow
*Music by Irving Caesar, words by Gerald
Marks, Sammy Lerner*

This Is Our Private Love Song
*Music by Irving Caesar, words by Sammy
Lerner*

BRIGHT LIGHTS OF 1944
September 16, 1943

MUSIC BY JERRY LIVINGSTON
WORDS BY MACK DAVID

Don't Forget the Girl from Punxatawney
Thoughtless

ONE TOUCH OF VENUS
October 7, 1943

MUSIC BY KURT WEILL
WORDS BY OGDEN NASH

Foolish Heart
Speak Low
That's Him
Trouble with Women, The
West Wind

ARTISTS AND MODELS
November 5, 1943

MUSIC AND WORDS BY PHILIP CHARIG, DAN
SHAPIRO, MILTON PASCAL

Let's Keep It That Way
*Music by Abner Silver, words by Milton Berle,
Ervin Drake*
Swing Low, Sweet Harriet
You Are Romance
You'll Know That It's Me

WHAT'S UP
November 11, 1943

MUSIC BY FREDERICK LOEWE
WORDS BY ALAN JAY LERNER

Joshua
My Last Love
You Wash and I'll Dry
You've Got a Hold on Me

*A CONNECTICUT YANKEE *(Revival)
November 17, 1943

MUSIC BY RICHARD RODGERS
WORDS BY LORENZ HART

New Songs:
Can't You Do a Friend a Favor?
To Keep My Love Alive
You Always Love the Same Girl

CARMEN JONES
December 2, 1943

MUSIC BY GEORGES BIZET
WORDS BY OSCAR HAMMERSTEIN II

Beat Out Dat Rhythm on a Drum
Dat's Love
My Joe
Stan' Up An' Fight

JACKPOT
January 13, 1944

MUSIC BY VERNON DUKE
WORDS BY HOWARD DIETZ

I've Got a One Track Mind
Sugarfoot
There Are Yanks (from the Banks of the Wabash)
What Happened?

Based on the Mark Twain novel

MEXICAN HAYRIDE
January 28, 1944

MUSIC AND WORDS BY COLE PORTER

Abracadabra
Carlotta
Count Your Blessings
Girls
Good-Will Movement, The
I Love You
It Must Be Fun to Be You
Sing to Me, Guitar
There Must Be Someone for Me

FOLLOW THE GIRLS
April 8, 1944

MUSIC BY PHILIP CHARIG
WORDS BY DAN SHAPIRO, MILTON PASCAL

Follow the Girls
I Wanna Get Married
I'm Gonna Hang My Hat
Twelve o'Clock and All Is Well
Where You Are
You're Perf

ALLAH BE PRAISED
April 20, 1944

Let's Go Too Far
  *Music by Don Walker, words by George
  Marion, Jr.*
Secret Song
  *Music by Baldwin Bergersen, words by George
  Marion, Jr.*

DREAM WITH MUSIC
May 18, 1944

MUSIC BY CLAY WARNICK
WORDS BY EDWARD EAGER

Baby, Don't Count on Me
I'm Afraid I'm in Love
Love at Second Sight

SONG OF NORWAY
August 21, 1944

MUSIC AND WORDS BY ROBERT WRIGHT AND
GEORGE FORREST (BASED ON GRIEG)

At Christmastime
Freddy and His Fiddle
I Love You
Midsummer's Eve
Now
Strange Music
Three Loves

BLOOMER GIRL
October 5, 1944

MUSIC BY HAROLD ARLEN
WORDS BY E. Y. HARBURG

Eagle and Me, The
Evelina
I Got a Song
Right as the Rain
T'morra, T'morra
When the Boys Come Home

*SADIE THOMPSON
November 16, 1944

MUSIC BY VERNON DUKE
WORDS BY HOWARD DIETZ

If You Can't Get the Love You Want
Life's a Funny Present from Someone
Love I Long For, The
Poor As a Church Mouse
Sailing at Midnight
When You Live on an Island

THE SEVEN LIVELY ARTS
December 7, 1944

MUSIC AND WORDS BY COLE PORTER

Band Started Swinging a Song, The
Ev'ry Time We Say Goodbye
Frahngee-Pahnee

*Based on play "Rain" by John Colton (based, in turn, on short
  story, "Miss Thompson" by W. Somerset Maugham)

Hence It Don't Make Sense
Is It the Girl?
Only Another Boy and Girl
Scenes de Ballet
  Music by Igor Stravinsky
When I Was a Little Cuckoo
Wow-Ooh-Wolf

LAFFING ROOM ONLY
December 23, 1944

Feudin' and Fightin'
  Music by Burton Lane, words by Al Dubin,
  Burton Lane

ON THE TOWN
December 28, 1944

MUSIC BY LEONARD BERNSTEIN
WORDS BY BETTY COMDEN AND ADOLPH GREEN

I Can Cook, Too
Lonely Town
Lucky to Be Me
New York, New York
Some Other Time
Ya Got Me

A LADY SAYS YES
January 10, 1945

MUSIC BY FRED SPIELMAN, ARTHUR GERSHWIN
WORDS BY STANLEY ADAMS

I Wonder Why You Wander
Take My Heart with You
Without a Caress
You're More Than a Name and Address

UP IN CENTRAL PARK
January 27, 1945

MUSIC BY SIGMUND ROMBERG
WORDS BY DOROTHY FIELDS

April Snow
Big Back Yard, The
Carousel in the Park
Close As Pages in a Book
Fireman's Bride, The
It Doesn't Cost You Anything to Dream
When You Walk in the Room

*THE FIREBRAND OF FLORENCE
March 22, 1945

MUSIC BY KURT WEILL
WORDS BY IRA GERSHWIN

Rhyme for Angela, A
Sing Me Not a Ballad
There'll Be Life, Love and Laughter
You're Far Too Near Me

**CAROUSEL
April 19, 1945

MUSIC BY RICHARD RODGERS
WORDS BY OSCAR HAMMERSTEIN II

Carousel Waltz
If I Loved You
June Is Bustin' Out All Over
Mister Snow
Real Nice Clambake, A
Soliloquy
What's the Use of Wond'rin'
When the Children Are Asleep
You'll Never Walk Alone

MEMPHIS BOUND
May 24, 1945

MUSIC BY DON WALKER
WORDS BY CLAY WARNICK

Growin' Pains
Nightingale, the Moon and I, The
Old Love

MARINKA
July 18, 1945

MUSIC BY EMMERICH KALMAN
WORDS BY GEORGE MARION, JR.

Cab Song
One Last Love Song
One Touch of Vienna
Sigh by Night
Treat a Woman Like a Drum
Turn On the Charm

*Based on play "The Firebrand" by Edwin Justus Mayer
**Based on play "Liliom" by Ferenc Molnar

MR. STRAUSS GOES TO BOSTON
September 6, 1945

MUSIC BY ROBERT STOLZ
WORDS BY ROBERT SOUR

Going Back Home
Into the Night
What's a Girl Supposed to Do?
Who Knows?

CARIB SONG
September 27, 1945

MUSIC BY BALDWIN BERGERSEN
WORDS BY WILLIAM ARCHIBALD

Sleep Baby, Don't Cry
Woman Is a Rascal

POLONAISE
October 6, 1945

MUSIC BY BRONISLAW KAPER (BASED ON CHOPIN)
WORDS BY JOHN LATOUCHE

Just for Tonight
Next Time I Care, The
Stranger
Wait for Tomorrow

THE GIRL FROM NANTUCKET
November 9, 1945

MUSIC BY JACQUES BELASCO
WORDS BY KAY TWOMEY

From Morning Till Night
That's How I Know That I'm in Love
Your Fatal Fascination

ARE YOU WITH IT?
November 10, 1945

MUSIC BY HARRY REVEL
WORDS BY ARNOLD B. HORWITT

Here I Go Again
Just Beyond the Rainbow
Slightly Perfect
This Is My Beloved

THE DAY BEFORE SPRING
November 22, 1945

MUSIC BY FREDERICK LOEWE
WORDS BY ALAN JAY LERNER

Day Before Spring, The
God's Green World
I Love You This Morning
Jug of Wine, A
My Love Is a Married Man
This Is My Holiday
You Haven't Changed At All

BILLION DOLLAR BABY
December 21, 1945

MUSIC BY MORTON GOULD
WORDS BY BETTY COMDEN, ADOLPH GREEN

Bad Timing
I Got a One Track Mind
I'm Sure of Your Love

NELLIE BLY
January 21, 1946

MUSIC BY JIMMY VAN HEUSEN
WORDS BY JOHNNY BURKE

Just My Luck
You May Not Love Me

LUTE SONG
February 6, 1946

MUSIC BY RAYMOND SCOTT
WORDS BY BERNARD HANIGHEN

Bitter Harvest
Lute Song, The
Mountain High, Valley Low
See the Monkey
Where You Are

THE DUCHESS MISBEHAVES
February 13, 1946

MUSIC BY FRANK BLACK
WORDS BY GLADYS SHELLEY

You Are My Only Romance

THREE TO MAKE READY
March 7, 1946

MUSIC BY MORGAN LEWIS
WORDS BY NANCY HAMILTON

Barnaby Beach
Lovely, Lazy Kind of Day, A
Oh, You're a Wonderful Person
Old Soft Shoe, The
Tell Me the Story

ST. LOUIS WOMAN
March 30, 1946

MUSIC BY HAROLD ARLEN
WORDS BY JOHNNY MERCER

Any Place I Hang My Hat Is Home
Cakewalk Your Lady
Come Rain or Come Shine
I Had Myself a True Love
*I Wonder What Became of Me
Legalize My Name
Ridin' on the Moon
Woman's Prerogative, A

CALL ME MISTER
April 18, 1946

MUSIC AND WORDS BY HAROLD ROME

Along with Me
Face on the Dime, The
Red Ball Express, The
South America, Take It Away
When We Meet Again

ANNIE GET YOUR GUN
May 16, 1946

MUSIC AND WORDS BY IRVING BERLIN

Anything You Can Do
Colonel Buffalo Bill
Doin' What Comes Naturally
Girl That I Marry, The
I Got Lost in His Arms

I Got the Sun in the Morning
I'll Share It All with You
I'm a Bad, Bad Man
I'm an Indian Too
Moonshine Lullaby
My Defenses Are Down
*Take It in Your Stride
There's No Business Like Show Business
They Say It's Wonderful
Who Do You Love, I Hope
You Can't Get a Man with a Gun

**AROUND THE WORLD
May 31, 1946

MUSIC AND WORDS BY COLE PORTER

If You Smile at Me
Look What I Found
Pipe-Dreaming
Should I Tell You I Love You?
There He Goes, Phileas Fogg
Wherever They Fly the Flag of England

HAPPY BIRTHDAY
(Play with one song)
October 31, 1946

I Haven't Got a Worry in the World
  Music by Richard Rodgers, words by Oscar
  Hammerstein II

PARK AVENUE
November 4, 1946

MUSIC BY ARTHUR SCHWARTZ
WORDS BY IRA GERSHWIN

Don't Be a Woman If You Can
For the Life of Me
Goodbye to All That
There's No Holding Me

*Dropped from New York production
**Based on the Jules Verne novel

IF THE SHOE FITS
December 5, 1946

MUSIC BY DAVID RAKSIN
WORDS BY JUNE CARROLL

I Took Another Look
I Wish
I'm Not Myself Tonight
In the Morning
My Business Man

*BEGGAR'S HOLIDAY
December 26, 1946

MUSIC BY DUKE ELLINGTON
WORDS BY JOHN LATOUCHE

Maybe I Should Change My Ways
On the Wrong Side of the Railroad Track
Take Love Easy
Tomorrow Mountain
Tooth and Claw
Wanna Be Bad
When I Walk with You

TOPLITZKY OF NOTRE DAME
December 26, 1946

MUSIC BY SAMMY FAIN
WORDS BY GEORGE MARION, JR.

I Wanna Go to City College
Let Us Gather at the Goal Line
Love Is a Random Thing
Wolf Time
You Are My Downfall

**STREET SCENE
January 9, 1947

MUSIC BY KURT WEILL
WORDS BY LANGSTON HUGHES

Boy Like You, A
Lonely House
Moon-Faced, Starry-Eyed
We'll Go Away Together
What Good Would the Moon Be?

*Based on "The Beggar's Opera" by John Gay
**Based on play of same title by Elmer Rice

FINIAN'S RAINBOW

MUSIC BY BURTON LANE
WORDS BY E. Y. HARBURG

Begat, The
How Are Things in Glocca Morra?
If This Isn't Love
Look to the Rainbow
Necessity
Old Devil Moon
Something Sort of Grandish
That Great Come and Get It Day
When I'm Not Near the Girl I Love
When the Idle Poor Become the Idle Rich

BRIGADOON
March 13, 1947

MUSIC BY FREDERICK LOEWE
WORDS BY ALAN JAY LERNER

Almost Like Being in Love
Brigadoon
Come To Me, Bend To Me
Down on MacConnachy Square
Heather on the Hill, The
I'll Go Home with Bonnie Jean
Jeannie's Packin' Up
There But for You, Go I
Waitin' for My Dearie

BAREFOOT BOY WITH CHEEK
April 3, 1947

MUSIC BY SIDNEY LIPPMAN
WORDS BY SYLVIA DEE

After Graduation Day
I Knew I'd Know
It's Too Nice a Day to Go to School
Story of a Carrot, The
When You're Eighteen

THE MEDIUM
May 1, 1947

MUSIC AND WORDS BY GIAN-CARLO MENOTTI

Black Swan, The

THE TELEPHONE
May 1, 1947

MUSIC AND WORDS BY GIAN-CARLO MENOTTI

Vocal Score Only

LOUISIANA LADY
June 2, 1947

MUSIC BY ALMA SANDERS
WORDS BY MONTE CARLO

Cuckoo-Cheena, The
Night Was All to Blame, The
That's Why I Want to Go Home
When You Are Close to Me

MUSIC IN MY HEART
October 2, 1947

MUSIC BY FRANZ STEININGER (BASED ON
TCHAIKOVSKY)
WORDS BY FORMAN BROWN

Balalaika Serenade, The
Flower Waltz, The
Love Is a Game for Soldiers
Love Song
Once Upon a Time
Song of the Troika
Stolen Kisses
While There's a Song to Sing

UNDER THE COUNTER
October 3, 1947

MUSIC BY MANNING SHERWIN
WORDS BY HAROLD PURCELL

Moment I Saw You, The

HIGH BUTTON SHOES
October 9, 1947

MUSIC BY JULE STYNE
WORDS BY SAMMY CAHN

Can't You Just See Yourself?
I Still Get Jealous
Papa, Won't You Dance with Me
There's Nothing Like a Model "T"
You're My Girl

ALLEGRO
October 10, 1947

MUSIC BY RICHARD RODGERS
WORDS BY OSCAR HAMMERSTEIN II

Come Home
Fellow Needs a Girl, A
Gentleman Is a Dope, The
Money Isn't Everything
So Far
You Are Never Away

ANGEL IN THE WINGS
December 11, 1947

MUSIC AND WORDS BY BOB HILLIARD AND
CARL SIGMAN

Big Brass Band from Brazil, The
Civilization
If It Were Easy To Do
Thousand Islands Song

MAKE MINE MANHATTAN
January 15, 1948

MUSIC BY RICHARD LEWINE
WORDS BY ARNOLD B. HORWITT

Gentleman Friend
I Don't Know Her Name
I Fell in Love with You
My Brudder and Me
Phil the Fiddler
Saturday Night in Central Park

LOOK MA, I'M DANCIN'
January 29, 1948

MUSIC AND WORDS BY HUGH MARTIN

If You'll Be Mine
I'm Not So Bright
I'm Tired of Texas
Little Boy Blues, The
Shauny O'Shay
Tiny Room
Way It Might Have Been, The

INSIDE U.S.A.
April 30, 1948

MUSIC BY ARTHUR SCHWARTZ
WORDS BY HOWARD DIETZ

Blue Grass
First Prize at the Fair
Haunted Heart
My Gal Is Mine Once More
Rhode Island Is Famous for You

HOLD IT!
May 5, 1948

MUSIC BY GERALD MARKS
WORDS BY SAM LERNER

About Face
Always You
Buck in the Bank
Down the Well
Friendly Enemy
Hold It!
It Was So Nice Having You
Nevermore
You Took Possession of Me

BALLET BALLADS
May 18, 1948

MUSIC BY JEROME MOROSS
WORDS BY JOHN LATOUCHE

I've Got Me
My Yellow Flower
Ridin' on the Breeze

SLEEPY HOLLOW
June 3, 1948

MUSIC BY GEORGE LESSNER
WORDS BY MIRIAM BATTISTA, RUSSELL MALONEY

Gray Goose, The
Here and Now
I'm Lost
    Words by Ruth Aarons
Things That Lovers Say, The

SMALL WONDER
September 15, 1948

I Like a Man Around the House
    Music by Baldwin Bergersen, words by Phyllis McGinley
Nobody Told Me
    Music by Baldwin Bergersen, words by Phyllis McGinley
Show Off
    Music and words by Albert Selden
When I Fall in Love
    Music and words by Albert Selden

HEAVEN ON EARTH
September 16, 1948

MUSIC BY JAY GORNEY
WORDS BY BARRY TRIVERS

Heaven on Earth
Home (Is Where the Heart Is)
You're So Near (So Near and Yet So Far)
You're the First Cup of Coffee

MAGDALENA
September 20, 1948

MUSIC BY HEITOR VILLA-LOBOS
WORDS BY ROBERT WRIGHT, GEORGE FORREST

Emerald Song, The
Magdalena
My Bus and I
Singing Tree, The

LOVE LIFE
October 7, 1948

MUSIC BY KURT WEILL
WORDS BY MAXWELL ANDERSON

Economics
Green-Up Time
Here I'll Stay
Is It Him or Is It Me?
Love Song
Mr. Right
Susan's Dream
This Is the Life

*WHERE'S CHARLEY?
October 11, 1948

MUSIC AND WORDS BY FRANK LOESSER

Lovelier Than Ever
Make a Miracle
My Darling, My Darling
New Ashmolean Marching Society and Students
  Conservatory Band, The
Once In Love with Amy
Pernambuco
Where's Charley?

†MY ROMANCE
October 19, 1948

MUSIC BY SIGMUND ROMBERG
WORDS BY ROWLAND LEIGH

Desire
From Now Onward
If Only
In Love with Romance

AS THE GIRLS GO
November 13, 1948

MUSIC BY JIMMY McHUGH
WORDS BY HAROLD ADAMSON

As the Girls Go
Father's Day
I Got Lucky in the Rain
It Takes a Woman to Take a Man
It's More Fun Than a Picnic
Nobody's Heart but Mine
Rock, Rock, Rock
There's No Getting Away from You
You Say the Nicest Things, Baby

LEND AN EAR
December 16, 1948

MUSIC AND WORDS BY CHARLES GAYNOR

Give Your Heart a Chance to Sing
I'm on the Lookout
Molly O'Reilly
Neurotic You and Psychopathic Me

*Based on play "Charley's Aunt" by Brandon Thomas
†Based on play "Romance" by Edward Sheldon

When Someone You Love Loves You
Who Hit Me?

**KISS ME, KATE
December 30, 1948

MUSIC AND WORDS BY COLE PORTER

Always True to You in My Fashion
Another Op'nin', Another Show
Bianca
Brush Up Your Shakespeare
I Am Ashamed That Women Are So Simple
I Hate Men
I Sing of Love
I've Come to Wive It Wealthily in Padua
So in Love
Tom, Dick or Harry
Too Darn Hot
We Open in Venice
Were Thine That Special Face
Where Is the Life That Late I Led?
Why Can't You Behave
Wunderbar

ALONG FIFTH AVENUE
January 13, 1949

Best Time of Day, The
  Music by Gordon Jenkins, words by Tom Adair
Call It Applefritters
  Music by Richard Stutz, words by Milton Pascal
Santo Dinero
  Music by Richard Stutz, words by Milton Pascal
Skyscraper Blues
  Music by Gordon Jenkins, words by Tom Adair
Weep No More
  Music by Gordon Jenkins, words by Tom Adair

ALL FOR LOVE
January 22, 1949

MUSIC BY ALLAN ROBERTS
WORDS BY LESTER LEE

All for Love
Big Four, The
  Music and words by Peter H. Weiss

**Based on "The Taming of the Shrew" by William Shakespeare

ALL FOR LOVE (*continued*)

Dreamer with a Penny
Humphrey Bogart Rhumba
My Baby's Bored
My Heart's in the Middle of July
No Time for Nothin' but Love
Oh, How Unfortunate You Mortals Be
Run to Me, My Love
Why Can't It Happen Again
   Music by Michel Emer, words by Sammy Gallop

†**SOUTH PACIFIC**
April 7, 1949

MUSIC BY RICHARD RODGERS
WORDS BY OSCAR HAMMERSTEIN II

Bali Ha'i
Carefully Taught
Cockeyed Optimist, A
Dites-Moi
Happy Talk
Honey Bun
I'm Gonna Wash That Man Right Outa My Hair
*Loneliness of Evening
*My Girl Back Home
Some Enchanted Evening
There Is Nothin' Like a Dame
This Nearly Was Mine
Wonderful Guy, A
Younger Than Springtime

MISS LIBERTY
July 15, 1949

MUSIC AND WORDS BY IRVING BERLIN

Extra! Extra!
Falling Out of Love Can Be Fun
Give Me Your Tired, Your Poor
   Words by Emma Lazarus
Homework
*Honorable Profession of the Fourth Estate, The
I'd Like My Picture Took

†*Based on "Tales Of The South Pacific," short stories by James A. Michener*
*Dropped from New York production

Just One Way to Say I Love You
Let's Take an Old Fashioned Walk
Little Fish in a Big Pond
Me an' My Bundle
Miss Liberty
Most Expensive Statue in the World
Only for Americans
Paris Wakes Up and Smiles
Policeman's Ball, The
*Pulitzer Prize, The
*What Do I Have to Do to Get My Picture in the Paper?
You Can Have Him

TOUCH AND GO
October 13, 1949

MUSIC BY JAY GORNEY
WORDS BY WALTER AND JEAN KERR

Be a Mess
Funny Old Little Old World
It Will Be All Right (In a Hundred Years)
This Had Better Be Love
Wish Me Luck

††**LOST IN THE STARS**
October 30, 1949

MUSIC BY KURT WEILL
WORDS BY MAXWELL ANDERSON

Big Mole
Little Gray House, The
Lost in the Stars
Stay Well
Thousands of Miles
Trouble Man

REGINA
October 31, 1949

MUSIC AND WORDS BY MARC BLITZSTEIN

Best Things of All, The
Blues
Chinkypin

††*Based on novel "Cry, The Beloved Country" by Alan Paton*
**Based on play "The Little Foxes" by Lillian Hellman

Greedy Girl
Summer Day
What Will It Be?

TEXAS, LI'L DARLIN'
November 25, 1949

MUSIC BY ROBERT EMMETT DOLAN
WORDS BY JOHNNY MERCER

Big Movie Show in the Sky, The
Hootin' Owl Trail
Horseshoes Are Lucky
It's Great to Be Alive
Month of Sundays, A
Yodel Blues, The

*GENTLEMEN PREFER BLONDES
December 8, 1949

MUSIC BY JULE STYNE
WORDS BY LEO ROBIN

Bye, Bye Baby
Diamonds Are a Girl's Best Friend
It's Delightful Down in Chile
It's High Time
Just a Kiss Apart
Little Girl from Little Rock, A
Mamie Is Mimi
Sunshine
You Say You Care

ALIVE AND KICKING
January 17, 1950

WORDS BY PAUL WEBSTER, RAY GOLDEN

If You Don't Love Me
  Music by Hoagy Carmichael
Love, It Hurts So Good
  Music and words by Harold Rome
One! Two! Three!
  Music by Sonny Burke
There's a Building Going Up
  Music by Sammy Fain
World of Strangers, A
  Music by Sammy Fain

*Based on the novel by Anita Loos

DANCE ME A SONG
January 20, 1950

MUSIC AND WORDS BY JAMES SHELTON

I'm the Girl
Lilac Wine
Matilda
My Little Dog Has Ego
  Music and words by Herman Hupfeld
Strange New Look

†ARMS AND THE GIRL
February 2, 1950

MUSIC BY MORTON GOULD
WORDS BY DOROTHY FIELDS

Cow and a Plough and a Frau, A
Don't Talk
Nothin' for Nothin'
That's My Fella
There Must Be Somethin' Better Than Love
You Kissed Me

THE CONSUL
March 15, 1950

MUSIC AND WORDS BY GIAN-CARLO MENOTTI

Empty-handed Traveler, The
Lullaby
To This We've Come

GREAT TO BE ALIVE
March 23, 1950

MUSIC BY ABRAHAM ELLSTEIN
WORDS BY WALTER BULLOCK

Blue Day
Call It Love
Dreams Ago
It's a Long Time Till Tomorrow
What a Day!

*†Based on play "The Pursuit of Happiness" by Lawrence Lang-
ner and Armina Marshall*

†PETER PAN
April 24, 1950

MUSIC AND WORDS BY LEONARD BERNSTEIN

My House
Never-land
Peter, Peter
Who Am I?

TICKETS PLEASE
April 27, 1950

MUSIC AND WORDS BY JOAN EDWARDS AND
LYN DUDDY

Darn It Baby, That's Love
   Music by Lyn Duddy, words by Joan Edwards
Moment I Looked in Your Eyes, The
Restless
Television's Tough on Love
You Can't Take It with You

THE LIAR
May 18, 1950

MUSIC BY JOHN MUNDY
WORDS BY EDWARD EAGER

Lack-a-Day
Out of Sight, Out of Mind
What's in a Name?

MICHAEL TODD'S PEEP SHOW
June 28, 1950

Blue Night
   Music and words by
   Bhumibol-Chakraband, N. Tong Yai

Gimme the Shimmy
   Music and words by Harold Rome

Love at Sundown
   Music and words by Bhumibol-Chakraband,
   N. Tong Yai

Pocketful of Dreams
   Music and words by Harold Rome

Violins From Nowhere
   Music by Sammy Fain, words by Herb
   Magidson

†*Based on play by Sir James M. Barrie*

PARDON OUR FRENCH
September 27, 1950

MUSIC BY VICTOR YOUNG
WORDS BY EDWARD HEYMAN

I'm Gonna Make a Fool out of April
There's No Man Like a Snow Man

CALL ME MADAM
October 12, 1950

MUSIC AND WORDS BY IRVING BERLIN

Best Thing for You, The
Can You Use Any Money Today?
*Free
Hostess with the Mostes' on the Ball, The
It's a Lovely Day Today
Lichtenburg
Marrying for Love
Mrs. Sally Adams
Ocarina, The
Once Upon a Time Today
*Our Day of Independence
Something to Dance About
They Like Ike
Washington Square Dance
You're Just in Love

**GUYS AND DOLLS
November 24, 1950

MUSIC AND WORDS BY FRANK LOESSER

Adelaide's Lament
Bushel and a Peck, A
Follow the Fold
Fugue for Tinhorns
Guys and Dolls
If I Were a Bell
I'll Know
I've Never Been in Love Before
Luck Be a Lady
Marry the Man Today
More I Cannot Wish You

*Dropped from New York production
**Based on Damon Runyon's story "The Idyll of Miss Sarah
  Brown"

My Time of Day
Oldest Established, The
Sit Down, You're Rockin' the Boat
Sue Me
Take Back Your Mink

BLESS YOU ALL
December 14, 1950

MUSIC AND WORDS BY HAROLD ROME

I Can Hear It Now
Little Things (Meant So Much to Me)
Love Letter to Manhattan
Rose Is a Rose, A
Summer Dresses
Take Off the Coat
You Never Know What Hit You

†**OUT OF THIS WORLD**
December 21, 1950

MUSIC AND WORDS BY COLE PORTER

Cherry Pies Ought to Be You
Climb Up the Mountain
*From This Moment On
Hark to the Song of the Night
I Am Loved
No Lover
Nobody's Chasing Me
Use Your Imagination
Where, Oh Where
*You Don't Remind Me

††**THE KING AND I**
March 29, 1951

MUSIC BY RICHARD RODGERS
WORDS BY OSCAR HAMMERSTEIN II

Getting to Know You
Hello, Young Lovers
I Have Dreamed

*Dropped from New York production
†Based on Amphitryon legend
††Based on novel "Anna And The King Of Siam" by Margaret
  Landon

I Whistle a Happy Tune
March of the Siamese Children
My Lord and Master
Shall We Dance?
Something Wonderful
We Kiss in a Shadow

**MAKE A WISH
April 18, 1951

MUSIC AND WORDS BY HUGH MARTIN

Over and Over
Paris, France
Suits Me Fine
That Face
What I Was Warned About
When Does This Feeling Go Away?

***A TREE GROWS IN BROOKLYN
April 19, 1951

MUSIC BY ARTHUR SCHWARTZ
WORDS BY DOROTHY FIELDS

Growing Pains
If You Haven't Got a Sweetheart
I'll Buy You a Star
I'm Like a New Broom
Look Who's Dancing
Love Is the Reason
Make the Man Love Me

FLAHOOLEY
May 14, 1951

MUSIC BY SAMMY FAIN
WORDS BY E. Y. HARBURG

Come Back, Little Genie
Flahooley
Here's to Your Illusions
He's Only Wonderful
Springtime Cometh, The
Who Said There Is No Santa Claus?
World Is Your Balloon, The

**Based on play "The Good Fairy" by Ferenc Molnár
***Based on novel of same title by Betty Smith

COURTIN' TIME
June 14, 1951

MUSIC AND WORDS BY JACK LAWRENCE, DON WALKER

Fixin' for a Long, Cold Winter
Heart in Hand
I Do! He Doesn't!
Man Never Marries a Wife, A
Sensible Thing to Do, The
Wishbone Song, The

*SEVENTEEN
June 21, 1951

MUSIC BY WALTER KENT
WORDS BY KIM GANNON

After All, It's Spring
Headache and a Heartache
Nobody Ever Felt Like This Before
Ooh, Ooh, Ooh, What You Do to Me
Reciprocity
Summertime Is Summertime
Things Are Gonna Hum This Summer

TWO ON THE AISLE
July 19, 1951

MUSIC BY JULE STYNE
WORDS BY BETTY COMDEN AND ADOLPH GREEN

Catch Our Act at the Met
Everlasting
Give a Little, Get a Little
Hold Me-Hold Me-Hold Me
How Will He Know?
If You Hadn't, But You Did

TOP BANANA
November 1, 1951

MUSIC AND WORDS BY JOHNNY MERCER

Be My Guest
My Home Is in My Shoes

O.K. for T.V.
Only If You're in Love
Sans Souci
That's for Sure
Top Banana

PAINT YOUR WAGON
November 12, 1951

MUSIC BY FREDERICK LOEWE
WORDS BY ALAN JAY LERNER

Another Autumn
Carino Mio
I Still See Elisa
I Talk to the Trees
I'm on My Way
†Sh!
They Call the Wind Maria
Wand'rin' Star

PARIS '90
March 4, 1952

MUSIC AND WORDS BY KAY SWIFT

Calliope
Waltz I Heard in a Dream, The

THREE WISHES FOR JAMIE
March 21, 1952

MUSIC AND WORDS BY RALPH BLANE

April Face
Goin' on a Hayride
It Must Be Spring
It's a Wishing World
Love Has Nothing to Do with Looks
    *Music by Ralph Blane, words by Charles
    Lederer*
My Heart's Darlin'
Trottin' to the Fair

NEW FACES
May 16, 1952

Bal Petit Bal
    Music and words by Francis Lemarque

---

*Based on novel and play by Booth Tarkington

†Dropped from New York production

Boston Beguine
Music and words by Sheldon Harnick

Guess Who I Saw Today?
Music and words by Murray Grand,
Elisse Boyd

He Takes Me Off His Income Tax
Music by Arthur Siegel, words by June Carroll

I'm in Love with Miss Logan
Music and words by Ronald Graham

Lizzie Borden
Music and words by Michael Brown

Love Is a Simple Thing
Music by Arthur Siegel, words by June Carroll

Monotonous
Music by Arthur Siegel, words by June Carroll

Penny Candy
Music by Arthur Siegel, words by June Carroll

*WISH YOU WERE HERE
June 25, 1952

MUSIC AND WORDS BY HAROLD ROME

Could Be
Don Jose of Far Rockaway
Everybody Loves Somebody
Flattery
Relax
Shopping Around
Summer Afternoon
They Won't Know Me
Tripping the Light Fantastic
Where Did the Night Go?
Wish You Were Here

BUTTRIO SQUARE
October 14, 1952

WORDS BY FRED STAMER

I Keep Telling Myself
Music by Arthur Jones

Love Swept Like a Storm
Music by Gen Genovese

*Based on play "Having Wonderful Time" by Arthur Kober

More and More
Music by Gen Genovese

There's No Place Like the Country
Music by Arthur Jones

MY DARLIN' AIDA
October 27, 1952

MUSIC BY GIUSEPPE VERDI
WORDS BY CHARLES FRIEDMAN

King Cotton
Me and Lee
My Darlin' Aida
Why Ain't We Free?

TWO'S COMPANY
December 15, 1952

MUSIC BY VERNON DUKE
WORDS BY OGDEN NASH

**Good Little Girls
Words by Sammy Cahn
It Just Occurred to Me
Just Like a Man
Out of the Clear Blue Sky
Roundabout

†HAZEL FLAGG
February 11, 1953

MUSIC BY JULE STYNE
WORDS BY BOB HILLIARD

How Do You Speak to an Angel?
I Feel Like I'm Gonna Live Forever
Salomee
Think How Many People Never Find Love
You're Gonna Dance with Me, Willie

††MAGGIE
February 18, 1953

MUSIC AND WORDS BY WILLIAM ROY

Charm
My Mind's on You
What Every Woman Knows
You Become Me

**Dropped from New York production
†Based on film "Nothing Sacred" by Ben Hecht
††Based on play "What Every Woman Knows" by Sir James M.
Barrie

*WONDERFUL TOWN
February 25, 1953

MUSIC BY LEONARD BERNSTEIN
WORDS BY BETTY COMDEN, ADOLPH GREEN

It's Love
Little Bit in Love, A
My Darlin' Eileen
Ohio
Quiet Girl, A
Swing
Wrong Note Rag, The

CAN-CAN
May 7, 1953

MUSIC AND WORDS BY COLE PORTER

Allez-Vous En, Go Away
Can-Can
C'est Magnifique
Come Along with Me
I Am in Love
I Love Paris
If You Loved Me Truly
It's All Right with Me
Live and Let Live
Montmart'
Never Give Anything Away

ME AND JULIET
May 28, 1953

MUSIC BY RICHARD RODGERS
WORDS BY OSCAR HAMMERSTEIN II

Big Black Giant, The
I'm Your Girl
It Feels Good
It's Me
Keep It Gay
Marriage Type Love
No Other Love
That's the Way It Happens
Very Special Day, A

*Based on play "My Sister Eileen" by Joseph Fields and Jerome
 Chodorov (based, in turn, on short stories by Ruth McKenney)*

CARNIVAL IN FLANDERS
September 8, 1953

MUSIC BY JIMMY VAN HEUSEN
WORDS BY JOHNNY BURKE

For a Moment of Your Love
Here's That Rainy Day
I'm One of Your Admirers
It's an Old Spanish Custom
Ring the Bell
Sudden Thrill, The
Very Necessary You, The

KISMET
December 3, 1953

MUSIC AND WORDS BY ROBERT WRIGHT AND
GEORGE FORREST (BASED ON ALEXANDER BORODIN)

And This Is My Beloved
Baubles, Bangles and Beads
He's in Love
Night of My Nights
Sands of Time
Stranger in Paradise

JOHN MURRAY ANDERSON'S ALMANAC
December 10, 1953

Acorn in the Meadow
    Music and words by Richard Adler, Jerry Ross
Earth and the Sky, The
    Music and words by John Rox
Fini
    Music and words by Richard Adler, Jerry Ross
You're So Much a Part of Me
    Music and words by Richard Adler, Jerry Ross

THE GIRL IN PINK TIGHTS
March 5, 1954

MUSIC BY SIGMUND ROMBERG (AS DEVELOPED BY
    DON WALKER)
WORDS BY LEO ROBIN

Free to Love
In Paris and in Love
Lost in Loveliness
My Heart Won't Say Goodbye

THE THREEPENNY OPERA
March 10, 1954

MUSIC BY KURT WEILL
WORDS BY MARC BLITZSTEIN

Mack the Knife

BY THE BEAUTIFUL SEA
April 8, 1954

MUSIC BY ARTHUR SCHWARTZ
WORDS BY DOROTHY FIELDS

Alone Too Long
By the Beautiful Sea
Hang Up!
Happy Habit
More Love Than Your Love

THE GOLDEN APPLE
April 20, 1954

MUSIC BY JEROME MOROSS
WORDS BY JOHN LATOUCHE

Goona-Goona
It's the Going Home Together
Lazy Afternoon
Store-Bought Suit
When We Were Young
Windflowers

THE PAJAMA GAME
May 13, 1954

MUSIC AND WORDS BY RICHARD ADLER AND
JERRY ROSS

Hernando's Hideaway
Hey There
I'm Not At All in Love
Small Talk
Steam Heat
There Once Was a Man

THE BOY FRIEND
September 30, 1954

MUSIC AND WORDS BY SANDY WILSON

Fancy Forgetting
I Could Be Happy with You

It's Never Too Late to Fall in Love
Room in Bloomsbury, A

*PETER PAN
October 20, 1954

Captain Hook's Waltz
  *Music by Jule Styne, words by Betty Comden,
  Adolph Green*
Distant Melody
  *Music by Jule Styne, words by Betty Comden,
  Adolph Green*
I Won't Grow Up
  *Music by Mark Charlap, words by Carolyn
  Leigh*
I'm Flying
  *Music by Mark Charlap, words by Carolyn
  Leigh*
I've Gotta Crow
  *Music by Mark Charlap, words by Carolyn
  Leigh*
Never Never Land
  *Music by Jule Styne, words by Betty Comden,
  Adolph Green*
Tender Shepherd
  *Music by Mark Charlap, words by Carolyn
  Leigh*
Wendy
  *Music by Jule Styne, words by Betty Comden,
  Adolph Green*

**FANNY
November 4, 1954

MUSIC AND WORDS BY HAROLD ROME

Be Kind to Your Parents
Fanny
I Have to Tell You
I Like You
Love Is a Very Light Thing
Never Too Late for Love
Octopus

Based on play by Sir James M. Barrie
**Based on film trilogy by Marcel Pagnol*

FANNY (continued)

Restless Heart
To My Wife
Welcome Home
Why Be Afraid to Dance?

SANDHOG
November 29, 1954

MUSIC BY EARL ROBINSON
WORDS BY WALDO SALT

Johnny-O (Katie-O)
Katie O'Sullivan
Twins

MRS. PATTERSON
December 1, 1954

MUSIC AND WORDS BY JAMES SHELTON

Be Good, Be Good, Be Good
I Wish I Was a Bumble Bee
If I Was a Boy
Mrs. Patterson
My Daddy Is a Dandy
Tea in Chicago

HIT THE TRAIL
December 2, 1954

MUSIC BY FREDERICO VALERIO
WORDS BY ELIZABETH MIELE

Remember the Night
Set Me Free
Somehow I've Always Known
What's My Fatal Charm?

THE SAINT OF BLEECKER STREET
December 27, 1954

MUSIC AND WORDS BY GIAN-CARLO MENOTTI

Vocal Score Only

HOUSE OF FLOWERS
December 30, 1954

MUSIC BY HAROLD ARLEN
WORDS BY HAROLD ARLEN, TRUMAN CAPOTE

House of Flowers
I Never Has Seen Snow
Sleepin' Bee, A

Smellin' of Vanilla (Bamboo Cage)
Two Ladies in de Shade of de Banana Tree

PLAIN AND FANCY
January 27, 1955

MUSIC BY ALBERT HAGUE
WORDS BY ARNOLD B. HORWITT

City Mouse, Country Mouse
Follow Your Heart
It Wonders Me
Plain We Live
Plenty of Pennsylvania
This Is All Very New to Me
Young and Foolish

*SILK STOCKINGS
February 24, 1955

MUSIC AND WORDS BY COLE PORTER

All of You
As on Through the Seasons We Sail
It's a Chemical Reaction, That's All
Josephine
Paris Loves Lovers
Satin and Silk
Siberia
Silk Stockings
Stereophonic Sound
Without Love

SHOESTRING REVUE
February 28, 1955

Someone's Been Sending Me Flowers
   Music by David Baker, words by Sheldon Har-nick
When the Sea Is All Around Us
   Music by David Baker, words by Sheldon Har-nick

ANKLES AWEIGH
April 18, 1955

MUSIC BY SAMMY FAIN
WORDS BY DAN SHAPIRO

Eleven O'Clock Song, An
Headin' for the Bottom

*Based on film "Ninotchka"

Here's to Dear Old Us
His and Hers
Kiss Me and Kill Me with Love
La Fiesta
Nothing at All
Skip the Build Up

If It's a Dream
Love Sneaks Up on You
Man with a Dream, A
"Miss You" Kiss, A
Remarkable Fellow
Where Is That Someone for Me?

TROUBLE IN TAHITI
April 19, 1955

LEONARD BERNSTEIN

Vocal Score Only

PHOENIX '55
April 23, 1955

MUSIC BY DAVID BAKER
WORDS BY DAVID CRAIG

All Around the World
Funny Heart, A
Never Wait for Love

*DAMN YANKEES
May 5, 1955

MUSIC AND WORDS BY RICHARD ADLER AND
JERRY ROSS

Goodbye, Old Girl
Heart
Man Doesn't Know, A
Near to You
Shoeless Joe from Hannibal, Mo.
Two Lost Souls
Whatever Lola Wants (Lola Gets)
Who's Got the Pain?

**SEVENTH HEAVEN
May 26, 1955

MUSIC BY VICTOR YOUNG
WORDS BY STELLA UNGER

Blessings
C'est la Vie

CATCH A STAR
September 6, 1955

MUSIC BY PHILIP CHARIG
WORDS BY RAY GOLDEN, DAVE ORMONT

One Hour Ahead of the Posse

THE VAMP
November 10, 1955

MUSIC BY JAMES MUNDY
WORDS BY JOHN LATOUCHE

Have You Met Delilah?
I've Always Loved You
Ragtime Romeo
Why Does It Have to Be You?

†PIPE DREAM
November 30, 1955

MUSIC BY RICHARD RODGERS
WORDS BY OSCAR HAMMERSTEIN II

All at Once You Love Her
Everybody's Got a Home But Me
Man I Used to Be, The
Next Time It Happens, The
Suzy Is a Good Thing
Sweet Thursday

††MY FAIR LADY
March 15, 1956

MUSIC BY FREDERICK LOEWE
WORDS BY ALAN JAY LERNER

Get Me to the Church on Time
I Could Have Danced All Night

**Based on novel "The Year The Yankees Lost the Pennant" by
  Douglass Wallop*
**Based on play of same title by Austin Strong

†Based on novel "Sweet Thursday" by John Steinbeck
††Based on play "Pygmalion" by George Bernard Shaw

MY FAIR LADY (*continued*)

I've Grown Accustomed to Her Face
On the Street Where You Live
Rain in Spain, The
Show Me
With a Little Bit of Luck
Wouldn't It Be Loverly?

MR. WONDERFUL
March 22, 1956

MUSIC AND WORDS BY JERRY BOCK, GEORGE
WEISS, LARRY HOLOFCENER

Jacques De Raque
Mr. Wonderful
Too Close for Comfort

*THE MOST HAPPY FELLA
May 3, 1956

MUSIC AND WORDS BY FRANK LOESSER

Big "D"
Don't Cry
I Like Ev'rybody
Joey, Joey, Joey
Most Happy Fella, The
My Heart Is So Full of You
Somebody, Somewhere
Standing on the Corner
Warm All Over

THE LITTLEST REVUE
May 22, 1956

MUSIC BY VERNON DUKE
WORDS BY OGDEN NASH

Born Too Late
Good Little Girls
  Words by Sammy Cahn
Madly in Love
Summer Is A-Comin' In
  Words by John Latouche
You're Far From Wonderful

**Based on play "They Knew What They Wanted" by Sidney
  Howard*

**SHANGRI-LA
June 13, 1956

MUSIC BY HARRY WARREN
WORDS BY JEROME LAWRENCE AND
ROBERT E. LEE

Lost Horizon
Second Time in Love
Shangri-La
Walk Sweet

NEW FACES OF 1956
June 14, 1956

Boy Most Likely to Succeed, The
  Music by Arthur Siegel, words by June Carroll
Don't Wait
  Music by Arthur Siegel, words by June Carroll
Girls 'n' Girls 'n' Girls
  Music and words by Irvin Graham
Hurry
  *Music by Murray Grand, words by Murray
  Grand, Elisse Boyd*
Perfect Night
  *Music by Dean Fuller, words by Marshall
  Barer*
Scratch My Back
  *Music by Dean Fuller, words by Marshall
  Barer*
Tell Her
  Music by Arthur Siegel, words by June Carroll
White Witch, The
  Music by Arthur Siegel, words by June Carroll

BY HEX
June 18, 1956

MUSIC AND WORDS BY HOWARD BLANKMAN

Something New
What Is Love?

**Based on novel "Lost Horizon" by James Hilton

LI'L ABNER
November 15, 1956

MUSIC BY GENE DE PAUL
WORDS BY JOHNNY MERCER

If I Had My Druthers
It's a Typical Day
Jubilation T. Cornpone
Love in a Home
Namely You
Unnecessary Town

GIRLS OF SUMMER
(Play with one song)
November 19, 1956

Girls of Summer
  Music and words by Stephen Sondheim

CRANKS
November 26, 1956

MUSIC BY JOHN ADDISON
WORDS BY JOHN CRANKO

Who Is It Always There?
Would You Let Me Know?

BELLS ARE RINGING
November 29, 1956

MUSIC BY JULE STYNE
WORDS BY BETTY COMDEN AND ADOLPH GREEN

Bells Are Ringing
Drop That Name
Hello, Hello, There
I Met a Girl
Independent
Just in Time
Long Before I Knew You
Mu-Cha-Cha
Party's Over, The

*CANDIDE
December 1, 1956

MUSIC BY LEONARD BERNSTEIN

Buenos Aires
  Words by Leonard Bernstein
Glitter and Be Gay
  Words by Richard Wilbur
It Must Be Me
  Words by Richard Wilbur
What's the Use?
  Words by Richard Wilbur

HAPPY HUNTING
December 6, 1956

MUSIC BY HAROLD KARR
WORDS BY MATT DUBEY

Game of Love, The
Gee, But It's Good to Be Here
If'n
I'm a Funny Dame
Mr. Livingstone
Mutual Admiration Society
New-Fangled Tango, A
She's Just Another Girl
This Is What I Call Love
This Much I Know

**SHINBONE ALLEY
April 13, 1957

MUSIC BY GEORGE KLEINSINGER
WORDS BY JOE DARION

Flotsam and Jetsam
Stranger, The
Toujours Gai
Way Down Blues
Woman Wouldn't Be a Woman, A

*Based on the Voltaire novel
**Based on "archy and mehitabel" stories by Don Marquis

LIVIN' THE LIFE
April 27, 1957

MUSIC BY JACK URBONT
WORDS BY BRUCE GELLER

Late Love
Livin' the Life
Someone

*NEW GIRL IN TOWN
May 14, 1957

MUSIC AND WORDS BY BOB MERRILL

At the Check Apron Ball
Did You Close Your Eyes?
Flings
Here We Are Again
If That Was Love
It's Good to Be Alive
Look At 'er
New Girl in Town
Sunshine Girl
You're My Friend, Aintcha

SIMPLY HEAVENLY
May 21, 1957

MUSIC BY DAVID MARTIN
WORDS BY LANGSTON HUGHES

Did You Ever Hear the Blues?
Gatekeeper of My Castle
Good Old Girl
Let's Ball Awhile
Look for the Morning Star
Simply Heavenly
When I'm in a Quiet Mood

WEST SIDE STORY
September 26, 1957

MUSIC BY LEONARD BERNSTEIN
WORDS BY STEPHEN SONDHEIM

America
Cool

*Based on play "Anna Christie" by Eugene O'Neill

Gee, Officer Krupke
I Feel Pretty
Maria
One Hand, One Heart
Something's Coming
Somewhere
Tonight

COPPER AND BRASS
October 17, 1957

MUSIC BY DAVID BAKER
WORDS BY DAVID CRAIG

Baby's Baby
Don't Look Now
Me and Love
Sweet William
You Walked Out

JAMAICA
October 31, 1957

MUSIC BY HAROLD ARLEN
WORDS BY E. Y. HARBURG

Ain' It de Truth?
Cocoanut Sweet
I Don't Think I'll End it All Today
Little Biscuit
Napoleon
Pretty to Walk With
Push De Button
Savanna
Take it Slow, Joe
What Good Does it Do?

RUMPLE
November 6, 1957

MUSIC BY ERNEST G. SCHWEIKERT
WORDS BY FRANK REARDON

Coax Me
First Time I Spoke of You, The
How Do You Say Goodbye
In Times Like These
Wish

THE MUSIC MAN
December 19, 1957

MUSIC AND WORDS BY MEREDITH WILLSON

Gary, Indiana
Goodnight, My Someone
It's You
Lida Rose
My White Knight
Seventy-six Trombones
Till There Was You
Wells Fargo Wagon

THE BODY BEAUTIFUL
January 23, 1958

MUSIC BY JERRY BOCK
WORDS BY SHELDON HARNICK

All of These and More
Fair Warning
Just My Luck
Leave Well Enough Alone
Uh-huh, Oh, Yeah!

*OH CAPTAIN!
February 4, 1958

MUSIC AND WORDS BY JAY LIVINGSTON AND
RAY EVANS

All the Time
It's Never Quite the Same
Life Does a Man a Favor
Surprise
We're Not Children
You Don't Know Him
You're So Right for Me

†SAY, DARLING
April 3, 1958

MUSIC BY JULE STYNE
WORDS BY BETTY COMDEN AND ADOLPH GREEN

Dance Only With Me
It's the Second Time You Meet That Matters
Say, Darling
Something's Always Happening on the River
Try to Love Me Just As I Am

*Based on film "The Captain's Paradise"
†Based on book of the same title by Richard Bissell

THE BALLAD OF BABY DOE
April 3, 1958

MUSIC BY DOUGLAS MOORE
WORDS BY JOHN LATOUCHE

Augusta's Aria
Farewell Song
Letter Song
Silver Song
Warm as the Autumn Light
Willow Song

GOLDILOCKS
October 11, 1958

MUSIC BY LEROY ANDERSON
WORDS BY JOAN FORD, JEAN AND WALTER KERR

Heart of Stone
I Never Know When
Lady in Waiting
Lazy Moon
Pussy Foot, The
Save a Kiss
Shall I Take My Heart and Go?

SALAD DAYS
November 10, 1958

MUSIC BY JULIAN SLADE
WORDS BY DOROTHY REYNOLDS, JULIAN SLADE

I Sit in the Sun
It's Easy to Sing
Oh, Look at Me!
We Said We Wouldn't Look Back

**FLOWER DRUM SONG
December 1, 1958

MUSIC BY RICHARD RODGERS
WORDS BY OSCAR HAMMERSTEIN II

Don't Marry Me
Grant Avenue
Hundred Million Miracles, A
I Enjoy Being a Girl

**Based on novel of same title by C. Y. Lee

FLOWER DRUM SONG (*continued*)

Love, Look Away
*My Best Love
Sunday
You Are Beautiful

WHOOP-UP
December 22, 1958

MUSIC BY MOOSE CHARLAP
WORDS BY NORMAN GIMBEL

Caress Me, Possess Me, Perfume
Flattery
Love Eyes
Never Before
Sorry For Myself
What I Mean to Say
When the Tall Man Talks

SHE SHALL HAVE MUSIC
January 22, 1959

MUSIC AND WORDS BY DEDE MEYER

Who Are You?

REDHEAD
February 5, 1959

MUSIC BY ALBERT HAGUE
WORDS BY DOROTHY FIELDS

I Feel Merely Marvelous
I'm Back in Circulation
It Doesn't Take a Minute
Just for Once
Look Who's in Love
My Girl Is Just Enough Woman for Me
Right Finger of My Left Hand, The
Two Faces in the Dark

†JUNO
March 9, 1959

MUSIC AND WORDS BY MARC BLITZSTEIN

I Wish It So
Liffey Waltz, The

My True Heart
One Kind Word

**FIRST IMPRESSIONS
March 19, 1959

MUSIC BY GLENN PAXTON
WORDS BY ROBERT GOLDMAN, GEORGE WEISS

As Long As There's a Mother
Heart Has Won the Game, The
I Feel Sorry for the Girl
Love Will Find Out the Way
Not Like Me

DESTRY RIDES AGAIN
April 23, 1959

MUSIC AND WORDS BY HAROLD ROME

Anyone Would Love You
Are You Ready, Gyp Watson?
Fair Warning
Hoop de Dingle
I Know Your Kind
I Say Hello
Once Knew a Fella
Ring on the Finger
Rose Lovejoy of Paradise Alley

***ONCE UPON A MATTRESS
May 11, 1959

MUSIC BY MARY RODGERS
WORDS BY MARSHALL BARER

In a Little While
Normandy
Shy
Yesterday I Loved You

THE NERVOUS SET
May 12, 1959

MUSIC BY TOMMY WOLF
WORDS BY FRAN LANDESMAN

Ballad of the Sad Young Men, The
I've Got a Lot to Learn About Life
Travel the Road of Love

---

*Dropped from New York production
†Based on play "Juno and the Paycock" by Sean O'Casey

**Based on novel "Pride and Prejudice" by Jane Austen
    ("First Impressions" was original title of novel)
***Based on fairy tale "The Princess and the Pea"

†**GYPSY**
May 21, 1959

MUSIC BY JULE STYNE
WORDS BY STEPHEN SONDHEIM

All I Need Is the Girl
Everything's Coming Up Roses
Let Me Entertain You
Little Lamb
*Mama's Talkin' Soft
Mr. Goldstone
Small World
Some People
Together Wherever We Go
You'll Never Get Away From Me

**TAKE ME ALONG
October 22, 1959

MUSIC AND WORDS BY BOB MERRILL

But Yours
I Get Embarrassed
I Would Die
Little Green Snake
Nine O'Clock
Promise Me a Rose
Sid Old Kid
Staying Young
Take Me Along

THE GIRLS AGAINST THE BOYS
November 2, 1959

MUSIC BY RICHARD LEWINE
WORDS BY ARNOLD B. HORWITT

Girls and Boys
I Gotta Have You
Where Did We Go? Out

THE SOUND OF MUSIC
November 16, 1959

MUSIC BY RICHARD RODGERS
WORDS BY OSCAR HAMMERSTEIN II

Climb Ev'ry Mountain
Edelweiss

†*Based on Gypsy Rose Lee's book*
**Dropped from New York production*
***Based on play "Ah, Wilderness" by Eugene O'Neill*

Lonely Goatherd, The
Maria
Ordinary Couple, An
Sixteen Going On Seventeen
Sound of Music, The

LITTLE MARY SUNSHINE
November 18, 1959

MUSIC AND WORDS BY RICK BESOYAN

Colorado Love Call
Do You Ever Dream of Vienna?
Little Mary Sunshine
Look for a Sky of Blue
Such a Merry Party

FIORELLO!
November 23, 1959

MUSIC BY JERRY BOCK
WORDS BY SHELDON HARNICK

I Love a Cop
Little Tin Box
Politics and Poker
Till Tomorrow
Very Next Man, The
When Did I Fall in Love?
*Where Do I Go from Here?

††**SARATOGA**
December 7, 1959

MUSIC BY HAROLD ARLEN
WORDS BY JOHNNY MERCER

Game of Poker, A
Goose Never Be a Peacock
Love Held Lightly
Man in My Life, The
Saratoga

PARADE
January 20, 1960

MUSIC AND WORDS BY JERRY HERMAN

Next Time I Love
Show Tune in 2/4 Time

††*Based on novel "Saratoga Trunk" by Edna Ferber*

PARADE *(continued)*

Your Good Morning
Your Hand in Mine

†GREENWILLOW
March 8, 1960

MUSIC AND WORDS BY FRANK LOESSER

Faraway Boy
Gideon Briggs, I Love You
Greenwillow Christmas
Music of Home, The
Never Will I Marry
Summertime Love
Walking Away Whistling

BYE BYE BIRDIE
April 14, 1960

MUSIC BY CHARLES STROUSE
WORDS BY LEE ADAMS

Baby, Talk to Me
How Lovely to Be a Woman
Kids
Lot of Livin' to Do, A
††One Boy
One Last Kiss
Put on a Happy Face
Rosie

CHRISTINE
April 28, 1960

MUSIC BY SAMMY FAIN
WORDS BY PAUL FRANCIS WEBSTER

Christine
Happy Is the Word
I Never Meant to Fall in Love
I'm Just a Little Sparrow
My Little Lost Girl

†*Based on novel of same title by B. J. Chute*
††*Also published as "One Guy"*

THE FANTASTICKS
May 3, 1960

MUSIC BY HARVEY SCHMIDT
WORDS BY TOM JONES

Soon It's Gonna Rain
They Were You
Try to Remember

*ERNEST IN LOVE
May 4, 1960

MUSIC BY LEE POCKRISS
WORDS BY ANNE CROSWELL

Handbag Is Not a Proper Mother, A
Lost
Perfection
Wicked Man, A
You Can't Make Love

IRMA LA DOUCE
September 29, 1960

MUSIC BY MARGUERITE MONNOT
WORDS BY JULIAN MORE, DANIEL HENEKER,
MONTE NORMAN

Dis-Donc, Dis-Donc
From a Prison Cell
Irma La Douce
Our Language of Love
She's Got the Lot
There Is Only One Paris for That

**TENDERLOIN
October 17, 1960

MUSIC BY JERRY BOCK
WORDS BY SHELDON HARNICK

Artificial Flowers
Good Clean Fun

**Based on play "The Importance of Being Earnest" by Oscar
  Wilde*
**Based on novel of same title by Samuel Hopkins Adams

*I Wonder What It's Like
*Lovely Laurie
My Gentle Young Johnny
My Miss Mary
Tommy, Tommy

THE UNSINKABLE MOLLY BROWN
November 3, 1960

MUSIC AND WORDS BY MEREDITH WILLSON

Are You Sure
Bea-u-ti-ful People of Denver
Belly Up to the Bar, Boys
Bon Jour
Chick-a-Pen
Dolce Far Niente
I Ain't Down Yet
If I Knew
I'll Never Say No
I've A'ready Started In
Keep-a-Hoppin'

**CAMELOT
December 3, 1960

MUSIC BY FREDERICK LOEWE
WORDS BY ALAN JAY LERNER

Camelot
Follow Me

*Dropped from New York production
**Based on novel "The Once and Future King" by T. S.
   White

How to Handle a Woman
I Loved You Once in Silence
If Ever I Would Leave You
Lusty Month of May, The
What Do the Simple Folk Do?

WILDCAT
December 15, 1960

MUSIC BY CY COLEMAN
WORDS BY CAROLYN LEIGH

*Angelina
Corduroy Road
Give a Little Whistle
Hey, Look Me Over
One Day We Dance
Tall Hope
What Takes My Fancy
*You're Far Away From Home
You've Come Home

DO RE MI
December 26, 1960

MUSIC BY JULE STYNE
WORDS BY BETTY COMDEN, ADOLPH GREEN

All You Need Is a Quarter
Asking For You
Cry Like the Wind
Fireworks
Make Someone Happy
What's New at the Zoo?

COMPLETE VOCAL SCORES PUBLISHED

Allegro (Richard Rodgers–Oscar Hammerstein II) 1947

Alone at Last (Franz Lehar–Matthew Woodward) 1915

Annie Get Your Gun (Irving Berlin) 1946

Anything Goes (Cole Porter) 1934

Apple Blossoms (Fritz Kreisler, Victor Jacobi–William LeBaron) 1919

Arcadians, The (Lionel Monckton, Howard Talbot–Arthur Wimperis) 1910

Babes in Arms (Richard Rodgers–Lorenz Hart) 1937

Babes in Toyland (Victor Herbert–Glen Mac-Donough) 1903

Ballad of Baby Doe, The (Douglas Moore-John Latouche)

Ballet Ballads (Jerome Moross–John Latouche) 1948

Bells Are Ringing (Jule Styne–Betty Comden, Adolph Green) 1956

Bitter Sweet (Noel Coward) 1929

Blue Paradise, The (Edmund Eysler, Sigmund Romberg–Herbert Reynolds) 1915

Boy Friend, The (Sandy Wilson) 1954

Brigadoon (Frederick Loewe–Alan Jay Lerner) 1947

Call Me Madam (Irving Berlin) 1950

Camelot (Frederick Loewe–Alan Jay Lerner) 1960

Can-Can (Cole Porter) 1953

Candide (Leonard Bernstein–Richard Wilbur, John Latouche, Dorothy Parker) 1956

Carousel (Richard Rodgers–Oscar Hammerstein II) 1945

Cat and the Fiddle, The (Jerome Kern–Otto Harbach) 1931

Chocolate Soldier, The (Oscar Straus–Stanislaus Stange) 1909

Chu Chin Chow (Frederick Norton–Oscar Asche) 1916

Circus Princess, The (Emmerich Kalman–Harry B. Smith) 1927

Consul, The (Gian-Carlo Menotti) 1950

Conversation Piece (Noel Coward) 1934

Count of Luxembourg, The (Franz Lehar–Adrian Ross, Basil Hood) 1912

Countess Maritza (Emmerich Kalman–Harry B. Smith) 1926

Damn Yankees (Richard Adler, Jerry Ross) 1955

Desert Song, The (Sigmund Romberg–Otto Harbach, Oscar Hammerstein II) 1926

Destry Rides Again (Harold Rome) 1959

Do Re Mi (Jule Styne–Betty Comden, Adolph Green) 1960

Dollar Princess, The (Leo Fall–George Grossmith, Jr.) 1909

Eileen (Victor Herbert–Henry Blossom) 1917

Eva (Franz Lehar–Glen MacDonough) 1912

Fanny (Harold Rome) 1954

Finian's Rainbow (Burton Lane–E. Y. Harburg) 1947

Firefly, The (Rudolf Friml–Otto Harbach) 1912

Fireman's Flame, The (Richard Lewine–Ted Fetter) 1937

Florodora (Leslie Stuart–Owen Hall) 1900

Flower Drum Song (Richard Rodgers–Oscar Hammerstein II) 1958

Frederika (Franz Lehar–Edward Eliscu) 1937

Gentlemen Prefer Blondes (Jule Styne–Leo Robin) 1949

Girl Crazy (George Gershwin–Ira Gershwin) 1930

Girl on the Film, The (Walter Kollo, Willy Bredschneider, Albert Sirmay–Adrian Ross) 1913

Going Up (Louis A. Hirsch–Otto Harbach) 1917

Great Waltz, The (Johann Strauss–Desmond Carter) 1934

Guys and Dolls (Frank Loesser) 1950

Gypsy (Jule Styne–Stephen Sondheim) 1959

Gypsy Love (Franz Lehar–Harry &· Robert Smith, Adrian Ross) 1911

Have a Heart (Jerome Kern–Guy Bolton, P. G. Wodehouse) 1917

High Jinks (Rudolf Friml–Otto Harbach) 1913

Irene (Harry Tierney–Joseph McCarthy) 1919

Katinka (Rudolf Friml–Otto Harbach) 1915

King and I, The (Richard Rodgers–Oscar Hammerstein II) 1951˙

Kismet (Robert Wright, George Forrest-based on Borodin) 1953

Kiss Me, Kate (Cole Porter) 1948

Knickerbocker Holiday (Kurt Weill–Maxwell Anderson) 1938

Lady in the Dark (Kurt Weill–Ira Gershwin) 1941

Li'l Abner (Gene de Paul–Johnny Mercer) 1956

Lost in the Stars (Kurt Weill–Maxwell Anderson) 1949

Madame Sherry (Karl Hoschna–Otto Harbach) 1910

Mademoiselle Modiste (Victor Herbert–Henry Blossom) 1905

Maytime (Sigmund Romberg–Rida Johnson Young) 1917

Me and Juliet (Richard Rodgers–Oscar Hammerstein II) 1953

Medium, The (Gian-Carlo Menotti) 1947

Melody (Sigmund Romberg–Irving Caesar) 1933

Merry Widow, The (Franz Lehar–Adrian Ross) 1907

Most Happy Fella, The (Frank Loesser) 1956

Music in the Air (Jerome Kern–Oscar Hammerstein) 1932

Music Man, The (Meredith Willson) 1957

My Fair Lady (Frederick Loewe–Alan Jay Lerner) 1956

Naughty Marietta (Victor Herbert–Rida Johnson Young) 1910

Naughty-Naught (Richard Lewine–Ted Fetter) 1937

New Moon, The (Sigmund Romberg–Oscar Hammerstein II) 1928

Nina Rosa (Sigmund Romberg–Irving Caesar) 1930

No, No, Nanette (Vincent Youmans–Irving Caesar, Otto Harbach) 1925

Of Thee I Sing (George Gershwin–Ira Gershwin) 1931

Oh, Boy! (Jerome Kern–Guy Bolton, P. G. Wodehouse) 1917

Oh, Lady! Lady!! (Jerome Kern–Guy Bolton, P. G. Wodehouse) 1918

Oklahoma! (Richard Rodgers–Oscar Hammerstein II) 1943

Only Girl, The (Victor Herbert–Henry Blossom) 1914

Orange Blossoms (Victor Herbert–B. G. DeSylva) 1922

Paint Your Wagon (Frederick Loewe–Alan Jay Lerner) 1951

Pajama Game, The (Richard Adler, Jerry Ross) 1954

Pal Joey (Richard Rodgers–Lorenz Hart) 1940

Peter Pan (Mark Charlap, Jule Styne–Carolyn Leigh, Betty Comden, Adolph Green) 1954

Pink Lady, The (Ivan Caryll–C. M. S. McLellan) 1911

Pipe Dream (Richard Rodgers–Oscar Hammerstein II) 1955

Plain and Fancy (Albert Hague–Arnold B. Horwitt) 1955

Porgy and Bess (George Gershwin–DuBose Heyward, Ira Gershwin) 1935

Prince of Pilsen, The (Gustav Luders–Frank Pixley) 1903

Princess Pat, The (Victor Herbert–Henry Blossom) 1915

Quaker Girl, The (Lionel Monckton–Adrian Ross, Percy Greenbank) 1911

Red, Hot and Blue! (Cole Porter) 1936
Red Mill, The (Victor Herbert–Henry Blossom) 1906
Redhead (Albert Hague–Dorothy Fields) 1959
Regina (Marc Blitzstein) 1949
Rio Rita (Harry Tierney–Joseph McCarthy) 1926
Roberta (Jerome Kern–Otto Harbach) 1933
Rose Marie (Rudolf Friml, Herbert Stothart–Otto Harbach, Oscar Hammerstein II) 1924

Saint of Bleecker Street, The (Gian-Carlo Menotti) 1954
Salad Days (Julian Slade–Dorothy Reynolds, Julian Slade) 1958
Sally (Jerome Kern–Clifford Grey, P. G. Wodehouse, B. G. DeSylva) 1920
Sari (Emmerich Kalman–C. C. S. Cushing, E. P. Heath) 1914
Shinbone Alley (Published as "archy and mehitabel") (George Kleinsinger–Joe Darion) 1957
Show Boat (Jerome Kern–Oscar Hammerstein II) 1927
Sometime (Rudolf Friml–Rida Johnson Young) 1918
Song of Norway (Robert Wright, George Forrest-based on Grieg) 1944
Sound of Music, The (Richard Rodgers–Oscar Hammerstein II) 1959
South Pacific (Richard Rodgers–Oscar Hammerstein II) 1949

Spring Maid, The (Heinrich Reinhardt–Robert B. Smith) 1910
Stepping Stones, The (Jerome Kern-Anne Caldwell) 1923
Street Scene (Kurt Weill–Langston Hughes) 1947
Strike Up the Band (George Gershwin–Ira Gershwin) 1930
Student Prince, The (Sigmund Romberg–Dorothy Donnelly) 1924
Sunny (Jerome Kern–Otto Harbach, Oscar Hammerstein II) 1925
Sweethearts (Victor Herbert–Robert B. Smith) 1913

Telephone, The (Gian-Carlo Menotti) 1947
Three-Penny Opera, The (Kurt Weill–Marc Blitzstein) 1955
Trouble in Tahiti (Leonard Bernstein) 1955

Vagabond King, The (Rudolf Friml–Brian Hooker) 1925
Very Good Eddie (Jerome Kern–Schuyler Greene) 1915

Waltz Dream, A (Oscar Straus–Joseph W. Herbert) 1908
West Side Story (Leonard Bernstein–Stephen Sondheim) 1957
Wildflower (Vincent Youmans, Herbert Stothart–Otto Harbach, Oscar Hammerstein II) 1923
Wish You Were Here (Harold Rome) 1952

You're in Love (Rudolf Friml–Otto Harbach) 1917

ABOUT THE AUTHORS

RICHARD LEWINE is a composer and television producer. He has composed scores for Broadway musicals, including the hit revue *Make Mine Manhattan*; and produced for television: Rodgers and Hammerstein's *Cinder-ella*, the Noel Coward-Mary Martin "special" *Together with Music*, Cole Porter's *Aladdin*; for many seasons he was Executive Producer of the New York Philharmonic Young People's Concerts with Leonard Bernstein. He is a member of ASCAP and of the councils of the Dramatists Guild and the Authors League of America. Mr. Lewine has made piano recordings (of theatre music, of course) and is the author of several articles on show music.

ALFRED SIMON, like his co-editor, is an accomplished pianist. Together they have performed as duo-pianists in their own radio series, devoted to show tunes. He was the rehearsal pianist for several productions, including the original production of George Gershwin's *Of Thee I Sing*; has written notes for record albums containing the music of Jerome Kern, Arthur Schwartz, Leroy Anderson, Johann Strauss and John Philip Sousa; composed the theme for Andre Kostelanetz' radio series; and compiled information for hundreds of songs in the *Cole Porter Song Book* and the *George and Ira Gershwin Song Book*. Since 1942, Mr. Simon has been the Director of Light Music at WQXR, the *New York Times* radio station.